WOMEN AND MORMONISM

WOMEN AND MORMONISM

HISTORICAL AND CONTEMPORARY PERSPECTIVES

Edited by Kate Holbrook and Matthew Bowman

THE UNIVERSITY OF UTAH PRESS
Salt Lake City

Copyright © 2016 by The University of Utah Press. All rights reserved.

The Defiance House Man colophon is a registered trademark of the University of Utah Press. It is based on a four-foot-tall Ancient Puebloan pictograph (late PIII) near Glen Canyon, Utah.

Library of Congress Cataloging-in-Publication Data

Names: Holbrook, Kate, editor. | Bowman, Matthew, editor.
Title: Women and Mormonism : historical and contemporary perspectives/ edited by Kate Holbrook and Matthew Bowman.
Description: Salt Lake City : University of Utah Press, 2016. | Includes bibliographical references and index.
Identifiers: LCCN 2015044600| ISBN 9781607814771 (pbk. : alk. paper) | ISBN 9781607814788 (ebook)
Subjects: LCSH: Mormon women.
Classification: LCC BX8643.W66 W66 2016 | DDC 289.3082—dc23
LC record available at http://lccn.loc.gov/2015044600

Agency is how we define and learn who we are.

—AMELIA AUDEN HOLBROOK-BROWN

Contents

Figures and Tables

Figures

Table

Introduction

MATTHEW BOWMAN AND KATE HOLBROOK

On August 24–25, 2012, a diverse group of scholars consisting of lay members of the Church of Jesus Christ of Latter-day Saints and other interested researchers, convened at Fort Douglas, in Salt Lake City, Utah, for a conference entitled "Women and the LDS Church: Historical and Contemporary Perspectives." We, the editors, arranged this conference to discuss the "state of the field" for the study of Mormon women and to sketch out a potential future for the field. The conference generated excitement, allowing us to attract important voices in the discipline. This volume contains many of the essays presented at the conference—augmented by further research—plus additional solicited offerings. The resulting articles reflect summations of scholarship on Mormon women in a diverse range of academic disciplines, and reflective essays that contemplate the issues that face contemporary Mormon women. We hope this innovative work can help steer the conversation on women and Mormonism forward.

As with much of Mormon studies, work on the lives of Mormon women has usually been historical, and thus it is history that has framed the questions scholars have traditionally asked. Many of these questions were originally posed in the 1877 volume entitled, *The Women of Mormondom.*[1] This earliest book length analysis of Mormon women was authored by journalist and Mormon convert Edward W. Tullidge, with extensive assistance from Eliza R. Snow (a leader among Mormon women who served as longtime president of the official Mormon women's organization, the Relief Society.)[2] When twentieth-century scholars began to revisit the history of nineteenth-century Mormon women, many of Tullidge's themes were echoed: an emphasis on the everyday and mundane aspects of their lives, an analysis of women's contributions to the church's history and the settlement of Utah, and a depiction of Mormon women as hardworking, independent, spiritual agents who, contrary to the narratives of most non-Mormon sources, were presently at work building a tangible Zion in Utah. Tullidge interspersed this narrative with profiles of notable Mormon women, and a few speculative essays about women's role in Mormon theology. The next major work on the topic, *Mormon Sisters: Women in Early Utah* (1976), a collection of topical essays edited by Claudia L. Bushman, came ninety-nine-years later, and struck similar chords.[3] Both books stressed what has since become a common historiographical trope in Mormon women's history: the social and political activism of nineteenth-century Mormon women, who balanced the challenging spiritual commitments polygamy demanded with civic and spiritual leadership, often through the Relief Society organization.

Like Tullidge's book, Bushman's collection of essays offered profiles of women in Utah in the late nineteenth century, using each to illustrate some aspect of the lives of Mormon women. The essays emphasized their hard, practical work; they were also, however, more forthright than the enthusiastic Tullidge about the emotional and social trial of polygamy, and were not nearly so hagiographic.

Later works also emphasized a variety of the motifs Tulllidge developed. While paying attention to the sort of social history Tullidge's and Bushman's collections underscored, the essays in *Sisters in Spirit: Mormon Women in Historical and Cultural Perspective* (1987),[4] edited by Maureen Ursenbach Beecher and Lavina Fielding Anderson, explored some of the particularities of Mormon theology as they applied to women, offering revised conceptions of the Fall of Adam and Eve and marriage, and arguing that Mormon theology offered especially empowering possibilities for women. Meanwhile, *Women of Covenant: The Story of Relief Society* (1992), written by Jill Mulvay Derr, Janath Russell Cannon, and Maureen Ursenbach Beecher, documented the Relief Society's emphasis upon social activism, civic involvement, and spiritual development.[5] Like *The Women of Mormondom*, *Women of Covenant* presented the Relief Society's history as a generally optimistic story of women uplifting themselves through the institutional church. That same year saw the publication of Maxine Hanks's edited volume, *Women and Authority: Re-Emerging Mormon Feminism* (1992), a diverse collection of essays that mustered historical and theological resources to argue that Mormon women participated in their religion in far richer ways in the nineteenth century than they had in the twentieth.[6] Many of its essays had an activist tone, calling for Mormon women to reassert their presumably lost opportunities.

More recently, work on Mormon women has focused on biography and life writings of both high profile and unfamiliar women in Mormon history. An important antecedent here is Linda King Newell and Valeen Tippetts Avery's *Mormon Enigma: Emma Hale Smith* (1984), a groundbreaking biography of a female Mormon leader who was also Joseph Smith's wife.[7] The biography explored the contributions of women in the early Mormon movement and cast new light on the movement's inception of plural marriage. Utah presses have published autobiographies and biographies of the lives of important nineteenth-century Mormon women such as Donna Smart's *Mormon Midwife: The 1846–1888 Diaries of Patty Bartlett Sessions* (1997), Carol Cornwall Madsen's *An Advocate for Women: the Public Life of Emmeline B. Wells* (2006), and Dave Hall's *A Faded Legacy: Amy Brown Lyman and Mormon Women's Activism, 1872–1959* (2015).[8] Oral histories have also brought a welcome focus on Mormon women outside the United States, and increasing attention to twentieth-century women. Important works here include *Mormon Women: Portraits and Conversations* (2009), *Mormon Women Have Their Say: Essays from the Claremont Oral History Collection* (2013), and *Sisters Abroad: Interviews from The Mormon Women Project* (2013).[9]

Ours is the first volume in over twenty years to take a combined thematic, cultural, and historical approach to the study of Mormon women. We have also gathered essays from outside the historical and theological disciplines to address myriad aspects of the Mormon experience. We hope this book will offer a summation and suggest new avenues for scholarship.

When we conceived the conference, we chose to use the notion of "agency" to frame discussion. Philosophers have traditionally defined agency as a person's capacity for intentional action, but the word has multiple meanings when used in reference to Mormon culture and history.[10] In 2010, historian of religion Catherine Brekus delivered a plenary address at the Mormon History Association that called attention to the fact that many historians and activists have focused on the ways in which agency functions as liberation from institution. This approach often left the impression that the exercise of agency is the equivalent of resistance to authority and a generally liberal view of the autonomous, independent self. Many historians, particularly in women's studies and the history of slavery, have offered a more nuanced interpretation of agency, examining how agency can often function within institutional boundaries, whether voluntary or coerced. We believe, and the following contents substantiate, that agency always exists on a spectrum, that even the most oppressed beings have some measure of ability to act.[11] Eugene Genovese, Steven Hahn, and James C. Scott have explored the ways in which slaves pursued agency and bent the boundaries of their bondage in a number of ways, even if they fell short of freedom.[12] Similarly, Brekus's own work, as well as that of R. Marie Griffith, show how women in American history have sometimes embraced seemingly patriarchal institutions—like the LDS church—and found power and liberation in shaping them.[13]

This book contributes to the discussion by exploring agency in a multiplicity of forms. Some of the women in this collection embrace agency as resistance or initiative, pressing against the boundaries of the church institution. Others locate agency within that institution, taking action in harmony with institutional mores. They participate in church structure and hierarchy, embrace elements of church doctrine or practice, and seek to express their agency through other forms of identity, such as race or nationality. Like any historical concept, agency has taken on different configurations over time and space. To that end, we have sought to include voices of women often neglected in popular discussions about Mormon women's history: women of color and women outside the United States.

The notion of agency has special resonance in Mormon theology. The Book of Mormon declares that "God gave unto man that he should act for himself," and makes a distinction between "things to act and things to be acted upon" (2 Nephi 2:16, 14). Joseph Smith embraced a robust notion of agency, insisting that humanity's ability to make moral choices was unfettered by original sin. He taught that human beings bear the responsibility to act righteously, the aspect of agency that Mormon leaders stress today.[14] Joseph Smith's own decision to pursue religious experience away from the organized religions of his day is often repeated in Mormon environments to demonstrate that agency properly exercised should be a choice to follow God, enhancing the believer's capacity to see the world morally and act even more righteously in the future. This interpretation of agency is similar to that of many other religious thinkers in Western history. Phyllis Mack's study of Quaker women led her to conclude:

> Quaker women and others defined agency not as the freedom to do what one wants but as the freedom to do what is right. Since "what is right" was determined by absolute truth or God as well as by individual conscience, agency implied obedience as well as the freedom to make choices and act on them. And since doing what is right inevitably means subduing at least some of one's own habits, desires, and impulses, agency implied self-negation as well as self-expression.[15]

The LDS philosopher Blake Ostler argues that the Mormon idea of agency in theory is close to libertarian free will, meaning that human behavior is not determined by external or divine events; rather, people are free to choose and act as they will.[16] In practice, however, the Church of Jesus Christ of Latter-day Saints is an extremely demanding religion with high expectations of its adherents, and women in particular lack access to most formal, institutional authority.[17] Mormon notions of agency have been worked out against the backdrop of these tensions.

Depictions of Mormon women and agency have often included subordination and submission. In the nineteenth century, Mormon women were frequently portrayed as slaves to polygamous masters, and certain factions in the contemporary Mormon feminist movement have invoked a similar critique decrying patriarchal leadership. The essays in this book bridge that historical divide, presenting a number of ways in which Mormon women have conceived of and exercised agency from the early nineteenth century to the present.

The diversity of contributors' approaches and case studies in this book allows us to move beyond questions of whether or not women in a patriarchal church are capable of agency. Instead, the essays explore the complicated nature of agency and its consequences. Several of the chapters investigate women choosing to act because they felt guided by God—sometimes in consonance with institutions and sometimes in rejection.

Many of the women presented in these essays draw on the resources of the Mormon tradition to press back against institutions—sometimes even the church itself. Aimee Hickman's essay investigates the tension between the cultural scripts of Mormon culture and the pursuit of individual spiritual experience, following the often cited example of Joseph Smith. Hickman describes women who found in their personal religious experiences grounds for resisting church institutional authority, but also women who turned to male authority figures to interpret these experiences. Similarly, Mary Farrell Bednarowski draws comparisons between Mormon and Catholic women, both torn between love for their spiritual traditions and discomfort with priesthood hierarchies restricted to men. In contrast, Mariama Kallon interprets Latter-day Saint teachings about gender equality as ennobling and liberating from the oppressive script of female inferiority in her homeland Sierra Leone. For Kallon, church teachings concerning agency and personal revelation are liberating forces, allowing her to more fully exercise her own autonomy. Claudia Bushman argues for a similar point, drawing on many oral histories of Mormon women in America today to make the case that Mormon theology and practices can accommodate a robust conception of female agency, and that women can make room for themselves in a patriarchal church.

Other essays focus on the diversity of resources Mormon women have used to find sites of meaning and sacred experience. David Campbell's analysis of survey data indicates that while LDS women are equally as committed to the practice of the faith as are men, they have significantly different views on the issue of authority—Mormon women are markedly less likely than men to place confidence in church hierarchy. Other essays describe resources Mormon women draw upon beyond hierarchical authority. Jennifer Reeder and Kristine Wright both write about Mormon women's relationship to the material culture of their church. Reeder explores the quilts, blocks, stones, and architecture of the Relief Society's communal projects to unearth voices not recorded in textual records, demonstrating that the diversity of Relief Society products illustrates the variety of its activities. Wright explains how Mormon women, otherwise barred from administering in certain sacramental rites, found access to them by fashioning ritual objects, thereby generating sacred meaning for themselves. Further, Susanna Morrill's essay describes how Mormon women have drawn on particular doctrines (in this case, the idea of a Heavenly Mother) to create their own religious discourse existing within the larger cultural framework of the church.

Laurel Thatcher Ulrich takes us further into a private space, watching nineteenth-century Mormon men and women represent themselves and their contributions in their diaries, autographs, and even hair ornaments out of their great human yearning to be remembered. Also pursuing the narratives of individual women, Neylan McBaine illustrates the diversity of present day Mormon women in faith, lifestyle, and theology, showing how divergent interpretations of doctrine and culture offer various women diverse means of comfort. Finally, Jennifer Finlayson-Fife deals sensitively with the most private of spaces, teasing apart the complex interactions between faith, institutions, and sexuality, exploring the ways Mormon women navigate their relationship with their husbands, with male church leaders, and their choices about behavior and belief.

Contributors write about access to agency in complicated institutional spaces and within the contexts of polygamy and priesthood authority. Rachel Cope, Kate Holbrook, and Rebekah Ryan Clark explore the variety of ways Mormon women came to terms with polygamy. Cope offers a number of ways in which women made reconciliation, arguing that Mormon women often emphasized other aspects of their faith in order to make the sacrifice of plural marriage worth living. Holbrook and Clark argue that plural wives often had access to a number of sources of power: participation in the Relief Society, exercise of spiritual gifts, and access to male leaders, all of which they drew upon to counter accusations that they were passive and powerless. Jonathan Stapley and Matthew Bowman both venture further into the gray areas between soft power and institutional authority. Stapley illuminates the complicated nineteenth-century relationship between liturgical practices women engaged in—such as, blessings for the sick and rituals administered for pregnant women—and priesthood offices normally restricted to men. He argues that too many discussions of that relationship have suffered from presentism, and nineteenth-century Mormons imagined the gendered nature of priesthood in ways differently than do Mormons today. In the conflict between two powerful early-twentieth-century

Relief Society leaders, Susa Young Gates and Amy Brown Lyman, Bowman identifies a Mormon example of a national transition that occurred during the Progressive era: the drift away from lay and amateur social services—often in the late nineteenth century administered by women's church or social groups—toward a trained profession called social work, a more traditionally male sphere.

Finally, these essays explore the ways in which agency within Mormon culture is affected by intersectional factors, particularly race and nationality. These essays remind us that the church today is a majority non-American faith, increasingly diverse in language and ethnicity both within and without America's borders, revealing both the challenges and the promise of that reality. P. Jane Hafen's personal essay describes the ways in which generally American, and particularly Mormon, stereotypes and prejudices about American Indians have shaped her religious life. Amanda Hendrix-Komoto's discussion of interracial marriage between white American Mormon missionaries and indigenous Tahitian women in the mid-nineteenth century further illustrates the ambivalence of Mormon attitudes about the relationship between race and women's spiritual capacities. Quincy Newell's sketch of the life of Jane Manning James, among the best-known early African American converts to the church, illustrates the ways in which James used organizations (e.g., Relief Society) and spiritual practices (e.g., speaking in tongues) to gain a measure of respect within the Mormon community, even as her race kept her from the full ritual practices of Mormon temple worship. Finally, Melissa Inouye and Carine Decoo-Vanwelkenhuysen discuss the experience of Mormon women of Asian and European descent, respectively, arguing that Mormon religious culture is deeply inflected by American culture. For Mormon women of Asian descent, this panoply of cultural ideals allows some measure of picking and choosing, fashioning a religion and a culture that works for them. Decoo-Vanwelkenhuysen argues that European Mormon women often reject the "Americanness" of Mormon culture, instead identifying as "Mormon Europeans" who tend to share the social and cultural values of their home countries, rather than the conservative American values of many American Mormons.

Since the "Women and the LDS Church" conference in 2012, there have been a number of developments in the picture of Mormon women and agency. These include restructuring the church's semiannual General Conference to dub the general women's meeting (that now invites all female members, ages eight and over) as the opening session, and the inclusion of women offering official prayers in conference for the first time; the publication and widespread discussion of Neylan McBaine's *Women at Church: Magnifying LDS Women's Local Impact,* advocating greater gender equality in church governance within already established institutional structures;[18] and the early fruits of the 2012 changes in missionary service lowering the age for women to serve from twenty-one to nineteen, resulting in unprecedented numbers of female missionaries, many of whom are occupying leadership roles in their missions. Also, women are participating on internal church committees and boards in increasing numbers, and a number of women now oversee public affairs efforts on the regional and stake levels.

Additionally, from 2012 to 2014, the Ordain Women movement drew significant attention to the relationship between gender and priesthood authority. In various public actions that elicited significant media attention, the movement asserted that priesthood acquisition was necessary for the full exercise of female agency in the church. Ordain Women excited a great deal of public conversation about issues of agency and gender, and drove the conversation forward on a range of issues. But as the volume as a whole demonstrates, and chapters by Bednarowski and Stapley particularly emphasize, questions about women and agency in a faith community are more complex than a single metric of official authority can measure. To hold to one metric both ignores women's exercise of agency to act within institutional parameters, and neglects possibilities for more radical conceptions and exercise of agency outside of institutional parameters. Ordain Women approached the church's hierarchy to ask for specific permissions. Other women choose to work outside of that hierarchy to avoid its authority system entirely. Still others assert that focus on a narrow definition of priesthood distracts members from a theology that offers vast possibilities for female and male accomplishment.

In total, we hope these essays further the conversation about the relationship between gender and religion within Mormonism, to be sure, but also in broader contexts as well. The lessons of these essays are, in the end, broadly applicable.

The complex interplay they exhibit between agency and authority, gender and race, is a dynamic at work in religions beyond Mormonism, and in institutions beyond religion.

Notes

1. Edward W. Tullidge, *The Women of Mormondom* (New York: Tullidge and Crandall, 1877).
2. Claudia L. Bushman, "Edward W. Tullidge and *The Women of Mormondom*," *Dialogue: A Journal of Mormon Thought* 33, no. 4 (Winter 2000): 15–26.
3. Claudia L. Bushman, ed., *Mormon Sisters: Women in Early Utah* (Logan, UT: Utah State University Press, 1997).
4. Maureen Ursenbach Beecher and Lavina Fielding Anderson, eds., *Sisters in Spirit: Mormon Women in Historical and Cultural Perspective* (Urbana: University of Illinois Press, 1987).
5. Jill Mulvay Derr, Janath Russell Cannon, and Maureen Ursenbach Beecher, *Women of Covenant: The Story of Relief Society* (Salt Lake City: Deseret Book, 1992).
6. Maxine Hanks, *Women and Authority: Re-Emerging Mormon Feminism* (Salt Lake City: Signature Books, 1992).
7. Linda King Newell and Valeen Tippetts Avery, *Mormon Enigma: Emma Hale Smith, Prophet's Wife, "Elect Lady," Polygamy's Foe, 1804–1879* (Garden City, NY: Doubleday, 1984).
8. Patty Bartlett Sessions, *Mormon Midwife: The 1846–1888 Diaries of Patty Bartlett Sessions*, edited by Donna Toland Smart (Logan, UT: Utah State University Press, 1997); Carol Cornwall Madsen, *An Advocate for Women: The Public Life of Emmeline B. Wells, 1870–1920* (Provo, UT : Brigham Young University Press, 2005); Dave Hall, *A Faded Legacy: Amy Brown Lyman and Mormon Women's Activism, 1872–1959* (Salt Lake City: University of Utah Press, 2015).
9. James N. Kimball and Kent Miles, *Mormon Women: Portraits and Conversations* (Salt Lake City: Handcart Books, 2009); Claudia L. Bushman and Caroline Kline, eds., *Mormon Women Have Their Say: Essays from the Claremont Oral History Collection* (Salt Lake City: Greg Kofford Books, 2013); Neylan McBaine, ed., *Sisters Abroad: Interviews from The Mormon Women Project* (Englewood, CO: Patheos Press, 2013).
10. See the influential works by G. E. M. Anscombe, *Intention* (Oxford, UK: Blackwell, 1957); and Donald Davidson, *Essays on Actions and Events* (New York: Oxford, 2001).
11. This point echoes Walter Johnson, "On Agency," *Journal of Social History*, 37, no. 1 (Autumn 2003): 113–21.
12. Eugene Genovese, *Roll Jordan Roll: The World the Slaves Made* (New York: Pantheon, 1974); Steven Hahn, *A Nation Under Our Feet: Black Political Struggles in the Rural South from Slavery to the Great Migration* (Cambridge:

Harvard University Press, 2003); James C. Scott, *Domination and the Arts of Resistance* (New Haven: Yale University Press, 1990).

13. Catherine Brekus, *Strangers and Pilgrims: Female Preaching in America, 1740–1865* (Chapel Hill: University of North Carolina Press, 1998); R. Marie Griffith, *God's Daughters: Evangelical Women and the Power of Submission* (Berkeley: University of California Press, 1998).
14. Representative treatments of Mormon agency include the analysis of scholar Douglas Davies, *An Introduction to Mormonism* (Cambridge: Cambridge University Press, 2003), 144–71; Mormon theologian Truman Madsen, *Eternal Man* (Salt Lake City: Deseret Book, 1966), 63–70; and Apostle Boyd K. Packer, "Atonement, Agency, Accountability," *Ensign*, May 1988, 69–72.
15. Phyllis Mack, "Religion, Feminism, and the Problem of Agency: Reflections on Eighteenth-Century Quakerism," *Signs*, 29, no. 1 (Autumn 2003): 149–77, 156.
16. Blake Ostler, *Exploring Mormon Thought: The Attributes of God* (Salt Lake City: Greg Kofford Books, 2001), chapters 6–7. See also Tomis Kapitan, "Free Will Problem," in *The Cambridge Dictionary of Philosophy*, ed. Robert Audi (Cambridge: Cambridge University Press, 1995), 280–82.
17. See Carrie Miles, "LDS Family Ideals versus the Equality of Women: Navigating the Changes since 1957," and Loren Marks and Brent D. Beal, "Preserving Peculiarity as a People: Mormon Distinctness in Lived Values and Internal Structure," in *Revisiting Thomas F. O'Dea's The Mormons: Contemporary Perspectives*, edited by Cardell K. Jacobson, John P. Hoffmann, and Tim B. Heaton (Salt Lake City: University of Utah Press, 2004), chapters 5 and 10.
18. Neylan McBaine, *Women at Church: Magnifying LDS Women's Local Impact* (Draper, UT: Greg Kofford Books, 2014).

I

HISTORICAL METHODOLOGY PERSPECTIVES

1

Mormon Women and the Problem of Historical Agency

CATHERINE A. BREKUS

Few women in the nineteenth century were as controversial—and as maligned—as Mormon women. Angered by polygamy, nineteenth-century critics claimed that Mormon women were the victims of both lecherous husbands and a despotic church. "The cornerstone of polygamy is the degradation of woman," Jennie Anderson Froiseth argued in 1888, "and it can flourish only when she is regarded and treated as a slave." Mormon women were "deluded and downtrodden," "broken-hearted," "dull, senseless, sorrowful," "degraded," "shameless," "miserable," and "the meanest and most abject slaves."[1] In a work of fiction that advertised itself as journalism, a critic in 1877 denounced polygamy as a "crime that degrades woman to a level actually below the beasts of the field! A crime that makes woman at once the slave of lustful men rich enough to purchase her; the mere toy of base passion, to be cast aside the moment a newer and more attractive face is seen."[2] The author claimed that, when he asked a working man why he intended to join the Mormons, the man responded, "*Out there a chap can have as many wives as he wants.*" And when asked how his wife would cope, the man replied, "Oh, bother her, I'll teach her not to interfere with my ideas when I get her out to Salt Lake. That's the place, Sir, where we men can make these women folks keep their proper places and mind their own business. Women was made to be the servants of men, and a man ought to have just as many as he can get a hold of."[3] Most of these critiques were written by antipolygamy activists and doubtless contained a strong element of fiction, but the condemnations penned by women like Ann Eliza Young, Brigham

Young's runaway wife, were especially damaging. Ann Eliza claimed that polygamy was responsible for broken hearts and ruined lives.[4]

The antipolygamy literature of the nineteenth century was so vivid, so inflammatory, and so popular that historians have never been able to completely escape from its shadow. On one hand, historians outside of the LDS community seem to have been influenced by the caricature of the degraded polygamous wife; and although they have rarely articulated their reasons for ignoring Mormon women, they seem to assume that they are not worth studying. Neither women's historians nor American religious historians have seemed interested in including Mormon women in their narratives, implicitly suggesting that they should not be considered as serious historical actors who made things happen. On the other hand, scholars who specialize in Mormon history have been so determined to defend nineteenth-century LDS women against lingering stereotypes that they have sometimes exaggerated their agency. The result is that we are left with a fractured picture of Mormon women as either deluded, downtrodden slaves or fiercely independent matriarchs.

The conceptual confusion over how to imagine Mormon women raises larger questions about the challenges of writing women's history, especially the history of women and religion. Mormon women are an especially dramatic example of women's absence from narratives of American religion, but not the only one. Women's religious history has flourished during the past thirty years, but it has often remained on the sidelines of both women's history and religious history.[5] This essay explores why historians have found it difficult to integrate religious women into their narratives and, specifically, why the many excellent studies of Mormon women have not had a greater impact on the way historians teach and write about American religion. Since the answer to these questions seems to involve the way that historians imagine historical agency, this essay examines the problem of writing about Mormon women as agents of historical change.

Even though modern-day historians have often ignored early Mormon women, those same early Mormon women seem to have had a robust sense of their power to shape events—a power that they believed had come from God. When the first generation of Mormon women wrote memoirs about their experiences, they proudly described their contributions to the building of Zion. Ruth Page Rogers, for example, claimed that she had convinced her family to gather with the Saints after she threatened to go alone, and Mercy Rachel Fielding Thompson remembered how she and other women had raised money to build the temple at Kirtland. After receiving a revelation, she encouraged women "to subscribe one Cent per Week for the purpose of buying Glass and nails for the Temple." Although she had to hide the money from mobs, she and other women eventually raised $500.[6] Other women remembered standing up to officers or mobs who had harassed them. According to Patience Delilah Pierce Palmer, she stared "fearlessly" into the eyes of a man who held a gun near her chest and said, "I swore I'd kill a d-d Mormon when I left home and now is my chance." He left only after his captain ordered him to lower his gun. Sarah Studevant Leavitt remembered that, when an officer asked whether she and other women were armed, she lied to him. As she commented with satisfaction: "It is not hard to deceive a fool."[7]

Impressed by their mothers' strength, the daughters of these female pioneers remembered them with a mixture of affection and awe. "What a fearless, courageous woman mother was!" exclaimed Margaret Gay Judd Clawson. She praised her mother as a devout woman who had not only collected warm clothing for the "brethren" during the Echo Canyon War, but who had "sat up many nights knitting woolen stockings to protect them from the inclemency of the weather." Martha Cragun Cox marveled that her mother had not been daunted even by giving birth in a wagon on the way to Utah: "All day she suffered the jolting of the wagon under the August sun while her pains of travail were upon her without a sign of complaint and did not hinder the travel one hour. As the wagons rolled into camp her delivery came." Many other women echoed Cox's conclusion in the late nineteenth century: "It is women of that caliber that can build a nation."[8]

Despite damaging stereotypes of polygamous wives as passive and degraded, Mormon women insisted that their work was as valuable as men's—perhaps more so. "How great the responsibilities of the sisters of the church," wrote Belinda Marden Pratt, one of Apostle Parley P. Pratt's plural wives. "What a work they are accomplishing! . . . Teaching their children. Engaged in the Relief Society! Giving of their means to the poor. Visiting the sick. Administering comfort and consolation when needed. Engaged in the starting of Silk Culture. Buying up wheat etc. etc. Our labors are as great as those of the Brethren and more numurous [*sic*] for the responsibility of training the young rests almost entirely with the sisters."[9] In 1901 a group of women founded Daughters of Utah Pioneers to preserve the stories and memorabilia of their foremothers as well as those of the better-known men.[10]

When Mormons began to publish histories of the church, however, they rarely wrote about the women whose faith and work had made its existence possible. Influenced by the historical assumptions of their time, they wrote as if male leaders had created a new religious movement virtually on their own. Apostle George A. Smith's 1872 book, *The Rise, Progress and Travels of the Church of Jesus Christ of Latter-day Saints* does not mention any women by name, and only a handful of women appear in B. H. Roberts's seven-volume edition of LDS history, *History of the Church of Jesus Christ of Latter-day Saints,* which includes Joseph Smith's own chronicle and those of his close associates.[11]

This official chronicle praises several women for their faith, including Emily Coburn, who defied her family to become an early convert, and Lydia Knight, who had a prophetic dream about the Prophet Joseph; but the narrative focuses mostly on influential male converts like Sidney Rigdon, Oliver Cowdery, and Parley Pratt.[12]

In contrast, Edward Tullidge published a tribute to LDS women in 1877, *The Women of Mormondom,* which praised them as "religious empire-founders, in faith and fact."[13] But at a time when most people assumed that the natural subject of history was men and their accomplishments, Tullidge was an exception. Writing in 1893, Edward H. Anderson, a Mormon journalist, historian, and member of the Young Men's Mutual Improvement Association general board, avoided writing about women even when they should have been unavoidable—for example, in his discussion of celestial marriage. Explaining this doctrine, Anderson explained that Mormons saw marriage as "one of the chief means of man's exaltation and glory in the world to come, whereby he may have endless increase of eternal lives, and attain at length to the power of the Godhead."[14] Douglas Davies, a British scholar of Mormonism, pointed out in 2003 that, since men "cannot fully exercise their priesthood outside marriage and women cannot fully benefit from the power of the Melchizedek priesthood unless they are married to a member of it," the doctrine of celestial marriage makes men and women central to one another's salvation.[15] But one would not know this from reading Anderson's book.

By the early twentieth century, however, many LDS historians felt compelled to include women in their narratives, even if only briefly. Besides being influenced by the women's suffrage movement, they seem to have seen the political advantages of countering the stereotype of the degraded, polygamous wife. Orson F. Whitney, a bishop, future apostle, and son of a plural marriage, published his four-volume *History of Utah* in 1904, including a section on "Women of Note" that emphasized Mormon women's intelligence, patriotism, and character. He praised Eliza Roxcy Snow, poet, general president of the revived Relief Society, and a plural wife of both Joseph Smith and Brigham Young, as "gifted and educated."[16] Whitney also pointed out that Bathsheba Wilson Bigler Smith expressed affection and "respect" for her husband's other wives, reportedly saying: "We have worked and toiled together, have had our joy in our labors, have had our recreations and taken comfort in each other's society. Our faith is the same, our anticipations are the same."[17] When historian B. H. Roberts, editor, famous second-generation missionary, theologian, and member of the First Council of the Seventy, published his *Comprehensive History of the Church* in 1930, he included idealized portraits of Vilate Murray Kimball and Leonora Cannon Taylor (wives of Heber C. Kimball and John Taylor respectively) as "types of the early womanhood of the church: noble-minded, high-spirited, intelligent, courageous, independent, cheerful, but profoundly religious and capable of great self-sacrifice under the sense of religious duty." He concluded emphatically:

> Never was a greater mistake made than when it has been supposed that the women of the church were weak, and ignorant, and spiritless. Such religious movements as that which the world knows as "Mormonism," involving as it has done self-sacrifice, patient, heroic service, through trying years—through whole lifetimes, in fact—cannot be maintained on the womanhood side of it but by high-spirited, virtuous women.[18]

Although Roberts's glowing tribute to women was heartfelt, it also sounded defensive and was definitely politically driven. He wanted to guarantee that no one repeated the "mistake" of portraying Mormon women as "ignorant." His own autobiography barely mentions his own plural wives and children, and he strenuously argued against including female suffrage in Utah's Constitution.[19]

Roberts's book set a pattern. Until the rise of women's history in the mid-1970s, most Mormon historians who wrote about women seemed to be motivated by a desire to counter negative stereotypes of polygamy. For example, Russell R. Rich's 1972 book *Ensign to the Nations: A History of the Church from 1846 to the Present,* which was designed to be a survey text for undergraduate classes, only briefly refers to the Relief Society but includes several pages on women's defenses of polygamy. When Rich cites the testimonies of Sarah Melissa Granger Kimball, Mrs. Levi Riter, Phebe Carter Woodruff, Harriet Cook Young, and Eliza R. Snow, he mentions more women by name than on any other single page of his book. Rich's interest in female agency seemed to be limited to demonstrating that women were not forced into plural marriages.[20]

Rich asked probing questions about Mormon men's faith, but he did not ask why so many women were attracted to the LDS Church. Like other historians, he seems to have taken women's religious devotion for granted—as if faith has always been a natural and enduring feature of being female. Historians have traditionally naturalized women's piety instead of asking questions about why we equate femininity with faith, or how women's religious beliefs and practices have changed over time. In her history of the Reorganized Church, for example, Inez Smith Davis rarely wrote about women. The exception is a brief paragraph about their charitable endeavors as members of the Daughters of Zion: "The women of the church carry on the same church activities as have occupied the time and attention of church women everywhere," she wrote.[21] Her description implied that historians did not need to spend time analyzing something as timeless and stable as women's church work.

The modern field of Mormon women's history dates from the 1970s, when a group of female scholars including Maureen Ursenbach Beecher, Jill Mulvay Derr, Carol Cornwall Madsen, Claudia Lauper Bushman, and Laurel Thatcher Ulrich began writing about LDS women, often in collaboration with one another. When *Mormon Sisters: Women in Early Utah,* edited by Bushman, was published in 1976, it heralded the arrival of a new, academic interest in Mormon women's history. The authors who contributed to that collection wrote about topics that few before them had found worthy of study, including the Relief Society, healing, teaching, and midwifery.[22]

Since the 1970s the field of Mormon women's history has exploded. Hundreds of books and articles about Mormon women have been published, including insightful biographical accounts and groundbreaking studies of women's economic activities, professionalization, education, and support of suffrage.[23] Scholars have also published critical editions of Mormon women's diaries and autobiographies that have let women speak in their own voices. Landmark works include the diaries of midwife Patty Bartlett Sessions and the introspective journal of the well-connected Helen Mar Kimball Smith Whitney.[24]

Yet despite this impressive scholarship, Mormon women's history has not yet been integrated into the larger fields of either women's history or American religious history. In the introduction to the second edition of *Mormon Sisters,* Anne Firor Scott remembered her ignorance when she was asked to give the Tanner Lecture to the Mormon History Association in 1984. "The most startling thing I learned," she wrote, "was how little any of us non-Mormons knew about Mormon history in general but especially about the work being done on Mormon women. Most of my colleagues in the field were quite unaware that this work was going on."[25] More than twenty-five years later, the same could still be said. Few historians outside the LDS community have included Mormon women in their narratives. For example, Edwin Gaustad and Leigh Schmidt's textbook, *The Religious History of America,* includes a few pages on Joseph Smith and Brigham Young but nothing else, and Mary Beth Norton's *Major Problems in American Women's History* does not include any essays or documents about Mormon women.[26]

While Mormon women appear in the brand-new textbook, *Women and the Making of America,* they are confined to a three-page section on polygamy and women's suffrage. Although the authors mention Emmeline B. Wells in the context of her relationship with suffrage leaders like Susan B. Anthony, their brief discussion of Mormon women's activism is overshadowed by a full-page extract from Jennie Anderson Froiseth's 1882 polemic, *Women of Mormonism, or the Story of Polygamy as Told by the Victims Themselves.*[27] Froiseth's work is an important document for understanding Mormon women's history; but by giving it so much space, the authors imply that Mormon women should be imagined as "victims." Even though they include a question at the end of the document asking students to consider how Froiseth's antipolygamy stance might have influenced her depiction of plural marriage, their brief acknowledgment of possible bias is dwarfed by the full-page description of women's degradation. The authors could have discussed Mormon women in more depth elsewhere, but either they decided against it or they simply overlooked such possibilities. For example, they could have compared nineteenth-century Mormon women's charitable work in the Relief Society to Protestant women's participation in reform and benevolent associations.

Like historians outside of Mormon studies, many specialists in Mormon history have also found it difficult to imagine women as central characters in their narratives. Often their solution has been to place them in separate chapters or sections. For example, in their 1979 one-volume history, *The Mormon Experience,* Leonard J. Arrington and Davis Bitton include far more material on women than previous historians, but they place most of their discussion of women in separate chapters on "Mormon Sisterhood" and "Marriage and Family Patterns." Without intending it, they end up portraying women as marginal to the building of the faith. In Part 1, for example, when they discuss "the appeal of Mormonism," they focus exclusively on the experiences of male converts like Wilford Woodruff, Newel Knight, Parley P. Pratt, and Lorenzo Snow.[28] By waiting until Chapter 12 to tell the stories of early female converts, the authors end up isolating them from the main action of the narrative—a choice that implies that women's lives had little effect on the rise of Mormonism. Since Arrington was a strong supporter of women's history who published several articles and books about women, this effect was clearly not what he intended; but despite his admiration for historical Mormon women, he struggled to connect women's history to the larger field of Mormon history.[29]

Why have historians, despite their best intentions, found it difficult to integrate Mormon women's history into their narratives? There are several possible explanations, including androcentrism (the assumption that the universal human subject is male), inherited assumptions about what counts as serious history, and top-down models of historical change.[30] Because orthodox Latter-day Saints and Community of Christ members believe that Joseph Smith's encounters with the divine led him to create a new church based on the example in the New Testament, Mormon historians seem to have been particularly attracted to models of history that emphasize the power of prophetic leaders to create change. And indeed, many of the most dramatic changes in both churches have come from divine revelation: for example, the advent of polygamy for Mormons (and its rejection by the first RLDS prophet-president, Joseph Smith III), the acceptance of black men into the priesthood for Latter-day Saints in 1978, and the 1984 revelation authorizing the ordination of women for Community of Christ, the first of which occurred in 1985.

When LDS Assistant Church Historian Andrew Jenson published his *Church Chronology*, he began by recording the names of the First Presidents, the Council of the Twelve Apostles, the Presiding Patriarchs, and the First Council of Seventies.[31] Historians rarely reflect on why they arrange their narratives the way they do, or why they include some characters and not others, but the choice to ignore women seems to be connected to their assumptions about agency. The *Oxford English Dictionary* defines agency as "the faculty of an agent or of acting; active working or operation; action, activity," and as "working as a means to an end; instrumentality, intermediation." An "agent," also according to the *Oxford English Dictionary*, is "one who (or that which) acts or exerts power, as distinguished from the *patient*, and also from the *instrument*."[32] In other words, agency is the ability to take action—to *do* something—and an agent is someone or something that has the power to make something occur.

Most scholars, however, invest far more in the word "agency" than these simple technical definitions might suggest.[33] The field of women's history grew in tandem with the feminist movement; and, especially in the 1970s and 1980s, women's historians hoped to recover the stories of crusading female leaders who had challenged male authority. Although historians of male leaders had never felt compelled to argue that men's agency was politically subversive or liberating (and in fact, their narratives often revolved around men who had fostered war and destruction), historians of overlooked groups—including women, Native Americans, African Americans, and Latina/os—were searching for a "usable past," and so they looked for evidence of individual or collective resistance to white male hegemony. For example, African American historians inspired by the civil rights movement focused on black protests against slavery.

As a result, "agency" today has become virtually synonymous with emancipation, liberation, and resistance. When historians write about agency, they often imagine an individual in conflict with his or her society who self-consciously seeks greater freedom. As Sharon Hays, a sociologist, has pointed out, agency is often portrayed as the opposite of "structure," the enduring patterns of human life that are reproduced across generations. Social structure is associated with constraint, permanency, and collectivity, while human agency is associated with individuality, change, and freedom.[34] An agent is someone who resists the constraints of the social structure, who challenges social norms to create something new.

Given these implicit definitions of agency as freedom, empowerment, and intentionality, it is not surprising that the few women who appear in American religious history textbooks tend to be pioneering female leaders who self-consciously challenged the restrictions on their authority: white, mainstream Protestant women like Catharine Beecher, Harriet Beecher Stowe, and Frances Willard. Because historians have implicitly defined agency against structure, they have found it hard to imagine women who *accepted* religious structures as agents. This is why there are so few Mormon women in American religious history textbooks—or for that matter, Catholic women, Orthodox Jewish women, or Fundamentalist women. The field of women's history still has a feminist bent, and scholars in search of a "usable past" have rarely been interested in studying women who seem to have accepted female subordination.

Mormon historians have been determined to change this marginalization; and over the past thirty years, they have written scores of books and articles about Mormon women. They have been especially interested in recovering the stories of notable Mormon feminists like Emmeline B. Wells, suffragist, journalist, and Relief Society general president, who challenged the restrictions on women's political and economic equality.[35] Contrary to what many historians seem to have assumed, Mormon history has proven to be fertile ground for feminists in search of their foremothers. Today one of the most vital fields in Mormon women's history focuses on suffrage.

Much of this recent scholarship has been excellent, and we need still more studies of Mormon feminism in both the nineteenth century and today. Yet even though Mormon women's historians have demonstrated why Mormon women deserve to appear alongside female worthies like

Elizabeth Cady Stanton and Susan B. Anthony, they have unwittingly allowed other historians to set the terms of their debate. Instead of broadening the definition of female agency, they have tried to fit Mormon women's lives into an emancipatory paradigm by demonstrating their subjects' engagement in feminist politics. This is a laudable (and inspiring) project, but an incomplete one. While Mormon women's historians have made a compelling case for why LDS women should be included in discussions of the suffrage movement, they have not explained why historians should care about the large numbers of ordinary women who never openly challenged male authority in the family, state, or church.

Besides privileging the stories of female leaders, historians who have equated agency with resistance have encountered a different kind of problem. Because of their desire to dismantle lingering stereotypes of nineteenth-century Mormon women as victims of patriarchy, they have sometimes exaggerated women's agency. This is especially true in recent studies of polygamy. Ever since the nineteenth century, LDS historians have emphasized that women were not coerced into polygamy; but since the rise of second-wave feminism, they have portrayed this marriage practice in an increasingly positive light. Although Mormon historians always acknowledge that women described polygamy as a "trial," many also emphasize that it encouraged women to become independent and, in some cases, to seek fulfillment outside of the home.

For example, in a path breaking essay published in *Mormon Sisters* in 1976, Stephanie Smith Goodson pointed out that "polygamy developed independent women who bore much of the financial responsibility for their families," adding, "Childcare problems for polygamous wives away from home for one reason or another were virtually eliminated with the help of other sister-wives." Describing polygamous wives as powerful "matriarchs," she argued that "the advantages of polygamy often offset the problems of the system."[36] Offering an even more positive interpretation, Joan Iversen published an essay in 1984 claiming that polygamy led to "intense female bonding, increased female independence, and closer mother/child bonds." By assaulting the ideology of exclusive romantic love, Mormon leaders inadvertently encouraged women to carve out autonomous identities for themselves apart from men.[37] More recently historian and cultural critic Terryl L. Givens has explained that plural marriage "engendered great independence and resilience on the part of women necessarily deprived of the presence of a constant companion." Pointing out the large numbers of Mormon women who attended college, he claims that polygamy made it possible for women to become doctors or lawyers.[38] Turning the interpretations of nineteenth-century critics upside down, historians have insisted that polygamy was not necessarily degrading or oppressive, but sometimes liberating. Polygamy could be a form of freedom; it could liberate women from the burdens of housekeeping and childcare and enable them to find fulfillment outside of the home.

On one hand, it is clear that Mormon women were not forced into polygamy, and in fact most insisted that they had chosen it of their own free will. "I freely gave my assent," testified Artimesia Beman Snow.[39] By pointing out that polygamy encouraged women to become more independent, historians have helped to dismantle nineteenth-century caricatures of Mormon women as "slaves" or concubines. On the other hand, this positive interpretation of polygamy has also had the effect of minimizing or even ignoring the structural constraints on women's agency. Postmodernists have often overstated the limits on human agency (to the point that they have been accused of portraying humans as prisoners of language), but they have reminded us that freedom is never absolute.[40] Mormon women were free to make choices, but they exercised that freedom within a religious environment that strongly encouraged them to cultivate the supposedly "feminine" values of piety, self-denial, and obedience. According to Mary Ellen Kimball, her husband, Heber, warned his wives that if they did not recognize him as their "head," they "would bring death and destruction and misery" upon themselves.[41] The power of Mormon culture was not absolute; and many women, including Emma Smith, refused to submit to the authority of the male priesthood by accepting plural marriage. Yet these women were warned that the price of dissent might be their salvation. According to Joseph Smith's revelation on polygamy, Emma would be "destroyed" if she refused to obey the commandment to accept and even facilitate her husband's polygamy (LDS Doctrine and Covenants 132:54).[42] In 1842, when sixteen-year-old Lucy Walker hesitated to become Joseph Smith's plural wife, she reported his response as: "I have no flattering words to offer. It is a command of God to you. I will give you until tomorrow to decide this matter. If you reject this message the gate will be closed forever against you." Walker consented after receiving her own individual revelation, but her choice took place within webs of power that she herself had not spun.[43]

Later Mormon women made the same choice within the same limited matrix. When Orson Pratt, himself already a polygamist, preached on "Celestial Marriage" in 1852, he warned, "Let no woman unite herself in marriage with any man, unless she has fully resolved herself to submit herself wholly to his counsel, and to let him govern as the head. It is far better for her not to be united with him in the sacred bonds of eternal union, than to rebel against the divine order of family government, instituted for a higher salvation; for if she altogether turn therefrom, she will receive a greater condemnation."[44] Belinda Marden Pratt (his sister-in-law) later defended polygamy on the grounds that "in the Patriarchal order of family government, the wife is bound to the law of her husband. She honors him, 'calls him lord,' even as Sarah obeyed and honored Abraham. She lives for him, and to increase his glory, his greatness, his kingdom, or family."[45]

Influenced by this emphasis on feminine difference and obedience, most nineteenth-century Mormon women did not describe polygamy in the emancipatory language used by modern historians. Even those who praised polygamy for encouraging women's independence argued that it was a difficult and often painful discipline. According to an anonymous author in the 1884 *Woman's Exponent*, polygamy forced women "to depend more upon their own judgment and to take more fully the charge of their own home and affairs; this brings into requisition many latent powers in woman's nature, which would, under other circumstances, have lain dormant, and she finds herself capable of being something more than a plaything, or a hothouse plant." Yet the same author also emphasized that polygamy taught women painful lessons about how to make "the greatest sacrifice for the good of another."[46] Similarly, Lucy Walker Kimball described polygamy as a "grand school" that had taught her "self-control" and "self-denial," and many others described it as a "trial": it was a hardship or an ordeal that taught them traditionally feminine virtues like chastity, submission, and especially self-sacrifice.[47] Although it was painful to share their husbands with sister-wives, women argued that their suffering purified them and helped them prepare for their spiritual exaltation.

Most of the early Latter-day Saints had once belonged to Protestant churches, and they seem to have absorbed common Protestant ideas about the redemptive power of suffering. As Artimesia Beman Snow explained, "The Lord has said, He would have a tried people, that they should come up through great tribulation, that they might be prepared to endure His presence and glory. If I had no trials, I should not expect to be numbered with the People of God, and therefore not be made a partaker of his blessings and glory." Elizabeth Graham MacDonald claimed that her "trials" had made her "a far better woman than I otherwise should be."[48] She understood polygamy as a form of discipline that taught her how to subordinate herself to her husband, her family, and above all, to God.

Given the controversies surrounding polygamy, it is not surprising that Mormon historians have struggled to find the right tone to use when writing about plural wives. Yet their difficulties suggest that they need to think more deeply about their understanding of women's agency. In terms of its treatment of women, the field of Mormon history stands at a crossroads. While previous generations of historians virtually ignored women, recent scholars have been so determined to portray women as historical agents that they have sometimes exaggerated their freedom to make choices about their lives. Although there is no simple solution to this conceptual problem, one way forward is to try to craft a new model of agency—a model that recognizes *both* the capacity of ordinary women to create change *and* the structural constraints on their agency.

What should this model look like? I suggest seven characteristics. First, a new definition of agency should recognize that agency includes the reproduction of social structures as well as the transformation of them. As Saba Mahmood, an anthropologist of religion, has argued, scholars assume that "human agency primarily consists of acts that challenge social norms and not those that uphold them."[49] But even though we are interested in how things change, we must also be attentive to continuity—how and why things remain the same. Most of the time, people use their agency to uphold the structures that bring meaning and stability to their lives.[50] Historians sometimes treat structures as inherently oppressive, as if we are always injured or harmed by the institutions and practices that shape us, but in fact, structures also give us a sense of security.[51] Social structures may seem permanent and unchangeable, but they do not exist independently of human beings; they have to be reproduced by people in every generation.[52]

It is hard to understand the rise of the Latter-day Saints in the nineteenth century without paying attention to the women who sat in the pews every Sunday, raised their children in the faith, volunteered their time and energy to the Relief Society, and agreed to participate in plural marriages. When Lucy Ashby Clark encouraged her husband to marry another woman because "I believed in the plurality of wives, and I thought my husband worthy to enter this order of the priesthood," she helped to perpetuate the distinctive beliefs and practices of her church.[53] Neither American religious historians in general nor Mormon historians in particular have treated ordinary female believers as "agents," but of course they were: They helped to reproduce their religious communities across the generations. As sociologists Mustafa Emirbayer and Ann Mische have explained, "Habitual and routinized activities are not devoid of agency."[54]

Second, we should reconsider the implicit association of agency with freedom and emancipation.[55] Agency is certainly liberating on a personal level—people who make things happen gain an expanded sense of personal power—but as we have seen, agency is not limited to challenging social structures; it also includes reproducing them. So, for example, women's historians outside of the LDS community have been fascinated by nineteenth-century women's religious organizations like the Woman's Christian Temperance Union and the Female Antislavery Society, but they have written little about the Relief Society.

Given the large numbers of women who belonged to the Relief Society—more than 115,000 by 1942 when it was a voluntary dues-paying organization—this silence is perplexing, but women's historians have often found it difficult to write about conservative women.[56] Because they have implicitly equated women's agency with the quest for liberation, they have either ignored Mormon women or implied that their agency was not authentic—that they were victims of false consciousness. Ironically, historians treat apostates like Ann Eliza Young as agents because of their decision to leave their marriages and the church, but they seem to assume that women who remained Mormon could not have made a free choice. Although we must ask hard questions about *why* women have acted in certain ways, there is no doubt that the choice to reproduce structures—such as male headship in the church and home in the case of Mormon women—is, in fact, a form of agency.

To be clear, claiming that a woman has exerted agency is not the same as claiming that her actions were necessarily admirable. Historians of white men do not hesitate to acknowledge that men have often used their agency for ill, but because women's history began as an attempt to recover the stories of inspiring female heroines, and perhaps because of cultural assumptions about women's superior morality, historians have sometimes been reluctant to write about the less appealing aspects of women's history: for example, women's nativism or their involvement in racist organizations. Historians should be empathetic toward the women they study, especially as a factor in understanding the constraints on their choices, but they must also make carefully considered judgments about the ways that women have used their agency.[57]

Third, in addition to broadening our definition of agency to include the reproduction of social structures, we should also rethink the close association between agency and intentionality. Ever since the Enlightenment, freedom has been defined as "rational self-interest"; and in the United States in particular, historians have been fascinated by the stories of seemingly self-made men who triumphed over adversity to gain fame or wealth.[58] "Agency" has usually been equated with the deliberate pursuit of power. Yet one of the most important insights of the new social history that emerged in the 1970s is that historical change not only comes from the top down, but also from the bottom up. Even though agency includes intentionality (a sense of purpose and direction), this intentionality can be more subtle and modest than highly visible and deliberate campaigns to enact large scale change. Emphasizing the collective power of groups, social historians claim that, when large numbers of people make similar decisions about their lives, they set events in motion that have far-reaching consequences—sometimes unwittingly. Historical agents are not only visionary leaders who deliberately decide to change the world, but also ordinary people who might not be fully aware of how their individual decisions create historical change. American religious historians do not hesitate to describe Joseph Smith or Brigham Young as historical agents because they purposefully tried to create something new. But without minimizing the contributions of famous individuals, we must also pay attention to the collective agency exercised by groups of religious actors who seek common ends. For example, as Susanna Morrill has shown, large numbers of nineteenth-century Mormon women wrote poems, journals, articles, short stories, and letters that subtly challenged the patriarchal tone of the church by placing women at the center of eternal progression. Although these female writers did not intend to create something new, their common questions and concerns led them to create an alternate, female-centered theology.[59]

Fourth, a new definition of agency should also include the insight that agency should always be seen as relational and social rather than simply individual.[60] Historians sometimes write about famous religious leaders as if they were autonomous individuals who bent history to their will, but in fact their leadership was dependent on the recognition of others. Brigham Young would not be celebrated today as the "American Moses" if not for the ordinary men and women who embraced his ideas as their own.[61] His agency was largely dependent on *theirs*. Remembering the confusion that followed Joseph Smith's murder, Nancy Naomi Alexander Tracy insisted that she had no doubt about the legitimacy of Brigham Young's leadership. She found certitude in her perception that, when he spoke to the assembled Mormons at Nauvoo in August 1844, "the mantle of Joseph fell upon Brigham that day as that of Elijah did fall upon Elisha, for it seemed that his voice, his gestures, and all were Joseph."[62] Without her testimony (and the testimony of scores of other men and women in Utah who testified that they saw and heard the same thing), Sidney Rigdon might have succeeded in becoming the "guardian" of the church.

Fifth, agency must be understood as existing on a continuum. Historians tend to write as if their subjects either have agency or they do not. Nineteenth-century Mormon women were either proto-feminists (suffragists) or dupes of a patriarchal church who suffered from false consciousness. But, of course, agency is not so clear-cut. With the horrifying exception of those who, under torture, are utterly deprived of any capacity to act, almost everyone has some degree of agency—some capacity, even if limited, to make things happen. As sociologists Thomas Dietz and Tom R. Burns explain, "All actors possess agency to some degree, and no actor has total, unconstrained agency."[63]

So, for example, several LDS women claimed that they had been married to violent husbands before joining the Mormons. When Elizabeth Terry Heward remembered her first husband, she lamented that he "kept getting drunk and coming home at night and abusing me."[64] Other women were reportedly sexually assaulted as part of the mob violence against them in Missouri and elsewhere. Many Mormon women knew the shame and terror of physical violation, and their lives bear testimony to the fragility of human agency. But Mormon women also converted others to the faith, demonstrated against antipolygamy laws, and sometimes physically fought back against their enemies. Laura Farnsworth Owen remembered that, when an apostate verbally attacked Brigham Young's character in her house, she hit him with a "long-handled slice" (a cooking tool for placing food in the oven) and then "backed him out of the door the blood trickling down his cheeks."[65]

Mormon women did in fact have agency, and historians interested in the rise of Mormonism in the nineteenth century have to reckon with them as full-fledged historical actors. At the risk of stating the obvious, though, most Mormon women did not have as much agency as Mormon men, who had greater access to material and cultural resources, including money, education, and the power of the priesthood. Agency is relative and is marked by gender, racial, and class disparities.[66]

Sixth, we should also recognize that agency is always shaped by cultural norms and structural constraints. Although all humans are born with the capacity for agency, the way that humans use their agency is always shaped by the multiple structures that exist at a particular historical moment. As sociologist William Sewell has argued, "What kinds of desires people can have, what intentions they form, and what sort of creative transpositions they can carry out vary dramatically from one social world to another depending on the nature of the particular structures that inform those social worlds."[67] What this means is that there are limits to what we can imagine and what we can do. For example, both church authorities and historians have pointed out that relatively few contemporary Latter-day Saint women have explored the possibility of ordination to the Melchizedek Priesthood, but few have asked deeper questions about why Mormon women seem less interested in gaining access to male leadership roles than Protestant, Jewish, or Catholic women.

Offering a possible explanation, historian Richard Lyman Bushman suggests that Mormon women

> knew from everyday experience that women had plenty of responsibility in the lay-run congregations where there were rarely enough men and women to perform all the necessary tasks.

> Women preached and prayed in church, they taught classes, and they had a limited but consistent place in the congregational leadership councils. What Mormon women wanted, as measured by the writings in *Exponent II*, was a voice. They wanted to count when decisions were made, and they insisted that attention be paid to the peculiar problems of young mothers, single women, abused women, and others in need of help.

As a further explanation, Bushman adds, "Most Mormon women think of marriage and children as the life they most desire."[68]

Bushman's description of Mormon women's subjectivity is undoubtedly right: most Mormon women have not demanded the priesthood, and most seem to value marriage and motherhood as their most important calling. But Bushman does not pursue his line of inquiry further to ask how women's desires have been shaped and molded by their religious culture. Why, for example, did women in Community of Christ seek (and win) priesthood ordination despite their equally strong commitment to marriage and motherhood?[69]

Since women's desires do not stand outside of history (as the differences between individual women make clear), we cannot explain Mormon women's decisions about their lives solely in the language of personal preference. Instead, we must also ask how their decisions have been influenced by the political, economic, and religious structures that have framed their lives. In terms of the institutional LDS Church, this means asking questions about how women's beliefs and practices have shaped and disciplined them into being particular kinds of selves. It seems likely, for example, that the paucity of female characters in the Book of Mormon, the exclusively male priesthood starting with twelve-year-old boys, and the widely publicized excommunications of outspoken feminists have all influenced Mormon women's subjectivities. To be clear, human agency is not *determined* by structures, which would make dissent impossible. But as sociologist Anthony Giddens has argued, agency and structure should be understood as dialectical. Human action transforms structures, but structures also influence human action. Or to rephrase the same point, individuals make history, but history also makes individuals.[70]

Finally, we should remember that agency takes place within structures as well as against them. Although this is not a new observation, it bears repeating because it reminds us that women creatively appropriated LDS history to make space for assertions of their own importance and authority. Lucy Walker Kimball, for example, made sure that younger Mormons knew that Joseph Smith frowned on men who belittled their wives. Looking back, she remembered that he

> often referred to the feelings that should exist between husbands and wives, that they, his wives, should be his bosom companions, the nearest and dearest objects on earth in every sense of the word. He said men must beware how they treat their wives. They were given them for a holy purpose that the myriads of spirits waiting for tabernacles might have pure and healthy bodies. He also said many would awake in the morning of the resurrection sadly disappointed; for they, by transgression, would have neither wives nor children, for they surely would be taken from them and given to those who should prove themselves worthy. Again he said a woman should have her choice; this was a privilege that could not be denied her.[71]

Similarly, Martha Cox told a story to her granddaughter about Caroline Barnes Crosby, who "was a very hardworking woman taking much more responsibility in her home than most women take. Her husband, thinking to give the prophet some light on home management said to him. 'Brother Joseph, my wife does much more hard work than your wife.' Bro. Joseph replied by telling him that if a man cannot learn in this life to appreciate a wife and do his duty by her in properly taking care of her, he need not expect to be given one in the hereafter."[72] Recounting a cherished memory of Joseph Smith, Polly Angell remembered his praise in 1835 when he saw her and other women sewing drapes and carpets for the Kirtland Temple: "The sisters are always first and foremost in good works."[73] By telling stories like these, LDS women tried to guarantee that they would be treated with the respect and dignity that they deserved.

The model of agency outlined in this essay does not solve all the problems that Mormon historians (and American religious historians) face when writing about women. Yet if we can develop an understanding of agency that moves beyond its association with freedom, liberation, and intentionality, we will write books that deepen our understanding of how religious change takes place. If we remember that agency is not an either/or proposition, but a continuum, we will write books featuring a diverse set of characters—women as well as men—as the creators of historical change. If we view agency as relational and social, we will analyze famous leaders like Brigham Young in the context of their relationship to the ordinary men and women who made their agency possible. If we recognize agency as collective as well as individual, we will gain insight into the way that Mormon women have transformed American religion—sometimes intentionally, sometimes not—by making common decisions about their beliefs and practices. If we emphasize that agency includes the reproduction as well as the transformation of structures, we will ask questions about why and how Mormon women have reproduced the LDS Church across the generations. If we clarify that agency always exists in a dialectical relationship to structure, we will not only resist the temptation to exaggerate Mormon women's ability to create change, but we will confront the reality of their sacrifices in the name of their faith. And if we explain that women's agency is not always oriented toward emancipation or resistance, we will treat conservative as well as radical women as serious historical actors. My hope is that if we can rethink our assumptions about agency and historical change, we will write new, more inclusive narratives that show how Mormon women both made and were made by history.

Notes

1. Jennie Froiseth Anderson, ed., *The Women of Mormonism, or the Story of Polygamy as Told by the Victims* (Detroit, MI: C. G. G. Paine, 1887), 20, 23, 26, 144, 191, 259. Previously published in the *Journal of Mormon History* 37, no. 3 (Summer 2011): 59–88.
2. Wesley Bradshaw, "Letter to the Publisher," in Ella Young Harris, *Life, Confession and Execution of Bishop John D. Lee, the Mormon Fiend!* (Philadelphia: Old Franklin Publishing House, 1877), unpaginated prefatory material.
3. Ibid., 64.
4. Ann Eliza Young, *Wife No. 19, or the Story of a Life in Bondage* (Hartford, CT: Dustan, Gilman, 1875).
5. On this theme, see Catherine A. Brekus, "Searching for Women in Narratives of American Religious History," in *The Religious History of American Women*, edited by Catherine A. Brekus (Chapel Hill: University of North Carolina Press, 2007), 1–50.
6. Ruth Page Rogers, "Sketches and Incidents of the Life of Ruth P. Rogers," 1887, MS 1854, fd. 1, LDS Church History Library, Salt Lake City; Mercy Rachel

Fielding Thompson, Autobiographical Sketch, 1880, 8–9, MS 4580, LDS Church History Library. See also Mercy Rachel Fielding Thompson, Subscriptions for the Temple [ca. December 1843], MS 18642, LDS Church History Library.

7. William Moroni Palmer, "Sketch of the Life of Patience Delilah Pierce Palmer," n.d., MS 18461, LDS Church History Library; Sarah Studevant Leavitt, "History of Sarah Studevant Leavitt, copied from her history by Juanita Leavitt Pulsipher, 1919," 28, LDS Church History Library. See also Mary A. Phelps Rich, "Autobiography," in *Autobiographies of Mormon Pioneer Women* (Salt Lake City: Pioneer Press, 1994), 217.
8. Margaret Gay Judd Clawson, "Rambling Reminiscences, 1904–1911," typescript, 2, MS 3712, LDS Church History Library. Martha Cragun Cox, "Biographical Sketch of Martha Cox," 1928–1930, 38, MS 1661, LDS Church History Library.
9. Belinda Marden Pratt, "The Autobiography and Diary of Belinda Marden Pratt," typescript (undated) and introduction by Taunalyn Ford Rutherford, 37, LDS Church History Library.
10. For more information on Daughters of Utah Pioneers, see http://www.dupinternational.org.
11. George A. Smith, *The Rise, Progress and Travels of the Church of Jesus Christ of Latter-day Saints, Being a Series of Answers to Questions, including the Revelation on Celestial Marriage,* 2nd ed. (Salt Lake City: Deseret News, 1872); Joseph Smith et al., *History of the Church of Jesus Christ of Latter-day Saints,* edited by B. H. Roberts, 7 vols., 2nd ed. rev. (Salt Lake City: Deseret Book, 1948), hereafter cited as *History of the Church* by volume and page number.
12. *History of the Church,* 1:87, 101.
13. Edward Tullidge, *The Women of Mormondom* (New York: Tullidge and Crandall, 1877), 1.
14. Edward H. Anderson, *A Brief History of the Church of Jesus Christ of Latter-day Saints* (Salt Lake City: George Q. Cannon and Sons, 1893), 130.
15. Douglas J. Davies, *An Introduction to Mormonism* (New York: Cambridge University Press, 2003), 212–13. It should be noted that "celestial marriage," though understood as plural marriage in the nineteenth century, has been redefined as monogamous marriage between a man and a woman, sealed by a temple ordinance.
16. Orson F. Whitney, *History of Utah,* 4 vols. (Salt Lake City: G. Q. Cannon and Sons, 1904), 4:573.
17. Bathsheba B. Smith, quoted in Whitney, *History of Utah,* 4:573, 579.
18. B. H. Roberts, *A Comprehensive History of the Church of Jesus Christ of Latter-day Saints,* 6 vols. (Salt Lake City: Deseret Book, 1930), 5:253–54.
19. B. H. Roberts, *The Autobiography of B. H. Roberts,* edited by Gary James Bergera (Salt Lake City: Signature Books, 1990).
20. Russell R. Rich, *Ensign to the Nations: A History of the Church from 1846 to the Present* (Provo, UT: Brigham Young University Publications, 1972), 330, 365, 369, 402, 591.

21. Inez Smith Davis, *The Story of the Church* (Independence: Herald Publishing House, 1948), 574. She was the great-granddaughter of Joseph Smith, the granddaughter of Alexander Hale Smith, and the daughter of Vida E. Smith and Heman C. Smith. Heman was the RLDS Church historian in the late 1800s and early 1900s.
22. Claudia L. Bushman, ed., *Mormon Sisters: Women in Early Utah*, rev. ed. (Logan: Utah State University Press, 1997).
23. For biographies of Mormon women, see Vicky Burgess-Olson, ed., *Sister Saints* (Provo, UT: Brigham Young University Press, 1978); Lavina Fielding Anderson, "A 'Salt of the Earth' Lady: Martha Cragun Cox," in *Supporting Saints: Life Stories of Nineteenth-Century Mormons*, edited by Donald Q. Cannon and David J. Whittaker (Provo, UT: BYU Religious Studies Center, 1985), 101–32. On suffrage, see Carol Cornwall Madsen, ed., *Battle for the Ballot: Essays on Woman Suffrage in Utah, 1870–1896* (Logan: Utah State University Press, 1997). On polygamy, see Kathryn M. Daynes, *More Wives than One: Transformation of the Mormon Marriage System* (Urbana: University of Illinois Press, 2001); Sarah Barringer Gordon, *The Mormon Question: Polygamy and Constitutional Conflict in Nineteenth-Century America* (Chapel Hill: University of North Carolina Press, 2002); and Jessie L. Embry, *Mormon Polygamous Families: Life in the Principle* (Salt Lake City: University of Utah Press, 1987). Other groundbreaking studies of Mormon women include Maureen Ursenbach Beecher and Lavina Fielding Anderson, eds., *Sisters in Spirit: Mormon Women in Historical and Cultural Perspective* (Urbana: University of Illinois Press, 1987) and Maxine Hanks, ed., *Women and Authority: Re-emerging Mormon Feminism* (Salt Lake City: Signature Books, 1992).
24. For examples of women's personal writings, see Kenneth W. Godfrey, Audrey M. Godfrey, and Jill Mulvay Derr, eds., *Women's Voices: An Untold History of the Latter-day Saints, 1830–1900* (Salt Lake City: Deseret Book, 1982); Maria S. Ellsworth, ed., *Mormon Odyssey: The Story of Ida Hunt Udall, Plural Wife* (Urbana: University of Illinois Press, 1992); Maureen Ursenbach Beecher, *The Personal Writings of Eliza Roxcy Snow* (Salt Lake City: University of Utah Press, 1995); Jennifer Moulton Hansen, ed., *Letters of Catharine Cottam Romney, Plural Wife* (Urbana: University of Illinois Press, 1992); Carol Cornwall Madsen, ed., *In Their Own Words: Women and the Story of Nauvoo* (Salt Lake City: Deseret Book, 1994); Donna Toland Smart, ed., *Mormon Midwife: The 1846–1888 Diaries of Patty Bartlett Sessions* (Logan, UT: Utah State University Press, 1997); and Charles M. Hatch and Todd Compton, eds., *A Widow's Tale: The 1884–1896 Diary of Helen Mar Kimball Whitney* (Logan, UT: Utah State University Press, 2003). For a useful overview of scholarship on Mormon women, see Todd Compton, "The New Mormon Women's History," in *Excavating Mormon Pasts: The New Historiography of the Last Half Century*, edited by Newell G. Bringhurst and Lavina Fielding Anderson (Salt Lake City: Greg Kofford Books, 2004), 273–302.
25. Anne Firor Scott, "Introduction," in Bushman, *Mormon Sisters*, xxii.

26. Edwin S. Gaustad and Leigh Eric Schmidt, *The Religious History of America* (New York: HarperCollins, 2002), 177–80; Mary Beth Norton, *Major Problems in American Women's History: Documents and Essays* (Boston: Houghton Mifflin, 2007).
27. Mari Jo Buhle, Teresa Murphy, and Jane Gerhard, *Women and the Making of America* (Upper Saddle River, NJ: Pearson Prentice Hall, 2009), 340.
28. Leonard J. Arrington and Davis Bitton, *The Mormon Experience: A History of the Latter-day Saints* (New York: Alfred A. Knopf, 1979), 28–29.
29. Arrington's work on women includes "Blessed Damozels: Women in Mormon History," *Dialogue: A Journal of Mormon Thought* 6, no. 2 (Summer 1971): 22–31; "Women as a Force in the History of Utah," *Utah Historical Quarterly* 38, no. 1 (Winter 1970): 3–6; with Susan Arrington Madsen, *Sunbonnet Sisters: True Stories of Mormon Women and Frontier Life* (Salt Lake City: Bookcraft, 1984); with Susan Arrington Madsen, *Mothers of the Prophets* (Salt Lake City: Deseret Book, 1987).
30. Brekus, "Searching for Women in Narratives of American Religious History," 13–23.
31. Andrew Jenson, *Church Chronology*, 2nd ed. (Salt Lake City: Deseret News, 1899).
32. "Agency," *Oxford English Dictionary Online*, accessed July 1, 2010.
33. Mustafa Emirbayer and Ann Mische, "What Is Agency?," *American Journal of Sociology* 103, no. 4 (1998): 970, offer this useful definition: "The temporally constructed engagement by actors of different structural environments—the temporal-relational conflicts of action—which, through the interplay of habit, imagination, and judgment, both reproduces and transforms those structures in interactive response to the problems posed by changing historical situations" (italics removed). William H. Sewell Jr., *Logics of History: Social Theory and Social Transformation* (Chicago: University of Chicago Press, 2005), 142–43, defines agency as "the actor's capacity to reinterpret and mobilize an array of resources in terms of cultural schemas other than those that initially constituted the array."
34. Sharon Hays, "Structure and Agency and the Sticky Problem of Culture," *Sociological Theory* 12, no. 1 (1994): 57. Christopher Lloyd, "The Methodologies of Social History: A Critical Survey and Defense of Structurism," *History and Theory* 30, no. 2 (1991): 190, defines structures as "the ensemble of rules, roles, relations, and meanings that people are born into and which organize and are reproduced and transformed by their thought and action."
35. Carol Cornwall Madsen, "Emmeline B. Wells: 'Am I Not a Woman and a Sister?,'" *BYU Studies* 22, no. 2 (Spring 1982): 161–78.
36. Stephanie Smith Goodson, "Plural Wives," in Bushman, *Mormon Sisters*, 104–5.
37. Joan S. Iversen, "Feminist Implications of Mormon Polygyny," *Feminist Studies* 10, no. 3 (Autumn 1984): 507.
38. Terryl L. Givens, *The Latter-day Saint Experience in America* (Westport, CT: Greenwood Press, 2004), 204–5.

39. Artimesia Beman Snow, quoted in Arrington and Bitton, *The Mormon Experience*, 201.
40. See, for example, the works of Michel Foucault, including *Discipline and Punish* (New York: Vintage, 1977) and *The Order of Things: An Archaeology of the Human Sciences* (New York: Pantheon, 1970). For critiques of postmodernism, see Lloyd, "The Methodologies of Social History," 210–12; Michael L. Fitzhugh and William H. Leckie Jr., "Agency, Postmodernism, and the Causes of Change," *History and Theory* 40, no. 4 (December 2001): 59–81; and Perez Zagorin, "History, the Referent, and Narrative: Reflections on Postmodernism Now," *History and Theory* 38, no. 1 (February 1999): 1–24. See also Keith Jenkins, "A Postmodern Reply to Perez Zagorin, *History and Theory* 39, no. 2 (May 2000): 181–200, and Perez Zagorin, "Rejoinder to a Postmodernist," *History and Theory* 39, no. 2 (May 2000): 201–9. See also the essays collected in Keith Jenkins, ed., *The Postmodern History Reader* (London: Routledge, 1997).
41. Mary Ellen Kimball, *Journal of Mary Ellen Kimball, Including a Sketch of Our History in This Valley* (Salt Lake City: Pioneer Press, 1994), 52.
42. On Emma Smith, see Linda King Newell and Valeen Tippetts Avery, *Mormon Enigma: Emma Hale Smith, Prophet's Wife, "Elect Lady," Polygamy's Foe* (New York: Doubleday, 1984).
43. Lucy Walker Kimball, "Statement of Mrs. L. W. Kimball," n.d., typescript, MS 3142, LDS Church History Library. After Joseph Smith's assassination, Lucy became one of Heber C. Kimball's numerous plural wives.
44. Orson Pratt, "Celestial Marriage," sermon August 29, 1852, in *The Essential Orson Pratt*, foreword by David J. Whittaker (Salt Lake City: Signature Books, 1991), 275.
45. Belinda Marden Pratt, *Defence of Polygamy, by a Lady in Utah to Her Sister in New Hampshire* (Salt Lake City: n.p., 1854), 7. On the patriarchal emphasis of polygamy, see B. Carmon Hardy, "Lords of Creation: Polygamy, the Abrahamic Household, and Mormon Patriarchy," *Journal of Mormon History* 20, no. 1 (Spring 1994): 119–52.
46. Anonymous, "A Mormon Woman's Views," *Woman's Exponent* 13, no. 11 (November 1, 1884): 81.
47. Kimball, "Statement of Mrs. L. W. Kimball." Belinda Marden Pratt, "Autobiography and Diary," 30, also described polygamy as a "sacrifice." For an account of a woman's suffering in polygamy, see Annie Clark Tanner, *A Mormon Mother: An Autobiography* (Salt Lake City: University of Utah Tanner Trust Fund, 1969), 57–69.
48. Artimesia Beman Snow quoted in Arrington and Davis, *The Mormon Experience*, 201. Elizabeth Graham MacDonald, 1831–1917, Autobiography, 1875, letterpress, 40, MS 31, LDS Church History Library. For a good overview of recent scholarship on polygamy, see Martha Sonntag Bradley, "Out of the Closet and into the Fire: The New Mormon Historians' Take On Polygamy," in Bringhurst and Anderson, *Excavating Mormon Pasts*, 303–22.
49. Saba Mahmood, *Politics of Piety: The Islamic Revival and the Feminist Subject* (Princeton, NJ: Princeton University Press, 2005), 5. See also Talal Asad,

Genealogies of Religion: Discipline and Reasons of Power in Christianity and Islam (Baltimore: Johns Hopkins University Press, 1993), 15.

50. On this point, see Hays, "Structure and Agency and the Sticky Problem of Culture," 63. According to Emirbayer and Mische, "What Is Agency?," 975, "The past, through habit and repetition, becomes a stabilizing influence that shapes the flow of effort and allows us to sustain identities, meanings, and interactions over time."
51. Elizabeth Pritchard, "Agency without Transcendence," *Culture and Religion* 7, no. 3 (2006): 267. Pritchard criticizes Judith Butler's theory of "subjectivization" in her *The Psychic Life of Power: Theories in Subjection* (Stanford, CA: Stanford University Press, 1997). Pritchard argues that socialization does not always entail antagonism or violation: "There is no warrant for supposing that making is tantamount to subordination. There is no warrant for supposing that one is deprived of agency in being made or for supposing that subordination entails 'the deprivation of agency'" ("Agency without Transcendence," 266). See also Hays, "Structure and Agency and the Sticky Problem of Culture," 61.
52. Christopher Lloyd, "The Methodologies of Social History," 191, argues that "society is a real structure of rules, roles, relations, and meanings that has to be produced, reproduced, and transformed by individuals while causally conditioning individual actions, beliefs, and intentions." Hays, "Structure and Agency and the Sticky Problem of Culture," 63, describes the reproduction of structures as "structurally reproductive agency."
53. Lucy Ashby Clark, "A Short Sketch of My Life—Written in 1881," *Our Pioneer Heritage*, compiled by Kate B. Carter, vol. 10 (Salt Lake City: Daughters of Utah Pioneers, 1967), 130.
54. Emirbayer and Mische, "What Is Agency?," 978.
55. On this point, see Mahmood, *Politics of Piety*.
56. Jill Mulvay Derr, Janath Russell Cannon, and Maureen Ursenbach Beecher, *Women of Covenant: The Story of Relief Society* (Salt Lake City: Deseret Book, 1992), 287. As of 1971, all LDS women over the age of eighteen were automatically enrolled in the Relief Society and the requirement of paying dues was cancelled.
57. On the challenges of making judgments, see Linda M. G. Zerilli, "Toward a Feminist Theory of Judgment," *Signs: Journal of Women in Culture and Society* 34, no. 2 (2009): 295–317.
58. On Enlightenment definitions of agency, see Emirbayer and Mische, "What Is Agency?," 964–65.
59. Susanna Morrill, *White Roses on the Floor of Heaven: Mormon Women's Popular Theology, 1880–1920* (New York: Routledge, 2006); see also her "Relief Society Birth and Death Rituals: Women at the Gates of Mortality," *Journal of Mormon History* 36, no. 2 (Spring 2010): 128–60. In contrast to my argument, Thomas Dietz and Tom R. Burns, "Human Agency and the Evolutionary Dynamics of Culture," *Acta Sociologica* 35, no. 3 (1992): 191–92, claim that "actions must be intentional for agency to be operating." Yet they also add, "That does not mean that all implications of the action are understood or anticipated."

60. William Hamilton Sewell, *Logics of History: Social Theory and Social Transformation* (Chicago: University of Chicago Press, 2005), 145; Mary Jo Neitz, "Gender and Culture: Challenges to the Sociology of Religion," *Sociology of Religion* 65, no. 4 (Winter 2004) 392–97; Emirbayer and Mische, "What Is Agency?," 973; Pritchard, "Agency without Transcendence," 280.
61. Leonard J. Arrington, *Brigham Young: American Moses* (New York: Alfred A. Knopf, 1985).
62. Nancy Naomi Alexander Tracy, "Autobiography," in *Autobiographies of Mormon Pioneer Women*, edited by Ogden Kraut, 2 vols. (Salt Lake City: Pioneer Press, 1998), 2:149.
63. Hays, "Structure and Agency and the Sticky Problem of Culture," 64; Dietz and Burns, "Human Agency and the Evolutionary Dynamics of Culture," 192.
64. Elizabeth Terry Heward, *Autobiography and Journal* (n.p.: n.p., 1900–1980?), 8.
65. Laura Farnsworth Owen, "Autobiography," 1868, MS 1048, LDS Church History Library. Mary Ann Phelps Rich, "Autobiography," in Kraut, *Autobiographies of Mormon Pioneer Women*, 2:220, reports how she helped rescue her husband.
66. On agency as "relative," see Pritchard, "Agency without Transcendence," 278–79.
67. Sewell, *Logics of History*, 144. See also Dietz and Burns, "Human Agency and the Evolutionary Dynamics of Culture," 192.
68. Richard L. Bushman, *Mormonism: A Very Short Introduction* (New York: Oxford University Press, 2008), 93–94.
69. On women in Community of Christ, see Danny L. Jorgensen, "Sisters' Lives, Sisters' Voices: Neglected Reorganized Latter Day Saint Herstories," *John Whitmer Historical Association Journal* 17 (1997): 25–42. According to William D. Russell, whose history of the schism is in preparation, an estimated 25 percent of RLDS members defected, either formally or informally, over the 1984 revelation; but not surprisingly, women's role in this schism was primarily accompanying husbands and fathers out of the Church rather than leading a protest movement.
70. In his theory of "structuration," Anthony Giddens, *Central Problems in Social Theory* (Berkeley: University of California Press, 1979), argues that structure and agency constitute each other. Hays, "Structure and Agency and the Sticky Problem of Culture," 61, argues that "people . . . produce certain forms of social structure at the same time social structures produce certain types of people."
71. Lucy Walker Kimball, "Statement of Mrs. L. W. Kimball."
72. Martha Cragun Cox, "Stories from the Notebook of Martha Cox, Grandmother of Fern Cox Anderson," typescript, not paginated, MS 658, LDS Church History Library. *Joseph Smith: The Prophet of the Restoration*, a church-produced film shown at the Visitors' Center in Temple Square (and at other visitors centers), shows Smith speaking these lines while standing outside and beating a rug—a choice that emphasizes his sexual egalitarianism.
73. Polly Angell, quoted in Derr, Cannon, and Beecher, *Women of Covenant*, 16.

2

Remember Me

Inscriptions of Self in Nineteenth-century Mormonism

LAUREL THATCHER ULRICH

Many years ago, while doing research on women in colonial New England, I came across a sampler made in Boston in the early 1700s. The embroidery portrayed a whimsical Adam and Eve beside a fruit-filled tree. Alongside inscriptions honoring God and nation was this little verse, rendered in cross-stitch:

> When I am Dead and Laid in Grave
> And all my Bones are Rotten
> When this you see
> Remember Me
> And never let me be forgotten.

Coming from a nine-year-old girl, the reference to rotten bones was mildly shocking. I attributed it to a Puritan tendency to frighten children into obedience with the specter of death and thought of grim sermons in unheated churches and gaunt skulls on gravestones.

Then my husband and I decided to remodel the upstairs of our New Hampshire house. As we tore out the rough-sawn pine paneling in one of the rooms we found notes, acorns, and coins that our children had dropped through knotholes twenty years before. With a blue felt-tipped pen, our daughter Melinda had provided a little history of the house, writing: "I am 9 years old. But when you find this early History I'll probably be dead." Mindy's little note forced me to think about that eighteenth-century sampler in a new way. Like the young embroiderer (and at the very same age), my daughter was learning to place herself in time as well as space.

There is no simple explanation for why people drop acorns into knotholes or inscribe their names on linen samplers. Letting others know that you once walked the earth may be an essential part of what it means to be human.

The words "Remember Me" have a long and intriguing history. In the Bible, they were often uttered in prayer, as when Hannah, longing for a child, "vowed a vow, and said, 'O Lord of hosts . . . remember me.'" Like Job, David, Samson, and the thief on the cross she was a supplicant seeking God's favor.[1] Jesus reversed things when he broke bread and asked his disciples to remember him.[2] But in this case, too, the relationship was vertical. In the early modern world, ordinary people began using their pens, needles, or chisels to make a claim, not on God, but on people much like themselves. On school books, samplers, gravestones, albums, and the underside of desks, they begged, "When this you see, Remember me." Sometimes their inscriptions were jaunty, as in an autograph from the nineteenth-century Ozarks, "Remember me early, remember me late/Remember me as your old schoolmate."[3] (That sentiment could appear today on Facebook.) Other invocations were more sober, as on a powder horn from the American Revolution:

> Oliver Graham it tis My Name
> At Saybrook I Was born,
> When this you See
> Remember Me,
> If I AM Dead and Gon.[4]

Regardless of tone, a request to be remembered implies absence—an earthly journey or death.

The rotten bones verse is a devil-may-care way of acknowledging death, a form of whistling in a graveyard. It is found all over the English-speaking world, in ring games and ballads and even in modern novels as a way of delineating characters or setting scenes. A sampler with the rotten bones verse is now stored in the Revolutionary War Pension Papers at the Library of Congress. It was submitted because its genealogical details affirmed the identity of a soldier.[5] I haven't found the rotten bones jingle in the LDS Church archives, but that may be because I haven't looked hard enough. Nineteenth-century Mormons had no qualms about imagining death, and they too wanted to be remembered.

Zina Huntington Young was too refined to imagine her own bones disintegrating, but she knew from firsthand experience as a nurse what it meant to watch beside the bed of someone she loved. More than once she wrote in a friend's album:

> Say, would it afford you a pleasing sensation
> Some trace of a Friend to behold
> When the heart that now dictates has ceased it's pulsation
> And the hand which now writes this is cold.

She wrote with an understanding that a heart was not a valentine but a physical organ that pumped blood. When its pulsation ceased, a hand grew cold. But a mark that hand made on a sheet of paper remained.[6] In her world, an ink stroke or a twist of hair could call up the presence of a person, living or dead.

Today, DNA analysis lends credibility to the notion that by touching a piece of paper with one's lips, a person might actually send a kiss through the mail, as many letter writers attempted to do when they marked the spot where they had kissed a letter. Physical traces connected living persons to each other. But Mormons believed that certain kinds of traces might also bind the heavens. In his instruction regarding baptism for the dead, Joseph Smith rephrased a New Testament scripture by telling the Latter-day Saints that "whatsoever you record on earth shall be recorded in heaven, and whatsoever you do not record on earth shall not be recorded in heaven; for out of the books shall your dead be judged, according to their own works."[7] Although the language is elusive (was it really the record that did the binding or the spiritual act of remembering?), it nevertheless enhanced the meaning of writing things down, of turning memory into a tangible thing.

Historians are fortunate in being able to draw upon the wealth of records that nineteenth-century Mormons created, but we are not always as diligent as we might be in addressing the astonishing variety and form of these records, nor as attentive as we might be to the circumstances in which they were fashioned and preserved. Those tasks are essential to any effort to recover the history of Latter-day Saint women. Mormon sisters wanted God to remember them; they wanted their family and friends to remember them; and though they didn't always admit it, many of them also wanted future generations to remember them. They made a claim upon history and upon those of us who presume to write Mormon history today.

Wilford Woodruff was a recent convert to Mormonism and a newly called missionary when he wrote across the top of his journal, "The first book of Wilford." He took literally the concept expressed in the Book of Commandments that whatever God's missionaries spoke when moved upon by the Holy Ghost was scripture.[8] Two decades later, he told a gathering of church leaders in Salt Lake City,

> I have kept a Journal of almost every day of my life for the last 24 years. I could tell each day what I had done, what Company I was in & what was transpiring around me . . . You may say that this is a great deal of trouble. Vary well. It has been to me in one sense . . . But what of it? I have never spent any of my time more profitably for the benefit of mankind than in my Journal writing.[9]

Few historians would disagree. Woodruff's journal is not only an essential source in Mormon history but a great American diary.

Compare Woodruff's statement with Rachel Simmons's comment as she began her own diary in 1881 at the ripe old age of forty-five:

> At this late time of my life, being in my 45th year, I feel impressed, or have a desire to keep a journal. I do this for my own satisfaction (and probably for future reference) and knowing it will be a pleasure to my children to have it to look at and read, no matter how little merit it may contain or how poorly done, they will cherish it, not for great and noble deeds or sacrifices made for others, but they will like it to read. *Just because it was Mother.*[10]

This contrast between a man's diary as a "benefit to mankind" and a woman's diary as a gift to her children reflects the nineteenth-century concept of "separate spheres," an ideological construction that developed as the locus of production and authority shifted from the household to the marketplace and the ballot box.

In the early nineteenth century, writers began to imagine men as valiantly facing the harsh world of work and politics, while women preserved the comforts of family and home. In reality, the two spheres were interwoven. Female labor, whether paid or unpaid, was essential to the functioning of the larger economy, for Latter-day Saints as well as other Americans. At the same time, the idea of the home assumed political power in struggles over slavery, temperance, polygamy, and eventually woman suffrage.[11] Yet the ideology of separate spheres and the differential institutional power of women and men has had a powerful impact on the way later generations have understood gender relations. Men and women both wanted to be remembered, but few women extended that desire beyond the intimate circle of family and friends, nor did well-established institutions make it easy for them to do so. The resurgence of women's history in the late twentieth century had a profound effect on archival acquisition and preservation of women's writings, but there is still a great deal more work to be done.

A number of years ago, Maureen Beecher analyzed Davis Bitton's then comprehensive bibliography of nineteenth-century Mormon sources, concluding that only one in ten of these documents was written by a woman.[12] Understandably, the ability to keep records depended on mastery of written English. In earlier centuries young girls were taught to read but not to write, and even in the nineteenth century when opportunities for education were expanding, girls may have had less formal education and fewer opportunities in adulthood to use writing skills. Many early male leaders among the Latter-day Saints (including Joseph Smith) had little education, yet managed to keep some sort of record; if not in their own handwriting, in that of scribes. Men wrote because keeping records was a church responsibility. Their writings survived because they were deemed important to the institutional history of the church.

In the correspondence of former Presiding Bishop William B. Preston, the ratio of his letters to those of his wife Harriet is twenty to one. This is not because Harriet failed to write letters—frequent reference in her husband's correspondence attests to their existence—but because hers did not survive. It may be she kept his letters while he did not keep hers; she was at home—he was traveling. Or it may be because his seemed of greater consequence.[13] Complicating the problem is the difficulty of actually finding women's writings in the archives. How many of us have puzzled over which part of the alphabet to consult when looking for a person with a compound name like Zina Huntington Jacobs Smith Young.

Although few Latter-day Saint men were either as diligent or effective as Woodruff in creating and preserving records, hundreds of them tried, at least for a while. It is no accident that the vast majority of Mormon diaries were kept by men because the vast majority of Mormon missionaries were men and diary keeping was one of the duties of a missionary.[14] In this way, institutional practices compounded gender differences. The loss is not just to women's history, but to history more broadly. Consider how much richer our records of the Mormon past might have been if female converts had been given a journal at the moment of baptism and told to keep an account of their own spiritual experiences and their activity in the church. If that had happened, we would not only have Wilford Woodruff's record of holding a meeting at Polly Vose's house in Boston in 1838, we might have her account of the testimonies she heard and her relationship with her fellow church members most of whom were other women, persons Woodruff identified only as "the sisters."[15]

Think, too, how Mormon history would look if the *wives* of missionaries had been called to keep journals while their husbands were away. That sometimes happened. At her husband's request, Mary Richards composed both a day-by-day journal and a brief account of her early life while her husband Samuel was serving in England. Her account of the difficult crossing from Nauvoo and life at Winter Quarters is, without question, one of the most powerful and revealing documents from that period. It is a rare example of what might have been. But when Samuel came home, her diary stopped.[16] Diary keeping was a difficult task for anyone, as Woodruff himself acknowledged, but a belief that God or his representative wanted you to do it was a powerful incentive.

I do not believe it is accidental that the first surviving diaries by LDS women (with the exception of a little journal kept by Leonora Cannon before she became a Mormon) were begun after the founding of the Female Relief Society of Nauvoo. Eliza Snow's first journal opens in June 1842, three months after she became secretary of the Relief Society. Zina Huntington Jacobs, who was an active member of the Relief Society, began her journal in 1844, just before the death of Joseph Smith.

Other women, including midwife Patty Sessions, may have kept diaries earlier, but these have not survived. In some respects it is a miracle

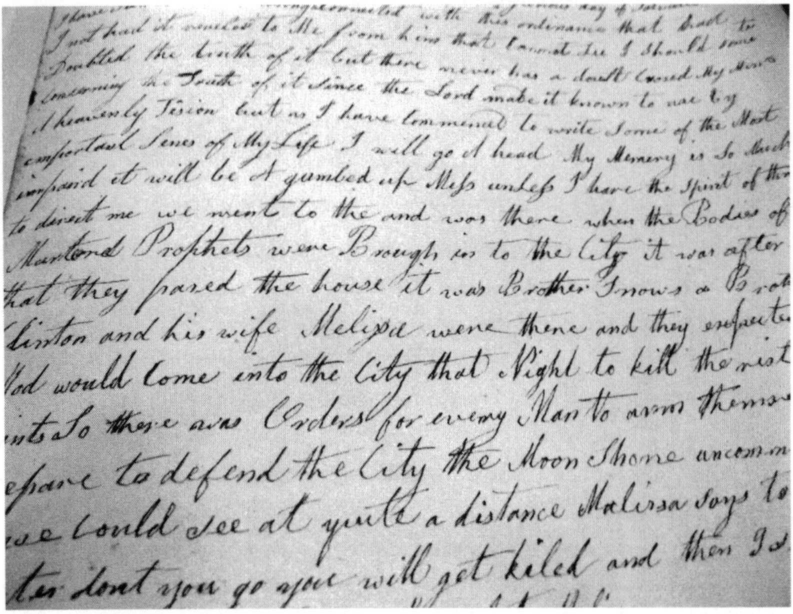
not had it revealed to Me from him that had to
Doubted the truth of it but there never has a doubt Crossed My Mind
concerning the Truth of it Since the Lord made it known to me by
a heavenly Vision but as I have commenced to write Some of the Most
important Senes of My Life I will go A head My Memory is So Much
impaired it will be A jumbled up Mess unless I have the Spirit of the
to direct me we went to the and was there when the Bodies of
Martered Prophets were Brough in to the City it was after
that they pased the house it was Brother Snows a Brot
Clinton and his wife Melissa were there and they expecte
Mob would Come into the City that Night to kill the rest
ints So there was Orders for every Man to arm themse
prepare to defend the City the Moon Shone uncomm
we could see at quite a distance Malissa says to
ter dont you go you will get kiled and then I

FIGURE 2.1. Sarah S. Leavitt's words about memory in her own hand. Her autobiography is nearly sixty pages in length, and this comes halfway through the text. Used by permission, Utah State Historical Society.

that Eliza's and Zina's eventually came to public archives. Historians can only work with surviving records, and sadly many records kept by women have disappeared. After Eliza's death, her Nauvoo diary passed from her brother Lorenzo to his daughter-in-law Elizabeth Wilson, who gave it to her home teacher in 1943 when he was helping her prepare her house for sale. In 1965 the home teacher and his wife gave it to a couple in their neighborhood who had visited Nauvoo and become enthusiastic about church history. They handed it over to the director of Nauvoo Restoration, who eventually gave it to Belle S. Spafford, then general president of the Relief Society, who had it conserved and then gave it to the church archives.[17] It could have been lost at any point in this long journey.

Zina's diary was not so much lost as hidden in plain sight. After her death, her family kept some of her papers in an old red tin bread box she had brought from Nauvoo, "a treasure box passed down through the generations, filled with letters, diaries, clippings, and other precious documents," preserved but seldom read. A great-granddaughter, Mary Woodward, remembered seeing these things as a child but lost track of the bread box until she found it in the basement of her mother's house while looking for Christmas decorations. Other relatives found more papers hidden behind the log walls when they were restoring a house in Canada, and in 1980 a great-great-granddaughter found Zina's Nauvoo diary in a locked trunk she had been using as a sofa table for several years.[18]

The modern practice of separating written documents from museum artifacts has also complicated the task of recovering women's history. Different professionals, preservation practices, and forms of cataloguing make it difficult to connect materials that may have originated in the same family. In this, as in so many other areas, Latter-day Saint practice conforms to procedures common everywhere. In the nineteenth century, distinctions between diaries and other kinds of records were much less clear. Men as well as women engaged in sentimental (and sometimes deeply religious) exchanges of physical relics, locks of hair, autographs, fragments of wood, or fabric. Although diaries and minute books ended up in archives, memorabilia of this sort were preserved, if at all, in local history collections or in the hands of honorary societies, like the Pioneer Memorial Museum. But such things were not separated at their creation.

When Wilford Woodruff departed on his first mission to England in 1839, he deliberately left his unfinished journal where his wife Phebe would find it, adding a note at the bottom of the page, "Remember me in your prayers especially as the sun sets on the western horizon." In essence, his still unfinished journal became a token of his love for Phebe. In exchange, she tucked into his luggage some sort of woven ornament made from her hair with a similar note imploring him to remember her and their infant daughter.[19] Not surprisingly, the diary survived and is now housed in the church archives. Phebe's tokens have disappeared, although the Church History Museum has many snippets of hair carefully labeled in Woodruff's handwriting. After Joseph Smith's death, he collected locks from both the prophet and Hyrum, some of which he passed on to other men, some he encased in a cane preserved in the museum.[20]

Autograph albums also cross presumed gender boundaries. A 1986 study found sixty-five autograph albums in Utah repositories, roughly half of which were kept by women.[21] Barbara Neff Moses, a convert from Lancashire County, Pennsylvania, was especially assiduous in collecting autographs of church leaders. Her book has inscriptions beginning in Nauvoo and extending to the end of the nineteenth century, with signatures from Joseph Smith, Brigham Young, John Taylor, Wilford Woodruff, Sidney Rigdon, W. W. Phelps, Orson Hyde, Eliza R. Snow, and many others. The prophet's inscription shows both his willingness to engage in a common social practice and his awkwardness in doing so. He wrote:

> The truth and virtue both are good
> When rightly understood
> But Charity is better, Miss,
> That takes us home to bliss
> And so forthwith
> remember Joseph Smith
> Nauvoo 1844[22]

To fully understand nineteenth-century Mormon culture, we need to find ways to bring seemingly ephemeral records like this together with more conventional documents.

Fortunately, some women had the education, the inspiration, and the audacity to insist on being remembered. Few were as assertive as Augusta Adams Cobb, a woman who left her husband and children in Massachusetts to join the church and marry Brigham Young in polygamy. In letters written not long after she arrived in Utah, she displayed both relentless faith and astounding self-possession. Annoyed at what she perceived to be Young's neglect of her she wrote, "If you keep yourself from under the Sound of my voice, you cannot from under the influence of my pen thank God." She expressed hope that when the books were opened through which all men might be judged, hers might be opened as well. "For my life is a living epistle and I am willing to be known and read of all men." In a second letter, she insisted that what she wrote was "dictated by the Spiret of the Lord, as much so as when men get up in the stand and preach." If it wasn't dictated by the spirit, then she wished it "to go into the land of forgetfulness, together with my weaknesses and follies, which I confess to be many, to be remembered no more forever."[23]

She was not alone. In June 1852, an Ogden pioneer named Abigail Abbott wrote Brigham Young. She had heard that the church was going to celebrate the Fourth of July by honoring the men who had marched with the Mormon Battalion. Since she was the "Companion of one of Those men," she thought she would pen a few of her own experiences during the three-and-a-half-years she held her family together in Nauvoo and Winter Quarters while her husband was absent. She told Young that at first she had "staid not lived" in the frame of a meeting house west of Montrose, Iowa, with three other families. Then, with another woman and their combined six children, she had packed everything into a wagon and walked across Iowa, spending most nights husking the six or seven bushels of corn they had packed into the mouth of their wagon. When they reached the Mormon refugee camps on the Missouri River, she supported her family by teaching school in more than one temporary settlement and chopping firewood at night to keep her family warm. She nursed her oldest daughter and one of her husband's plural wives through childbirth and extended illnesses. She grew and sold garden produce, put in an acre of corn and beans, cleared two acres of land still "in a wild state" and grew and harvested twenty-three bushels of buckwheat, which she threshed on a blanket with a pole. She spun twenty pounds of wool, exchanging some to pay for having her animals wintered over by another family, hauled two tons of hay, and gleaned turnips from other people's fields, getting every third bushel she gathered. She then crossed the Missouri River with three yoke of oxen and got her family to Utah. She closed by saying that this had only been a brief sketch. "The Rest is Better Realized than told. If it will be of any use or satisfaction to My Brethren and Sisters who were connected with the Battalion or belonging to it they are welcome to it for what it is worth. If it is not worth attention please throw it under the Table." She added that she would like to see the celebration include "an Expression from Sister Eliza R Snow if there is no objection," and hoped that if the wives of the men who went with the battalion deserved any applause or reward, they would get it. She signed herself "your Faithful Sister in the bonds of the New and Everlasting Covenant."[24]

So much for separate spheres! It wasn't until after the reorganization of the Relief Society in the 1860s, and the founding of the *Woman's Exponent* in 1872, that a significant number of women began to compose stories of their lives. The Relief Society made a special effort to collect autobiographies during the church's jubilee in 1880.[25] Belinda Marden Pratt was moved to tears by reading the *Exponent* account of the jubilee.

"What an age we are living in! How great the responsibilities of the sisters of the church. What a work they are accomplishing! And how many there are that do not realize the amount of work before them as helpers in this great dispensation."[26]

There was a lot of self-deprecation in the writings the women produced. Rhonda Seamons warned future readers, "I write this after I am Seventy too years old for my Children to look at. It is wrote very poor. Perhaps you cant read it."[27] Sarah Leavitt interrupted her narrative to explain, "My memory is so much impaired it will be A jumbled up Mess unless I have the spirit of truth to direct me."[28] But being told that their work mattered to others and to God was a powerful incentive. In July 1887, Ruth Page Rogers observed, "When I commenced to write I done it for my own satisfaction and amusement, not thinking of writing to have it preserved for others, knowing I am a humble person . . . but [as] the Lord has been mindful of me and blessed me in this life and by the spirit has whispered to me that I should have my writings preserved."[29] The Spirit had whispered, but her fellow Latter-day Saints had also ratified and nurtured those whisperings.

To the end of her life, Zina Huntington kept a woven hair ornament and accompanying poem made by a friend named Sophia Bull:

> Dear friend accept the lock of hair
> Which you so oft have seen me wear.
> I've worn it when in friendships bower
> And passed with you the social hour
> This little present kindly take
> And keep it for the givers sake
> And when this lock of hair you see
> My dear dear friend do remember me.[30]

Latter-day Saint women wanted to be remembered by those closest to them. They also wanted their service and commitment to be acknowledged by the church. In the 1880s, women of the Manti Relief Society offered a framed bouquet made of their own hair to the newly constructed temple in Manti. The accompanying inscription echoed those exchanged between friends: "These locks of hair, O Lord, thou hast seen us wear, so now we commit them to thy holy Temple's care." What looks like a golden vase holding the hair flowers is actually a miniature baptismal font complete with supporting oxen.[31] In this way they transformed a sentimental practice into a sacred offering.

Twentieth-century historians should take such materials more seriously. Instead of being put off by what appears to us an odd, or perhaps even creepy, use of human hair, we might consider the bodily labor of Latter-day Saint women to sustain an institution that too often forgot them. They asked to be remembered by their friends, by God, and by future generations of Latter-day Saints. They also deserve to be remembered by historians.

Notes

1. 1 Samuel 1:11; Job 14:3, Psalms 106:44, Judges 16:28, Luke 23:42.
2. Luke 22:19. The concept of remembrance is reinforced in Latter-day Saint scripture and practice in 3 Nephi 18:7, 11 and in the prayer on the bread and water in Moroni 4:3 and Doctrine and Covenants 20:77.
3. Vance Randolph and May Kennedy McCord, "Autograph Albums in the Ozarks," *The Journal of American Folklore* 61, no. 240 (April–June 1948): 183–84.
4. W. M. Beauchamp, "Rhymes from Old Powder-Horns," *The Journal of American Folklore* 2, no. 5 (April–June 1889): 119.
5. Katherine H. Wintemberg and W. J. Wintemberg, "Folk-lore from Grey County, Ontario," *The Journal of American Folklore* 31, no. 119 (January–March 1918): 83–124; Annie G. Gilchrist, "Note on the 'Lady Drest in Green' and Other Fragments of Tragic Ballads and Folk-Tales Preserved amongst Children," *Journal of the Folk-Song Society* 6, no. 22 (June 1919): 87; "Folk-lore in the News," *Western Folklore* 10, no. 1 (January 1951): 83–84; Richard Wall, "Fleming's Inscription," in *James Joyce Quarterly* 19, no. 3 (Spring 1982): 348–49; Margaret Atwood, *Alias Grace* (New York: Doubleday, 1996); National Society of the Colonial Dames of America, Sampler Survey found at http://www.nscda.org/samplers/samp-home.php; Jennifer Davis Heap, "'Remember Me': Six Samplers in the National Archives," *Prologue Magazine* 34, no. 3 (Fall 2002). http://www.archives.gov/publications/prologue/2002/fall/samplers-1.html#f11
6. Sarah Melissa Kimball Autograph Album, MS 131, Church History Library, Salt Lake City, Utah.
7. Doctrine and Covenants 128:8
8. The passage that now appears as Doctrine & Covenants 68:4 was given in Hiram, Ohio, December 1, 1831. See the original text on the Joseph Smith Papers website at: http://josephsmithpapers.org/paperSummary/revelation-1-november-1831-a-dc-68.

9. *Wilford Woodruff's Journal, 1833–1898,* edited by Scott G. Kenney, 9 vols. (Midvale, UT: Signature Books, 1983–1985), 5:36–37 (hereafter cited as *Wilford Woodruff's Journal* with volume and page).
10. "Journal of Rachel Emma Woolley Simmons," *Heart Throbs of the West,* vol. 11, edited by Kate Carter (Salt Lake City: Daughters of the Utah Pioneers, 1951), 153–208.
11. There is a wealth of literature on this topic. Landmark essays include Barbara Welter, "The Cult of True Womanhood: 1820–1860," *American Quarterly* 18, no. 2 (1966): 151–74; Paula Baker, "The Domestication of Politics: Women and American Political Society, 1780–1920," *American Historical Review* 89, no. 3 (June 1984): 620–47; Linda K. Kerber, "Separate Spheres, Female Worlds, Woman's Place: The Rhetoric of Women's History," *Journal of American History* 75, no. 1 (June 1988): 9–39; and essays by Mary Kelley, Julie Roy Jeffrey, Laura McCall, and Carol Lasser in "Redefining Womanly Behavior in the Early Republic: Essays from a SHEAR Symposium," *Journal of the Early Republic,* 21, no. 1 (2001): 73–123.
12. Maureen Ursenbach Beecher, ed., *The Personal Writings of Eliza Roxcy Snow* (Salt Lake City: University of Utah Press, 1995), xv.
13. William B. Preston Papers, 1857–1919, Utah State University.
14. There are only 5 diaries kept by women among the 114 missionary diaries recently digitized by the Brigham Young University Library. "About the Collection," Mormon Missionary Diaries, Digital Collection, BYU Harold B. Lee Library, http://lib.byu.edu/digital/mmd/about.php
15. *Wilford Woodruff's Journal,* 1:248–49.
16. Maureen Carr Ward, ed., *Winter Quarters: The 1846–1848 Life Writings of Mary Haskin Parker Richards* (Logan, UT: Utah State University Press, 1996).
17. Beecher, *Personal Writings of Eliza R. Snow,* 47–49.
18. Martha Sontag Bradley and Mary Brown Firmage Woodward, *Four Zinas: A Story of Mothers and Daughters on the Mormon Frontier* (Salt Lake City: Signature Books, 2000), vii, viii.
19. "Phebe's Supplication," Wilford Woodruff Collections, Church History Library, MS 19509, Correspondence, item 6, and separate entries for August 8, 1839 in Journal January 1838–1839 and Journal 1839–1840; Wilford Woodruff Journals and Papers, MS 1352, box 1, fd. 2, fd. 9, Church History Library. Kenny's transcription (1:349) amalgamates the two.
20. *Wilford Woodruff's Journal,* 2:450; 3:3.
21. Melvin L. Bashore, "Index to Autographs and Memorializations in Autograph Albums in Utah Repositories," 1986, typescript, Church History Library.
22. Barbara Neff Moses, Autograph Album, Church History Library.
23. Augusta Adams Cobb Young to Brigham Young, September 16, 1851, and October 3, 1852. I thank Connell O'Donovan for sharing his transcription of these letters.
24. Abigail Smith Abbott to Brigham Young, June 28, 1852, Brigham Young Papers, Church History Library, quoted in Kathleen Halverson Hadfield, "I Trusted in

God and Improved Every Opportunity," in *Women of Faith in the Latter Days,* vol. 1, edited by Richard E. Turley Jr. and Brittany A. Chapman (Salt Lake City: Deseret Book, 2011), 10–12.

25. There were several "Jubilees" in the nineteenth century. See Jill Mulvay Derr, Janath Russell Cannon, and Maureen Ursenbach Beecher, *Women of Covenant: The Story of Relief* Society (Salt Lake City: Deseret Book, 1992), 261–62, which describes Relief Societies in the 1930s opening Jubilee Boxes prepared in 1880. For one example of such a memoir, see "Mercy F. Thompson Autobiographical Sketch, 1880," Microfilm of holograph, Church History Library, cited in Jennifer Reeder, "The Blessing of the Lord Has Attended Me," in *Women of Faith,"* 423–30.
26. Belinda Marden Pratt, Journal, September 5, 1880, quoted in Taunalyn Ford Rutherford, "The Joy and Peace I Experienced Was Inexpressible," in *Women of Faith,* 245.
27. "History of Mary Ann Brown Pulsipher," 1872, typescript, L. Tom Perry Special Collections, Harold B. Lee Library, Brigham Young University, quoted in Rhonda Seamons, "That We May All, in Glory Dwell," in *Women of Faith,* 263.
28. Sarah S. Leavitt, Autobiography, Juanita Leone Levitt Pulsipher Brooks Papers, Utah State Historical Society, quoted in Andrea Ventilla, "Like Fire in My Bones," in *Women of Faith,* 163.
29. Quoted in Carol Cornwall Madsen, *Journey to Zion: Voices from the Mormon Trail* (Salt Lake City: Deseret Book, 1997), 456.
30. Zina Card Brown Family Collection, MS 4780, box 3, fd. 17, Church History Library.
31. Mary Wintch, Manti Temple Hair Wreath, 1885. Church History Museum, LDS 85-244-2. A picture of the wreath can be found in Richard G. Oman and Robert O. Davis, *Images of Faith: Art of the Latter-day Saints* (Salt Lake City: Deseret Book, 1995), 38. It is also discussed, along with the use of hair in other memorials, in Jennifer Reeder, "'To Do Something Extraordinary': Mormon Women and the Creation of a Usable Past" (PhD dissertation, George Mason University, 2013), 29–74. Reeder's dissertation is a landmark work in the integration of material and documentary sources in Mormon women's history.

3

Reexploring Mormon Women and Agency in the Context of Polygamy

RACHEL COPE

Histories that focus on Mormon women have often fallen into an either/or trap, particularly on the subject of plural marriage. According to standard interpretations, this practice either empowered Mormon women by making them autonomous, or it stripped them of agency altogether.[1] "The result," Catherine Brekus noted, "is that we are left with a fractured picture of Mormon women as either deluded, downtrodden slaves or fiercely independent matriarchs."[2]

In an effort to encourage more accurate interpretations of Mormon women's lived religiosity, this essay will examine plural marriage to hint at the depth and breadth of female religious experiences. Specifically, it will consider three women—Hannah Tapfield King, Edith Turpin McMurrin, and Martha Cragun Cox—whose personal writings demonstrate that Mormon women's agency has been too simplistically conceived. Plural wives did not simply define themselves in relation to the practice of polygamy; rather, they saw themselves as converts, as spiritual pilgrims, and as covenant makers and keepers. Their stories reveal how devout women wrestled with, felt devastated by, and also embraced LDS teachings about plural marriage. Grappling with this practice shaped their understandings of personal revelation, salvation, and atonement.

Plural Marriage

Early Mormon theology included both individual and corporate salvation. Conversion to and membership within the community was a means of discovering oneself and then becoming connected to a web of human relationships that ultimately link back to the divine.[3] Salvation involved cooperation and community; it included "a preservation of human ties."[4]

Joseph Smith's soteriological teachings eventually included a radical revision of marriage; indeed, he introduced the Biblical practice of plural marriage. For Smith, this marriage system provided a way to preserve human relationships through the establishment of spiritual dynasties.[5] This sealing of the human family—a welding together of multiple relationships through marriage and the law of adoption—created lateral links within the LDS community that bound people together into an extensive cosmological sphere.[6]

Although practiced selectively in Nauvoo, many people, including some church members, were unaware of the practice of plural marriage prior to Mormon settlement in the Rocky Mountains.[7] In fact, the church did not make an official announcement about plural marriage until Brigham Young asked Orson Pratt to do so in 1852.[8] Pratt explained plural marriage by placing it within its religious framework, drawing mainly upon the revelation (now Doctrine and Covenants 132) Smith had dictated in 1843.

As plural marriage became an increasingly common and public practice, many people wrote scathing critiques, exposés, and editorial pieces in order to reveal the "truth" about the church. Eventually, Mormon women as well as men took up the pen to defend this radical practice, hoping to assure readers they were not forced to enter plural marriages, but rather had made a conscious choice. Mormon writings defending polygamy appeared in newspapers, periodicals, and other forms of public print.[9] Perhaps it is from those contemporary depictions of polygamy, both partisan and polemical, that our modern historiographical perceptions have perpetuated. Mormon women were either highly empowered agents or submissive dupes.[10]

Hannah Tapfield King, Covenant Keeper

Hannah Tapfield King's interest in the church was sparked in 1849, when her dressmaker, Lois Bailey, introduced her to the LDS faith. Although initially upset by the claim that this was God's only true church, Hannah's perspective began to evolve as her mind became "engrossed" with the doctrines and principles Lois shared with her—a message that appealed to Hannah's heart and mind. Hannah read, prayed, and discussed the church with Lois for fifteen months. Her conversion process unfolded slowly, enriched by religious discussions that took place, woman to woman. "[Lois] alone was my teacher, my priestess," Hannah explained.[11]

On April 17, 1851, Hannah was baptized by Joseph W. Johnson, a Mormon missionary from America. Of this experience she recalled, "I was buried in the liquid grave and raised up out of it in the likeness of the burial and resurrection of our Savior—and then I found that this was but the beginning of a new life and new trials."[12] Almost immediately, Hannah encountered the disapproval and dismay of close family members and friends who feared she and her daughter Georgiana, who had likewise been baptized a member of the LDS Church, had gone insane. Intimate ties were weakened, and in some cases, severed.[13]

And yet, no trial appears to have been as perplexing as the eventual confirmation Hannah received that rumors about Mormon polygamy were indeed true, a discovery that came when church leaders announced the practice publicly to her congregation in England in 1852.[14] Echoing the reactions of women who learned of plural marriage at the time of its inception in Nauvoo, Illinois, Hannah felt that this disturbing news had hit her like a "thunderbolt."[15] She undoubtedly wondered how any woman could participate in, or even accept a marital practice that required a radical reconfiguration of personal sanctity. Like so many other Mormon women, she questioned how anything so nauseating, so contrary to the virtue and morality she had been taught to cultivate throughout her life, could be a commandment of God.

Doubt. Despair. Devastation. Each of these words captures Hannah's feelings as she attempted to comprehend what to her seemed incomprehensible. Of this experience she recalled:

> In the afternoon *the revelation* was read which will I expect set the world in a blaze—Oh! Brother I shall never forget my feelings! it had an extraordinary effect upon me! for tho' I had Known for a year that such a principle existed in the Church, when I heard it read, and some things in it which I did *not* know, I confess to you I became Sceptical, and my heart questioned with Tears of agony, did *this* come from God?—I could not speak or shed a tear at first, I felt overpowered *stunned* as it were!—We had a Cab home Mr Spencer, Claudius, Georgey, and I in it—Claudius seeing my

> state of mind, got up as he sat opposite to me and Kissed me affectionately, and asked me how I felt[.][16] That was sufficient—the floodgates of my heart were burst open & I wept like a child—he soothed me—and but for the Kiss & the Kindness God Knows how long the Evil One would have held my spirit in bondage—my Eyes seemed to *rain* tears—when we got out of the Cab—I asked Mr Spencer Senr if I might speak to him—he Kindly walked up and down the square with me while I asked him if he *Knew* that the revelation was from *God*! he was very Kind—and said every thing to Comfort and Console me, and build up my trembling faith, till I became calmer—I then went to my Lodging close by . . . and there I wept unrestrainedly till the agony of my feelings subsided.[17]

Public defenses of plural marriage were not enough to console Hannah's troubled heart and mind. As she explained it, she could only come to terms with this strange revelation by turning to her God; she had to engage in a healing process that was private, personal, interior. Even as time passed, she continued to feel the "shock" of the announcement.[18] The heartache and confusion she experienced could not be resolved easily.

Notwithstanding her distress concerning polygamy, Hannah remained a committed believer in the church—so committed that she convinced her husband Thomas, who was not LDS, to sell the family farm and immigrate with her to the United States so she could live amongst fellow believers in the Rocky Mountains. Upon settling there, Hannah learned about the Mormon doctrine of sealing, and immediately lamented that her husband did not meet the requirements to participate in the temple ceremony. A journal entry written on October 7, 1855, captured the concern Hannah felt about not being able to experience this salvific rite. In the context of this private space she confided that she did not want to abandon her husband, and yet she also did not want to "lose one jot or tittle of my salvation." Reflecting further on this important matter, she continued, "No I must make my calling and Election Sure—I must have the sealing ordinance abiding upon me—then I shall be at rest so far—but Who?—and when—and how shall all these things be? 'God will provide[']—and I throw Myself into His Hands!"[19] Despite Thomas's eventual baptism on March 14, 1857, during the era of the Mormon Reformation, he never reflected real interest in or commitment to the church. Hannah lamented that they "were two in the regions of the Soul."[20]

Hannah's ability to accept plural marriage came as she recognized that it could offer a solution to her dilemma. In 1872, while Thomas was still living, she became a plural wife of Brigham Young, so she could have, as she later explained, the "sealing ordinance abiding upon me."[21] Her sealing to Young applied only to the afterlife; Hannah never had a conjugal relationship with the Mormon prophet, even following Thomas's death in 1874.

Hannah's spiritual journey—from conversion, to learning about and feeling aversion for polygamy, then deciding to settle with the Latter-day Saints, and ultimately, becoming a plural wife—hints at the paradoxes of agency inherent in the lives of devout Mormon women. Many elements of her story, including convincing her husband to uproot for the sake of her faith, intimate her role as agent. But what should scholars make of her continuing commitment to the church and her eventual plural marriage in light of her initial aversion to this practice? One could argue that Hannah's situation was different because her husband was not a member of the LDS Church; it is possible that she initially felt private relief that this practice could not apply to her own marital relationship. Later, however, as her understanding of Mormon soteriology developed, her views evolved. She recognized that plural marriage would enable her to be sealed to an eternal companion when she could not make that covenant with Thomas.[22] Hannah's interpretation of personal revelation and her desire to have the "sealing ordinance abiding upon me" resulted eventually in her coming to terms with a practice she had initially abhorred.[23]

Edith Turpin, Community

Like Hannah King, Edith Turpin converted to the church in her native England, but the thirty years that separate their conversion stories resulted in strikingly different initial encounters with the practice of plural marriage. Whereas Hannah heard rumors about plural marriage, and then received shocking confirmation that the rumors were indeed true, Edith undoubtedly knew about plural marriage before making the decision to be baptized in 1884. During that time, the practice received frequent public attention, both national and international. British

FIGURE 3.1. Edith Turpin. Courtesy John and Debbie Dester.

newspapers contained countless accounts and criticisms of Mormon polygamy, and warned people to be cautious of the "dangerous" elders who sought to kidnap English women so they could take them to their Utah harems.[24] Due to this rampant publicity, Edith had to come to terms with plural marriage prior to, rather than, following her baptism. Her radical religious decision was fully informed and alarming for her family.

Eventually, Edith immigrated to Utah. Once settled, she finally penned a letter to her half-brother John and his wife, Elizabeth. She described Utah and the Mormons from the perspectives of both an objective observer and an active participant of the church. She used this dual approach to assure her family that she had exercised wisdom and caution in her new home and had not become a submissive prisoner to the Mormon people. Edith informed her brother and sister-in-law that she would give them all the information she could "regarding the peculiar people among whom my lot is now cast" and explained to them that she had made note of the "inwardness of this people and their popular religion."[25] By assuring her family that she had not been "idle in this direction," Edith made it clear that she would provide an accurate representation of the Mormon people to them. She described their exemplary deeds, while also acknowledging some of their weaknesses and admitting that there were those who did not live their religion. This balance made her claim "that I have never seen a better lot of people, taken as a whole, than the Latter Day Saints" more convincing than if she had insisted on their complete perfection. She wanted her brother and sister-in-law to see the Mormon people as she saw them—a group of individuals striving to live the gospel of Jesus Christ. Disparaging accounts about the church, she explained, were recounted by those who "grievously lied about" it. Edith wanted to correct misconceptions her family had by sharing "the truth and nothing but the truth" concerning their "situation and conduct here in the mountains."

After arguing in behalf of the exemplary and wholesome character of the "honorable, upright, God-fearing" people that surrounded her, Edith shifted into the most controversial aspect of the church—plural marriage. She attempted to convince her brother and sister-in-law that it was "one of the most beneficial doctrines to women if properly carried out." Rather than relying on emotive expressions or religious sentiment to explain why this was the case, Edith chose to employ logic and reason. She recognized that spiritual explanations would not suffice for her unbelieving family. Thus, she engaged with Biblical and philosophical interpretations employed by church leaders and LDS apologists in an attempt to explain the positive reasons for this most unusual practice. At one point, she even declared, "I had rather to be the 20th wife of an honorable God-fearing Man, than to be the only wife of any one of two thirds of the Men in the world."[26]

At first glance, a historian might interpret Edith's letter as evidence that Mormon women submissively embraced and repeated justifications for polygamy that originated with lecherous male leaders. A careful reading, however, reveals that Edith's writing, and thus her thinking, was highly sophisticated. She wove together different strains of apologetic thought into a cohesive narrative that reflected her own feelings and understandings about plural marriage. The very structure of her letter reveals that Edith was an educated, thoughtful, and articulate writer.[27] Certainly she had been a careful observer and a cautious student of the church. Although not all arguments she used were original to her, Edith's writing displays confidence and surety, and she exhibits a form of agency in her conviction. Intricately woven throughout the explanations she provided was a powerful declaration of personal testimony, both implicit and explicit. To truly understand her role as an agent, one must consider how her defense of plural marriage, combined with her decision to become the second wife (by one day) of James Leaing McMurrin, both created and reinforced this distinct LDS practice.[28] Scholarship on Mormon women should consider how people like Edith helped to shape and reshape the church, even while working within a structured framework.

Martha Cragun Cox: Mormon Cosmology

Slowly and subtly over the course of the nineteenth century, the Mormon marriage system changed. Some of this transformation can be traced to the decisions and actions of Mormon women. In the years prior to Wilford Woodruff issuing the 1890 manifesto, which sought to end plural marriage, already fewer women became polygamous wives. Many LDS families even discouraged their daughters from entering such relationships and women who chose to be plural wives often faced comments of derision.[29] It was in such an environment that Martha Cragun decided to marry Isaiah Cox in 1869, a man who already had two wives and seven children. Although friends and family members disapproved of Martha's choice, she "had studied out the matter" for herself. In her autobiography she explained, "If the Lord would have manifested . . . that the principle of plural marriage was wrong . . . I felt I should be happy . . . My only relief was in prayer, and prayer only strengthened my resolve to leave father, mother and all for—I scarcely knew what."[30]

Martha would not deviate from the direction she believed God had given her, even though she may have wished, at least at times, that he had answered her prayer differently. Instead, she became increasingly devoted to Mormon cosmology, and developed her own theological worldview and commitments. Although Martha developed strong relationships with her sister-wives, she rarely saw or received any support from her husband. She taught school to provide for her family, and was able to support her children by herself. Thus, Martha's story could easily be placed into the framework that stresses too much or too little agency. It could be argued that her circumstances as a polygamous wife ultimately lead to autonomy. Or, perhaps she remained committed despite difficult circumstances because she had fallen into a plural marriage trap—so much so that warnings from friends and family members made no difference. While those scenarios are plausible, more careful consideration of Martha's personal writings suggests a more complex story. Martha willingly sacrificed what she wanted, and what others wanted for her, for the things she believed God wanted her to do. In that sense, she considered herself an agentic being.

Martha believed the trials she endured as a plural wife enabled her spiritual commitment to increase. For instance, she recorded a dream she had during the "underground years"—a time in which she struggled with deep feelings of despair and depression.[31] In the dream, Martha saw herself carrying an enormous chain around her neck with heavy bundles welded to various links. As a result of the weight of this chain, she could not even look up toward the sky. An unnamed individual (also in the dream) suggested that she hang the burdens on a rod over her fireplace, and Martha heeded this advice. The bundles included events in her life that had made her angry, sad, and frustrated. Some of them reflected her suffering as a plural wife. She recalled that after removing the last one, "lo, the chain was gone and I was free."[32] This dream signified to Martha the role of the divine in her daily life. She believed God had delivered this important message to her; he wanted her to know she could transcend her burdens. She could forgive what might have seemed unforgiveable and endure her trials through the grace of her Savior. Her autobiography reflects a powerful belief in atonement and a personal expression of lived theology. Martha believed her suffering and sacrifice, combined with her willingness to change, would lead to personal sanctification.

Martha's intense commitment to understanding and living her beliefs—from making the decision to become a plural wife to relying on the atoning power of Christ to overcome her burdens—surfaces throughout her autobiography. She grasped the importance of reuniting her fractured world through covenantal relationships. Through horizontal means, she believed her husband, children, sister-wives, and she were welded together into an eternal family unit. Vicarious sealings performed for her deceased ancestors bound her vertically to the generations that preceded her parents. Martha perceived her decision to become a plural wife had allowed the vertical and the horizontal to join together into a full and salvific web of human relationships that would continue after her own death.

Conclusion

To suggest that plural marriage was the route either to endless agency or to grave oppression is to miss the meaning that Mormon women assigned to their participation in the practice. Plural marriage did not define LDS women; it was just one aspect of some of their lives. Hannah Tapfield King, Edith Turpin McMurrin, and Martha Cragun Cox found that grappling with the doctrine of plural marriage increased their first-hand experience with revelation and atonement, while entering plural marriage facilitated their salvation through communal relationships.

Notes

1. Catherine A. Brekus, "Mormon Women and the Problem of Historical Agency," *Journal of Mormon History* 37, no. 2 (Spring 2011): 59–87.
2. Ibid., 61.
3. Ibid., 44–45.
4. Samuel Morris Brown, *In Heaven as It Is on Earth: Joseph Smith and the Early Mormon Conquest of Death* (New York: Oxford University Press, 2012), 208.
5. Todd Compton, *In Sacred Loneliness: The Plural Wives of Joseph Smith* (Salt Lake City: Signature Books, 1997), 487; J. Spencer Fluhman, "'A Subject That

Can Bear Investigation': Anguish, Faith, and Joseph Smith's Youngest Plural Wife," *Mormon Historical Studies* 11, no. 1 (Spring 2010): 45; Kathryn M. Daynes, *More Wives Than One* (Urbana-Champaign: University of Illinois Press, 2008), 28.

6. Early Latter-day Saints believed that humankind must all be sealed to one another (preferably to a church leader) to ensure salvation and exaltation, while current Mormons believe humankind must be sealed together in nuclear families, in an unbroken line back to Adam. For more information, see Samuel Morris Brown and Jonathan Stapley, "Mormonism's Adoption Theology: An Introductory Statement," *Journal of Mormon History* 37, no. 3 (2011): 1–53; Daynes, *More Wives Than One*, 28.
7. See John G. Turner, *Brigham Young: Pioneer Prophet* (Cambridge, MA: Harvard University Press, 2012), 152–57.
8. Using the Mormon teaching of a premortal existence, Orson Pratt explained that Mormons were "more worthy" in God's eyes before mortality, and were spiritually prepared to live polygamy. Arguments were also made using the Old Testament Patriarchs Abraham, Isaac, and Jacob. Perhaps most important, it was traced back to a revelation given to Joseph Smith in 1843. See Orson Pratt, "Celestial Marriage," in *Journal of Discourses*, vol. 1 (London: Latter-day Saints' Book Depot, 1854), 53–66.
9. Sherilyn Cox Bennion, "Sisters under the Skin: Utah's Mormon and Non-Mormon Women and Their Publications," *BYU Studies* 33, no. 1 (1993): 111–30.
10. "In casting monogamous women as the only real agents, anti-polygamists denied or ignored other Mormon women's voices and choices—the very dismissals they laid at the feet of the Mormon hierarchy." J. Spencer Fluhman, *A Peculiar People: Anti-Mormonism and the Making of Religion in Nineteenth-Century America* (Chapel Hill: University of North Carolina Press 2012), 121.
11. Hannah Tapfield King, "Autobiography," 122–26, Church History Library, Salt Lake City, Utah.
12. As cited in Dorothy Brewerton, Carolyn Gorwill, and Leonard Reed, *The Songstress of Dernford Dale: The Life of Poetess, Diarist and Latter-day Saint Pioneer Hannah Tapfield King*, (n.p.: privately published, 2011), 50, L. Tom Perry Special Collections, Harold B. Lee Library, Brigham Young University.
13. Leonard Reed, "'As a Bird Sings': Hannah Tapfield King, Poetess and Pioneer," *BYU Studies* 51, no. 3 (2012): 105–7.
14. Turner, *Brigham Young*, 205.
15. Brown, *In Heaven as It Is on Earth*, 243; Benjamin F. Johnson, *My Life's Review: The Autobiography of Benjamin F. Johnson*, edited by Lyndon W. Cook and Kevin V. Harker (Provo, UT: Grandin Book, 1997), 83–84; Lucy Walker Kimball, "Autobiographical Sketch," Church History Library.
16. Claudius Spencer was married to Hannah's daughter, Georgiana (Georgey). Mr. Daniel Spencer was Claudius's father.
17. Tapfield King, "Autobiography," 174–76.

18. Carolyn Gorwill, ed., The Journals of Hannah Tapfield King (privately published, 1985), December 25, 1852.
19. Tapfield King, "Autobiography," 275–76; Brewerton, Gorwill, and Reed, *Songstress of Dernford Dale,* 106.
20. Tapfield King, "Autobiography," 275–76.
21. Ibid.
22. Tapfield King, "Autobiography," 275–76.
23. Reed, "As a Bird Sings," 113–16; Tapfield King, "Autobiography," 275–76. For other women's initial reactions to plural marriage, see Maureen Ursenbach Beecher, "'All Things Move in Order in the City': The Nauvoo Diary of Zina Diantha Huntington Jacobs," *BYU Studies* 19, no. 3 (1979): 291–92; Helen Mar Whitney, "Scenes and Incidents in Nauvoo," *Women's Exponent* 11, no. 5 (1 August 1882): 39.
24. While Mormon polygamy rarely made the front page, it frequently occupied the middle pages of British and American periodicals. See "The Condition of Mormon Women," *New York Tribune,* November 17, 1871, 2; "The Danger of War in Utah," *The Evening Telegraph* (Philadelphia), February 9, 1870, 2; "The Mormon Women and Polygamy," *Manchester Evening News* (England), October 27, 1871, page 3; "The Mormon Women's Love of Polygamy," *Dundee Courier* (Angus, Scotland), November 20, 1871, 4.
25. Edith Turpin to John and Elizabeth Turpin, n.d., in private collection of John and Debbie Dester, Provo, Utah. Subsequent quotations in this paragraph are taken from this source
26. Ibid.
27. Rachel Cope, "'I Cannot Refrain from Testifying': Edith Mary Turpin's Observations about Mormonism and Plural Marriage," *Mormon Historical Studies* 14, no. 2 (2014): 154–88.
28. Brekus, "Mormon Women," 79.
29. See Virginia Eggertsen Sorensen, *Where Nothing is Long Ago: Memories of a Mormon Childhood* (Salt Lake City, UT: Signature Books, 1998).
30. Martha Cragun Cox, "Autobiography," 117–18, Church History Library.
31. As a result of federal prosecution after the 1882 Edmunds Act, many Mormons lived in a complex system of hiding places referred to as the "underground."
32. Cox, "Autobiography," 178–79.

4

Turning the Key

Understanding Mormon Women's Material Culture

JENNIFER REEDER

On April 28, 1842, Joseph Smith told the women who joined the new Relief Society in Nauvoo, "I now turn the key to you in the name of God and this Society shall rejoice and knowledge and intelligence shall flow down from this time—this is the beginning of better days, to this Society."[1] The phrase, "I now turn the key to you," has since encouraged discussion of women, agency, authority, and intelligence. Having several potential meanings, the key could represent a means to unlock a door, a symbol of administrative authority, or a means of understanding new information, like cracking a code.[2]

The key, in a variety of physical formats, has become an icon of Relief Society authority, a symbol of female legitimacy. As a distinctive piece of Relief Society material culture, the key has been reproduced at various times and places. At the 1892 Relief Society Jubilee, a large floral key was displayed on the Tabernacle pipes with portraits of Joseph Smith, Emma Smith, and Eliza R. Snow.[3] In 1936, Joseph A. F. Everett portrayed women receiving the key from Joseph Smith on the cover of the *Relief Society Magazine*.[4] In 1980, the Reorganized Church of Jesus Christ of Latter Day Saints (now known as the Community of Christ) rebuilt the Nauvoo Red Brick Store and later sold replicas of the store's nineteenth-century skeleton key. The icon, reproduced in flowers, ink, and metal, resides in Mormon cultural memory as a symbol of women's agency with deep interpretive meaning.

A variety of artifacts in addition to the key—quilts, samplers, banners, aprons, even glass grapes—represent Mormon women and their past.[5] Curators display them in museums and exhibits; artists and writers position them in historical re-creations and artistic works; families pass them down matrilineal lines as heirlooms. These material objects are valuable tools to examine female history and agency. First, artifacts offer insight not contained in written records, allowing women to speak in different ways. Second, objects situate women within their era and provide contextual details. Third, careful study of these items reveals the breadth of female activity and gives insight into economic, social, political, cultural, and religious ideologies. Finally, both the preservation and the loss of Mormon women's material culture reveal an additional level of agency in the selection and construction of the past.

Material Culture Speaks for Women beyond a Textual Record

Due to the religious emphasis on record keeping, numerous texts document Mormon history. However, many women did not write, or their records did not survive. Material culture can help fill this void with clues about the experiences of otherwise voiceless people in the same way a key opens a locked door or a secured treasure box. For instance, Mary Whitmer did not leave a written record. She did, however, keep a tattered piece of string that bound together the original Book of Mormon manuscript, illustrating her participation in the Restoration.[6] This ragged cord provides details about domestic manufacture, relationships among families and friends, women's contribution to the physical details of translation, and preservation of important items.[7] Artifacts preserve insights into skills, relationships, and domestic and public practices not often described in textual records.

As a key code to provide interpretation of indecipherable mysteries, artifacts furnish information about creators and keepers, their desires, beliefs, hopes, and fears.[8] L. Thomas Frye noted that quilts "serve as documents, no less than diaries, manuscripts and letters. Yet to read them, we must examine every shred of evidence, both physical and associational, and look for the larger connections quilts had as functional material culture."[9] Analysis of artifacts provides personal relationships and domestic items with public meaning. Relief Society album quilts allowed women to display their sewing skills, as well as their personalities, in ways not captured in written records. The Salt Lake City Fourteenth Ward

FIGURE 4.1. In 1870, members of the Salt Lake City Twentieth Ward Relief Society pieced together individually-made blocks to create an album quilt for their president, Margaret T. Smoot. Courtesy of the International Society of Daughters of Utah Pioneers, Salt Lake City, Utah.

Relief Society created such a quilt in 1852. The quilt was raffled to raise money and eventually split into two parts for descendants of the raffle winner. Mary Elizabeth Knight Bassett's block features bright sunflowers with an intricate stem. She lived a fractured life of poverty while moving from Missouri to Illinois to Utah, as well as the difficulties of living in polygamy with a husband who favored a younger plural wife. Her block, while cheery, was cut in half on the diagonal when the quilt was split in half for two descendants of the owner, revealing more about her life experience than the fragments of written biographical information she left. Scrutiny of individual blocks, of their fabrics and designs, provides historical background of individuals and contextual circumstances of otherwise silent women.[10]

Likewise, the women in the Twentieth Ward in Salt Lake City pieced a quilt for their president, Margaret T. Smoot, in 1870.[11] They inscribed blocks with tributes of friendship and family as well as political and cultural references. The majority of the families on these blocks arrived in Utah after 1856; most of the women were newer converts who had not experienced the persecutions in Ohio, Missouri, or Illinois. Contributors came from many different countries, including England, Ireland, Scotland, and Denmark. Material culture allowed the women, some of whom struggled with English as a second language, to express their views, relationships, contributions, and heritage without using the written word.

Material Culture as a Window into the Historical Environment

By their very nature, keys are not interchangeable. Different keys open different secured spaces: doors, safety deposit boxes, cars, codes, or memories. Material objects communicate historical context in ways that text cannot iterate. Artifacts, Ulrich wrote, "tell us most when they are embedded in the rich texture of local history."[12] The Fourteenth Ward quilt provides a snapshot of a very specific time and place: 1857, in the heart of downtown Salt Lake City. The abundance of floral designs in the different blocks displayed a popular Victorian motif in quilts, but also expressed the landscape and ideology of the desert valley of the Great Salt Lake and pioneer efforts to blossom and thrive. Examination of specific fabrics, stitches, embellishments, and colors—some unique and others shared—provides insight into the environmental, social, political, religious, cultural, and technological layers of the quilt.[13] The Twentieth Ward album quilt was created in 1870 as Mormon women in Utah publicly protested federal antipolygamy legislation.[14] Annie K. Smoot, for instance, created a block with a sprig of yellow flowers. She came from Norway and did not speak much English upon arrival, and therefore was not comfortable with public speaking at protest meetings or contributing to the *Woman's Exponent*.[15] Her block spoke for her, providing insight into her background and desires.

Quilts also reveal information about very specific local historical context. The Twentieth Ward quilt provides details about the northeast Salt Lake City neighborhood not available in other sources. The quilt furnishes an 1870 textile ward map and directory as the layout mirrors the blocks of the ward boundaries. The George Luff family and the Harry Luff family resided on the same block, so the blocks of mother-in-law Mary Luff and daughter-in-law Lovina Luff are next to each other. The leaves on their blocks were cut from the same fabric. Additionally, the location of each square communicates something about the relationship and the degree of intimacy of the block maker with the recipient.[16] Blocks created by the ward Relief Society presidency occupy the center row and are flanked by blocks made by the only three women featured in this quilt who belonged to the Nauvoo Relief Society. The proximity and layout of the blocks marks their central social hierarchy. Thus the quilt serves as a map to the Relief Society just as a neighborhood map indicates proximity, revealing important relationships, identities, and locations.

Nineteenth-century Relief Society buildings also provide historical context for local environments and change over time. Construction of Relief Society halls, beginning in 1869, signaled permanence and legitimacy, both for the settlers as a whole and for the female organization. Literal keys to these edifices provided women with administrative authority and demonstrated their agency. Building materials were drawn from local surroundings: soft pink rock in Beaver, adobe in Thurber, and black lava rock with clay sand mortar in Washington.[17] Like the variation in building materials, women's design decisions indicate change over time. Initially, pioneer architectural trends were limited to utilitarian design.[18] Over time, as elsewhere in nineteenth-century America, designers attended to fine detail to demonstrate culture and refinement.[19] The addition of these elements demonstrated a shift from vernacular architecture to elaborate design, and a transformation of the Utah desert environment into a refined location. To illustrate, the Washington Relief Society hall added elements over time such as molded cornices; later Relief Society halls incorporated additional popular high Victorian details.[20] The Relief Society hall in Deseret, Millard County, included a gable roof, cornice returns, Queen Anne detailing, lathe-turned columns with spindled brackets, and a transom over the door.[21] These architectural details transformed developing frontier towns with popular styles. The buildings reveal women's design choices and efforts at creating and maintaining a refined identity while establishing a sense of permanence and legitimacy.

Material Culture Reveals the Breadth and Diversity of Mormon Women's Activity

Artifacts reveal the breadth of women's political, economic, religious, and social activity. The Nauvoo Relief Society minute book is perhaps the most important piece of Relief Society history, as women have prolifically quoted, copied, and published excerpts from it. The way women physically used the book insinuates its position as the most significant item in Relief Society material culture. Eliza R. Snow packed the ledger across the plains in 1848, protecting it against buffalo stampedes, inclement weather, and multiple river crossings. When Brigham Young called for the Relief Society's official reorganization in 1867, Snow relied upon the record she had preserved to demonstrate Joseph Smith's original intentions for the organization. Like a holy relic, the presence of the minute book bestowed a veritable link to the past as it traveled to different settlements along the Wasatch Front Corridor.[22] The soft leather and gilded pages bonded women to their Nauvoo roots and displayed a wide range of nineteenth-century female activity.

The minute book demonstrates the organization's political efforts through its references to public circulars and petitions to the Illinois governor from Relief Society members. It also accounts for expenditures, donations, service, and work exchange as the women ran the Relief Society. The ledger shows that Relief Society members, like women of other benevolent societies, were astute businesswomen.[23] In addition, the minutes provide insight into Latter-day Saint theology concerning women and the social sisterhood developed in the Relief Society. The ledger provides a key code from which to more fully comprehend the full range of activity of Nauvoo women and their influence on expanding progressive activity later in Utah.

Later artifacts perpetuate the wide array of activity nineteenth-century Mormon women undertook. Print culture depicts their political activity and efforts to shape their identity for a larger audience. The advent of sophisticated and accessible commercial technology, as well as cheaper transportation with the completion of the transcontinental railroad in 1869, facilitated the dissemination of textual and visual accounts through newspapers, magazines, and books. The *Woman's Exponent*, distributed across the country, proclaimed its platform supporting "The Rights of the Women of Zion, and the Rights of the Women of All Nations" in its masthead[24] and also published a suffrage song book.[25]

Analysis of change over time in ephemera provides valuable insight into the way Mormon women fashioned their identity. Augusta Joyce Crocheron's 1883 lithograph poster, *Representative Women of Deseret*, demonstrates another attempt to depict LDS women as politically respectable and refined at a time when they were portrayed in the national press as ignorant, uneducated, and uncivilized. Photographs of twenty Mormon women decorated with ink etchings of religious iconography, refined décor, and benevolent work displayed a refined society. Utilizing media appropriated by mainstream culture, such visual representations provided a useful medium of self-expression and collective identity.[26] These women thus skillfully presented themselves and their heritage through strategic cultural identity.

Other objects reveal Mormon women's economic activity with roots in Nauvoo. The Relief Society building construction efforts, described above, began in 1869 when Sarah Kimball, president of the Fifteenth Ward Relief Society, decided to build a "modern" red brick store as a gathering place for women to meet, sell homemade goods, work, and fill their prophetic charge to care for the poor and save souls. The women planned and funded a building that followed the architectural outline of Joseph Smith's red brick store in Nauvoo with a store on the main level and a meeting room upstairs. Mormon women eventually constructed nearly 140 Relief Society halls, stores, and granaries.[27] These buildings demonstrated women's construction and preservation of female space for commercial, civic, and Relief Society activity. Emmeline Wells described the Gunnison Relief Society hall as "a good illustration of the executive ability women have shown who have managed the various practical enterprizes that has made this great organization such a success financially."[28] The buildings signaled a very specific sense of female autonomy.

Objects also reveal the religious activities of women. Items associated with temples provided windows into sacred locations where women, as matriarchs, participated with men, as patriarchs, in religious ritual and worship. Women sewed veils, handcrafted altar pieces, and produced rugs for floors and hair wreaths for walls. Hair wreaths hanging in the

Salt Lake and Manti Temples demonstrated a sense of female religious hierarchy and ritual participation. The Salt Lake Temple piece created with women's hair intertwined with men's hair, suggested links between patriarchy and matriarchy.[29] The Manti hair wreath illustrated the ordinance of baptisms for the dead, depicting a baptismal font filled with bounteous hair flowers.

Women as Historians—Material Culture, Preservation, and Agency

Keys also represent authority. By the mid-nineteenth century, American society perceived American women as "custodians of culture" and "guardians of heritage," revealing a sense of public responsibility for women to remember and teach proper cultural values from the past.[30] Women played a key role in the preservation of objects. The choice to preserve or abandon an artifact—or even an entire format or genre of artifacts—demonstrates historical agency. Pierre Nora used the term *lieux de memoire,* or sites of memory, to define the collapse in time and historical distance between the past and the present found in historic sites and artifacts.[31]

The preservation of quilts demonstrates women's choices of which memories and artifacts to retain. Within a couple of decades of settlement of a new area, women were able to accumulate materials, tools, and skill to make ornamental quilts, in addition to utilitarian ones.[32] Families preserved these decorative quilts as tributes to their heritage, unlike utilitarian quilts used until they fell apart. Margaret Smoot had no daughters, so she bequeathed her quilt from the Twentieth Ward to daughter-in-law Polly Jones Smoot, who donated the quilt to the Daughters of Utah Pioneers.[33]

Mormon women also worked to preserve their buildings as important artifacts. The towns of Santa Clara, Laketown, and Deseret, Utah, proudly hailed their Relief Society halls as the oldest remaining LDS church buildings in the community.[34] However, most Relief Society halls were sold, abandoned, or destroyed. While the halls, cooperative stores, and granaries thrived for a time, they fell victim to a variety of forces, including the expansion of a national marketplace (such as the advent of mail-order catalogs) that diminished the need for local business. Approximately 140 Relief Society halls were constructed but only 25 survive today.[35]

The loss of key artifacts, both physical and symbolic, reveals much about the ebb and flow of women's authority. Abandoned buildings testify of lost autonomy as wards consolidated auxiliary programs under one roof.[36] The Relief Society was generally given its own room, removing the need for a separate hall. Many societies were not able to maintain modern grain storage methods and their granaries became less effective. In 1911, the Presiding Bishopric centralized Relief Society wheat, funds, and granaries, then later during World War I sold the wheat to the federal government without consulting the women.[37] A centennial history of the Relief Society includes photographs of the ragged ruins of extant granaries with this tribute: "The buildings remain, mute evidence of the faith, obedience, and industry of pioneer Relief Society women."[38] In their ruin, the crumbling remnants serve as a *lieux de memoire*—a reminder of loss. Lost space marked lost autonomy. The presence of empty lots, once home to successful women's edifices, sometimes reconstructed into other buildings, continues to testify to women's previous activity and innovation.

Another format that did not pass the test of time is the hair wreath. An intertwining of hair into a decorative piece to be hung on a parlor wall preserved a tangible scene with a very physical sense of the body—human hair. Europeans utilized artifacts made of human hair, including pictures, rings, necklaces, brooches, pins, earrings, and wreaths in the late eighteenth century; they later became fashionable in the United States.[39] For a time, hair wreaths were displayed in fine nineteenth-century parlors as a mark of refinement. Two significant women's pieces once hung in the Manti Temple and in the Salt Lake Temple. The practice of making hair wreaths declined after the Civil War, a victim of the industrialization of the manufacture of goods and fear of disease.[40] By the late nineteenth century, styles had changed; dark, fussy ornaments appeared awkward and weighty compared to new lighter twentieth-century fashions.[41] Hair wreaths illustrate a segment of popular material culture that became virtually forgotten.

As with quilts and buildings, the choice to preserve or abandon objects provides insights about Mormon female agency and shifts in cultural attitudes. In a similar way, the relationship between women and authority has shifted over time. While Joseph Smith turned the key to women on April 28, 1842, on March 9, 1845, after Smith's death, Brigham

Young commented that women could never hold the keys of the priesthood apart from their husband.[42] In September 1855, a team of historians under the direction of George A. Smith revised Joseph Smith's statement from actually presenting keys to women to turning the key "in behalf" of Relief Society women, contributing to an even larger declension narrative or apparent loss of agency.[43] Yet by February 1, 1877, Eliza R. Snow declared to the Twelfth Ward Relief Society that Joseph Smith's key to them was one of knowledge, which would not be removed from them.[44] In that sense, Mormon women were in the midst of an unprecedented era of progressive activity. Interpretations of memory and retelling have changed depending on the circumstances and ideologies of the present.

Conclusion

In the upper room of the Nauvoo red brick store, LDS women organized their society, elected leaders, received authority, and gained instruction from the prophet. Some of them received the endowment there and participated in the highest religious ritual that existed before the completion of the temple. At the sixth Relief Society meeting, Joseph Smith proclaimed, "I now turn the key to you in the name of God."[45] The connection of a physical key, unlocking the door to a room or a building, opened the women to a new realm of religious participation among their secular labors. As with the presentation of a city key to a prominent citizen, this statement described a physical icon, which represented authority and autonomy.

Mormon women have remembered Smith's turning of the key both in word and in physical re-creation. Material culture records the activity and the preservation of memory with a distinct form of female agency. Material culture allows otherwise voiceless women to speak, providing insight into the diversity of female activities in their families, congregations, communities, and in their preservation of the past. Additional scholarly studies of the material culture of Mormon women will continue to give insight. The key to understanding the past has been turned to include new dimensions.

Notes

1. "Nauvoo Relief Society Minutes, 1842–1844," April 28, 1842, 40, LDS Church History Library, Salt Lake City, Utah; Sarah M. Kimball, "Early Relief

Society Reminiscences," in "Salt Lake Stake Relief Society Record, 1880–1892," March 17, 1882, 29, Church History Library.

2. See Jason Lindquist, "'Unlocking the Door of the Gospel': The Concept of 'Keys' in Mormonism and Early American Culture," in *Archive of Restoration Culture: Summer Fellows' Papers, 1997–1999* (Provo, UT: Joseph Fielding Smith Institute for Latter-day Saint History, 2000), 29–41.
3. "Relief Society Jubilee," *Woman's Exponent* 20, no. 18 (April 1, 1892): 140.
4. *Relief Society Magazine* 23, no. 3 (March 1936): cover.
5. See Elizabeth Pinborough, ed., *Habits of Being: Mormon Women's Material Culture* (n.p.: Exponent II, 2012); Mark A. Staker, "'By Their Works Ye Shall Know Them': The World View Expressed in Mormon Folk Art," *BYU Studies* 35, no. 3 (1996): 74–93; Mary Bywater Cross, *Quilts & Women of the Mormon Migrations: Treasures of Transition* (Nashville: Rutledge Hill Press, 1996); Carol Holindrake Nielson, *The Salt Lake City 14th Ward Album Quilt, 1857: Stories of the Relief Society Women and Their Quilt* (Salt Lake City: University of Utah Press, 2004).
6. Robin Scott Jensen, "A Bit of Old String: Mary Whitmer's Unheralded Contributions," *Treasures of the Collection: LDS Church History Library*, April 25, 2013, http://history.lds.org/article/mary-whitmer-book-of-mormon?lang=eng.
7. See Laurel Thatcher Ulrich, *The Age of Homespun: Objects and Stories in the Creation of an American Myth* (New York: Random House, 2001), 108–41.
8. Judy Elsley, *Quilts as Text(iles): The Semiotics of Quilting* (New York: Peter Lang, 1996), 1.
9. L. Thomas Frye, ed., *American Quilts: A Handmade Legacy* (Oakland, CA: The Oakland Museum, 1981), 8. See also Jacqueline Tobin and Raymond G. Dobard, *Hidden in Plain View: The Secret Story of Quilts and the Underground Railroad* (New York: Doubleday, 1999); Marita Sturken, *Tangled Memories: The Vietnam War, the AIDS Epidemic, and the Politics of Remembering* (Berkeley: University of California Press, 1997), 183–219.
10. Nielson, *The Salt Lake City 14th Ward Album Quilt*, 72–74; see also Laurel Thatcher Ulrich, "An American Album, 1857," *The American Historical Review* 115, no. 1 (February 2010): 1–25.
11. Cross, *Quilts & Women of the Mormon Migrations*, 18–19.
12. Ulrich, *The Age of Homespun*, 39; ibid., 4, 7, 111.
13. Ulrich, "An American Album."
14. Salt Lake City Fifteenth Ward, Salt Lake Stake, "Relief Society Minute Book," vol. 1, 1869–1875, January 16, 1870; Sarah B. Gordon, *The Mormon Question: Polygamy and Constitutional Conflict in Nineteenth-Century America* (Chapel Hill: University of North Carolina Press, 2002), 273–74n6.
15. Olive Smoot Bean, "Biographical Sketch of Margaret T. Smoot, Abraham O. Smoot Papers," n.d., L. Tom Perry Special Collections, Harold B. Lee Library, Brigham Young University, Provo, UT.

16. See Gloria Seaman Allen and Nancy Gibson Tuckhorn, *A Maryland Album: Quiltmaking Traditions, 1634–1934* (Nashville: Rutledge Hill Press, 1995), 91; Catherine Schwoeffermann, "A Community of Quilters," in *Quilted Together: Women, Quilts, and Communities*, edited by Joyce Ice and Linda Norris (Delhi, NY: Delaware County Historical Association, 1989), 39.
17. Jan Harold Brunvand, "The Architecture of Zion," *American West* 13, no. 2 (March–April 1976): 29; Utah State Historical Society, "Beaver Relief Society Meetinghouse" (Historic Preservation Research Office, October 18, 1983); Cotton Mission Sons of the Utah Pioneers, "Utah's Dixie Historical Sites: Pioneer Relief Society Building," http://www.sonsofutahpioneers.info/hs/b01-pioneerreleifsocietybuilding.html; Ronald S. Hanson, *The Relief Society: Its Meeting Halls, Granaries, Cooperative Stores and Its Impact on Nineteenth-Century Utah* (North Salt Lake City: DMT, 2007), 17, 23.
18. Sarah Kimball initially visualized a utilitarian building for the first Fifteenth Ward Relief Society hall, though she did name her hall a "temple." Sarah M. Kimball, "Salt Lake City, 13th November, 1868," *Woman's Exponent* 14, no. 2 (June 15, 1885): 14.
19. For cultural context, see Richard L. Bushman, *The Refinement of America: Persons, Houses, Cities* (New York: Vintage Books, 1993), xii–xviii, 25, 152.
20. United States Department of the Interior, Heritage Conservation and Recreation Service, "Washington Relief Society Hall, National Register of Historic Places Inventory—Nomination Form," August 27, 1980, 2. The Weber Stake Relief Society hall presented an excellent Victorian Gothic example with a prominent steeply pitched gable roof and three pointed arched windows in the principle façade, highlighted with low relief brick arches. United States Department of the Interior, Heritage Conservation and Recreation Service, "Weber Stake Relief Society Hall," December 20, 1988, 2.
21. United States Department of the Interior, Heritage Conservation and Recreation Service, "Deseret Relief Society Hall," November 6, 1995, 5.
22. Jill Mulvay Derr, Janath Russell Cannon, and Maureen Ursenbach Beecher, *Women of Covenant: The Story of Relief Society* (Salt Lake City: Deseret Book, 1992), 89; Jill Mulvay Derr and Carol Cornwall Madsen, "Preserving the Record and Memory of the Female Relief Society of Nauvoo, 1842–92," *Journal of Mormon History* 35, no. 3 (Summer 2009): 88–117.
23. See Peggy Pascoe, *Relations of Rescue: The Search for Female Moral Authority in the American West, 1874–1939* (New York: Oxford University Press, 1990), 4; Lori D. Ginzberg, *Women and the Work of Benevolence: Morality, Politics, and Class in the Nineteenth-Century United States* (New Haven: Yale University Press, 1990), 36–67.
24. The first issue this masthead appeared in is November 15, 1879, 8 no. 12.
25. *Utah Woman Suffrage Song Book* (Salt Lake City: Woman's Exponent, 1890).
26. Carol A. Edison, "Material Culture: An Introduction and Guide to Mormon Vernacular," in *Mormon Americana: A Guide to Sources and Collections in the*

United States, edited by David J. Whittaker (Provo, UT: BYU Studies, 1995), 307.

27. Hanson, *The Relief Society,* 33, 65–69. The Utah State Historical Society has identified seventeen existing halls. National Register of Historic Places, "Mormon Architecture in Utah," Utah State Historical Society, sec. F, 1.
28. Emmeline B. Wells, ed., *Charities and Philanthropies: Woman's Work in Utah* (Salt Lake City: George Q. Cannon, 1893), 19.
29. See Jennifer Reeder, "'To do something extraordinary': Mormon Women and the Creation of a Usable Past," (dissertation, George Mason University, 2013).
30. See Ann Pamela Cunningham, "To the Ladies of the South," *Charleston Mercury,* December 2, 1853; Dee Garrison, "The Tender Technicians: The Feminization of Public Librarianship, 1876–1905," in *Clio's Consciousness Raised: New Perspectives on the History of Women,* edited by Mary Hartman and Lois W. Banner (New York: Harper, 1974), 161; Ann Douglas, *The Feminization of American Culture* (New York: Noonday Press, 1998); Patricia U. Bonomi, *Under the Cope of Heaven: Religion, Society, and Politics in Colonial America* (New York: Oxford University Press, 2003).
31. Pierre Nora, "Between Memory and History: Les Lieux de Mémoire," *Representations,* no. 26 (Spring 1989): 7–24.
32. Ibid., 4; Karoline Patterson Bresenhan and Nancy O'Bryant Puentes, *Lone Stars: A Legacy of Texas Quilts, 1836–1936* (Austin: University of Texas Press, 1986), 15.
33. "Pioneer Quilts," in *Our Pioneer Heritage,* compiled by Kate B. Carter, vol. 18 (Salt Lake City: Daughters of Utah Pioneers, 1958), 71.
34. United States Department of the Interior, Heritage Conservation and Recreation Service, "Deseret Relief Society Hall," 8; United States Department of the Interior, Heritage Conservation and Recreation Service, "Santa Clara Relief Society Hall," 5; Utah State Historical Society, "Relief Society Hall Markers," *Markers and Monuments Database.*
35. Sources culled from Kate B. Carter, comp., *Heart Throbs of the West,* 12 vols. (Salt Lake City: Daughters of Utah Pioneers, 1939–1951); *An Enduring Legacy,* 12 vols. (Salt Lake City: Daughters of Utah Pioneers, 1978–1989); Kate B. Carter, comp., *Our Pioneer Heritage,* 20 vols. (Salt Lake City: Daughters of Utah Pioneers, 1958–1977); Kate B. Carter, comp., *Treasures of Pioneer History,* 6 vols. (Salt Lake City: Daughters of Utah Pioneers, 1952–1957); Relief Society, *A Centenary of Relief Society, 1842–1942* (Salt Lake City: General Board of Relief Society, 1942); and the *Woman's Exponent.*
36. Several scholars have examined deserted buildings as a testament to loss. See Judith Schachter Modell, *A Town without Steel: Envisioning Homestead* (Pittsburgh: University of Pittsburgh Press, 1998), 3, 5; Thomas J. Sugrue, *The Origins of the Urban Crisis: Race and Inequality in Postwar Detroit* (Princeton: Princeton University Press, 2005), 3, 5; Dydia DeLyser, "Authenticity on the Ground: Engaging the Past in a California Ghost Town," *Annals of the*

Association of American Geographers 89, no. 4 (December 1999): 602–3, 606, 609, 612–13.

37. Derr, Cannon, and Beecher, *Women of Covenant*, 180, 210–12; Relief Society, *History of the Relief Society, 1842–1966* (Salt Lake City: General Board of Relief Society, 1966), 110–11.
38. Relief Society, *A Centenary of Relief Society*, 73.
39. Ruth Gordon, "Victorian Hairwork," *Piecework* 4, no. 2 (April 1996): 36; Mlle. Defour, "Hair Work, No. 1," *Peterson's Magazine*, November 1850, 202.
40. Irene Guggenheim Navarro, "Hairwork of the Nineteenth Century," *Antiques* 159, no. 3 (March 2001): 491, 486; Gordon, "Victorian Hairwork," 38.
41. Helen Sheumaker, *Love Entwined: The Curious History of Hairwork in America* (Philadelphia: University of Pennsylvania Press, 2007), viii.
42. Brigham Young, "General Record of the Seventies, 1844–1848," March 9, 1845, 77–78, Church History Library.
43. "History of Joseph Smith," *Deseret News*, September 19, 1855.
44. Twelfth Ward, Salt Lake Stake, "Relief Society Record Book," 1868–1877, February 1, 1877, 255–57, LR 12908 24, Church History Library.
45. "Nauvoo Relief Society Minutes, 1842–1844," April 28, 1842, 40.

5

"We Baked a Lot of Bread"

Reconceptualizing Mormon Women and Ritual Objects

KRISTINE WRIGHT

During the year leading up to the dedication of the San Antonio Texas Temple in 2005, Mormon women in the area engaged in a handwork project that was a material form of religious practice—a tangible version of Joseph Smith's promise of a welding link of eternal salvation that tied the human family together through eternally binding ordinances.[1] This physical representation of communal salvation was not made of priesthood power, but of crochet thread. Women spent hours and months creating altar cloths, shawls, lap blankets, and tissue box covers. Before the temple dedication, they compiled written accounts detailing their experiences. One woman wrote:

> My mother taught me to crochet and I found myself thinking about her often while crocheting this altar cover. My mother was baptized when she was 84 . . . and received her endowments at the Houston Temple . . . She passed away nine days later. It would be my great joy to be sealed to my parents over this cloth which I created with my own hands . . . It is my prayer that thousands of others may be sealed over the altar cover which I have donated.[2]

Creating religious objects for the temple connected these women to their own ancestors as well as to the historical textile work of the Mormon women's organization, Relief Society. During this period, many of them had religious experiences, including dreams and revelations, demonstrating how the creation of material culture facilitates religious belief and engenders religious encounters.

Scholars of religious studies have noted that one of the most effective strategies that women have used to construct a meaningful religious life is the sacralisation of their own life experiences, which often derive from the domestic sphere.[3] While male rituals are frequently "presented with explanatory 'paradigms' for the society at large, women's rituals . . . often appear as 'domestic' and insignificant, except to women themselves."[4] The mundane materials and processes that often define women's work can be problematic to study as they are frequently viewed as tedious, demeaning, or oppressive.[5] Such tasks do not fit easily into emancipatory models of women's history. At the same time, they often become problematic for scholars, who, using a lens of artistic hierarchy, see them as occupying the arena of craft.[6] Recently, Catherine Brekus argued that those who study women's history have frequently associated historical agency with freedom, empowerment, intentionality, and contesting male authority.[7] Women who reproduce and uphold conservative religious structures present a serious challenge to this model of interpreting the past and are difficult to cast as historical agents. As historian Phyllis Mack asserted:

> To dismiss [the religious woman's] gestures of surrender and self-denial as a rhetoric of self-abnegation, as false consciousness, or as a covert expression of resistance to the dominant male order is not only an over-simplification of her psychology; it is an avoidance of our responsibility [as historians] not merely to search for examples of female strategies of self-assertion under patriarchy but to look steadily at women's own ideas about ethics, autonomy, and spirituality.[8]

This approach insists that historians recognize that "habitual and routinized activities are not devoid of agency."[9] Agency is not only located in how women challenged religious structures and communities, but also in how they maintained them. Historical agency exists on a continuum. Historians of Mormon women cannot ignore the real limitations on women's agency and should be cautious when using emancipatory historical paradigms to describe the constraints of religious structures and cultural beliefs as liberating.[10] The following Mormon women's material practices should be understood as their commitment to the social structures and rituals of their religious communities.

The Mormon liturgy of the Lord's Supper or sacrament has been described as one where, "the elements did not matter, [yet] the identity of both the administrators and the communicants did. It was not that anybody could officiate; it was that any male could, potentially, become an officiator, and any Saint a member of the Zion community."[11] Women have always been a part of the Mormon salvific community that received the Lord's Supper since its introduction on April 6, 1830. However, the administration of the sacrament has been largely understood as a ritual of female absence. Following the ordination of Joseph Smith and Oliver Cowdery as First and Second Elders of the church, men and boys administered bread and wine to the congregation with the Book of Mormon serving as a template for the ordinance.[12] But women also had direct embodied experiences with religious objects that were and are central to this priesthood ordinance. Frequently, women were the ones who produced and cared for them. Baking sacrament bread and caring for sacrament vessels created a sense of religious self and community.

Bread remained an important part of the ordinance throughout Mormon migrations. In Kirtland, Zebedee Coltrin painted a vivid picture of the centrality of bread to early Mormon celebrations of the Lord's Supper:

> The sacrament was also administered at times when Joseph appointed, after the ancient order that is, warm bread to break easy was provided and broken into pieces as large as my fist and each person had a glass of wine and sat and ate the bread and drank the wine; and Joseph said that was the way that Jesus and his disciples partook of bread and wine.[13]

Early Mormon women in Kirtland and throughout Mormon history have been intimately connected to the production of sacrament bread and transformed their kitchens into sacred space by baking it. Women have often claimed ritual spaces that originated in domestic tasks, many of which were invisible. These quotidian rites could be either constructed deliberately, or sometimes incrementally.[14] As Lesley Northup has noted, much of female ritualizing is not esoteric. It is rooted in the here and now, in everyday materials, and in ordinary locations where women live and work. Women will sometimes claim the "horizontal" or nonhierarchical space in a religious community to create their own rituals.[15]

Recent scholarship recognizes that sacred space is very often ordinary; it becomes set apart through human action that constructs the sacred through belief and practice.[16] Early Mormonism fused the sacred and the mundane—religious devotion could be found in all forms of work—in groves of trees, in the attics of stores, and domestic spaces of homes.[17] Constrained agency was evident in the tensions surrounding female exclusion from some aspects of the rituals held at the Kirtland Temple dedication in 1836. While women worked to build the temple, experienced an outpouring of spiritual gifts, and participated in the public meetings, they were upset about not being full participants in the washings and anointings men enjoyed there. George A. Smith remembered that Joseph Smith, "told us to wash ourselves, and that almost made the women mad, and they said, as they were not admitted into the Temple while this washing was being performed, that some mischief was going on, and some of them were right huffy about it."[18]

However, women were able to express themselves religiously in other ways. When recalling the Pentecostal events surrounding the dedication of the Kirtland Temple, Nancy Naomi Alexander Tracy affirmed, "Blessings were poured out. Solemn assemblies were called. Endowments were given. The elders went from house to house, blessing the Saints and administering the sacrament. Feasts were given. Three families joined together and held one at our house. We baked a lot of bread . . ."[19]

Historians and foodways scholars alike have examined the role of food in women's religious experiences and have argued compellingly that food practices have enabled women to exert power and make meaning in their families and religious communities.[20] Although Mormon women have a long history of creating sacramental meals for their community, their food practices have been studied outside of the boundaries of liturgy. Women took these responsibilities seriously and performed them over long periods of time and with great care.[21] Charity Kinder Savage baked sacrament bread in Henrieville, Utah, during the 1890s. Her daughter remembered:

> At that time the Bishopric took turns in furnishing the sacrament. When it was father's turn, mother had her own way in preparing

> it. She cut the crusts off the loaves of bread, then sliced it into half inch strips. Preparing it this way made it easier for the Priests to break it evenly. She had crystal plates she kept for the sacrament only. She would put the bread on the plates, cover it with a pretty white linen towel that she kept especially for that purpose. Father was always so proud to take it to church.[22]

Decades later, Ruth Mace Waddell recalled

> The women in the ward took turns providing the bread for the sacrament. Mom would take special care when it was her turn. She made sure the final product was white in color, and that the texture was even. She cut off the crusts, so it would look beautiful in the tray. Mom always made good bread, but for the sacrament, it had to be just right.[23]

Such accounts of special plates, cloths, and attention to details of texture and preparation all underscore the defining influence of routinized activity, the significance of human making and doing, the tendency of women to create ritual from domestic work, and the idea that belief is more than a linguistic act. Baking sacrament bread provided a venue for women to connect themselves to the Lord's Supper. However, it was also more than this. Mormon women claimed horizontal space by creating their own individualized rituals around sacramental bread baking. As David Morgan has observed, "Belief is not merely the symbolic act of representation, but the symbol as well as all that it evokes and draws on."[24]

In addition to sacramental baking, women, and sometimes girls, prepared the sacrament table.[25] Sacrament vessels and trays required cleaning and polishing. Similarly, sacrament tablecloths needed to be created and laundered. The need for creating ritual textiles and caring for sacramental vessels provided embodied interactions with these religious objects that became fixtures of female religious identity. Annette Steeneck Huntington remembered that the "young girls in MIA . . . filled the water cups in the kitchen and placed the bread on the trays. We then prepared the Sacrament table with the cloth and trays on it. It was a wonderful privilege I shall always remember."[26] Aware of their constrained agency in relation to the administration of the sacrament, women recognized these opportunities for material connections as sacred occasions. Kate Coreless of the Salt Lake City Fourth Ward cared for the sacrament table for twenty-five years. Not only did she crochet the sacrament cloth, but she regularly cleaned the trays, baked and sliced the bread, and set the sacrament table.[27] As the church turned to the use of disposable cups during the 1940s, the need for dishwashing disappeared.[28] Between the changes in materials and adjustments to sacrament table preparation policies implemented a few years later, which favoured the increased participation of Aaronic priesthood holders, female interaction with sacrament vessels became obsolete.[29]

Women often embellished sacrament cloths with needlework, emphasizing communal religious identity through words and symbols. Women in the Salt Lake City Twenty-Sixth Ward embroidered the name of the ward in the lower left hand corner of their sacrament table cloth—as well as the words, "The Lord's Supper," in satin stitch in the centre of the cloth. Similarly, one embroidered temple altar cloth had beehives and sego lilies in the corners.[30] Embroidery allowed women to create and experience a sense of belief, knowledge, and communal identity that was transmitted through the sensory interactions with fabric, needle, and thread.[31] It is useful to consider these material creations as a "text," along with the written theological, poetic, or narrative accounts generally studied in Mormon history. Textile studies can refer to the surface fabric that is produced through weaving, or to the embroidery, which is the art of producing patterns or marks on cloth with wool, linen, or silk by means of a needle, which often have multiple meanings.[32]

Women's material contributions to the sacrament table were not limited to handmade creations. Relief Societies not only created sacramental cloths and cared for sacramental vessels, but they also funded the purchase of these ritual objects. The Park City First Ward Relief Society donated two sterling silver sacrament cups with two handles on the side in 1898.[33] Similarly, a sacrament pitcher was etched with the words "Presented to the Timpanogos Ward by the Relief Society, January 1899."[34] Such engravings permanently acknowledged the work of Mormon women in their congregations and allowed them to have a material presence in the Lord's Supper.

Textile work, particularly collective sewing, also served as a material locus of Mormon women's religious commitment. This work was often kept within the domestic circle of a family, but also reflected communal networks. Cloth and clothing played an important role in embodied belief practices. The manufacturing and use of cloth illustrated how women invested cloth and clothing with their beliefs. Clothing became part of the body. It touched all aspects of the wearer. Clothing reveals gender, social, and religious identities and is often a central item in life cycle rituals.[35] Each time women made ritual textiles and wore sacred clothing, or engaged in the religious rites that involved them, they renewed and internalized their beliefs and values. Mormon women created their religious identity not only through conversion narratives and tales of the overland journeys, but also through textile work. Laurel Thatcher Ulrich noted that when Lucy Meserve Smith wrote her memoir, "she measured her life not so much through the suffering she experienced when the Latter-day Saints were driven from their homes in Nauvoo, nor through the privations of the early years in Utah, but through the work she had accomplished in a long life."[36] Smith's vast textile biography included the cutting and making of "dresses cloaks coats pants and Temple suits with their aprons &c."[37]

In October 1830, four missionaries traveled west to preach and bring the Book of Mormon to Native Americans who had been relocated by the Indian Removal Act.[38] Lavina Fielding Smith observed that "Emma Smith, and several other sisters, began to make arrangements to furnish those who were set apart for this mission, with the necessary clothing, which was no easy task, as the most of it had to be manufactured out of the raw material."[39] In addition to creating apparel for departing missionaries, women also sewed clothing for men who worked building the Kirtland Temple.[40] This quickly evolved into creating textiles for the temple itself. A month before the dedication, Joseph Smith noted, "This afternoon the sisters met again at the chapel to work on the v[e]il . . . I made some remarks from the pulpit upon the rise and progress of the church of Christ of Latter day Saints and pronounced a blessing upon the Sisters for the liberality in giving their servises so cheerfully to make the veil for the Lord's house."[41] Women sewed carpets and draperies for the temple interior. Polly Angell recalled Joseph Smith saying, "The sisters are always first and foremost in all good works. Mary was first at the resurrection and the sisters now are the first to work on the inside of the temple."[42]

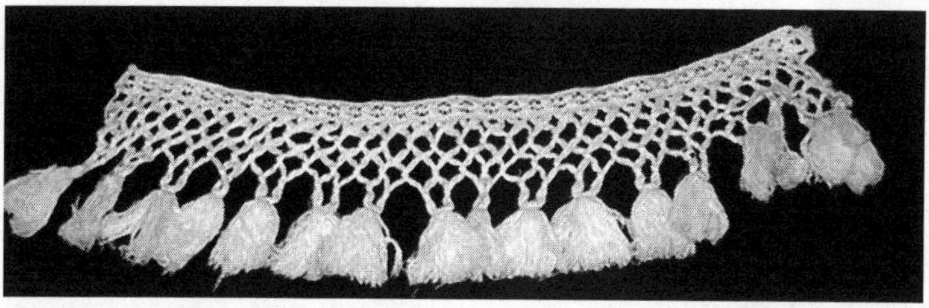

FIGURE 5.1. White fringe, made of knotted lace, from the Kirtland Temple, 1870. Courtesy of the International Society of Daughters of Utah Pioneers, Salt Lake City, Utah.

Histories of temple workmanship often focused upon the work of artisans, "a term that carries gendered overtones implying skilled men who know how to do things with steel, wood, concrete and stone."[43] While historians of Mormon temple building may be familiar with such names as Truman O. Angell, Joseph Don Carlos Young, John R. Moyle, and Avard Fairbanks, women who created religious, functional, or artistic objects for temples largely remain anonymous. Expanding the definition of temple building to include women's domestic work highlights the importance of female material religion as well as the economic impact of such work.[44] Temples were not just constructed of stone and wood—they were also made of textiles. Construction of the Nauvoo Temple provided women with increased opportunities to create embodied forms of material religion. In fact, the initial impulse to create the Relief Society in 1842 came from Sarah Granger Kimball and her seamstress, Miss Cook, who committed to sew shirts for the men who were building the Nauvoo Temple and invited other women to join them. Mormon women built upon their work in Kirtland by sewing veils for the Nauvoo temple and were intimately involved in the design and creation of temple clothing from the very start. A variety of sources allude to different original seamstresses. The group might have included Emma Smith, Eliza R. Snow, Bathsheba Smith, and Elizabeth Warren Allred.[45] Regardless, Joseph Smith undeniably sought out women to assist him in making the original temple garments. William Clayton records that Elizabeth Durfee made his garments, while Hosea Stout's wife made his.[46]

The process of creating sacred clothing was part of an early emphasis on the consecrated community. Ritual clothing did not have to be constructed within the family circle, but by those from the salvific community. Heber C. Kimball counselled the men of Nauvoo, "Go to a good faithful sister, and secrete yourself, and make your garments."[47] Originally, temple clothing was cut and sewn in the sacred space of the Nauvoo Temple; eventually, the process became so unwieldy that Brigham Young had to select houses where the work could be done.[48] The process of creating sacred clothing bound women to their religious beliefs, rites, and community. Ritual knowledge was not just conveyed through oral communication and embodied ceremony, but also through textile work.[49] William Clayton wrote, "Sisters Whitney and Kimball have been very busy through the day overseeing the washings and anointings in the female department, and instructing the Sisters in cutting and making robes and garments."[50] These interactions could take place in both sacred and domestic spaces. Mary Jane Mount Tanner later described an afternoon at her home in Provo, Utah, where such instruction occurred, "Presently Sister Holden came and I laid my work aside. Sister Clark came too and I marked a temple apron and showed her how to work it."[51]

Even the most mundane interactions with temple clothing could mediate religious experience. On one of her first days working as a servant in the home of Joseph Smith, Jane Manning James had a mystical experience while doing the laundry. She recalled,

> Among the clothes [to be washed] I found brother Josephs Robes. I looked at them and wondered. I had never seen any before, and I pondered over them and thought about them so earnestly that the spirit made manifest to me that they pertained to the new name that is given the saints that the world knows not off. I didn't know when I washed them or when I put them out to dry.[52]

Jane's performance of this quotidian task, the resulting trance, and the spiritual knowledge she acquired illustrates the power that material things wield in the lives of believers.

Women produced many other textile items associated with temples such as altar cloths, veils, and carpets, although they did some of the installation work in collaboration with men. Concerning the Nauvoo Temple, Heber C. Kimball recorded: "At half past 11 My wife, Sister Whitney, Hellen my Daughter, Sarah Ann Kingsbury, Come in fore the purpus of Heming the Veil."[53] While women sewed the Nauvoo Temple

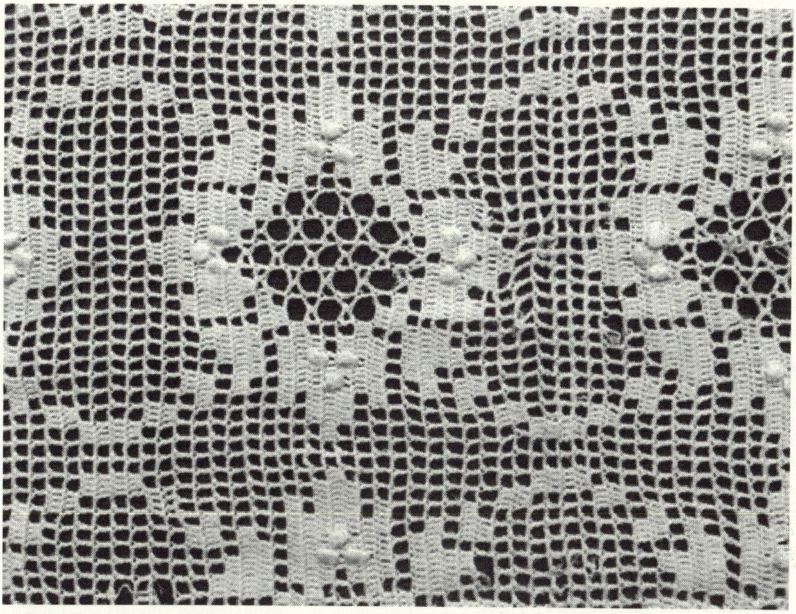

FIGURE 5.2. Altar cloth from the Logan Temple, 1884. Courtesy of the International Society of Daughters of Utah Pioneers, Salt Lake City, Utah.

veil, it was Brigham Young who installed it. Similarly, four days before the Logan Temple dedication, Samuel Roskelley noted in his journal that "I set my wife Margaret and Sister Elizth G. Benson and Lucy B. Cardon to making the vails for Logan Temple after I cut them out."[54] Roskelley was the first Logan Temple recorder and supervised much of the construction and decorative work, often working closely with women. The month before the Logan Temple dedication, his diary is filled with references to coordinating with women from the Cache Stake as they feverishly worked to finish textiles, install carpets, and clean the temple. In March 1878, he noted, "I worked in the temple at the carpets and had sixteen of the sisters sewing on them also."[55] Edna Cardon Langton remembered:

> During the time I was in Logan, my mother sponsored many carpet rag bees. The women would all bring their carpet rags to a central place, like my mother's home, where they would first sort out the different colors into the respective piles and then the rags of the same color would be sewn and wound into a ball. The

> white rags and lighter shades were saved to make the carpet for the Logan Temple. All of the early carpets used in the temple were made in carpet looms by the people of Cache Valley. This was tedious and exacting work, but the women were glad to perform it because they knew it was their work which made the Logan Temple the beautiful spot that it was with their homemade rugs on the floors.[56]

Mirroring the major transitions that the church experienced at the end of the nineteenth century, the creation of sacred clothing and garments moved away from the communal and towards more solitary endeavours.[57] The sisters in the St. Charles Ward were advised:

> Because of the sacred character of temple clothing and the importance of having it safe-guarded against being unnecessarily exposed, Relief Society officers are instructed to have Relief Society members refrain from sewing temple clothing, including embroidering and handwork on the clothing, during any Relief Society meeting. Relief Society women are also advised against sewing on temple clothing in groups where members of the group may not have received their endowments.[58]

Gradually, this work was most often completed in the privacy of homes, as it transitioned into a task that was performed in isolation. As the creation of ceremonial clothing moved from the realm of the sacred community to a more privatized space, the work of ritual sewing became more specialized. Relief Society textile work became correlated as it moved away from sewing groups. Individual women were more likely to engage in textile work for family members or engage in paid employment for undertakers.[59] Eventually, this practice was subsumed by the drive for efficiency and standardization that accompanied "administrative modernization." Consistent with other dislocations that characterized the tenure of Relief Society general president Emmeline B. Wells, the production and distribution of sacred textiles became correlated and bureaucratized with the establishment of the Temple and Burial Clothing Department of the Relief Society in 1912.

Concerned about the potential desecration of temple clothing that was sold publicly, the First Presidency sent a letter to stake and Relief

Society presidents informing them that the general board of the Relief Society had taken "charge of the business of supplying temple clothing to all members of the Church . . . preventing it from being loosely handled or unnecessarily exposed."[60] Even with increased industrialization, women remained the primary producers of garments as they moved into textile factory work when garment production shifted to knitting mills.[61] In the private sphere, they continued the more personal and tactile work of embroidering marks onto purchased clothing for themselves and family members, bridging the nineteenth and twentieth century.[62] In contrast to the communal ritual textile work of Nauvoo, temple handwork became more individualized and focused upon the nuclear family.

Changes in Mormon identity can be traced through the material practices and textiles designed, created, and distributed by a workforce of female seamstresses who performed the industrialized work of creating ritual objects under male supervision. Men oversaw the garment design changes initiated during the second half of the twentieth century, although women did the work of the design and creation. When William Hartley conducted an oral history interview with swimsuit designer Rose Marie Reid, she remembered meeting with general Relief Society president Belle Spafford and examining different styles of garments to help her formulate a new design: "So she had garments laid out on a table, all the ones that were made by various factories. It was a very interesting thing. It gave me a chance to be with Sister Madsen and Sister Belle Spafford and Sister Marianne Sharp, but I was with Sister Spafford more than the others, and it was a very interesting experience."[63]

Reid consulted with President David O. McKay over certain details, but performed the creative handwork herself in 1965. When asked what she did and what her role was she explained, "I remade the patterns completely and changed the style."[64] Reid saw this as spiritual work—a vocation that allowed her to touch the sacred both over time and space, connecting her to the Mormon past and cosmos. Near the end of the interview, she declared:

> The woman who designed the garments at [the] Prophet Joseph's instructions was one of my ancestors. Her name was Elizabeth Warren Allred . . . And when I learned that, I was so astonished. I thought, "Isn't that amazing." She made the patterns for the first

> garments. Do you suppose the Lord keeps that privilege in one family?[65]

Like the women who preceded her, Rose Marie Reid experienced the construction of sacred clothing as a meaning-making practice.

Religious women often reproduce and uphold religious structures through domestic material practices, particularly when they intersect with religious rituals. Scholars who only study or place value upon interactions with sacred objects that happen during the public moment that a rite is performed, may overlook the many ways that belief is embodied and practiced. Mormon women participated in the spiritual life of their religious community through formal religious rituals and meetings. However, they also experienced their religion in the form of the yeasty odour of the kneading process, the feel of warm, soapy water, the sound of clinking glass cups, the cutting of patterns, the threading of needles, and the texture of fabric. All of these sensations and practices intermingled to embody faith and belief. Creating, cooking, and caring for sacred and religious objects was often transient work. For many, their work and the impact that these objects had on their religious lives has disappeared—some absorbed into bodies and some of it changed by policy, industrialization, or centralization. However, some vestiges of it remain. While the creation of sacred or religious objects was woven into the everyday life of Mormon women in the nineteenth and early twentieth centuries, women of the San Antonio Temple district one hundred years later understood that contributing to a new temple building was a rare opportunity. One woman commented, "I felt that this was a unique, once-in-a-lifetime opportunity to be involved in the building and preparation of [a] temple."[66] The creation of a sacred object, as well as its use in formal ritual forms, forges belief—while the aspects of touching, feeling, and creating in turn generate knowledge, faith, and memory.

Notes

1. Samuel Morris Brown, *In Heaven as It Is on Earth: Joseph Smith and the Early Mormon Conquest of Death* (New York: Oxford University Press, 2011), 203–47; Richard Lyman Bushman, *Joseph Smith: Rough Stone Rolling* (New York: Knopf, 2005), 420–23.
2. The San Antonio Texas Temple was dedicated May 22, 2005. "Thoughts, Experiences and Testimonies of Sisters Who Made Items for the San Antonio Texas

Temple," History Files, San Antonio Texas Temple, CR 904 2, Church History Library, Salt Lake City, Utah.

3. Susan Starr Sered, *Women as Ritual Experts: The Religious Lives of Elderly Jewish Women in Jerusalem* (New York: Oxford University Press, 1992), 87–102; Heather Miayano Kopelson, *Faithful Bodies: Performing Religion and Race in the Puritan Atlantic* (New York: NYU Press, 2014), 86–90.
4. Azam Torab, *Performing Islam: Gender and Ritual in Iran* (Boston: Brill, 2006), 21.
5. Susan Strasser, *Never Done: A History of American Housework* (New York: Pantheon Books, 1982); Rebecca Solnit, "Mysteries of Thoreau, Unsolved: On the Dirtiness of Laundry and the Strength of Sisters," *Orion* 32, no. 3 (June 2013): 18–23.
6. Quilt making is a notable exception that has been elevated in status from craft to art form and has been the focus of historical analysis. See Carol Holindrake Nielson, *The Salt Lake City 14th Ward Album Quilt, 1857: Stories of the Relief Society Women and Their Quilt* (Salt Lake City: University of Utah Press, 2004); Laurel Thatcher Ulrich, "An American Album, 1857," *American Historical Review* 115, no. 1 (February 2010): 125; Mark L. Staker, "By Their Works Ye Shall Know Them: The World View Expressed in Mormon Folk Art," *BYU Studies* 35, no. 3 (1995): 74–94.
7. Catherine A. Brekus, "Mormon Women and the Problem of Historical Agency," *Journal of Mormon History* 37, no. 2 (Spring 2011): 78–79.
8. Phyllis Mack, "Religion, Feminism, and the Problem of Agency: Reflections on Eighteenth-Century Quakerism," *Signs* 29, no. 1 (2003): 156. For a discussion of conservative women and feminist scholarship, see R. Marie Griffith, *God's Daughters: Evangelical Women and the Power of Submission* (Berkeley: University of California Press, 1997), 201–5.
9. Mustafa Emirbayer and Ann Mische, "What is Agency?," *American Journal of Sociology* 103, no. 4 (1998): 978.
10. Brekus, "Mormon Women and the Problem of Historical Agency," 79–82.
11. Matthew Bowman, "Liturgy as History: An Approach to Mormon Worship, 1830–2008," unpublished manuscript, 22–23.
12. Dean C. Jessee, Mark Ashurst-McGee, and Richard L. Jensen, eds., *Histories, Volume 1: 1832–1844* (Salt Lake City: Church Historian's Press, 2012), 326–27; Gregory A. Prince, *Power from on High: The Development of Mormon Priesthood* (Salt Lake City: Signature Books, 1995), 95–97; and Bowman, "Liturgy as History," 14–15. Also see Justin Bray, "The Lord's Supper in Early Mormonism," in *You Shall Have My Word: Exploring the Text of the Doctrine and Covenants*, edited by Scott C. Esplin, Richard O. Cowan, and Rachel Cope (Provo: Brigham Young University, 2012), 64–74.
13. Merle H. Graffam, ed., *Salt Lake School of the Prophets Minute Book, 1883* (Palm Desert, CA: ULC Press, 1981), 38. Also see Dean C. Jessee, Mark Ashurst-McGee, and Richard L. Jensen, eds., *Journals Volume 1: 1832–1839*, The Joseph Smith Papers (Salt Lake City: The Church Historian's Press, 2008), 146–47;

Elizabeth Ann Whitney, "A Leaf from an Autobiography," *Woman's Exponent* 7, no. 11 (November 1, 1878): 83.

14. Ronald L. Grimes, *Reading, Writing, and Ritualizing: Ritual in Fictive, Liturgical, and Public Places* (Washington, D.C.: Pastoral Press, 1993), 5; Lesley A. Northup, *Ritualizing Women: Patterns of Spirituality* (Cleveland: Pilgrim Press, 1997), 19.
15. Lesley A. Northup, ed., *Women and Religious Ritual* (Washington, D.C.: Pastoral Press, 1993), 42.
16. Louis P. Nelson, ed., *American Sanctuary: Understanding Sacred Space* (Bloomington: Indiana University Press, 2006), 3–7; Jonathan Z. Smith, *Map is Not Territory: Studies in the History of Religions* (Leiden: E. J. Brill, 1978), 92.
17. Bowman, "Liturgy as History," 24–25.
18. *Journal of Discourses,* vol. 2 (London: LDS Booksellers Depot, 1886), 215.
19. Nancy Naomi Alexander Tracy, *"Life History of Nancy Naomi Alexander Tracy Written by Herself,"* 1885, typescript, L. Tom Perry Special Collections, Harold B. Lee Library, Brigham Young University (hereafter cited as Perry Special Collections).
20. Christopher Tilley et al., eds., *Handbook of Material Culture* (London: Sage, 2006), 145–60; Caroline Walker Bynum, *Holy Feast and Holy Fast: The Religious Significance of Food to Medieval Women* (Berkeley: University of California Press, 1987). Robert Orsi discusses women's power within the "domus" in *The Madonna of 115th Street: Faith and Community in Italian Harlem, 1880–1950* (New Haven, CT: Yale University Press, 1985), 129–49.
21. Joseph F. Smith's wife, Julina, wrote about baking the sacrament bread. Women like Frances Ann Adams baked the sacrament bread in her ward for twenty-five years. See Kenneth W. Godfrey, Audrey M. Godfrey, and Jill Mulvay Derr, eds., *Women's Voices: An Untold History of the Latter-day Saints, 1830–1900* (Salt Lake City: Deseret Book, 1982), 346; "Obituaries: Frances Ann Adams," *Woman's Exponent* 31, no. 3 (March 1903): 78.
22. Josephine Savage Jones, *Henry Savage and His Family, Including Bridcutt, Paverly or Peverly, Power, Preston, Richardson, Savage, Smith, West, Woodhouse,* (n.p.: 1968), 71, Perry Special Collections. Another example is found in Talula Frandsen Nelson, "Pa" in *Saga of the Sanpitch*, 17 (1985): 49–50:

> Mother would carefully bake bread on Saturday, making sure it was light and good. She would choose a loaf, cut all the crusts away, then slice the beautiful white loaf and place it on a napkin tying the four corners together. She had it in a nice white bag, ready for Pa to take to Sunday school and again for church. What a thrill to see him and another Elder make their way to the children where I sat. The beautiful white bread was always special.

23. David Henry Garner, ed., *Treasures among the Tetons: Treasured Memories of the Family of David Lambert Waddell and Mary Ann Mace* (n.p.: 2000), 395, accessed

September 29, 2013, https://dcms.lds.org/delivery/DeliveryManagerServlet?dps_pid=IE61123.

24. David Morgan, ed., *Religion and Material Culture: The Matter of Belief* (New York: Routledge, 2009), 5. See also Northup, *Ritualizing Women*, 85. Lesley Northup has written extensively upon the topic of ritualizing women and the horizontality of these rituals: Lesley Northup, "Expanding the X-Axis: Women, Religious Ritual, and Culture," in *Women and Religious Ritual*, 141–51; and Lesley Northup, "Claiming Horizontal Space: Women's Religious Rituals," *Studia Liturgica* 25, no. 1 (1995): 86–102.
25. William G. Hartley, "From Men to Boys: LDS Aaronic Priesthood Offices, 1829–1996," *Journal of Mormon History* 22, no. 1 (1996): 130.
26. Hartley, "From Men to Boys," 130. He asserted, "As late as 1943, the Presiding Bishopric publicized for bishops the example of young women in one ward who "take care of washing and sterilizing the sacrament sets after each service." Also see "Bee-Hive Girls Report," *Young Woman's Journal*, 29 no. 4 (April 1918): 183. While it is not the focus of this paper, it is also important to note the importance of Relief Society funding for temple building, including penny drives, the collection of "Sunday eggs," and other monetary donations.
27. Hartley, "From Men to Boys," 130. For another example of women's long-term commitment to the care of sacramental objects, the obituary for Julia S. McKee states: "For more than twelve years she has had charge of the sacrament dishes and furnished bread for the same not once failing to have it ready at the proper time." Mary E. Westover and Mary S. Fowler, "In Memoriam," *Woman's Exponent* 30 no. 13, (May 1, 1902): 103.
28. For other changes to sacrament vessels see Justin Bray, "The Lord's Supper during the Progressive Era, 1890–1930," *Journal of Mormon History*, 38, no. 4 (2012): 88–104.
29. Hartley, "From Men to Boys," 131. He notes: "Although women still launder and press the linen, beginning in 1950, the Presiding Bishopric assigned teachers to prepare the sacrament table, specifically requesting that this task not be delegated to LDS girls or their mothers. However, in 1955, the Presiding Bishopric told Church members that young women 'where desired' could be assigned care of the table linens and trays following meetings." The current handbook states: "Sacrament tablecloths should be white, non-transparent, clean, and pressed." It does not specify who should do the work of laundering and pressing the cloth. *Handbook 2: Administering the Church* (Salt Lake City: Church of Jesus Christ of Latter-day Saints, 2010), 173.
30. Altar cloth, circa 1888, LDS 2003-64, Church History Museum. This is a white rectangular altar cloth with embroidered corners. The fabric is plain weave, probably cotton or linen. In possession of Mary B. Pratton at the time of her death.
31. Maureen Daly Goggin, "An Essamplaire Essai on the Rhetoricity of Needlework Sampler-Making: A Contribution to Theorizing and Historicizing Rhetorical Praxis," *Rhetoric Review* 21, no. 4 (2002): 313.

32. Maureen Daly Goggin and Beth Fowkes Tobin, eds., *Women and Things, 1750–1950: Gendered Material Strategies* (Surrey, England: Ashgate, 2009), 6.
33. Two sterling silver sacrament cups, LDS 81-10-1 and LDS 81-10-2, Church History Museum, donated by the Park City first Ward Relief Society, at the first meeting held in the rebuilt chapel after the great fire of 1898.
34. Silverplate sacrament pitcher, LDS 90-3-1, Church History Museum. Sacrament cups and trays donated to the Park City 1st Ward by the Relief Society in 1900 LDS 81-10-1–81-10-3.
35. Anna Karina Hermkens, "Clothing as Embodied Experience of Belief," in *Religion and Material Culture*, 16; Linda B. Arthur, *Religion, Dress and the Body* (New York: New York University Press, 1999).
36. Laurel Thatcher Ulrich, *The Age of Homespun: Objects and Stories in the Creation of an American Myth* (New York: Vintage Books, 2001), 409.
37. Lucy Meserve Smith, "Historical Sketch," 1889, 60, Special Collections, Marriott Library, University of Utah (hereafter cited as Marriott Special Collections).
38. Mark Lyman Staker, *Hearken, O Ye People: The Historical Setting of Joseph Smith's Ohio Revelations* (Salt Lake City: Greg Kofford Books, 2009), 49–50.
39. Lavina Fielding Anderson, ed., *Lucy's Book: A Critical Edition of Lucy Mack Smith's Family Memoir* (Salt Lake City: Signature Books, 2001), 502.
40. "Our women were engaged in spinning and knitting in order to clothe those who were laboring at the building and the Lord only knows the scenes of poverty, tribulation and distress which we passed through in order to accomplish this thing." "Extracts from H. C. Kimball's Journal," *Times and Seasons* (April 15, 1845): 867. Vilate Kimball and another woman spun one hundred pounds of wool and then "wove and got the cloth dressed, and cut up and made up into [clothing] and gave them to those men who labored on the Temple." Jill Mulvay Derr, Janath Russell Cannon and Maureen Ursenbach Beecher, *Women of Covenant: The Story of Relief Society* (Salt Lake City: Deseret Book, 1992), 16.
41. Jessee, Ashurst-McGee, and Jensen, *Journals*, 188–89.
42. Edward Tullidge, *Women of Mormondom* (New York: Tullidge & Crandall, 1877), 76.
43. Goggin and Tobin, *Women and Things*, 6.
44. Leonard J. Arrington and Melvin A. Larkin, "The Logan Tabernacle and Temple," *Utah Historical Quarterly* 41, no. 3 (1973): 301–14. Arrington describes six temple industries springing from temple building that reflect a focus on the work of male artisans. However, Arrington does acknowledge the economic work of Mormon women elsewhere; integrating the material practices of women in temple building could yield interesting results. Leonard J. Arrington, "The Economic Role of Pioneer Mormon Women," *Western Humanities Review*, 9 (Spring 1955): 145–64. See also Noel A. Carmack, "Labor and Construction of the Logan Temple, 1877–1884," *Journal of Mormon History* 22, no. 1 (1996): 52–79. Carmack's article is a notable example, as he does address the impact of women's economic contributions to temple building.

Also see Kristine Wright, "'All Proceeded at Once to Cut and Sew': Temple Building and Gendered Material Practices," unpublished paper, 2012.

45. Colleen McDannell, *Material Christianity: Religion and Popular Culture in America* (New Haven: Yale University Press, 1995), 201, 297; Eliza Mariah Allred Munson, *Early Pioneer History*, undated, MS 4558, Church History Library; Benjamin LeBaron, "How we obtained our garments," 1940, MS 4057 2, Church History Library; Rose Marie Reid, interviewed by William G. Hartley at Provo, Utah, June–August 1973, OH 71, 169, Church History Library.

46. "P.M. Sister [Elizabeth] Durphy came to make my Robe and Garment." (William Clayton—Thursday Jan 25, 1844). Devery S. Anderson and Gary James Bergera, eds., *Joseph Smith's Quorum of the Anointed, 1842–1845: A Documentary History* (Salt Lake City: Signature Books, 2005), 57.

47. Devery S. Anderson and Gary James Bergera, eds., *The Nauvoo Endowment Companies, 1845–1846: A Documentary History* (Salt Lake City: Signature Books, 2005), 173; George D. Smith, ed., *An Intimate Chronicle: The Journals of William Clayton* (Salt Lake City: Signature Books, 1991), 228. Similarly, on December 26, 1845 President Brigham Young announced "there would be no business done to day, and that they were all dismissed . . . except the two Brother Hansons, Lewis Robbins and Brother Averett, whom he wanted for door keepers and John L. Butler for fireman. Also Sisters M[ercy] R. Thompson and Eliza R. Snow whom he wanted to do some sewing." Ibid., 233.

48. Anderson and Bergera, *The Nauvoo Endowment Companies*, 192–93.

49. Kathleen Flake, "'Not to be Riten': The Mormon Temple Rite as Oral Canon," *Journal of Ritual Studies* 9, no.2 (1995): 1–21.

50. Smith, *An Intimate Chronicle*, 217.

51. Mary Jane Mount Tanner Diary, March 19, 1878, Mary Jane Mount Tanner Papers, MS 200, box 17, Marriott Special Collections.

52. Jane Manning James, Autobiography, circa 1902, MS 4425, 18–19, Church History Library, https://eadview.lds.org/dcbrowser/MS%204425/. Many thanks to Quincy Newell for sharing this reference with me. The experiences of modern Mormon women also bear out this observation. Women who made items for the San Antonio Temple referred to spiritual experiences and manifestations of the spirit, as well as personal revelation received through their handwork. See "Thoughts, Experiences and Testimonies of Sisters Who Made Items for the San Antonio Texas Temple."

53. Stanley B. Kimball, *On the Potter's Wheel: The Diaries of Heber C. Kimball*, (Salt Lake City: Signature Books, 1987), 162–63. Kimball also noted on December 6, 1845 "Sister Elzebeth Ann Whitney come in and sode [sewed] on the fringe, going over the Top of the canvas running threw the room crost from North to South . . . Sister Clarisa and Emily Cutler mad[e] a Coten [cotten] Veil going before the Linnen Veil. Jullia Durphy assisted in making the Veil Linnen".

54. Samuel Roskelley: Papers and Temple Records, 1862–1962, Diary, May 13, 1884, MSS 65, box 2, book 2, Special Collections and Archive, Merrill-Cazier Library, Utah State University.

55. Ibid., March 14, 1884.
56. James L. MacFarlane, comp., *History of Lucy Smith Cardon Cache Valley's Aunt Lucy and Tommy Gordon, Bugler, Co. G, U.S. Infantry (Thomas B. Cardon) Civil War Hero to Business Leader* (n.p.: James MacFarlane, 2011), 38.
57. Thomas G. Alexander, *Mormonism in Transition: A History of the Latter-day Saints, 1890–1930* (Urbana: University of Illinois Press, 1996), 125–56.
58. "Instructions for Making Temple and Temple-Burial Clothing, Special Instructions Relief Society Paper, ca. 1885–1923," Saint Charles Ward, Bear Lake Stake Local Records, 6, LR 7742 32, Church History Library.
59. Audrey M. Godfrey, "'The Queen of Invention': The Sewing Machine Comes to Utah," *Journal of Mormon History* 32, no. 3 (2006): 87.
60. Derr, Cannon, and Beecher, *Women of Covenant*, 197–98. Derr et al. refer to a First Presidency letter authored by Joseph F. Smith, Anthon H. Lund, and Charles W. Penrose entitled "Dear Sister," undated, as reproduced in the Relief Society General Board Minutes, November 7, 1912. See also Alexander, *Mormonism in Transition*, 242.
61. Miriam B. Murphy, "Women in the Utah Work Force from Statehood to World War II," *Utah Historical Quarterly* 50, no. 2 (1982): 139–59.
62. Reid, Oral History, 169–70.
63. Reid, Oral History, 167.
64. Ibid. See also Anderson and Bergera, *The Nauvoo Endowment Companies*, 351–53 for excerpts from David O. McKay's diary detailing the approval process for the design changes in temple garments.
65. Reid, Oral History, 169.
66. "Thoughts, Experiences and Testimonies of Sisters Who Made Items for the San Antonio Texas Temple."

6

Women and Mormon Authority

JONATHAN A. STAPLEY

Early Mormonism's complex liturgy, cosmology, and lexicon render facile attempts to define its system of authority futile. Moreover, because terms such as "priesthood" have catechismal values in modern Mormonism, presentism is a perennial threat, even within academic discussions of Mormon authority.

In order to show how Mormon women have negotiated changing concepts of authority throughout its history, I employ a taxonomy for categorizing different aspects of that authority that is not native to the revelations or handbooks of the Latter-day Saints. I make distinctions between "ecclesiastical authority," "liturgical authority," and "priestly authority." I show how these authorities interact with "priesthood," itself a dynamic term in Mormon parlance and saturated with various meanings.

In particular, I review the complicated meaning of priesthood introduced as part of the cosmology associated with the Nauvoo Temple liturgy. There Joseph Smith revealed an expanded conception of heaven that comprised an interconnected network of relationships as materialized through temple ritual. This heaven was discursively synonymous with priesthood for several years, and aspects of it for decades. Female incorporation into this priesthood was essential, but as language shifted, this relationship became incomprehensible with time.

Additionally, I show that the manner whereby early Mormon liturgical knowledge was communicated increased the authority of those individuals, whether male or female, who had the most proximate access to Joseph

Smith. In Utah this resulted in authority distribution outside of priesthood organizations. In particular I will show how the community recognized greater authority in some women with regard to the performance of healing ritual over even the highest church leaders. Lastly, I present some general observations on shifts in the participation of women in Mormon liturgy in an effort to identify areas of fruitful future research.

A Taxonomy of Mormon Authority

The Church of Christ was organized in April 1830 with an ecclesiastical structure comprised of individual teachers, priests, elders, and perhaps deacons. According to Joseph Smith's revelations, the men who were ordained to these positions performed certain rituals and presided at meetings and conferences in an ad hoc fashion. Over the subsequent years, Joseph Smith revealed quorum and administrative structures that served as the foundation for modern church organization.[1] The activities of these early ecclesiasts, however, did not comprise the totality of church worship and function. Women, as well as nonecclesiastically positioned men, joined church officers in a host of rituals and ritualized behaviors. Latter-day Saint liturgical terrain is complex and shifting, and sometimes overlapping borders are readily evident.

Whereas the term priesthood in today's church refers to broad conceptions of power and authority, both on earth and in heaven, in the early church it referred simply to the office of priest in the hierarchy of the nascent church.[2] When early Mormon evangelists baptized converts they did so by the implicit authority of the office to which they were ordained. Similarly, when they offered up prayers for the Sacrament of the Lord's Supper or ordained new officers, the priest or elder did not explicitly invoke any particular authority. Even after Smith revealed the more familiar structures of the bifurcated priesthood, or Aaronic and Melchizedek priesthoods, these early rituals were performed simply in the name of Jesus Christ.[3] However, the community recognized that a particular authority was required for the performance of these rituals. This particular authority was associated with ecclesiastical offices and therefore was ecclesiastical in nature.

Authority in the early church was, however, not completely localized to ecclesiastical office. When a woman prayed, laid hands on the sick to bless or heal, exhorted, or translated glossolalia, she did so with implicit authority. The community recognized that she had authority within the church to perform certain actions in the name of the Lord. However, the community did not recognize this authority as a type of priesthood, nor was it ecclesiastical in nature. For the first decade of the church, women held no offices in the church organization. Kristine Wright and I have used the term "liturgical authority" as an appellation for this nonecclesiastical church authority.[4] Liturgy includes the ritualized systems of church worship in which believers participate—often relating to regular church services and major life events, such as birth, death, marriage and coming of age. Early Mormonism in particular had a very diffuse liturgy. For instance, while a Catholic priest was required to perform the liturgy of extreme unction, any Latter-day Saint could dedicate the dying to the Lord or administer a healing anointing in the name of Jesus Christ. Women as well as men were integral participants in wide areas of church liturgy.

While documentation for the participation of women in the early church and its liturgy is scant due to male-centric record keeping, there is some evidence. Elizabeth Rollins Lightner remembered seeking after the gift of interpreting tongues in early 1833 while living in Independence, Missouri. As a young woman, she translated the glossolalia of a group of men who had gathered to discuss the revelations then in print. Her translation was an indictment of the Latter-day Saints in Missouri and the men rejected her words. However, church leaders supported the young woman's authority and she became a prominent interpreter where she lived. Lightner exercised liturgical authority to translate glossolalia and deliver the resulting sermons and prophecy to the church. Her experiences also shed light on another area of church liturgy. Elizabeth described a healing event ten years later in Nauvoo: "I took a severe cold that caused inflamation of the bowels. I was so low that my life was despaired of by two Physicians[.] Mother was sent for. She brought some consecrated oil with which she anointed me, and prayed for me."[5] The performance of healing rituals are the most commonly documented examples of women wielding liturgical authority in the early church.[6]

The Cosmological Priesthood, and Priestly Authority

The separation of liturgical authority from ecclesiastical authority is a useful convention; however, the radically shifting usage of the term priesthood in nineteenth-century Mormonism complicates its utility.

In the church's earliest days, ecclesiastical office and priesthood office were synonymous. However, in Nauvoo, nonpriesthood ecclesiastical offices were introduced to the church with the formation of the Relief Society and the ordination of its presidency.[7] Moreover, Joseph Smith's revelation of the expanded temple liturgy in 1842 and 1843 included an expanded cosmology in which kinship, priesthood, government, and salvation became synonymous. Those who participated in the temple liturgy commonly referred to themselves, as well as the interconnected network of heaven as materialized in the temple on earth, as the "priesthood." As part of the temple liturgy, both male and female participants dressed in priesthood robes, shared priesthood symbols, and looked forward to the promise of the "fullness of the priesthood"—the status of being a king and priest, or queen and priestess for eternity. Men and women who had participated in the Nauvoo Temple liturgy expected to be able to extend this priesthood kinship to others.[8]

In distinction from the older ecclesiastical priesthood offices, I refer to this temple-linked conception of priesthood as the "cosmological priesthood."[9] I call the authority that church members received by being incorporated into this cosmological priesthood, "priestly authority."[10] Participants in the temple liturgy didn't gain any ecclesiastical position. This priestly authority allowed church members to perform the temple liturgy for others, and it also functioned within their physical bodies, as children born to parents sealed in the temple were considered sealed to their parents for eternity.

For a few years immediately after the Nauvoo Temple, cosmological priesthood language saturated the discourses of church leaders. In Utah, the common usage of the term priesthood reverted relatively quickly to be associated with ideas based on the older administrative priesthood ecclesiology. However, an understanding of the cosmological priesthood explains the few but important exceptions to this shift. These exceptions involved certain invocations of temple cosmology in relation to temple marriages, familial sealings, and Brigham Young's justification for the exclusion of black people from the temple and priesthood. Reviewing these cases clarifies important differences between ecclesiastical authority, liturgical authority, and priestly authority.

First, patriarchs like John Smith and Charles Hyde who had participated in the Nauvoo Temple commonly blessed women who had received temple marriages and announced that they were "heirs of the priesthood" or that they had or were to receive the "fullness of the priesthood." Occasionally, they made similar statements in proximity to statements regarding blessing the sick or other church functions relating to ecclesiastical office, and it is important not to conflate them. When Smith blessed Delilah Allen in 1847 he said: "I also seal the holy Priesthood upon thee in common with thy companion. Thou shall have faith to heal the sick. You shall have wisdom to instruct thy sisters in the principles of salvation."[11] Statements such as these are completely comprehensible within the framework of the cosmological priesthood, but collapsing the three sentences into one breaks that same framework. Smith was not stating that the priesthood he sealed on Allen was an ecclesiastical authority to teach nor liturgical authority to heal.[12]

In three statements, Smith recognized the three different types of authority discussed in this paper. Women could have ecclesiastical authority to teach, and did have liturgical authority to administer healing and blessing rituals, regardless of their participation in the temple liturgy. Beyond these common invocations of the cosmological priesthood in patriarchal blessings, some church leaders also referenced the concept in formal statements. In a public sermon in 1879, John Taylor asked, "Do they [women] hold the priesthood? Yes, in connection with their husbands and they are one with their husbands[.]"[13] When Orson Pratt edited an account of Joseph Smith's teachings for inclusion in the 1879 Doctrine and Covenants, he added an editorial clarification that the "Order of the Priesthood" required for the highest eternal blessings was "the new and everlasting covenant of marriage."[14]

Second, not just wives but entire families were understood to inherit priesthood through sealings. The primary justification for sealing children to parents from Nauvoo to the early twentieth century was to establish heirship to the cosmological priesthood. Thus, the cosmological priesthood incorporated familial relationships, and as reified in temple practice, the most exalted station of humankind was to be king and priest, or queen and priestess, over one's progeny (biological or adoptive).[15] As the governing quorums declared in preparation for the return of temples in Utah, "Which of them, if he understands the laws of God, can feel indifferent as to whether his wife shall be his for eternity or for time only; or whether his children shall be born in the covenant and be legal heirs to the priesthood or have to become such by adoption?"[16] Though addressed to men, implicit in this statement is the belief that both men and women had to become heirs to the priesthood network of heaven.

Through this context, Brigham Young's justification for excluding black people from the temple liturgy (the cosmological priesthood) and the administrative priesthood, which is so incongruous to current church members, becomes at least coherent. Historians frequently describe the exclusion of black people in Mormonism before 1978 as a "priesthood ban," but it was far more than a ban on the ecclesiastical priesthood of the church. Despite Joseph Smith establishing a precedent of priesthood ordination for black men, after leaving Nauvoo and over a protracted period, Brigham Young formulated a policy that prohibited all black people, both men and women, from participation in the temple liturgy, which also barred black men from priesthood office.[17]

As justification for this exclusion, Young translated the common Christian beliefs that black people were descendants of Cain and/or Ham into the cosmology of the Nauvoo Temple. In doing so, he crafted a new Genesis narrative. In a meeting on February 12, 1849, Apostle Lorenzo Snow "presented the case of the African Race for a chance of redemption & unlock the door to them." Brigham Young responded and "explained it very lucidly that the curse remains on them bec[ause] Cain cut off the lives of Abel to hedge up his way & take the lead but the L[or]d has given them blackness, so as to give the children of Abel an opportunity to keep his place with his desc[endent]s in the et[erna]l worlds."[18] Though Thomas Bullock's longhand notes are somewhat disjointed, the narrative that Young repeated frequently throughout his life was clear. Young taught that Cain's murder of Abel represented an attempt to cut off Abel's posterity qua kingdom in the cosmological priesthood. As a consequence, Young taught, black men and women were not to be integrated into the cosmological priesthood until Abel's posterity was somehow restored. One manifestation of this fractured human network was the administrative priesthood restriction. Focusing only on this restriction, however, obfuscates the degree to which black Mormon women and men like Jane Manning James were not to be integrated into the family of God.[19] That an ad hoc temple ritual sealed Jane Manning James as a servant to Joseph Smith was not because John Taylor, who followed Young as president of the church, or other church leaders viewed black people as eternal servants, but because this relationship was the only way they could conceive to link her to Joseph Smith without integrating her into the priesthood family.

Brigham Young's narrative remained the de facto explanation of the temple and priesthood restrictions for several decades after he passed away. In the early twentieth century, church leaders moved away from describing temple sealing in terms of priesthood and priesthood heirship with an associated decline in the cosmological priesthood as a means of comprehending the temple.[20] Outside of this context, Young's narrative made little sense and became incongruous to church members and leaders, who found other explanations, like premortal valiancy, to have much greater explanatory power.[21] Additionally the incomprehensibility of Young's narrative resulted in a focus on the exclusion of black men from the administrative priesthood as the locus of restriction and deemphasized the temple restriction on both women and men.

The shift away from priesthood language to describe temple cosmology, coupled with the clear recognition that women have not held ecclesiastical priesthood office, has presented a challenge to both church leaders and academics when analyzing female participation in the temple liturgy and the broader church. Both men and women who have passed through the temple liturgy in turn perform the rituals of the temple for others of their own sex. This ritual performance requires a measure of authority above the standard liturgical authority described above, and yet church leaders and members have consistently stated that women do not hold the priesthood.

This predicament has resulted in some creative resolutions. A 1980 *Ensign* article stated: "Although women do not hold the priesthood, they are partakers of every blessing necessary for salvation. The temple endowment makes this clear. The general ordinances of the temple are all performed by authority of the priesthood, and women have access to all of them."[22] In other words, this author states that women perform rituals by priesthood authority without actually having any priesthood. One hundred and thirty-four years earlier, the women performing rituals in the Nauvoo Temple were recognized as having a sealed position in the cosmological priesthood and their authority to extend that station to others was implicit. With the lexical shift of priesthood, the authority became somewhat mysterious to participants and a tendency grew to conflate the cosmological priesthood functions with the ecclesiastical priesthood of the church. The concept of priestly authority consequently allows for analyses that more completely integrate historical evidence from different periods. Moreover, these categorizations also help to historicize the recent conflation of priesthood with all possible authority in the church by church leaders in response to questions over female ordination.[23]

Jane Manning James's experiences in the church are again illustrative of the distinctions between ecclesiastical, liturgical, and priestly authorities within the church. James held no church office, and therefore wielded no ecclesiastical authority. She recognized that as a black woman she was barred from the priestly functions of the temple, and consequently lacked priestly authority. However, she nevertheless freely testified, exhorted, spoke in tongues, and prayed in church meetings. She also kept consecrated oil and used it for healing.[24] James exercised liturgical authority in the church despite not having these other authorities.

Loci of Authority

The relationships between ecclesiastical, liturgical, and priestly authorities were fairly fluid for the first eighty years of the church, and many primary issues remained unsettled. However, it is clear that during this time the direction of these authorities pivoted on the same fulcrum, namely the proximity of that authority to Joseph Smith. While each authority might be conferred upon an individual in a discrete event, the management or direction of that authority was less formal.

In the nineteenth century, Mormons generally lacked codified instruction. Instead, church leaders relied on oral instructions, either through personal conversations, public sermons, or sometimes letters. By the time Joseph Smith was killed, Mormon men and women variously laid on hands, anointed the body or the head, drank consecrated oil, baptized for health, washed and anointed for health, and offered temple prayers for the sick.[25] There is no record of Smith's justification for the ritual diversity within the healing liturgy, nor did he leave concrete instructions for ritual performance. He rejected church rule books.[26] Instead, Latter-day Saints relied on each other to learn how to participate in the church liturgy. They learned by example and by oral instruction. When a question arose over what was to be done, or why it was to be done, church members viewed those closest to Joseph Smith and later church leaders as being most authoritative.[27]

In 1884, Eliza R. Snow, the recently ordained Relief Society general president, instituted a new policy with regards to female healing. Whereas all Mormon women previously had the liturgical authority to administer healing and blessing rituals, Snow declared, "Any and all sisters who honor their holy endowments, not only have the right, but should feel it a duty, whenever called upon to administer to our sisters in these ordinances, which God has graciously committed to His daughters as well as to His sons[.]"[28] The introduction of a temple qualification is subtle, however, she clearly and apparently intentionally conflated the liturgical authority to heal and bless with the priestly authority of the temple.

The reasons for this conflation are not clear. Perhaps it was an effort to protect female liturgical authority by connecting it to the very prominent and visible rituals of the temple. Nevertheless, it was a dramatic departure from previous practice. Immediately after Snow's death, acting LDS Church President Wilford Woodruff reauthorized all female church members to heal regardless of their temple experience.[29] While church leaders continued to preach the policy that all women could perform healing rituals for the next several decades, many people remembered Snow's instructions and were confused. Even other members of the First Presidency deferred to Snow on this position while she lived and for a few years after.[30] The reason for this confusion lies in Snow's role as chief interpreter of Joseph Smith's teachings to the Female Relief Society of Nauvoo.[31] She was widely recognized as one of Smith's plural wives, even taking his last name during the later years of her life (after Emma's death). She was the secretary who inscribed Smith's words to the Society in Nauvoo, and she kept the minute book with her to preach from until she died.

Another example of this locus of liturgical authority occurred in the September 16, 1901, general board meeting of the Young Ladies Mutual Improvement Association. Among the topics the board members discussed was an apparent shift in church policy regarding the rituals women employed to heal or bless. Earlier that year, in conjunction with the April general conference, the *Deseret News* published an anonymous editorial that made public a decision of the First Presidency that women were not to "seal" blessings or anointings as they had in the past, but instead were to "confirm" them. This change in ritual practice was significant and complex both in the reasons for it and in its ramifications.[32] At the meeting in 1901, the board members discussed the question of women sealing blessings. An anonymous editorial was certainly not sufficient to overturn decades of liturgical instruction. Helen Woodruff, wife of young apostle Abraham Owen Woodruff, testified "that Aunt Zina [D. H. Young] & Aunt Bathsheba [Smith]" had sealed a healing anointing on her and that "She took them as very good authority."[33] When the Young Ladies board discussed this issue, a twenty-eight-year-old apostle was frankly not a particularly "good authority" on the participation of women in church liturgy, and consequently it was only natural for Helen Woodruff to look to other sources for authority than her husband. Both Zina D. H. Young and Bathsheba Smith lived in Nauvoo, knew Joseph Smith—Zina was one of his wives—and had years of practical experience in the liturgy.

Ultimately, the First Presidency's mandate that women confirm anointings instead of sealing them became normative across the church. As such it is an important transition point when the ecclesiastical authority of the First Presidency and other church leaders began to supplant the more informal and oral networks of liturgical authority based on traditional proximity to the church's founders.

Trends in Female Participation in Mormon Liturgy

The following Venn diagrams represent various rituals, ritualized activities, and responsibilities overlaid onto domains demarcating ecclesiastical authority, liturgical authority, and priestly authority as discussed in this paper.

Additionally a region for priesthood is included to represent the ecclesiastical authority of men who have been ordained to a priesthood office in the church. The dates of the three charts, 1832, 1880, and 2010, are useful in gauging shifts in women's authority in the church. By 1832, Joseph Smith had revealed the offices of high priest and bishop, as well as a foundational body of rituals. In 1877, the St. George Temple opened with the complete temple liturgy being active for the first time in the church's history and Brigham Young and Wilford Woodruff worked to systematize temple practice. Moreover, by 1880 Mormons had developed other rituals, such as grave dedication and a specific blessing for expectant mothers.[34] This period represents perhaps the height of ritual diversity in

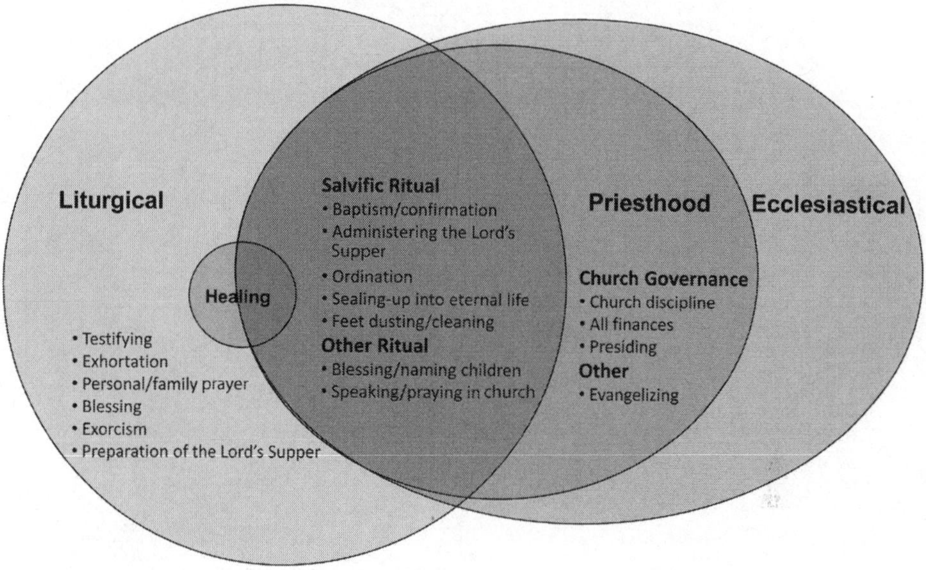

FIGURE 6.1. Church Authority, 1832.

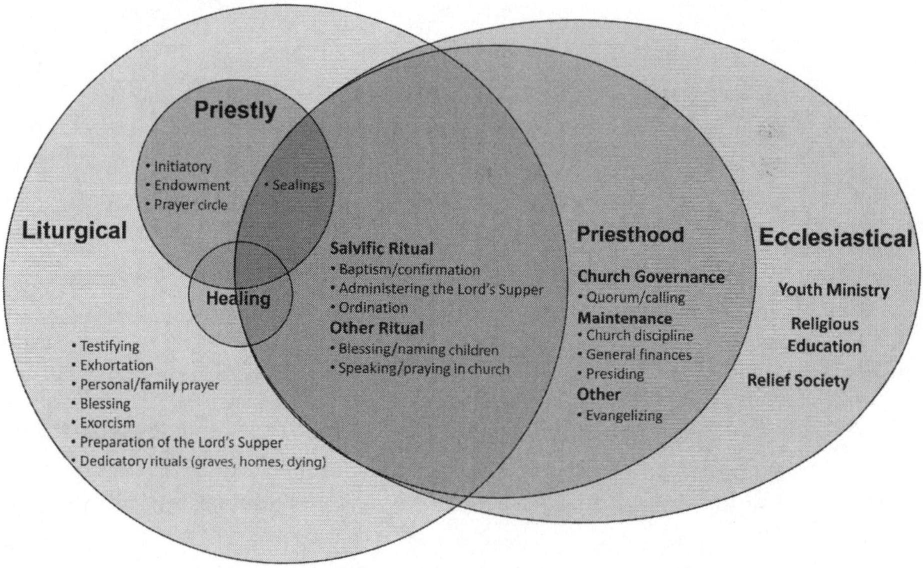

FIGURE 6.2. Church Authority, 1880.

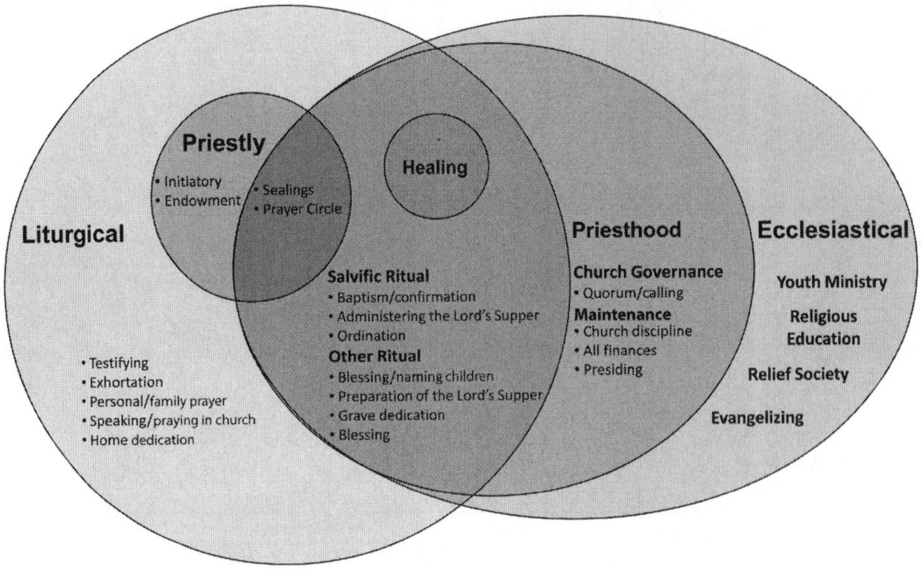

FIGURE 6.3. Church Authority, 2010.

Mormonism. After the death of Joseph F. Smith in 1918, church leaders formalized and codified church liturgy and relocated the loci of liturgical and priestly liturgy to be clearly subservient to ecclesiastical authority as managed by the priesthood bureaucracy of the church. In 2010, the First Presidency published the most recent general handbook of instructions for church government, which includes detailed liturgical texts. This text represents ecclesiastically defined policy and belief, refined through decades of official correlation.[35]

The differences between the diagrams highlight many trends, some that have been described in scholarly literature, and others that have not. Kristine Wright and I have documented and analyzed the shift in healing—which includes the temple as a special location for healing, prominent female healing practice, and diverse ritual forms—to the simplified priesthood-centric ritual form reinforced in the 2010 general handbook.[36] This locating of church ritual within ecclesiastical priesthood bureaucratic authority to the exclusion of women is a broad trend reflected in shifts in other rituals, like grave dedication and home dedication.[37] In some cases, like sacrament meeting prayers, the ritual became firmly located in the ecclesiastical sphere in the late 1960s, but the trend soon reversed.[38] Other areas have seen dramatic increases in female participation. To illustrate, the incorporation of women in the formal missionary program of the church and into regular Sunday preaching schedules represents a radical expansion in authority. In areas such as clothing and preparing the dead for burial, factors such as the professionalization of American funereal practice and the industrialization of temple clothing production dramatically altered both male and female activities.[39]

Beyond the histories of particular rituals, much work is yet needed to understand how women integrated themselves into Mormon lived religion. From the perspective of Mormon liturgy, historians must work harder to incorporate the voices and experiences of women. Even if a particular ritual was clearly performed solely by male priesthood holders, women were still frequently the most common participants. In the nineteenth century, the majority of temple proxies were women and over 70 percent of individuals baptized for their health in the temples were women.[40]

Conclusion

On April 28, 1842, Joseph Smith addressed the nascent Female Relief Society of Nauvoo and, among other topics, he affirmed the right and authority of women to perform healing rituals. He quoted the charge to the apostles: "'Go ye into all the world' &c.—no matter who believeth; these signs, such as healing the sick, casting out devils &c. should follow all that believe whether male or female." Smith then "ask'd the Society if they could not see by this sweeping stroke, that wherein they are ordained, it is the privilege of those set apart to administer in that authority which is confer'd on them[.]"[41] Teasing out what Smith meant in this sermon has been a challenge from the day it was delivered. In this paper, I have introduced a taxonomy in order to more completely and accurately analyze dynamics of authority throughout church history, including this sermon. Women have never held ecclesiastical priesthood office in the Church of Jesus Christ of Latter-day Saints. However, women have always participated in Mormon liturgy and eventually gained nonpriesthood ecclesiastical offices and authority in the church. This participation evolved with time—so too perceptions of it. The ideas of ecclesiastical, liturgical, and priestly authorities, coupled with the understanding of the cosmological priesthood, allow for a more accurate and integrated approach to understanding women and authority in the church.

Notes

1. William V. Smith, "Early Mormon Priesthood Revelation: Text, Impact, and Evolution," *Dialogue: A Journal of Mormon Thought* 46, no. 4 (Winter 2013): 1–84.
2. See M. Russell Ballard, "This Is My Work and Glory," *Ensign*, May 2013, 18–21.
3. The expansion of the priesthood, first between priests and high priests, and then between the more general Aaronic (or Levitical) Priesthood and the Melchizedek Priesthood, solidified during the first five years of the church. Smith, "Early Mormon Priesthood Revelations."
4. Jonathan A. Stapley and Kristine Wright, "Female Ritual Healing in Mormonism," *Journal of Mormon History* 37, no. 1 (Winter 2011): 1–86.
5. Mary Elizabeth Rollins Lightner, Autobiography, 4–5 and 21–22, holograph, box 14, fd. 4, Susa Young Gates Papers, Utah Historical Society Archives, Salt Lake City.
6. Kristine Wright and I have extensively documented female ritual healing from the Kirtland period through the twentieth century. Stapley and Wright, "Female Ritual Healing in Mormonism."
7. The establishment of the Female Relief Society of Nauvoo introduced lay ecclesiastical structure in the church, which grew with increased "auxiliaries" in modern Mormon parlance. These lay offices in the church operated with varying degrees of dependence on priesthood quorums for administrative authority and financial support. At the inaugural meeting of the Society, Joseph Smith stated: "Let this Presidency serve as a constitution—all their decisions be considered law; and acted upon as such. If any Officers are wanted to carry out the designs of the Institution, let them be appointed and set apart, as Deacons, Teachers &c. are among us. The minutes of your meetings will be precedents for you to act upon—your Constitution and law." On April 28, 1842, he further stated, "Those ordain'd to lead the Society, are authoriz'd to appoint to different offices as the circumstances shall require." "Nauvoo Relief Society Minutes, 1842–1844," March 16, 1842, 8; April 28, 1842, 40. Church History Library, Salt Lake City, Utah. http://josephsmithpapers.org/paperSummary/nauvoo-relief-society-minute-book
8. Jonathan A. Stapley, "Adoptive Sealing Ritual in Mormonism," *Journal of Mormon History* 37, no. 3 (Summer 2011): 56–65. See also Samuel Brown's excellent, *In Heaven as It Is on Earth* (New York: Oxford University Press, 2012).
9. Stapley, "Adoptive Sealing Ritual," 56–65.
10. I am using the term "priestly" in a way similar to Kathleen Flake, "The Emotional and Priestly Logic of Plural Marriage," *Leonard J. Arrington Mormon History Lecture Series*, no. 15 (Logan, UT: Utah State University Press, 2009). The temple liturgy elevated men and women to priests and priestesses, kings and queens.
11. John Smith, patriarchal blessing for Delilah Allen, January 31, 1847, in Martha Bagley Halverson, *A Lasting Legacy: The Bagley Family History since 1628* (Salt Lake City: Heritage Associates, 1997), 81.

12. Note that patriarchs used such language to reconfirm blessings on people, in this case a temple marriage.
13. *Journal of Discourses*, vol. 20 (Liverpool: William Budge, 1880), 359. When John Taylor organized the general Relief Society presidency the following year, he discussed ordination of Nauvoo Relief Society officers: "The ordination then given did not mean the conferring of the Priesthood upon those Sisters yet the sisters hold a portion of the Priesthood in connection with their husbands. (Sisters E. R. Snow and Bathsheba Smith stated that they so understood it in Nauvoo and have always looked upon it in that light.)" Minutes, July 17, 1880, Relief Society, Record, 1880–1892, microfilm of manuscript, CR 11 175, Church History Library. See also Ruth May Fox, Diaries, March 8, 1896, microfilm of holograph, MS 6348 1–2, Church History Library.
14. Orson Pratt, ed., *The Doctrine and Covenants, of the Church of Jesus Christ of Latter-day Saints, Containing the Revelations Given to Joseph Smith, Jun., The Prophet, for the Building up of the Kingdom of God in the Last Days* (Liverpool: William Budge, 1879), 462–63 [D&C 131]. Cf., George D. Smith, ed., *An Intimate Chronicle: The Journals of William Clayton* (Salt Lake City: Signature Books, 1995), 101.
15. See Stapley, "Adoptive Sealing Ritual."
16. Brigham Young et al., Letter to Bishops and Members, October 25, 1876, in *Messages of the First Presidency of The Church of Jesus Christ of Latter-day Saints*, edited by James R. Clark, 6 vols. (Salt Lake City: Bookcraft, 1965–75), 2:279.
17. The most comprehensive treatment of this shift is W. Paul Reeve, *Religion of a Different Color: Race and the Mormon Struggle for Whiteness* (New York: Oxford University Press, 2015), esp. chap. 3–5.
18. General Church Minutes, February 13, 1849, digital images of manuscript, CR 100 318, box 2, fd. 8, Church History Library.
19. See Quincy D. Newell, "'Is There No Blessing for Me?': Jane James's Construction of Space in Latter-day Saint History and Practice," in *New Perspectives in Mormon Studies: Creating and Crossing Boundaries*, edited by Quincy D. Newell and Eric F. Mason (Norman: University of Oklahoma Press, 2012), 41–68.
20. Stapley, "Adoptive Sealing Ritual," 113–15.
21. Reeve, *Religion of a Different Color*, chap. 6.
22. Carolyn J. Rasmus, "Mormon Women: A Convert's Perspective," *Ensign*, August 1980, 68–69. See similar statements by Sheri Dew, *Women and the Priesthood: What One Mormon Woman Believes* (Salt Lake City: Deseret Book, 2013), 102–9.
23. See Dallin H. Oaks, "The Keys and Authority of the Priesthood," *Ensign*, May 2014, 49–52. I analyze this shift in great detail in a forthcoming volume.
24. See the following in the *Woman's Exponent*: Lydia D. Alder, "Ladies' Semi-Monthly Meeting" 22, no. 9 (December 1, 1893): 66; L. D. Alder, "Ladies' Semi-Monthly Meeting" 22, no. 10 (January 1, 1894): 226; L. D. Alder, "Ladies' Semi-Monthly Meeting" 22, no. 18 (June 1, 1894): 141; A. T. Hyde,

"Ladies' Semi-Monthly Meeting" 23, no. 5 (September 1, 1896): 34; Various, "Ladies' Semi-Monthly Meeting" 25, no. 11 (December 15, 1896): 78; Various, "Ladies' Semi-Monthly Meeting" 25, no. 11 (December 15, 1896): 79; Zina H. Bull, "Ladies' Semi-Monthly Meeting" 25, no. 21 (May 1, 1897): 138; L. D. Alder, "Ladies' Semi-Monthly Meeting" 25, no. 23 (June 1, 1897): 155.

25. Jonathan A. Stapley and Kristine Wright, "The Forms and the Power: The Development of Mormon Ritual Healing to 1847," *Journal of Mormon History* 35, no. 3 (Summer 2009): 42–87. Reprinted with revisions in Stephen C. Taysom, ed., *Dimensions of Faith: A Mormon Studies Reader* (Salt Lake City: Signature Books, 2011), 135–76.

26. On December 14, 1834, Smith "preached three hours . . . during which he exposed the Methodist Dicipline in its black deformity and called upon the Elders in the power of the spirit of God to expose the creeds & confessions of men." Jan Shipps and John W. Welch, eds., *The Journals of William E. McLellin, 1831–1836* (Provo, Urbana and Chicago: BYU Studies and University of Illinois Press, 1994), 152.

27. See also examples in Jonathan A. Stapley, "'The Last of the Old School': Joseph F. Smith and Latter-day Saint Liturgy," in *Joseph F. Smith: Reflections on the Man and His Times,* edited by Craig K. Manscill and Brian D. Reeves (Provo, UT: Religious Studies Center, 2013), 233–64.

28. E. R. Snow Smith, "To the Branches of the Relief Society," *Woman's Exponent* 13, no. 8 (September 15, 1884): 61.

29. See discussion in Stapley and Wright, "Female Ritual Healing in Mormonism," 37–40.

30. Ibid.

31. Jill Mulvay Derr and Carol Cornwall Madsen, "Preserving the Record and Memory of the Female Relief Society of Nauvoo, 1842–1892," *Journal of Mormon History* 35, no 3 (Summer 2009): 89–117.

32. See Stapley and Wright, "Female Ritual Healing in Mormonism," 40–50 for a more complete discussion.

33. Young Women, General Board Minutes, September 16, 1901, microfilm of typescript, CR 13 6, Church History Library.

34. Jonathan A. Stapley, "Last Rites and the Dynamics of Mormon Liturgy," *BYU Studies* 50, no. 2 (2011): 97–128. Stapley and Wright, "Female Ritual Healing in Mormonism," 11–19.

35. On priesthood correlation, see Matthew Bowman, *The Mormon People: The Making of an American Faith* (New York: Random House, 2012), 184–215; Daymon Mickel Smith, "'The Last Shall Be First and the First Shall Be Last': Discourse and Mormon History" (PhD dissertation, University of Pennsylvania, 2007).

36. Stapley and Wright, "Female Ritual Healing in Mormonism." See also Jonathan Stapley, "Pouring in Oil: The Development of the Modern Mormon Healing Ritual," in *By Our Rites of Worship: Latter-day Saint Views on Ritual*

in Scripture and Practice, edited by Daniel L. Belnap (Provo/Salt Lake City: Deseret Book/Religious Studies Center, 2013), 283–316.

37. Stapley, "Last Rites and the Dynamics of Mormon Liturgy." The following italicized text was added to the 2010 General Handbook entry on home dedication from the 2006 entry: "*A Melchizedek Priesthood holder may dedicate a home by the power of the priesthood. If there is not a Melchizedek Priesthood holder in the home, a family might invite a close relative, a home teacher, or another Melchizedek Priesthood holder to dedicate the home. Or* a family might gather and offer a prayer that includes the elements mentioned in the preceding paragraph and other words as the Spirit directs." *Handbook 2: Administering the Church* (Salt Lake City: The Church of Jesus Christ of Latter-day Saints, 2010), 20.11.
38. Though Spencer W. Kimball authorized the participation of women in sacrament meeting prayer in 1978, there appears to have been some institutional resistance over the next thirty years. I have spoken to several former stake presidents who remember being directed by traveling general authorities to exclude women from offering certain prayers during sacrament meeting in the 1990s. On the initial exclusion and Kimball's remonstration, see Edward L. Kimball, *Lengthen Your Stride: The Presidency of Spencer W. Kimball* (working manuscript), chap. 17: 16, digital copy included with Edward L. Kimball, *Lengthen Your Stride: The Presidency of Spencer W. Kimball* (Salt Lake City: Deseret Book, 2005). On the 2010 change, see *Handbook 2*, 18.5.
39. Stapley, "Last Rites and the Dynamics of Mormon Liturgy."
40. Jonathan A. Stapley and Kristine Wright, "'They Shall Be Made Whole': A History of Baptism for Health," *Journal of Mormon History* 34, no. 4 (Fall 2008): 94–95, 100.
41. "Nauvoo Relief Society Minutes, 1842–1844," April 28, 1842, 36, Church History Library, http://josephsmithpapers.org/paperSummary/nauvoo-relief-society-minute-book

II

HISTORICAL NARRATIVE PERSPECTIVES

7

Mormon Women's Agency and Changing Conceptions of the Mother in Heaven

SUSANNA MORRILL

While reading allusions to the Mother in Heaven in the *Ensign,* the official magazine of the Church of Jesus Christ of Latter-day Saints, I recognized some distinct similarities between these recent discussions (1970s to 2000s) about Heavenly Mother and the ways earlier Mormon women wrote about her.[1] Starting with Eliza R. Snow, a major nineteenth-century leader in the Mormon women's organization called Relief Society, earlier women authors envisioned Heavenly Mother as standing at the gates of mortality, sending off her children to their earthly existence, and then welcoming them back to the divine realm at the end of their mortal probation. Recent church leaders contemplate similar heavenly partings from and returns to Heavenly Mother.[2] At the same time, extra-church discussions about the Mother in Heaven have burgeoned in recent decades as recent women authors explore a more fractured, complex conception of this figure. To understand present-day conversations about Heavenly Mother, scholars need to interpret earlier women writers as the agents who created this persistent theological discourse.

The Argument

How do we find and describe these Mormon women as historical agents? Catherine Brekus's insights about women's agency in her 2010 Tanner Lecture at the Mormon History Association's annual meeting provide an excellent place to start. Early Mormon women writers used their charismatic and institutional authority, as well as their individual and collective agency, to help develop a picture of Heavenly Mother as a loving maternal figure who stood at the gates of mortality. This collaborative, organic, and extended literary conversation among Mormon women reinforces a number of Brekus's insights about women's agency. Brekus suggests we "should . . . rethink the close association between agency and intentionality" and argues that agency should be seen "as relational and social rather than simply individual"—agency can be collective and individuals gain agency because a community of some kind supports them.[3] In creating this portrait of Heavenly Mother, Mormon women leaders and members utilized the agency and authority that was available to them and wielded it in ways that were effective within the cultural expectations of their religious community.

Brekus suggests: agency is not an either/or proposition, different groups of people have varying degrees of agency, and "agency is always shaped by cultural norms and structural constraints."[4] As they developed this picture of Heavenly Mother, early Mormon women worked within the theological and institutional structures of the church, even as they helped to shape these structures. This case study emphasizes that "agency includes the reproduction of social structures as well as the transformation of them"[5] and highlights that "agency takes place within structures as well as against them."[6] Most of these early Mormon women were happy within their church. They did not set out to challenge the social and religious structures that shaped their lives, and did not see that their literary work liberated them from these structures. On the contrary, for the most part they envisioned their lives and work as enlarging and solidifying their religion of choice, not changing it.

Today LDS women inhabit a church somewhat less hybrid in charismatic and institutional agency than that of their predecessors. However, they do possess the ability to shape their own beliefs and how they express these beliefs and, thus, the ability to shape lived religious experience in their communities.[7] This case study attempts to demonstrate that as scholars we need to resist the urge to see agency as something that grows, as something that is cumulative and evolutionary. We need to avoid evolutionary, postmillennial models of historical development. Agency exists on a continuum, is dynamic over time, and expresses itself differently in institutional, ritual, liturgical, theological, and social arenas of religious life. As scholars, we need to be sensitive to this and methodologically light on our feet in order to track the moving target of women's agency.

This case study illustrates that nineteenth- and early-twentieth-century Mormon women expressed a spectrum of agency within the institutional structures of the church. We can track that agency, and changes to it, through time by exploring church publications read through a broadly Weberian model of analysis. In the more recent context (late twentieth to early twenty-first century), however, this approach fails to accurately capture the agency of Mormon women. Instead, we need to look to extra-church publications and move toward "lived religion" models of analysis—models that prize religious expression and experience that take place outside of institutions. We need to focus on those places where, as Robert Orsi has described, individuals interpret institutional structures and symbols in ways that are meaningful to their everyday lives.[8] With this methodological lens, we see that Mormon women are still actively creating and exploring the figure of the Mother in Heaven in literary conversations that present a much more fractured, but also a much more personal, proximate Heavenly Mother.

The Mother in Heaven: History and Background

Joseph Smith apparently revealed the doctrine of the Mother in Heaven during the early 1840s, the Nauvoo era of the LDS community.[9] However, the first extended public discussion of the Mother in Heaven was Eliza Snow's poem, "O My Father," published in 1845 in the Nauvoo Mormon newspaper, and, by 1851, set to music as a hymn.[10] Snow's hymn became the *de facto* definitive statement on the concept.[11]

Because of Snow's institutional religious authority and agency, her hymn had great influence on how the doctrine of the Mother in Heaven developed. Joining the church in 1835, Snow quickly moved to the inner circle and became one of Smith's plural wives in 1842.[12] Following Smith's death in 1844, she became a plural wife of Brigham Young and gradually became the most powerful female institutional leader in the church—probably the most powerful woman leader in the entire history of the church.[13] However, Snow was publicly and resolutely obedient to the male leadership of the church and regularly encouraged members of the Relief Society to follow the directives of their priesthood leaders.[14] After the LDS community moved to Utah, Snow headed up what Maureen Ursenbach Beecher has called an inner echelon of first generation women converts with close ties to church leaders. This group of women ran their own affairs and wielded great institutional authority over the women of the church.[15] Due to their influence, in the second half of the nineteenth century the Relief Society had a powerful, semi-independent existence within the church.[16]

Snow's institutional authority, in turn, rested partly on her charismatic authority. Into the twentieth century, Snow's hymn was considered to be an authoritative, revelatory statement on Mormon theology, thus cementing her charismatic authority among Mormon women and men.[17] The hymn began with Snow wondering when she would be able to be in the presence of her divine father, as she had been in her premortal life.[18] In the verse below, Snow revealed the existence of a Heavenly Mother and prayed for a reunion with her divine parents.

> When I leave this frail existence,
> When I lay this mortal by,
> Father, Mother, may I meet you
> In your royal courts on high?
> Then at length, when I've completed
> All you sent me forth to do,
> With your mutual approbation
> Let me come and dwell with you.[19]

Often called "The Grand Invocation," the hymn became extremely popular in the early church.[20] Though church leaders rarely talked at length about the Mother in Heaven, this divinity was ever present in the ritual life of church members during this early time period. Every time they sung this hymn, church members were reminded of Heavenly Mother and of Snow's charismatic authority and close connection to Joseph Smith, who revealed this doctrine to Snow. When singing the hymn, members of the church individually and communally spoke divine words; they bodily participated in a revelation.[21] In a poetic tribute for Snow's eightieth birthday in 1884, an unnamed poet rhapsodized on the hymn's experiential dimensions:

> How shall we e'er forget that hymn of praise
> Familiar to the saints of Latter-days,
> Even "O My Father?" The exalting strain

Uplifts the spirit into heaven again,
And makes us recollect our royal birth,
However humble is our lot on earth.[22]

The experience of singing the hymn assured this poet of the ultimate heavenly reunion by giving her a taste—a memory—of the relationship between her and her divine parents. When she sang the hymn, the reality of the Mother in Heaven, as described by Snow, was embodied and made real.

Snow's authority and agency rested on the confidence of many women and men. She was powerful because of her organizational ability, her ties to Joseph Smith and Brigham Young, her overt obedience to church leaders and cultural expectations about women's leadership, her prophetic vision, and because she gave to church members a ritual, embodied experience of the ultimate, eternal goal of Mormonism.

Literary Expansions of the Hymn

The literary development of the Mother in Heaven was as much a product of collective women's agency as it was the product of Snow's individual imagination and agency. Her respected leadership authority allowed women individually, and as a group, to explore and expand the portrait of the Mother in Heaven in the public discourse of the community. These writers were doing a variation on what Barbara Newman has called "imaginative theology." Newman argued that medieval women writers engaged in "imaginative theology" when they explored and shaped Catholic theology by means of literature and images.[23] Their work was not sanctioned by the church and was influenced by inherited religious and cultural patterns.

Because Snow's hymn was the major source through which church leaders and members had access to Heavenly Mother, and because it carried with it Snow's authority, writers used it as a template with which to explore the Mother in Heaven. They more fully developed the idea of her as standing at the gates of mortality, sending off, and then welcoming her children to the divine realm. In perhaps the clearest example of this, Emily Hill Woodmansee pulled phrases directly from Snow's hymn as she encouraged and celebrated the newly freed soul of a friend who had recently died.

Free from this most "frail existence"—
Free to lay "this mortal by"—
Free to the span the starry distance
To the "royal courts on high."
Ransomed spirit! Deathless essence!
Hie thee hence to realms so fair;
Gain thy "Father's radiant presence;"
Greet thy noble "Mother there."[24]

Woodmansee emphasized her friend's reception into the heavenly realm—the moment that Snow spelled out so clearly in her own hymn.

Heavenly Mother took a much more active and central role in a poem recorded by Jane Kartchner Morris in her journal (recorded probably in the early to mid-twentieth century). A redaction of a poem by William C. Harrison, Morris's poem, "O My Mother," retools Snow's hymn to focus solely on Heavenly Mother, who sent off her daughters with affection and warnings.[25]

Oh, My Mother Thou that dwellest,
In your mansions up on high,
How you pressed me to your bosom,
Bade me a true child to be
E're I left my home Eternal
To accept mortality.[26]

The poem ended with the speaker begging the Father and Mother Gods to welcome her back to the spirit world upon her death, ending with the specific request that:

Dearest Mother to your bosom,
Please welcome back *this* one.[27]

A logical extension of Snow's less detailed scenes of departure and return, Heavenly Mother is the last to bid her children goodbye and the first to greet them on their return. She is a divine figure who helps humans to transition between different "estates"; she oversees key moments for individual souls in the Mormon progressive plan of salvation.

In a story published in 1916 in the *Relief Society Magazine*, Laura Moench Jenkins explored Heavenly Mother at the gates of mortality in even more depth.[28] At the beginning of the story, Heavenly Mother met with two daughters who had been selected by Heavenly Father to enter mortality and start in earnest the process of salvation. She gave them each the gift they chose—to one integrity and love, to another, music. She then sent them off with their guardian angels from the gates of heaven to make the journey to earth. One of the daughters found a happy home on earth. The other spirit child was left without a body in which to continue her spiritual journey when her earthly mother had an abortion. Upon her return to the spirit world, she was greeted by an astonished Mother in Heaven. The story ends here, leaving the reader with a vision of a beautiful, divine female standing at the portals between heaven and earth.

Significantly, Jenkins's and Morris's portraits mirror in reverse the work that Mormon women performed at the birthbeds and deathbeds of their friends and neighbors, as they assisted in childbirth and gave comfort in death.[29] As with Snow's hymn, embodied experience and theological discourse mutually influenced and supported each other in this conception of the Mother in Heaven. Women writers shaped the template of Snow's hymn to mirror their religious practices surrounding birth and death; and, in doing so, authorized these practices with a divine model.

A collective portrait of Heavenly Mother standing at the gates of mortality emerges most prominently in the *Woman's Exponent*. Edward L. Sloan and Louisa Green started this periodical in 1872 with the sanction of Eliza R. Snow and Brigham Young.[30] In 1877, Emmeline B. Wells took over as editor and owner of the journal and continued in this capacity until the magazine's demise in 1914. The *Relief Society Magazine,* a periodical published and financed directly by the Relief Society, replaced the *Exponent*.[31]

Wells's leadership allowed women writers, individually and collectively, to exercise agency in creating the portrait of the Mother in Heaven. Like Snow, Wells held wide-ranging institutional leadership authority. Wells was secretary of the Relief Society from 1888 to 1910; she then became Relief Society president until shortly before her death in 1921.[32] Wells also had many connections to the inner circle of male leadership. She was married three times, twice as a plural wife to powerful men in the church.[33] Wells was part of the younger generation of early women converts who, according to Beecher, were a second echelon of leading women who learned about effective female self-rule from the older generation of leaders such as Snow.[34]

In her position as editor of the *Exponent*, Wells was instrumental in creating a lively literary dialogue among the women of the church, a dialogue protected by Brigham Young's seal of approval for the *Exponent* and by Wells's frequent public support of the male hierarchy within the periodical.[35] She aggressively encouraged women to contribute to the periodical; and actively helped women authors such as Emily Hill Woodmansee to publish their own books of poetry and prose.[36]

Snow and Wells's institutional and charismatic authority made room for the collective agency of women. These many women writers prophetically and individually clarified their understandings of the Mother in Heaven with literary images available to them through Snow. Subsequently, they communicated these understandings in the public literary forum provided by Wells as an appropriate place for dignified female discourse. These women writers were working within the structures of their church, and along the way—collectively and unintentionally—they created compelling theological discourse about the Mother in Heaven.

Changes

In the church today, women still have a strong presence within central institutional structures as overseers of the Relief Society, the Primary Association, and the Young Women's organization, but they are less independent in their leadership than their sisters in faith one hundred years ago. The nature of women's agency shifted for a number of reasons. Citing a Weberian process of rationalization, Thomas Alexander has shown that in the twentieth century, church leaders attempted to bring all church auxiliaries and publications under the control of the central male leadership as they strove to create a unified, smoothly functioning institution that would be accepted within the wider American religious landscape.[37] They strove to better control access to charismatic, prophetic authority—the kind of authority that helped to create Snow's leadership agency. The Relief Society became very explicitly an auxiliary of the church.[38]

By the 1970s, the Relief Society no longer raised and used its own funds nor had its own publication.[39] This centralization effectively prevented women leaders from maintaining the kind of matriarchy within a patriarchy that Snow and Wells and their contemporaries had formed.

In addition, "O My Father" became less pervasive and authoritative than it had been in the late nineteenth through early twentieth centuries. Snow's cultural and historical authority also became less prominent within the discourses of the community than it had been in the nineteenth and early twentieth centuries. Today the hymn is not as frequently sung or referenced as in the past—and it is no longer identified as a revelation. In the 1985 edition of the official LDS hymnbook, "O My Father" appears at the back of the hymnbook as hymn number 292, an afterthought rather than a well-loved standard.[40] Even more telling, it does not make the list of eighteen hymns identified as well-known songs that are recommended for worship in stake conferences—meetings of local units of the church, usually held twice yearly.[41] In comparison, in an 1891 edition of Mormon hymns, the hymns are ordered alphabetically and "O My Father" appears as number 130.[42]

The portrait of the Mother in Heaven that earlier women writers helped to develop continues in the way recent church leaders talk about Heavenly Mother, though in a more faint and diluted fashion. In the *Ensign* during the period between 1978 and 2004, authors continued to speak about Heavenly Mother in the context of longing for their divine home. Neal A. Maxwell of the Quorum of the Twelve Apostles (from 1981 to 2004) placed responsibility on Heavenly Mother for the happy, heavenly homecoming that humans can anticipate. He, however, was the exception to the rule because he directly quoted Snow's hymn to describe the homecoming:

> Finally remember: When we return to our real home, it will be with the "mutual approbation" of those who reign in the "royal courts on high." There we will find beauty such as mortal "eye hath not seen"; we will hear sounds of surpassing music which mortal "ear hath not heard." Could such a regal homecoming be possible without the anticipatory arrangements of a Heavenly Mother?[43]

As in earlier depictions, the Mother in Heaven was a heavenly greeter and, for Maxwell, she became the consummate, divine party planner.

Instead of exploring the vision of Heavenly Mother in Snow's hymn as earlier women authors and Maxwell did, most authors in the *Ensign* during this period (1978 to 2004) employed already published, authoritative treatments of the Mother in Heaven. This demonstrates that the theological discourse of the church became standardized—more static—as the church experienced the institutional regularization that Alexander outlined. In the *Ensign*, between 1978 and 2004, authors who referred to Heavenly Mother quoted Orson F. Whitney, a church leader of the late nineteenth century, at least six times—three of those times coming in the years 1987 to 1989, and three of them quoting Whitney as quoted by the late church president, Spencer W. Kimball, who was in office from 1973 to 1985.[44] In that excerpt, Whitney reflected on the meaning of suffering and trials, arguing that troubles had to be endured in order to make humans more like their divine parents; he did not describe God the Father or Mother in Heaven beyond acknowledging their divinity.[45] Thus in church-sanctioned public discourse, Heavenly Mother had retreated somewhat back into the mystery and obscurity that early women writers tried to illuminate.

Based on my study of the *Ensign*, we need to look beyond official church publications in order to track how women have shaped recent public discussion about Heavenly Mother. Against the backdrop of an increasingly standardized church and in response to the feminist movement and more general mainstream interest in divine female figures in the 1970s and 1980s, church members began to write speculatively about Heavenly Mother and began to speak about her and pray to her in church meetings.[46] As did their foremothers in the church, they engaged in "imaginative theological" discussions about the Heavenly Mother.

From the 1980s through the 1990s, the central church leadership tried to cut off these discussions and practices. Some prominent advocates of Heavenly Mother, or scholars who wrote about Heavenly Mother, were excommunicated.[47] This did not stop church members from speculating about Heavenly Mother. At the height of the controversy, LDS women and men publicly pondered Heavenly Mother with great frequency. Indeed, this circumscription seems to have encouraged members to come to grips with the Mother in Heaven in idiosyncratic and creative ways in extra-church publications such as *Sunstone*, *Exponent II*, and *Dialogue*. The prophetic, creative, literary space that earlier women writers found at the margins of institutional church discourse has been pushed out through the process of institutional standardization into these extra-institutional forums of public dialogue.

In *Dialogue* during these years (1980s–1990s), the portrait of Heavenly Mother was much more varied and contested—even contradictory—than the rather vague portrait that emerged in the *Ensign*. In one issue, Melodie Moench Charles protested against the structures of Victorian sentimental motherhood through which her religious forebears strove to describe Heavenly Mother. "Mother in Heaven can be nothing other than the faceless, nameless, unavailable-for-theological purposes blank that she currently is . . . She has no self apart from her husband."[48] Just two issues later another author went back to the earlier, domestic depictions and painted Heavenly Mother as a caring mother embodied through the remembered experiences of childhood.[49]

Against all official statements of LDS theology, during the 1980s and 1990s these writers in *Dialogue* most commonly interpreted the Mother in Heaven as the Holy Ghost. Ruth Knight, frustrated by her failure on the bar exam, speculated on her need for Heavenly Mother: "What I needed was *female power*. Holy Ghost/Mother in Heaven/whatever it really was/*inside power*."[50] Linda Johns expanded on this idea: "I believe that it is she who plants the seeds of faith and desire in our hearts that leads us to Christ, and that . . . we can find her living and waiting for us inside the church, filling it with her light and life."[51] For these writers, Heavenly Mother was the immediate and caring presence of God. In many ways this conception contradicted the earlier image as remote and waiting in the spirit world, though caring and concerned about her spiritual children. Heavenly Mother was no longer a constant ritual presence, but in extra-church publications, members actively and imaginatively drew this goddess close to themselves and their everyday concerns.

With no authoritative template, recent authors in *Dialogue* offer no consensus about the characteristics of the Mother in Heaven. This figure is open to individual, prophetic interpretation as never before. Authors collectively create a vision that is fractured and contradictory compared to the earlier portrait of Heavenly Mother.

Conclusion

Which, if any, of these extra-institutional depictions will take hold of the public imagination? Which will shape more official statements on the Heavenly Mother? Armand L. Mauss suggests that the central leadership has eased up on policing theological discourse about the Mother in Heaven, pointing to Paulsen and Pulido's *BYU Studies* article as evidence.[52] Lately, discussions of Mother in Heaven have been taken up in blogs, an even more individualized form of public discourse.[53] Perhaps this will create a still more fractured portrait of Heavenly Mother. Perhaps it will do the opposite. The immediacy of the electronic realm may allow quick communication of popular ideas across space. Perhaps these ideas will even gain traction within the institutional discourse of the church.

In the future, then, in order to track women's agency, we may very well need to again shift our focus to different sources, models, and methodologies in order to analyze how popular and institutional theological discourses about the Mother in Heaven connect. By tracking women's agency through this small slice of Mormon doctrine, we see how complex it is. Women's agency is a moving target, not something that grows inevitably and in evolutionary fashion. Women's agency shows up in varying degrees in different areas of religious life: theological, ritual, liturgical, social, lived religious, changing through time in each of these areas. As scholars we must be on the alert to these changes and nuances, we must be willing to shift our focus and our methodology to find the elusive, shifting phenomenon of women's historical agency.

Notes

1. David L. Paulsen and Martin Pulido, "'A Mother There': A Survey of Historical Teachings about Mother in Heaven," *BYU Studies* 50, no. 1 (2011): 70–97. Paulsen and Pulido's article in *BYU Studies* on Heavenly Mother further highlighted these connections for me. Indeed, they include some of these early Mormon women writers in their analysis.
2. Ibid., 82–83.
3. Catherine A. Brekus, "Mormon Women and the Problem of Historical Agency," *Journal of Mormon History* 37, no. 2 (Spring 2011): 80–82.
4. Ibid., 82–83.
5. Ibid., 78–79.
6. Ibid., 85.
7. Marilyn J. Westerkamp, "Puritan Women, Spiritual Power, and the Question of Sexuality," in *The Religious History of American Women: Reimagining the Past*, edited by Catherine A. Brekus (Chapel Hill: The University of North Carolina Press, 2007), 51–72.
8. Robert A. Orsi, *The Madonna of 115th Street: Faith and Community in Italian Harlem, 1880–1950* (New Haven: Yale University Press, 2002), xix–xx.

9. George D. Pyper, *Stories of Latter-day Saint Hymns* (n.p.: George D. Pyper, 1939), 4; Linda Wilcox, "The Mormon Concept of a Mother in Heaven," *Sunstone* 22, no. 3–4 (June 1999): 79; Maureen Ursenbach Beecher, "The Eliza Enigma," *Dialogue* 11, no. 1 (Spring 1998): 37.
10. Jill Mulvay Derr, "The Significance of 'O My Father' in the Personal Journey of Eliza R. Snow," *BYU Studies* 36, no. 1 (1996–97): 98; Jill Mulvay Derr, Janath Russell Cannon, and Maureen Ursenbach Beecher, eds., *Women of Covenant: The Story of Relief Society* (Salt Lake City: Deseret Book, 1992), 57–58; Wilcox, "The Mormon Concept of a Mother in Heaven," 81.
11. Derr, "The Significance of 'O My Father,'" 99.
12. Eliza R. Snow, "Sketch of My Life," in *The Personal Writings of Eliza Roxcy Snow*, edited by Maureen Ursenbach Beecher (Salt Lake City: University of Utah Press, 1995), 10.
13. Derr, "The Significance of 'O My Father,'" 85–86, 115.
14. Beecher, *The Personal Writings of Eliza Roxcy Snow*, 26.
15. Maureen Ursenbach Beecher, "The 'Leading Sisters': A Female Hierarchy in Nineteenth-Century Mormon Society," *Journal of Mormon History* 9, no. 1 (1982): 25–39.
16. Derr, "The Significance of 'O My Father,'" 100, 112.
17. "May Entertainments," *The Relief Society Magazine* 4, no. 5 (May 1917): 265. See also Pyper, *Stories of Latter-day Saint Hymns*, 6.
18. Pyper, *Stories of Latter-day Saint Hymns*, 1.
19. Ibid.
20. "The Relief Society: Programme of Exercises," *Woman's Exponent* 20, no. 17 (March 1, 1892): 124.
21. Derr, "The Significance of 'O My Father,'" 86; "'O, My Father,'" *The Relief Society Magazine* 6, no. 6 (June 1919): 369.
22. "To Sister Eliza," *Woman's Exponent* 12, no. 17 (Feb. 1, 1884): 129. See also Florence Ridges Dean, Journal, August 1893–June 1896, 13, 29, 46, Church History Library, Salt Lake City, Utah.
23. Barbara Newman, *Gods and Goddesses: Vision, Poetry, and Belief in the Middle Ages* (Philadelphia: University of Pennsylvania Press, 2003), 298.
24. Emily H. Woodmansee, "Apostrophe . . . ," *Woman's Exponent* 16, no. 15 (January 1, 1888): 113.
25. William C. Harrison, "Companion Poem to Eliza R. Snow's 'Invocation,'" *Juvenile Instructor* 27, no. 5 (March 1892): 163. Thanks to Lisa Tait for bringing Harrison's poem to my attention.
26. Jane Kartchner Morris, Journals and Reminiscences, October 1916–February 1971, 3:148, Church History Library.
27. Ibid.
28. Laura Moench Jenkins, "Beyond the Portals," *Relief Society Magazine* 3, no. 6 (June 1916): 325–34.
29. Susanna Morrill, "Relief Society Birth and Death Rituals: Women at the Gates of Mortality," *Journal of Mormon History* 36, no. 2 (Spring 2010): 128–59.

30. Sherilyn Cox Bennion, "The *Woman's Exponent*: Forty-Two Years of Speaking for Women," *Utah Historical Quarterly* 44, no. 3 (Summer 1976): 227; Lula Greene Richards, "How 'The Exponent' Was Started," *Relief Society Magazine* 14, no. 12 (December 1927): 605–8; Maureen Ursenbach Beecher, "Eliza R. Snow," in *Mormon Sisters: Women in Early Utah*, edited by Claudia L. Bushman (Logan, UT: Utah State University Press, 1977), 24–41; Jill Mulvay Derr, et al., eds., *This Labor of Love and Duty: Selected Documents from Latter-day Saint Women's History, 1842–1892*, (forthcoming 2016).
31. Bennion, "The *Woman's Exponent*," 234.
32. Ibid.
33. Carol Cornwall Madsen, *An Advocate for Women: The Public Life of Emmeline B. Wells, 1870–1920* (Provo: Brigham Young University Press, 2006), 20.
34. Beecher, "The 'Leading Sisters,'" 35, 38.
35. "Approaching the Narrows," *Woman's Exponent* 15, no. 12 (November 15, 1886): 92.
36. Madsen, *An Advocate for Women*, 46–50; "Home Affairs," *Woman's Exponent* 10, no. 4 (July 15, 1881): 29.
37. Thomas G. Alexander, *Mormonism in Transition: A History of the Latter-day Saints, 1890–1930* (Urbana: University of Illinois Press, 1986), 14.
38. Alexander, *Mormonism in Transition*, 125–35.
39. Derr et al., *This Labor of Love and Duty*, 340–43.
40. *Hymns of the Church of Jesus Christ of Latter-day Saints* (Salt Lake City: Church of Jesus Christ of Latter-day Saints, 1985), 292.
41. *Hymns*, 381.
42. *Sacred Hymns and Spiritual Songs for the Church of Jesus Christ of Latter-day Saints*, 20th ed. (Salt Lake City: Deseret News, 1891), http://www.hymnary.org/hymnal/SHSS1891?page=1.
43. Neal A. Maxwell, "The Women of God," *Ensign*, May 1978, 10.
44. Elaine Marshall, "Lessons on Healing," *Ensign*, April 2004, 57; Howard W. Hunter, "The Opening and Closing of Doors," *Ensign*, November 1987, 54; Abigail Morris, "Don't Ask 'What's Wrong with Me?' Find Out 'What's Right with Me?,'" *Ensign*, March 1989; Adney Y. Komatsu, "Looking to the Savior," *Ensign*, May 1987, 78; LaVar Thornock, "In Your Time of Crisis," *Ensign*, February 1988, 28; Adney Y. Komatsu, "'After Much Tribulation Come the Blessings,'" *Ensign*, November 1979, 68.
45. Hunter, "The Opening and Closing of Doors," *Ensign*, 54. Whitney's original quote cited in Spencer W. Kimball, *Faith Precedes the Miracle* (Salt Lake City: Deseret Book, 1972), 68.
46. Wilcox, "The Mormon Concept of a Mother in Heaven," 14–15; Carol Lynn Pearson, *Mother Wove the Morning* (Pearson Publishing, 1992).
47. Jan Shipps, "Dangerous History: Laurel Ulrich and Her Mormon Sisters," *Christian Century* 110, no. 29 (October 10, 1993): 1012–15.
48. Melodie Moench Charles, "The Need for a New Mormon Heaven," *Dialogue* 21, no. 3 (Autumn 1988): 73–87.

49. Gay Taylor, "If I Were God," *Dialogue* 22, no. 1 (Spring 1989): 106–13.
50. Ruth Knight, "Carrying On," *Dialogue* 23, no. 3 (Fall 1990): 163.
51. Linda Johns, "My Search for the Mother and Daughter," *Dialogue* 27, no. 1 (Spring 1994): 41–43.
52. Armand L. Mauss, "Rethinking Retrenchment: Course Corrections in the Ongoing Campaign for Respectability," *Dialogue* 44, no. 4 (Winter 2011): 1–42.
53. For some examples of recent blog posts on Heavenly Mother, see Carmen Bradley, "Heavenly Parents: The Answer to End Sexism of the Mormon Church," *The Agitating Faithfully/Finding Heavenly Mother Project,* December 24, 2014, http://www.agitatingfaithfully.org/blog.html; Joanna Brooks, "Is Heavenly Mother Making a Comeback in Mormonism?," *Religion Dispatches,* May 9, 2011, http://www.religiondispatches.org/is-heavenly-mother-making-a-comeback-in-mormonism/; Esther Dale, "Heavenly Mother Walks with Me," *Rational Faiths,* July 23, 2014, http://www.rationalfaiths.com/heavenly-mother-walks-with-me/; Kathryn Skaggs, "Heavenly Mother, Are You Really There?," *Mormon Women Stand Blog,* undated, http://www.mormonwomenstand.com/topics/heavenly-mother/; Michelle Wiener, "By Goddess. I Will Not Be Left Behind," *Rational Faiths,* September 24, 2014, http://www.rationalfaiths.com/goddess-will-left-behind/.

8

Jane James's Agency

QUINCY D. NEWELL

The concept of agency is crucial to theology in the Church of Jesus Christ of Latter-day Saints.[1] In a commentary on 2 Nephi, Elder Dallin H. Oaks, a member of the Quorum of the Twelve Apostles, second highest body in the LDS church, wrote that "free agency, the power to choose, is a gift from God, conferred on his children and exercised by them in the preexistence. It is an essential precondition of the further progression we seek in mortality."[2] Visitors to the church's website who click on "Agency" under "Gospel Topics" find this statement:

> Agency is the ability and privilege God gives us to choose and to act for ourselves. Agency is essential in the plan of salvation. Without agency, we would not be able to learn or progress or follow the Savior. With it, we are "free to choose liberty and eternal life, through the great Mediator of all men, or to choose captivity and death, according to the captivity and power of the devil" (2 Nephi 2:27).[3]

In LDS thinking, agency is thus figured as inherent in the subject, an innate quality given by God in the preexistence. It is made visible by an individual's choices and actions, and it is intended to effect the individual's spiritual liberation.

A similar definition of agency is fundamental to scholarship on women and marginalized groups, where scholarship and activism frequently intertwine in an effort to find models for present-day, this-worldly liberation.[4] Here too, the concept of agency frequently depends on an ideal of an autonomous subject and assumes a goal of freedom, figured in terms of resistance to, dismantling of, or escape from oppressive social and political structures that prevent the full expression of the autonomous self. For example, in her study of women in India, Metti Amirtham writes,

> for a woman *agency* means . . . having a sense of autonomy and self-confidence in her own life[;] having freedom to use her bodily abilities to the fullest for her well-being as well as that of society[;] having adequate power and status to fight against all deprivations, abuse and discrimination[;] being independent, particularly in economic matters, and having authority in decision-making in the family and in personal life[; and] daring to deconstruct and decode myths and notions that keep her under control so that they do not influence her life adversely.[5]

This emphasis on agency in the study of marginalized groups can lead us to overlook subjects who seem to eschew liberal ideals of freedom and individual autonomy, such as women in conservative religious movements. Historian Phyllis Mack cautions against this mistake. She writes:

> to dismiss [the religious woman's] gestures of surrender and self-denial as a rhetoric of self-abnegation, as false consciousness, or as a covert expression of resistance to the dominant male order is not only an over-simplification of her psychology; it is an avoidance of our responsibility [as historians] not merely to search for examples of female strategies of self-assertion under patriarchy but to look steadily at women's own ideas about ethics, autonomy, and spirituality.[6]

In what follows, I take up Mack's challenge by examining the life of Jane Elizabeth Manning James, a nineteenth-century black Mormon woman. Doubly marginalized within the church by her gender and her race, James nevertheless had a rich, satisfying spiritual life. I use the work of Mack and others on women's agency to illuminate the seeming paradox of James's apparently willing submission to the church's

FIGURE 8.1. Photo believed to be of Jane Manning James. Public Domain.

discriminatory racial policies and her simultaneous creation of a full, compelling religious experience. Ultimately, the question is not *whether* James had agency, but rather *what forms* that agency took. James's life makes little sense until we place it in the cosmic framework in which she understood her own life, modifying scholarly notions of agency to de-emphasize individual liberation and instead focusing on the religious community and religious understandings of salvation.

Jane Elizabeth Manning James converted to Mormonism in the winter of 1842–43 when she heard a Latter-day Saint missionary speak where she lived as a young woman in southwestern Connecticut. As soon as she was able, she travelled with her family and several others from the region to Nauvoo, Illinois, where the church was then based. She worked as a servant in Joseph Smith's home and, after he was killed, in Brigham Young's home. She and her husband Isaac, whom she had met and married in Nauvoo, joined the Latter-day Saints' exodus to Utah, and she remained a faithful Latter-day Saint until her death in 1908.[7] Because James was black, she was never allowed to participate in the temple ceremonies Mormons believed would ensure her exaltation or cement her eternal connections with her family members.[8]

Using standard scholarly notions of agency that define an agent as someone who "resists the constraints of the social structure, who challenges social norms to create something new," and that see agency as "virtually synonymous with emancipation, liberation, and resistance,"[9] we can interpret James's life in diametrically opposed ways. She appears to be either a passive victim, deprived of agency by Latter-day Saints' racism and unable even to choose to leave the church; or she emerges as an active agent, persistently requesting temple privileges and leading the charge against institutional racism. Neither of these interpretations provides a satisfactory account of James's experience.

James petitioned for access to temple ceremonies repeatedly over the course of at least a quarter-century, but she also praised and sustained the men who consistently denied her the access she desired.[10] James never challenged the racial policies that mandated her exclusion from temple ceremonies; in fact, she tacitly accepted them, petitioning only for an exception, not for a reversal.[11] In joining the Mormon Church and never leaving it, even after the rebuff of her multiple petitions to participate in temple ceremonies, James also appears to have chosen *against* her own emancipation or liberation, opting instead for subordination and second-class status. Perhaps James was trapped by her circumstances. By the time the church's racial policies became clear, James had left her childhood home in Connecticut and lived in Utah, far removed from any significant non-Mormon population, let alone any major African American community. Although her husband and children had also travelled with her to Utah, her siblings and parents had not. It may be that James felt that she had invested too much in the church to leave it, or that she had nowhere else to turn. This reading of the documents suggests that James did not resist the system in any meaningful sense. Rather, she accepted and even perpetuated the racist beliefs of the church and the system to which these beliefs gave rise, perhaps because she felt overwhelmed by forces beyond her control, or perhaps because she had been duped into believing in her own oppression.

Another reading of the documents supports the opposite interpretation. Jane James's inclination to resist the impositions of the social structure became evident early in her life, when she challenged social norms to become a Latter-day Saint. James herself claimed to have defied her Presbyterian pastor in order to listen to the Mormon missionary in the first place.[12] This propensity to resist the existing structure continued in James's petitions for access to temple ceremonies. The extant evidence documents a concerted campaign that lasted two decades or more. James dictated letters to church authorities; she asked powerful women to write on her behalf; and she met with church leaders to press her case.[13] She appealed to her intimate acquaintance with Joseph Smith's family; she highlighted her conformity with the religious ideals of the church; and she even engaged in biblical exegesis.[14] Throughout, she attempted to overturn the decisions that kept her out of the temple ceremonies she desired. Even James's decision to remain a Latter-day Saint may be seen, in this light, as an active choice: James's husband and most of her children left the church, demonstrating that there were other choices available even in nineteenth-century Utah.[15] James's close relationships with people who opted out of the church suggest that we must interpret her choice to remain faithful as an active decision, not a passive acceptance of circumstance.

A notion of agency less committed to liberal ideals of freedom and individual autonomy makes possible a more nuanced reading of James's experience. Analyzing the ways white and black women are depicted in literature and discussed in literary criticism, Jennifer L. Fleissner writes, "the real problem is that women, persons of color, and other members of historically oppressed groups are not generally allowed to be both subject and object at once."[16] Recognizing James as both subject and object allows us to see the ways in which Mormonism shaped her exercise of agency, bringing together the "passive victim" and the "active agent" readings of her history. James chose to affiliate with the church and to remain faithful to it for the rest of her life. In that sense, she was an active agent, a subject. But she was also an object: Mormonism acted upon James and shaped the ways she exercised her agency.[17] It appears that for James, as for the Quaker women Mack studied, the theological concept of agency meant "not . . . the freedom to do what one wants but . . . the freedom to do what is right."[18] As a Latter-day Saint James recognized in the church's leaders an authority to define "what is right." She therefore expended considerable energy in pursuing temple access, which church leaders had defined as a spiritual good. This goal, which would not have made sense in any other situation, was utterly shaped by James's religious context, as was her inability to achieve it.

James's pursuit of religiously defined goals of "what is right" (or, perhaps more accurately, what is *good*) entailed a complex performance of submission to Latter-day Saint authority and assertive spiritual expression. For example, James dictated a letter to church President John Taylor in 1884, requesting permission to participate in temple ceremonies. "I realize my race & color & can[']t expect my Endowments as others who are white," she wrote.[19] This acceptance of Latter-day Saint ideas about racial difference went hand in hand with James's subsequent request for endowments, based on a millennialist biblical exegesis: "My race was handed down through the flood & God promised Abraham that in his seed all the nations of the earth should be blest & as this is the fullness of all dispensations is there no blessing for me[?]"[20] Anthropologist Saba Mahmood argues that agency "is entailed not only in those acts that resist norms but also in the multiple ways in which one *inhabits* norms."[21] For James, inhabiting church norms meant an acceptance of racially discriminatory ideas that opened up the possibility of an egalitarian reading of scripture and history. Thus, for James and other Mormons, as Phyllis Mack wrote of the Quaker women she studied, "agency implied self-negation as well as self-expression"[22] as a part of a larger project of self-shaping in the pursuit of spiritual goals. This seeming contradiction moves us to consider Mack's notion that the agency of religious people (and women in particular) is "a conception of agency in which autonomy is less important than self-transcendence and . . . the energy to act in the world is generated and sustained by a prior act of personal surrender."[23] Jane James's robust spiritual practice was only made possible by her acceptance of the Latter-day Saint gospel and the hierarchical, discriminatory structure that came with it.[24]

When we give up the popular image of Jane James as a heroine fighting for racial equality, we may wonder about the historical significance of her life. Why spend time and energy excavating the story of a poor black woman who was excluded from the center of Mormon ritual life? Surely our efforts are better spent elsewhere, understanding the lives of Mormons of greater consequence for the development of the religion, or uncovering the examples of African Americans whose lives offer a clearer model of self-determination. Religious historian Catherine Brekus anticipates and counters this argument in her assertion that agency and intentionality may not be linked. Brekus contends that actions need not be intended to accumulate power, nor to change history or society, in order to be agentic. In fact, social change can result from the small choices made by hundreds or thousands of ordinary people, not just from leaders acting deliberately to create change.[25] Likewise, political theorist Sharon R. Krause argues that "individual agency never resides exclusively within the individual but depends on the actions and reactions of other people."[26]

James's participation in the Relief Society is one example of this distributed agency: although poor, James contributed money to the Relief Society for the construction of the Logan Temple.[27] Her support of this effort may have made James more comfortable in requesting permission to perform baptisms for her dead once the Logan Temple was completed, a ritual she completed in 1888.[28] But James's petitions for other kinds of ritual access, combined with the questions and petitions of other black Mormons, may have also had a cumulative effect. Krause warns that "the agency of the oppressed frequently functions politically to reinforce their subordinate status,"[29] and W. Paul Reeve has shown this was true for black Mormons in the nineteenth century. Discriminatory racial policies in the church crystallized over the course of the second half of the nineteenth century, largely as church leaders' case-by-case responses to questions members brought before them were systematized at the highest levels.[30] Ironically, by petitioning for temple ceremonies, Jane James may have inadvertently contributed to the institutionalization of racial discrimination in the church.

James's dependence on the leaders of the church for help in accomplishing her goal of participating in temple ceremonies illustrates the degree to which her agency, in some cases, rested on the agency of those around her.[31] This dispersal of agency cut both ways: other Latter-day Saint women wrote the letters that James dictated, expanding her campaign to get access to temple ceremonies beyond the personal visits she could pay to church leaders.[32] These women also wrote letters of their own composition on James's behalf.[33] James's female coreligionists further affirmed her agency as they listened to and recorded her spiritual testimony, published it in the *Woman's Exponent* and the *Young Woman's Journal*, and thus bolstered James's reputation as a faithful and spiritually gifted Latter-day Saint.[34] Despite the ways in which women in the church enhanced her agency, James remained unable to persuade church leaders to grant her access to endowment and sealing ceremonies. Her agency was thus diminished to the degree that it depended on the consent of these men, consent she was unable to obtain.

To some degree, this experience of limited agency is typical: there are always curbs on individual autonomy.[35] But Brekus notes that "agency must be understood as existing on a continuum" and helpfully reminds us that "agency is relative and is marked by gender, racial, and class disparities."[36] Jane James was on the losing end of each of these disparities: she was female, black, and relatively poor, further limiting her ability to make and act upon her own choices.[37]

James's agency was also shaped by other "cultural norms and structural constraints," the most obvious of which were the societal ideals of femininity and the structural constraints of racism. James's membership in the church community shaped her sense of what it meant to be black and what it meant to be a woman; and her racial and gender identities likewise shaped her sense of what it meant to be Mormon.[38] These overlapping identities both opened and foreclosed James's possibilities for action. She proclaimed her conformity to the church norm of femininity in her autobiography, and clearly expected to receive positive recognition for her ability to live up to that standard. "I want to say right here," she concluded in her autobiography,

> that my faith in the Gospel of Jesus Christ as taught by the Church of Jesus Christ of Latter-day Saints, is as strong today, nay, it is if possible stronger than it was the day I was first baptized[.] I pay my tithes and offerings, keep the word of wisdom, I go to bed early and rise early[.] I try in my feeble way to set a good example to all; I have had eighteen grand children[. E]ight of them are living, also seven great grand children.[39]

James was careful to position herself in these familial terms, emphasizing her role as mother and grandmother. She also described herself as a widow after Isaac James's death, even though the couple had been divorced for more than two decades.

Jane James's life story makes the most sense when we place it within the cosmic context that the church provided. The same is true when it comes to the question of her agency. Mormonism's emphasis on individual agency inclines Latter-day Saints, and the scholars who study them, to focus on the autonomous choices that each person makes. However, Mack's concept of "spiritual agency" implies that a reframing is in order, expanding our concept of agency to include not only the immediate, earthly setting but also a wider, cosmic backdrop.[40] Situating James in the wider, spiritual framework of Latter-day Saint cosmology, and using models of agency like those I have employed in this essay, we see that James was both subject and object. She actively pursued religious goals and aspirations, but her identity as a black Mormon woman shaped those goals and aspirations and her strategies for achieving them. By asking what forms James's agency took, we shift our study of her life away from a singular focus on the ways the temple restriction impoverished her spiritual practice and made her a second-class citizen. Instead, we create a fuller picture of James's life that includes both her apparent acceptance of religious restrictions based on race and gender, and her robust spiritual practice that utilized the tools of Mormonism to build a Latter-day Saint identity independent of temple participation.

Acknowledgments

I thank Kate Holbrook for persuading me to undertake this project. Laurel Thatcher Ulrich's comments on an early version of this essay made it immeasurably better. Erin Forbes, Teena Gabrielson, and Frieda Knobloch worked through multiple drafts of this essay, pointing me to additional resources and helping me develop fragments of ideas into intelligent prose. I am deeply grateful for their friendship and scholarly companionship. Lastly, Kate Holbrook and Matt Bowman, as editors of this volume, helped push and pull this essay into its final form—I appreciate their help. All shortcomings and errors herein are, of course, my own.

Notes

1. See, for example, Douglas James Davies, *The Mormon Culture of Salvation: Force, Grace, and Glory* (Burlington, VT: Ashgate, 2000), 152.
2. Dallin H. Oaks, "Free Agency and Freedom," in *The Book of Mormon: Second Nephi, the Doctrinal Structure*, edited by Monte S. Nyman and Charles D. Tate Jr. (Provo, UT: Religious Studies Center, Brigham Young University, 1989), 9.
3. Church of Jesus Christ of Latter-day Saints, "What Is Agency?," accessed March 14, 2013, http://www.lds.org/topics/agency?lang=eng.
4. See, for example, Saba Mahmood, "Feminist Theory, Embodiment, and the Docile Agent: Some Reflections on the Egyptian Islamic Revival," *Cultural Anthropology* 16, no. 2 (2001): 202.
5. Metti Amirtham, *Women in India: Negotiating Body, Reclaiming Agency* (Eugene, OR: Resource Publications, 2011), 37.
6. Phyllis Mack, "Religion, Feminism, and the Problem of Agency: Reflections on Eighteenth-Century Quakerism," *Signs* 29, no. 1 (September 1, 2003): 157.
7. For a more extensive biography of James, see Quincy D. Newell, "The Autobiography and Interview of Jane Elizabeth Manning James," *Journal of Africana Religions* 1, no. 2 (2013): 251–91.
8. These ceremonies have been performed for James by proxy since the 1978 revelation canonized as Official Declaration 2.
9. Catherine A. Brekus, "Mormon Women and the Problem of Historical Agency," *Journal of Mormon History* 37, no. 2 (Spring 2011): 72, 71; see also Saba Mahmood, *Politics of Piety: The Islamic Revival and the Feminist Subject* (Princeton, NJ: Princeton University Press, 2005), 5; Mack, "Religion, Feminism, and the Problem of Agency," 149–53; Sharon R. Krause, "Bodies in Action: Corporeal Agency and Democratic Politics," *Political Theory* 39, no. 3 (2011): 300.
10. Toward the end of her autobiography, Jane James remarked, "I have seen Bro. Brigham, Bros[.] Taylor[,] Woodruff[,] and Snow, [r]ule this great work and

pass on to their reward, and now Brother Joseph F. Smith[.] I hope the Lord will spare him if [']tis his holy will for [m]any, many years, to guide the Gospel ship to a harbor of safety, and I know they will if the people will only listen and obey the teachings of these good great and holy men." Newell, "Autobiography and Interview," 267. This sounds formulaic, and it is—but a fair reading of the autobiography suggests it is also heartfelt.

11. See Jane E. James to President John Taylor, Salt Lake City, December 27, 1884; Jane E. James to Apostle Joseph F. Smith, Salt Lake City, February 7, 1890; Zina D. H. Young to Apostle Joseph F. Smith, Salt Lake City, January 15, 1894; Jane E. James to President Joseph F. Smith, Salt Lake City, August 31, 1903, all reprinted in Henry J. Wolfinger, "A Test of Faith: Jane Elizabeth James and the Origins of the Utah Black Community," in *Social Accommodation in Utah*, edited by Clark S. Knowlton, American West Center Occasional Papers, no. 4 (Salt Lake City: University of Utah, 1975), 148–51.
12. James was a member of the New Canaan Congregational Church, so if she defied a pastor, he was a Congregationalist. In New England at the time, Congregationalists were frequently referred to as "Presbyterians" because of their theological similarities and their cooperation in the 1801 Plan of Union that divided the fledgling United States between the Congregationalists and Presbyterians for the purposes of efficient evangelization. George M. Marsden, *The Evangelical Mind and the New School Presbyterian Experience: A Case Study of Thought and Theology in Nineteenth-Century America*, Yale Publications in American Studies 20 (New Haven: Yale University Press, 1970), 10.
13. For examples of these strategies, see especially the documents reprinted in Wolfinger, "A Test of Faith," 148–50.
14. One of James's earliest extant petitions, in an 1884 letter to President John Taylor, demonstrates this strategy of biblical exegesis. See my discussion on 141–42 and Jane E. James to President John Taylor, December 27, 1884, reprinted in Wolfinger, "A Test of Faith," 148. For examples of James's appeals to her acquaintance with Joseph Smith, see Newell, "Autobiography and Interview"; and Quincy D. Newell, "'Is There No Blessing for Me?': Jane James's Construction of Space in Latter-day Saint History and Practice," in *New Perspectives in Mormon Studies: Creating and Crossing Boundaries*, edited by Quincy D. Newell and Eric F. Mason (Norman: University of Oklahoma Press, 2013), 41–65.
15. On the lives of James's husband and her children, see Henry J. Wolfinger, "A Test of Faith," 133–34, 138–40.
16. Jennifer L. Fleissner, "Is Feminism a Historicism?," *Tulsa Studies in Women's Literature* 21, no. 1 (Spring 2002): 55.
17. Brekus points out that "we should also recognize that agency is always shaped by cultural norms and structural constraints." Brekus, "Mormon Women and the Problem of Historical Agency," 83.
18. Mack, "Religion, Feminism, and the Problem of Agency," 156.

19. Jane E. James to President John Taylor, Salt Lake City, December 27, 1884, reprinted in Wolfinger, "A Test of Faith," 148.
20. Ibid.
21. Mahmood, *Politics of Piety*, 15. This insight informs Brekus's proposal that an expanded model of agency should "recognize that agency includes the reproduction of social structures as well as the transformation of them" and that "agency takes place within structures as well as against them." Brekus, "Mormon Women and the Problem of Historical Agency," 78, 85.
22. Mack, "Religion, Feminism, and the Problem of Agency," 156.
23. Ibid.
24. This observation accords with the work of Saba Mahmood, who writes, "In order to analyze the participation of women in religious movements, such as the Egyptian mosque movement I describe, I want to suggest we think of agency not as a synonym for resistance to relations of domination, but as a capacity for action that historically specific relations of subordination enable and create." Mahmood, "Feminist Theory, Embodiment, and the Docile Agent," 203.
25. Brekus, "Mormon Women and the Problem of Historical Agency," 80.
26. Krause, "Bodies in Action," 308.
27. Wolfinger, "A Test of Faith," 135.
28. Linda King Newell Papers, "James, Jane E. M.: Miscellaneous Material," box 12, fd. 27, Marriott Library, University of Utah, Salt Lake City.
29. Krause, "Bodies in Action," 306.
30. W. Paul Reeve, *Religion of a Different Color: Race and the Mormon Struggle for Whiteness* (New York: Oxford University Press, 2015), 111–12, 135–39, 145–61, 193–214.
31. Brekus emphasizes the relational and social aspects of agency, a point that is particularly salient in James's case. Brekus, "Mormon Women and the Problem of Historical Agency," 81–82.
32. Wolfinger, "A Test of Faith," 169–76; John Turner, personal communication, October 4, 2011.
33. See, for example, Zina D. H. Young to Apostle Joseph F. Smith, Salt Lake City, January 15, 1894, reprinted in Wolfinger, "A Test of Faith," 150.
34. An interview with Jane James was published in the *Young Woman's Journal* in 1905. It is reprinted in Newell, "Autobiography and Interview," 268–70. For examples of James's appearances in the *Woman's Exponent*, see Lydia D. Alder, "Ladies' Semi-Monthly Meeting," *Woman's Exponent* 22, no. 18 (June 1, 1894): 141; Zina Hyde, "Ladies' Semi-Monthly Meeting," *Woman's Exponent* 24, no. 17 (February 1, 1896): 110; A. T. Hyde, "Ladies' Semi-Monthly Meeting," *Woman's Exponent* 25, no. 5 (September 1, 1896): 34; Lydia D. Alder, "Ladies' Semi-Momthly [*sic*] Meeting," *Woman's Exponent* 25, no. 11 (December 15, 1896): 78; Hannah M. Wright, "Ladies Semi-Monthly Meeting," *Woman's Exponent* 27, nos. 11–12 (November 1 and 15, 1898): 62; J. S. Woolley, "Ladies' Semi-Monthly

Meeting," *Woman's Exponent* 28, nos. 8–9 (September 15 and October 1, 1899): 56; Sec. *pro tem.*, "Ladies' Semi-Monthly Meeting," *Woman's Exponent* 29, nos. 4–5 (July 15 and August 1, 1900): 18.

35. Phyllis Mack reminds us, "In ordinary life, agency is rarely experienced as an entirely free series of movements or choices." Mack, "Religion, Feminism, and the Problem of Agency," 159.
36. Brekus, "Mormon Women and the Problem of Historical Agency," 82, 83.
37. Jane and Isaac James did fairly well for themselves when they arrived in the Salt Lake Valley, but Isaac's departure in 1870 exacerbated Jane's economic struggles by removing one source of income from the household. See Wolfinger, "A Test of Faith," 131–32, 134–35, 139, 160n16, 160n18.
38. I argued this point at much greater length in my paper "Daughters of Cain, Daughters of Zion: Black Mormon Women in the Nineteenth Century," Berkshire Conference on Women's History, Amherst, MA, June 11, 2011.
39. Newell, "Autobiography and Interview," 39.
40. Mack, "Religion, Feminism, and the Problem of Agency," 163.

9

A Rough Stone from Nature's Quarry

The Problem of Agency in the Nineteenth-century Pacific

AMANDA HENDRIX-KOMOTO

In 1846, a Mormon missionary named Benjamin F. Grouard married Tearo, a young Polynesian woman. Grouard's missionary companion, a grizzled whaler named Addison Pratt, wrote skeptically about the marriage in his journal. Grouard had previously been married, and Pratt may have worried that this second marriage would be seen as a form of adultery; additionally, the racial identity of Grouard's bride may have been an issue. Previous marriages between white Mormon men and native women had primarily occurred among beachcombers and other marginal white men who had converted to Mormonism.[1] Grouard, however, was an American shipwright who had enormous influence within the Mormon community in the Pacific. In his journal, Pratt wrote that if white Mormon women were to see Grouard's bride they would think that he had made "a rude choice." The girl was, after all, "a rough stone from nature's quarry." She had difficulty understanding why she should "shield her sable beauty from the [sun's] scorching rays" or wear stockings that made it difficult for her to climb coconut trees. Although initially opposed to Grouard's decision to remarry, Pratt ultimately resigned himself to his fellow missionary's choices. "What is to be done?" he wrote with a sense of futility. "It is not good for man to be alone."[2] He compared Grouard and himself to Uriah, a Biblical figure forced into battle and ultimately killed because of King David's lust for Uriah's wife Bathsheba. They had become "the sport of fortune."[3]

The marriage between Grouard and Tearo has offered historians the opportunity to examine how imperial contexts, which Mormon missionaries encountered as they spread the gospel, affected their ideas concerning interracial marriage and sexuality. In the Pacific, sex became a space in which individual missionaries sought to discredit each other's position within indigenous communities and among colonial officials. Although Mormon missionaries had themselves been the subjects of sexual gossip within the United States, they were just as willing as other missionaries to use sexual rumor and innuendo to attempt to discredit their opponents.

Most historians who have examined the missionary work that Grouard and Pratt undertook in the Pacific, myself included, have focused on its meaning for white communities. In this chapter, however, I will examine Tearo's marriage in the context of revealing how indigenous communities understood their relationship to Mormonism. The decision of the London Missionary Society (LMS) to create Tahiti and Moʻorea as the center of their missionary work in the Pacific had marginalized other island chains, including a chain of small coral atolls known as the Tuamotus. These communities were viewed as being too small to warrant the presence of a white missionary. White Mormon missionaries created an opportunity for Pacific Islanders to establish a Christianity whose geographic center was the smaller coral atolls and island communities, rather than Tahiti Nui or Moʻorea. I argue that Tearo's marriage represented her community's decision to align itself with Mormonism as an alternative to the Protestant Church that the LMS had founded in the 1790s.

Focusing on Tearo's marriage allows historians to foreground the experiences of Pacific Islanders, rather than those of white missionaries. Although this shift in perspective adds new, complex layers to our understanding of Mormonism in the Pacific, it is one that historians have frequently been unwilling to make. As Gina Colvin argued in a presentation to the Mormon History Association in 2013, Mormon historians have traditionally foregrounded the experiences of white Mormons, and included the experiences of indigenous people only when they serve the larger story of American exceptionalism.[4] This absence is not unique to Mormon history, especially in regard to indigenous women. In June 2014, Phyllis Herda edited a special volume of *The Journal of the Polynesian Society* on women's lives, in response to the absence of Polynesian women in general histories of the Pacific. In the introduction to this volume, she blamed the marginalization of Polynesian women in historical writing partially on the nature of archival work. The Europeans, who created many of the records that survive, tended to focus on male leaders and either ignored Polynesian women or reduced them to "sexual objects."[5] Recapturing the experiences of Polynesian women, then, means reading between the lines of the material that is available to us. It can be a messy, frustrating task. The conclusions I have made here are partial and subject to revision.

Much of the work that has tried to recover the experiences of indigenous people has approached the subject from the rubric of agency. At times, however, the idea of agency has been an awkward fit with the attempt to create narratives centered on the Pacific. As historian Walter Johnson states, the term agency "smuggles" into the "conversation" a "liberal notion of selfhood" that fails to recognize the constraints individuals experience, and elevates the experiences of white, middle-class men over those of women and people of color.[6] Pacific Islanders living in the nineteenth century would not necessarily have recognized themselves or their goals in the term agency. At the same time, the term has its utility. Scholars often use it as shorthand for the attempt to understand what events meant for individuals whose experiences have been traditionally marginalized in historical writing. The lack of materials written in Tearo's hand means that any discussion of how she understood her marriage to Grouard has to involve guesswork and the use of probabilities. In this essay, Tearo speaks most often through her community. In an attempt to comprehend how Tearo would have understood her marriage, I construct its possible meanings for the nineteenth-century Tuamotus. Although this method is imperfect, it is one of the few ways available to us for reconstructing how people whose voices are not fully captured in the historical record may have understood the past.

"More Warlike than the Tahitians": The Tuamotus in the Nineteenth Century

Historians are not certain where Tearo was born. F. Edward Butterworth suggests in *Roots of the Reorganization* that she was born in Tubuai in the Austral Islands and traveled to the Tuamotus with Addison Pratt.[7] It is also possible that Tearo was born in the Tuamotus. In his journal, Pratt refers to her as a "Chain Island lass." Chain Island was a name frequently used in the nineteenth century to refer to Anaa, an atoll in the Tuamotu

Archipelago.[8] According to some scholars, Polynesians from the Society Islands may have settled the Tuamotus by 700 CE.[9] Other scholars have given alternative dates.[10] In spite of the distance between Tahiti Nui and the Tuamotus, there was frequent communication between the two groups. When James Cook visited Tahiti in the eighteenth century, the well-educated high priest that he employed as a navigator was able to provide him with detailed sailing directions for several islands in the archipelago.[11] The people of the Tuamotus also produced large double canoes made from tree trunks that had been cut into planks and sewn together in a manner similar to that used in the Middle East.[12] When Mormon missionaries arrived in the Pacific in the mid-nineteenth century, they heard rumors about the ferocity of the archipelago's population. Benjamin F. Grouard wrote in his diary that "the accounts" they had heard of the Tuamotus "were generaly so unfavorable that we had not as yet had any desire to go there. Thay were represented to us, as being very low land, scarcely above the level of the sea, producing nothing but cocoanuts, & the natives being savage & revengefull being under no restraint whatever."[13] The accounts of other white men partially echoed his sentiments. In 1838, the American naval officer Charles Wilkes undertook an exploratory expedition to the South Pacific. In his published account, Wilkes described the people of the Tuamotus as being "more warlike than the Tahitians in spite of their being known as a 'trustworty race.'"[14] Although the distance between Tubuai and Tahiti Nui was over four hundred miles, the former was not known as being as "uncivilized" as the Tuamotus.

The decades surrounding Tearo's birth were a time of transition for both the Tuamotus and Tubuai. The arrival of Congregationalist missionaries in the Pacific shifted the region's power dynamics. The decision of the LMS to center their mission on Tahiti Nui and Moʻorea, provided those communities with immense prestige and access to material resources. Pomare II, the Tahitian king, used the knowledge he gained from his contacts with the white missionaries—and the increased trade revenues that their presence attracted—to build Western-style vessels and whaling boats.[15] Although these vessels were not necessarily more adept at navigating the coral reefs and uncertain currents of the Pacific Islands, they demonstrated that Pomare II had access to resources that some political leaders in the Pacific did not. In the early nineteenth century, he expanded his political authority over the Tuamotus in an attempt to gain a royal monopoly over the pearl trade.[16] He made similar claims in the Society and Austral Islands where pork, coconut oil, and sandalwood were important commodities. The joy of the people of Anaa at seeing Grouard suggests that at least part of the population was discontented with the archipelago's position in relation to Tahiti and the decision of the LMS not to send them a white missionary. Although Pomare II cast his expansionism in religious terms, giving his allegiance to the "king of Kings," the extension of his authority over many of the island chains surrounding Tahiti represented a fundamental loss of sovereignty for those communities. Throughout the early nineteenth century, individuals challenged the legitimacy of the Pomare dynasty by illicitly trading on untaxed ships, continuing banned religious practices, and asserting their own claims to political authority.[17]

Tearo was born into this changed world. Although the lack of information historians have about her parentage makes it impossible to assess how Pomare's ascendancy would have changed the position of her own family, Tearo would have viewed her community in relationship to larger changes occurring within the Pacific. Throughout the nineteenth century, the LMS relied on the labor of Polynesian men to spread the gospel, sending men from the Society Islands, Tonga, and Samoa to serve as teachers among communities the LMS had deemed too remote to warrant the presence of a white missionary. The labor for missionary work in the Tuamotus and the island of Tubuai likely came from the Society Islands. In the mid-1830s, Anaa had three mission stations.[18] For Tearo, the shift from traditional Polynesian religious practices to Christianity changed the rituals that marked her transition from childhood to adulthood, the way that she was expected to dress her body, and the recreation in which she was permitted to engage. The LMS proscribed certain Maʻohi cultural practices, such as sexually suggestive dances in which women appeared partially naked.[19] They also identified the marital ties that joined husbands and wives together through polygamy as adulterous.

Although these changes were a loss for many Polynesians, it is important to note that the religious and social changes that occurred in the Pacific were not uniformly disenfranchising. In fact, Pacific Islanders often enthusiastically embraced Christianity, converting en masse in scenes that the missionaries interpreted as evidence of God's providence.[20] The conversion of much of the region to Christianity empowered some individuals, while disempowering others. The LMS worried that the conversions they had witnessed in the Pacific in the early nineteenth century were not authentic. Their concern was based primarily on the idea that conversion should be grounded on the soul's recognition of its complete dependence on God for salvation. This emphasis led them to be suspicious of mass conversions. For the LMS, conversion also relied on the agency of the individual. It was the individual's decision to recognize her sinful nature and dependence upon God that led her to be saved.

It is critical to not import this understanding of conversion into the Pacific. Laurie Maffly-Kipp has stressed the difficulty of pinpointing how Pacific Islanders understood "particular religious behaviors" or how they "incorporated" them into their worldview.[21] We do not know how Pacific Islanders living in the nineteenth century understood terms like "agency" and "conversion," or how they translated them into their own experiences.

The difficulty of translation was not limited to the Pacific Islands. As Johnson has pointed out, the definition of agency upon which the LMS relied was a highly contingent one that had arisen in a specific historical moment in early modern Europe.[22] The emphasis the LMS placed upon conversion as individual action was not reflective of a universal human reality. Some Pacific Islanders saw their conversions in terms similar to the LMS. For others, however, conversion to the Congregationalist Church was as much an acceptance of the spiritual power of the ascendant Pomare dynasty as it was a reflection of a complete understanding of the doctrine of the atonement. Conversion occurred within a context in which spiritual and political power were intertwined.[23]

These social structures do not perfectly illuminate Tearo's experiences. She was probably an infant or a small child when many of these changes occurred. It is likely, however, that she would have understood at least some of the shifts that had transpired within her community. Pomare's attempt to create an empire that extended over much of the Pacific had partially enabled the religious and cultural transformations that had occurred in the region. Although the people of the Tuamotus and Tubuai had access to material goods through trade, they found themselves marginalized within Pomare's kingdom. After his 1821 death,

Pomare's successors continued his imperium. The LMS considered the Tuamotus and Tubuai too small—too insignificant—to warrant the presence of a white missionary. This shifting world was the one in which Mormon missionaries arrived in 1844. Understanding its contours cannot tell us with any certainty how Tearo understood her experiences, but it does provide us with some of the possible meanings that she would have attached to them.

"Damn Him as a Heretic": The Mormon Mission in the Pacific

The Mormon missionaries who traveled to the Pacific had initially intended to book passage to the Sandwich Islands, where Pratt had abandoned a whaling ship to live as a beachcomber several years earlier. The missionaries found themselves, however, unable to book passage to their original destination.[24] One of the blessings they had received when they were called to serve as missionaries had promised them they would be able to "heal the sick, cast out devils, and cause the lame to walk."[25] Pratt found the Austral Islands a ready field for conversion. The extension of a French protectorate over Tahiti Nui, Mo'orea, and much of the Pomares domains, however, made Grouard's mission on the island of Tahiti Nui more difficult. Unwilling to surrender their independence, hundreds of Tahitian men and women attacked French forces in a form of guerilla warfare. In response, French military forces committed acts of routine violence, cutting down fruit trees, burning villages, and killing wounded Tahitian soldiers. In the uncertainty that followed the establishment of the French protectorate, Grouard found it difficult to find people willing to listen to his message. In his journal, he wrote that whenever they tried to talk about the Mormon gospel people would respond "with something about the French."[26] Grouard's frustration eventually led him to abandon Tahiti Nui for the Tuamotus.

The Mormon conception of agency was just as unfamiliar to Grouard's converts as that of other Christian missionaries. It offered them the opportunity, however, to create an alternative Pacific Christianity centered not on Tahiti Nui but on Anaa and the Tuamotus. Within a few months, Grouard had converted much of the population of Anaa. He described his house as being "thronged from daylight till eleven & twelve o clock at night." They asked him "questions without end" on "religious civil & political topics," and "seemed desirous for me to stand at their head, in civil as well as religious affairs."[27] It is likely that Grouard saw the success he had achieved on Anaa as evidence of God's blessings. He still lamented, however, their lack of Biblical knowledge. He felt that they knew "no more of its contents than a child" and sometimes spent nearly an "hour explaining a simple passage of scripture."[28] He saw their willingness to learn about the Bible as part of the process through which the people of Anaa would become moral agents. When he described their state before his arrival, he used the language of immaturity, describing them as "benighted children of heathenism" who were unable to understand concepts that would be grasped by the youngest pupil in the United States.[29] In teaching them about the scriptures, Grouard believed that he would redeem them from their state of ignorance and provide them with the knowledge that they needed to become moral subjects with the power to act in society and as members of the Mormon priesthood.

In many ways, his vision of missionary work as a redemptive project mirrored that of other missionary groups in the nineteenth century. It was common among white missionaries throughout the colonial world to emphasize the importance of cultural as well as religious change.[30] White missionaries emphasized the need for indigenous people to adopt new understandings of domesticity that would discipline their sexual desires, pulling them into the home through the creation of nuclear families.[31] Although Mormons shared this belief in the disciplinary function of the family with other white missionaries, they proposed a radically different timeline for the transformation of indigenous cultures. For early Mormons, missionary work and millenarianism were deeply intertwined. Mormon missionaries saw themselves as drawing out the people of God who would then gather to the Mormon community forming on the banks of the Mississippi. This gathering would culminate in the creation of the Kingdom of God and the redemption of the earth. As part of this millennial gathering, indigenous people—whom Mormons believed were the descendants of the people of Israel—would remember their divine past.[32] The Book of Mormon was at once a history of the indigenous peoples of the Americas, and a promise that they would eventually be recognized as Israelites. Pratt and Grouard believed that Pacific Islanders were a part of this grand unfolding and would participate in the gathering to the Americas.

Although it is unlikely that the people of the Tuamotus interpreted this promise in the same way as Grouard and his white companions, there is evidence that they did see themselves in the stories that the Mormon missionaries told of the millennium. In response to the presence of Mormon missionaries, the LMS sent some of its white agents to investigate the spread of Mormonism in the region. They encountered a man and asked him "where Zion was." The man explained to the agent that Zion was in America and that he would soon be traveling there.[33] The man's explanation of Zion, along with the descriptions of the preaching of white Mormon missionaries, suggests that the people who converted to Mormonism in the Pacific may have adopted a refracted Israelite identity.[34] For Tearo and other Pacific Islanders, the promises that the Mormon missionaries made would have reminded them of earlier prophetic movements in the region.

Depending on Tearo's birthdate, a millennial movement called Mamaia became popular in the Pacific Islands under the Pomares just before she was born or when she was an infant. One of the movement's prophets was a man named Teao who may have claimed that Christ had possessed him. His dramatic prophesies that God was going to destroy the Papeete for its population's sins, and his rejection of the Protestant missionaries' authority, caused the LMS to view Teao as a threat.[35] Although the movement was religious in nature, it focused on politics as well. In appropriating Christian motifs, the members of Mamaia created a religion that drew upon the sympathetic elements of Christianity but was more open to the prophesies, healings, and possessions that had been a part of Tahitian religious life before the arrival of the Christian missionaries. Although the LMS succeeded in suppressing the movement in the 1830s, it continued to attract adherents until Teao's death in 1841.[36] Mormonism's acceptance of prophetic utterances, spirit possession, and faith healing likely reminded people of the movement; deepening its association with indigenous people and the perception that it offered a radical alternative to Protestant Christianity in the Pacific.

Mormonism also offered the Tuamotus and Tubuai an opportunity to improve their position vis-à-vis Tahiti Nui. In refusing to send a white missionary to the Tuamotus, the LMS had marked the communities as inconsequential. Letters from members of the LMS who traveled throughout the outer islands to determine how much of a purchase

Mormonism had there, suggest that this slight was deeply felt. When these men landed on the islands of Rurutu, Rimatara, and Raivavae, they were told that the congregations there "did not desire any more Tahitian teachers." They were "*fin roa*"—"thoroughly tired of them." Their cry that they had not been provided with Christian instructors reminded the LMS missionaries of "the Eunuch of old" who had asked "how can we understand unless some one instruct us?"[37] The willingness of Pratt and Grouard to live among these small communities provided them with a prestige that the LMS had denied them. When Grouard arrived on the island of Anaa, hundreds of people lined the shore, laughing and shouting happily as he neared. Within a month, he had amassed a congregation of a few hundred listeners.[38]

However, not all of Anaa's inhabitants viewed the arrival of Mormon missionaries as auspicious. Contained within Grouard's diaries are hints of some of the opposition he experienced. After he baptized some of his congregants, fully immersing them as Mormon theology required, Grouard reported that one of the Ma'ohi men (a teacher for the LMS) "made a great noise."[39] According to Grouard, the rumors being spread about him caused many of the other settlements on the island of Anaa to "damn [him] as a heretic." One community, in particular, vowed they would abandon their village and retreat "into the woods" if he approached them.[40] Grouard presents these instances as evidence of the power of the gospel, suggesting that after they heard the gospel these communities abandoned their opposition and accepted him as a missionary of God. Whether or not Grouard's recounting of events is accurate, the opposition that he initially encountered suggests some of the conflicts that arose after his arrival in the Tuamotus. The decisions of individuals to align themselves with the Mormon missionaries, the French, or the LMS divided communities. In asking them to accept Mormon theology, Mormons required the people of the Tuamotus to change fundamentally how they saw the world, and how they conceived their relationship between religious and social life. Tearo faced this challenge as much as any other member of her community. Although conversions in the Pacific often happened en masse, Mormon theology mirrored that of other Christians in demanding a transformation of individual conscience. Tearo married Grouard in 1846, thereby aligning herself with the Mormon Church, rather than the Protestant Church that the LMS had established.

"Hagar and Keturah": Understanding Tearo's Marriage

The evidence surrounding Tearo's marriage to Grouard is slim. As a result, the question of how she understood her marriage is a difficult one to answer. As a white historian, it is tempting to use Tearo's decision to marry Grouard as a moment to locate what scholars would traditionally label as her agency. As I have argued throughout this paper, however, the term agency sits awkwardly with attempts to understand how Pacific Islanders perceived Mormonism.[41] It is also impossible to know how much choice Tearo had in her decision to marry Grouard.

It is likely that the marriage had two disparate meanings for the white Mormon missionaries and for Tearo's community. White Mormons would have viewed her marriage to Grouard within the context of Mormon ideas about the millennial role of indigenous people. There is some suggestion that early Mormons may have viewed marriages between white Mormons and American Indians as a way to speed the Second Coming of Christ. In 1831, the *Ohio Star* alleged that Joseph Smith had encouraged Mormon missionaries to make a "matrimonial alliance" with American Indians.[42] Although no contemporary Mormon source corroborates this claim, the Mormon editor W. W. Phelps later remembered Smith telling him that Mormon missionaries would take native women as their wives just as Abraham had taken Hagar and Keturah, and Jacob had taken Bilhah and Zilpah.[43] Although Phelps's claims were likely heavily influenced by later Mormon theology, together these two sources suggests that the early Mormon community accepted interracial marriage to some extent and invested it with religious meaning. It is possible that Grouard viewed his marriage to Tearo as mirroring Abraham's to Hagar and Keturah, but the evidence that remains is too scanty to do more than speculate. The silence that surrounds her in his writings makes it impossible to know how he interpreted the marriage.

Whatever Grouard's ultimate interpretation of the marriage, it is unlikely that Tearo's community interpreted it in the same way. For her, marrying Grouard may have been a way to cement the alliance between her family and the white Mormon missionaries. Although the LMS feared that interracial marriages between white men and indigenous women would degrade the former, such marriages were not uncommon and offered native women and their families enormous prestige. For white men, they increased access to trading networks and native resources by integrating them into local kinship systems. Grouard's position as a missionary granted him immense spiritual power. Tearo's marriage to Grouard would have aligned her family with a new powerful religion, while offering her special status in the community. According to Pratt's journal, the people of the Tuamotus greeted her marriage to Grouard with a "great noise."[44] Their union would have positioned the Tuamotus, whom the LMS had dismissed as marginal and insignificant, at the center of Mormonism in the Pacific. It is little wonder that the marriage was celebrated.

White Mormons, however, were uncomfortable concerning the possible effects of interracial marriage. Although some evidence suggests that Mormon theology encouraged interracial unions, in practice, Mormons were deeply ambivalent about these marriages. The promises within the Book of Mormon about indigenous people were based on the idea that race was mutable. According to Book of Mormon descriptions of the Second Coming, the changes that occurred within indigenous people as they remembered their Israelite heritage would be physical as well as cultural. Their bodies would be physically lightened as the scales fell from their eyes. The mutability of racial identity that this suggested made Mormons uneasy. The possibility that individuals could lose their racial characteristics meant that it was possible for white men to become "Indian." Most Americans rejected the Mormon vision of the Second Coming as a time of redemption in which Native Americans would be reintegrated into the people of Israel. They shared Mormon fears, however, about interracial marriage. According to the historian Richard Godbeer, "Any English man or woman who became sexually intimate with an Indian" in early America, "was liable to stigmatization as 'debased' or 'defiled.'"[45] Pratt was reluctant to accept Grouard's marriage. In spite of his justifications of the marriage, he spent a considerable amount of time in his journal discussing Tearo's identity as a Polynesian woman. He may not have felt the same need to explain Grouard's decision if he had married a white woman. Moreover, Grouard's status within the community and previous marriage made his decision to remarry politically volatile. Pratt's initial disapproval, however, did little to quell Grouard's desire to marry Tearo or her willingness to accept the union. Separated from his wife, Grouard wanted someone to serve as his helpmeet and justified his actions using the Biblical adage that "it was not good for man to be alone."[46]

Their marriage, however, was short-lived. Tearo died shortly after their wedding, leaving behind a daughter named Sophronia. After Tearo's death, Grouard decided to take another native woman named Nahina as his wife. His decision to do so allowed him to reinforce the connections that he had formed with the Tuamotus through his marriage to Tearo. Although Nahina's marriage did not have the same role in forging an alliance between the white Mormon missionaries and the people of the Tuamotus, it is likely that her marriage was celebrated also. Exploring how interracial marriages forged connections between communities in the Pacific Islands allows us to understand the politics of Mormon missionary work. They also remind us of the importance of considering how indigenous communities understood the arrival of Mormon missionaries. Although there are few documents from the point of view of Ma'ohi women like Tearo and Nahina, reconstructing their world provides us with a different perspective than the stories that are told from the viewpoint of the white men who traveled to the Pacific Islands as Mormon missionaries. This perspective will become increasingly important as the church tries to create a history that reflects the global nature of its ministry.

Notes

1. Beachcombers were white men who had abandoned whaling ships to live among indigenous communities.
2. S. George Ellsworth, ed., *Journals of Addison Pratt* (Salt Lake City: University of Utah Press, 1990), 276–77.
3. Ibid.
4. Gina Colvin, "Maori and Pakeha Mormonism in New Zealand," (paper presented at the Mormon History Association Annual Conference, Layton, Utah, June 6–9, 2013).
5. Phyllis Herda, "Introduction: Writing the Lives of Some Extraordinary Polynesian Women," *Journal of the Polynesian Society* 123, no. 2 (June 2014): 113–28.
6. Walter Johnson, "On Agency," *Journal of Social History* 37, no. 1 (Fall 2003): 115.
7. F. Edward Butterworth, *Roots of the Reorganization: French Polynesia* (Independence, MO: Herald House Publishing, 1977), 70.
8. Ellsworth, *Journals of Addison Pratt,* 276.
9. Many historians have investigated the settlement of the Pacific. For the debate surrounding the dates when specific island chains were settled, see Geoffrey Irwin, *The Prehistoric Exploration and Colonisation of the Pacific* (Cambridge: Cambridge University Press, 1994); Donald Denoon, "Human Settlement," in *The Cambridge History of the Pacific Islanders,* edited by Donald Denoon

et al. (Cambridge: Cambridge University Press, 1997), 37–79; and James Minahan, *Ethnic Groups of South Asia and the Pacific: An Encyclopedia* (Santa Barbara, Denver, and Oxford: ABC-Clio, 2012), 340.

10. Craig Lockard, for example, has suggested that both the Austral Islands and the Tuamotus were settled around 300 BCE. See Craig Lockard, *Societies, Networks, and Transitions,* vol. 1 (Boston: Houghton Mifflin, 2008), 93.
11. James Hornell, "Was There Pre-Columbian Contact between the Peoples of Oceania and South America?," *Journal of the Polynesian Society* 54, no. 4 (1945): 169.
12. Hornell, "Was There Pre-Columbian Contact?," 169.
13. Benjamin F. Grouard, Journal, June 1843–September 1846, February 25, 1845, 67–68, Church History Library, Salt Lake City, Utah.
14. Charles Wilkes, *Narrative of the United States Exploring Expedition,* vol. 1 (London: Ingram, Cooke, 1852), 128.
15. David A. Chappell, *Double Ghosts: Oceanian Voyagers on Euroamerican Ships* (Armonk, NY: M.E. Sharpe, 1997), 12.
16. Niel Gunson, "Pomare II of Tahiti and Polynesian Imperialism," *Journal of Pacific History* 4 (1969): 65–82; Chappell, *Double Ghosts,* 12; Colin Newbury, *Tahiti Nui: Change and Survival in French Polynesia, 1767–1945* (Honolulu: University of Hawaiʻi Press, 1980), 28; and A. D. Couper, *Sailor and Traders: A Maritime History of the Pacific Peoples* (Honolulu: University of Hawaiʻi Press, 2009), 80–82.
17. Couper, *Sailors and Traders,* 82; Gunson, "Pomare II of Tahiti," 68.
18. Couper, *Sailors and Traders,* 75, 81–82.
19. Maʻohi is used here to refer to the indigenous people of what is now French Polynesia, including the Tuamotus and the Austral Islands.
20. Robert I. Levy, *Tahitians: Mind and Experience in the Society Islands* (Chicago: University of Chicago Press, 1973), 16–17.
21. Laurie Maffly-Kipp, "Looking West: Mormonism and the Pacific World," *Journal of Mormon History* 26, no. 1 (Spring 2000): 55.
22. Johnson, "On Agency," 115.
23. Bronwen Douglas, "Religion," in *Pacific Histories: Ocean, Land, People,* edited by David Armitage and Alison Bashford (New York: Palgrave MacMillan, 2014), 203–5.
24. Fred E. Woods, "Launching Mormonism in the Pacific: The Voyage of the Timoleon," in *Go Ye into All the World: The Growth and Development of Mormon Missionary Work,* edited by Reid L. Nielson and Fred E. Woods (Provo, UT: Religious Studies Center, 2012), 191–216.
25. Journal History of the Church, May 23, 1843, Church History Library. This source is a scrapbook consisting of transcripts of letters, copies of newspaper articles, and selections from diaries. It is arranged by date.
26. Grouard, Journal, May 24, 1844, 37.
27. Grouard, Journal, May 5, 1845, 93.
28. Grouard, Journal, January 13, 1846, 133; and May 5, 1844, 92.

29. Grouard, Journal, January 13, 1846, 133.
30. For more on cultural change and Protestant missionary work in the nineteenth century, see William Hutchinson, *Errand to the World: American Protestant Thought and Foreign Missions* (Chicago: University of Chicago Press, 1993).
31. There is extensive literature on this subject. For a sampling see Patricia Grimshaw, *Paths of Duty: American Missionary Wives in Nineteenth-Century Hawaii* (Honolulu: University of Hawai'i Press, 1989); Emily Manktelow, *Missionary Families: Race, Gender, and Generation on the Spiritual Frontier* (Manchester, UK: Manchester University Press, 2013); and Jennifer Thigpen, *Island Queens and Mission Wives: Gender and Empires Remade Hawai'i's Pacific World* (Chapel Hill: University of North Carolina Press, 2014).
32. 2 Nephi 30:6.
33. George Platt to the Directors of the London Missionary Society, January 16, 1849, CWM/LMS/South Seas, Incoming Correspondence, box 22, fd. 1, jacket A, School of Oriental and African Studies, London, UK.
34. In 1851, Louisa Barnes Pratt told a group of Pacific Islanders that the Nephites were the "ancient fathers of the Tahitians." Family histories also suggest that her husband Addison may have requested to be sent to the Sandwich Islands because of the similarities he saw between Native Hawaiians and American Indians. The latter story, however, may be more reflective of later theological developments than contemporary ideas about Polynesians. It is possible, but not certain, that Addison Pratt and Benjamin F. Grouard taught early Polynesian converts that they were descended from Israelites. See Russell T. Clement, "Polynesian Origins: More on the Mormon Perspective," *Dialogue: A Journal of Mormon Thought* 13, no. 4 (Winter 1980): 88–98; and Norman Douglas, "The Sons of Lehi and the Seed of Cain: Racial Myths in Mormon Scripture and Their Relevance to the Pacific Islands," *Journal of Religious History* 8, no. 1 (June 1974): 90–104.
35. Niel Gunson, "An Account of the Mamaia or Visionary Heresy of Tahiti, 1826–1841," *Journal of the Polynesian Society* 71, no. 2 (1962): 208–43.
36. Ibid., 238.
37. George Charter and Ernst Krause to the Directors of the London Missionary Society, July 10, 1849, CWM/LMS/South Seas, Incoming Correspondence, box 22, fd. 1, jacket C, School of Oriental and African Studies, London, UK.
38. Grouard, Journal, May 1, 1845, 80–82.
39. Grouard, Journal, May 25, 1845, 99.
40. Grouard, Journal, May 25, 1845, 102.
41. Johnson, "On Agency," 115.
42. "Mormonism—Nos. VIII–IX," *The Ohio Star* 11, no. 49 (December 8, 1831), reprinted in Eber D. Howe, *Mormonism Unvailed, Or, A Faithful Account of That Singular Imposition* (Painesville, OH: E. D. Howe, 1834), 200.
43. W. W. Phelps to Brigham Young, August 12, 1861, Brigham Young Papers, Church History Library, cited in Todd Compton, "Fanny Alger Smith Custer: Mormonism's First Plural Wife," *Journal of Mormon History* 22, no. 1 (Spring

1996): 80. Armand Mauss has written about later visions of intermarriage with American Indians in Armand Mauss, *All Abraham's Children* (Urbana: University of Illinois Press, 2003), 52–65, 116–27.

44. Ellsworth, *The Journals of Addison Pratt*, 276.
45. Richard Godbeer, "Eroticizing the Middle Ground: Anglo-Indian Sexual Relations along the Eighteenth-Century Frontier," in *Sex, Love, Race: Crossing Boundaries in North American History*, edited by Martha Hodes (New York: New York University Press, 1999), 93.
46. Ellsworth, *The Journals of Addison Pratt*, 275.

10

A Wider Sphere of Action

Women's Agency in 1870s Utah

KATE HOLBROOK AND REBEKAH RYAN CLARK

The year was 1878 in Farmington, Utah, and Aurelia Spencer Rogers worried about the young boys in the church. They were rowdy and insufficiently disciplined, and she wondered whom the girls would marry if these "hoodlums" weren't reformed. As Rogers entertained these questions, she recalled, "A fire seemed to burn within me." She considered showing up at a Young Men's Mutual Improvement Association meeting, and later wondered whether she had thought "too much, perhaps, of what people might say" when she refrained.[1]

A few weeks later, Eliza R. Snow and Emmeline B. Wells came to Farmington to attend a conference for the LDS women's Relief Society organization. As the head of Relief Society and the editor of the *Woman's Exponent*, respectively, Snow and Wells held great influence within the church. They stopped at Rogers's home on their way to the depot, talked about the "rough, careless ways" of the young men and boys, and wondered what should be done. Rogers seized the opportunity to suggest her idea of forming "an organization for little boys wherein they could be taught everything good, and how to behave."[2] Snow agreed that such a thing might be possible and promised to speak to the acting First Presidency of the church. Once Snow received approval and support from these male leaders, she established the Primary Association—an organization that continues to serve LDS children today. As they corresponded about the newly founded organization, Snow told Rogers, "I feel assured that the inspiration of heaven is directing you, and that a great and very important movement is being inaugurated for the future of Zion."[3]

FIGURE 10.1 Aurelia Spencer Rogers (center) and the Farmington Ward Primary presidency in the 1870s. Photograph by C. R. Savage. Courtesy of the International Society of Daughters of Utah Pioneers, Salt Lake City, Utah.

Rogers's story demonstrates the kind of agency Latter-day Saint women could exercise in the 1870s. When speaking of women exercising agency, it is tempting to use the most dramatic examples—Harriet Tubman, Mary Wollenstonecraft, or Elizabeth Cady Stanton—who defied the institutional authority of their day. But what about these exceptional women's lesser-known mothers, cousins, and sisters-in-law? What did agency mean and make in their lives? What about women who worked *with* an institution instead of *against* it? Aurelia Rogers provides an example of a woman who used her agency to enact lasting change working within, instead of against, her church. Rogers was not the president of an organization or married to a Mormon prophet. She was a believing Latter-day Saint woman with a vision of how to help build God's kingdom within the structures of her church rather than outside them.

In the essay that begins this volume, Catherine Brekus analyzes "women as agents of historical change."[4] Casual thinkers might mistake the meaning of agency for choice, but Brekus writes in terms of the dictionary definition, "the ability . . . to act or exert power."[5] The ability to act and exert power is precisely what Latter-day Saint women during the 1870s reported finding in their church. They also experienced agency communally. These women not only felt empowered to act as individuals, they felt a mandate to act on behalf of others, to contribute their work to a broader effort to build God's kingdom and achieve humanity's welfare.

Rogers's work to institute the Primary illustrates both the possibilities and limitations of Mormon women's agency during the 1870s. These women interpreted and acted on inspiration, accessed power through spiritual gifts, and worked within the existing system in a cooperative, yet active and influential way. At the same time, church doctrine required that their actions accord with the structure of an all-male hierarchy. Women professed to believe these structures and commandments came from God, so they were not obeying men, they were obeying God. However, they saw that God's will for the institution reached them through prophetic, but human, men. Obedience was simultaneously limiting—because it meant following rules—and liberating—because obedient church members received their own promptings and inspiration from the Holy Ghost. Latter-day Saints wielded agency when affiliating with the church, following its rules, and honoring its structure. They exercised agency when transforming, teaching, and healing within the organization.

A belief in personal answers to prayer facilitated female agency in a complicated way. Personal revelation through prayer enabled church members to commune directly with God without the need of an intermediary. "Following the Spirit" comprised a crucial element of the agency of women throughout the history of the church, since both women and men were to turn to God to receive confirmation of the validity of church teachings and scripture. To illustrate, in the last chapter of the Book of Mormon (1830), the prophet Moroni promises,

> And when ye shall receive these things, I would exhort you that ye would ask God, the Eternal Father, in the name of Christ, if these things are not true; and if ye shall ask with a sincere heart, with real intent, having faith in Christ, he will manifest the truth of it unto you, by the power of the Holy Ghost. And by the power of the Holy Ghost ye may know the truth of all things.[6]

This fundamental tenet of the LDS faith offered opportunities for women like Rogers to experience spiritual autonomy and power.

Believing in and acting on divine inspiration gave Mormon women a doctrinal foundation to follow their own course. When women reported that their actions were responses to spiritual promptings, it gave those actions credibility. Skeptics might see these conversations about one's spiritual life as opportunities for manipulation (i.e., pretending an idea was based on inspiration to garner support, when it was not), but insiders accepted them as sincere.

A soul in conversation with the Holy Spirit made agency a more layered matter, for when a woman received a spiritual prompting, she was on the receiving end of ideas originating from a transcendent source. Although she felt the idea did not originate with her, she exercised agency in how she responded to the prompting. In Rogers's case, responding involved quite a lot of work—making a children's organization part of general church structure and figuring out what that organization would look like and accomplish. For women in the church, from prominent leaders to regular members, this individual access to the spirit represented an ennobling freedom, providing them unmediated access to an understanding of God's will, and a sense of spiritual confidence as they worked to perform that will.

Individual access to God's spirit was essential to Aurelia Rogers's exercise of agency. In particular, her sense of God's spirit gave her courage to challenge social norms. Rogers's autobiography demonstrates that she felt worthy and capable of acting on God's inspiration, for when she described wrestling over the problem of what to do about rowdy boys, she said, "[a] fire seemed to burn within me."[7] Her ability to act on inspiration was not restricted to that private sphere where late-nineteenth-century women's concerns were most often relegated;[8] however, she acted on behalf of children, which was increasingly an acceptable reason for women to involve themselves in the public sphere. Rogers's founding of the Primary organization coincided with national trends of expansion and feminization in the institutional education and training of young children. Scholars have identified a transformation of the teaching population during the post-bellum years, concluding, "In the half century after the Civil War, the female teacher came to predominate in the elementary schooling of the nation."[9] Although Utah, like other Western territories, had lower ratios of female teachers than the national average in the 1870s, the number and ratio of women teachers employed in Utah steadily increased during this period as public education expanded and more teachers were needed.[10]

Throughout the country, public schools "were expected to . . . save the republic, develop character, uplift morals, and train the mind."[11] Historians have noted that in the post-bellum decades, "schools were basic to nation building, cultural and geographical integration, and socialization of the young to the dominant values of the age."[12] Contemporary reformers applauded women's traditional norms of nurturing, virtue, and domestic responsibilities of childrearing as evidence in favor of hiring them as elementary teachers. In 1872, Catharine Beecher, a prominent nineteenth-century writer and educator, promoted the idea of female schoolteachers as paragons of moral virtue with innate nurturing abilities essential for teaching children: "Woman's great mission is to train immature, weak, and ignorant creatures, to obey the laws of God; the physical, the intellectual, the social, and the moral—first in the family, then in the school, then in the neighborhood, then in the nation, then in the world."[13] With few alternatives for respectable employment outside the home, nineteenth-century women often found that teaching provided a greater level of independence, status, influence, and autonomy within an acceptable extension of the female domestic sphere.[14]

When Rogers observed and felt prompted to address a problem in the church community, she considered that an invitation to solve problems and a mandate to act. Yet broader American gender norms initially gave her pause, for she resisted her first impulse to approach the Young Men's Mutual Improvement Association because she thought "too much, perhaps, of what people might say."[15] Like many women, her fear of male disapproval or appearing to overstep her place initially limited her actions; however, the liberating strength of her personal spiritual witness enabled her to overcome these concerns and take action on that revelation. That sense of personal spiritual guidance continued after church leaders enthusiastically accepted Primary as part of the church. Writing about the experience fifteen years later, Rogers recalled her conviction that God was leading her:

> I seemed to be carried away in the spirit, or at least I experienced a feeling of untold happiness which lasted three days and nights. During that time nothing could worry or irritate me; if my little ones were fretful, or the work went wrong, I had patience, could control in kindness, and manage my household affairs easily. This was a testimony to me that what was being done was from God.[16]

Acting on inspiration complicated agency. God was leading her, but he was not telling her exactly what to do; she had to figure that out on her own. Only after her independent strategizing and action did the spirit confirm to her that her plans pleased God, or were "from God," as she understood it.

While outsiders often viewed the church as precluding female agency, many women in the church in fact viewed themselves as more liberated than women of the world because of the unique agency they exercised through their membership in the church.[17] Upon returning from a nine-month trip to Europe and the Middle East, Eliza R. Snow spoke at a Relief Society meeting in the Ogden Tabernacle, arguing that Latter-day Saint women had a far-reaching space in which to act. She stated,

"No where on the earth has woman so broad a sphere of labor and duty, of responsibility and action, as in Utah."[18] The whole notion of spheres strikes contemporary readers as restrictive, but gendered spheres of influence were a given in 1870s America, and the Mormon woman's sphere was radically expansive at the time. Six months after Snow's speech, her counselor Zina D. H. Young also preached to the Salt Lake City Tenth Ward Relief Society an extensive vision of what women could do: "The sisters of this organization . . . have been organized by the spirit of God, and set apart to do a great and glorious work. Women have more power than they are aware of, They have power to anoint and administer to forward the cause of God."[19]

Throughout the 1870s, Mormon women's influence expanded beyond the private sphere typically associated with traditional women's roles. Keenly aware of the escalating anti-Mormon campaign's portrayal of female Latter-day Saints as unthinking slaves to an oppressive patriarchal system, Mormon women increasingly began to speak out in their own defense. They particularly employed rhetoric that emphasized the unique liberty, autonomy, and widening sphere of influence they enjoyed as members of the church, although their self-awareness of widespread opposition likely led them to exaggerate their liberation at times.

A series of mass meetings, held early in 1870 to protest federal antipolygamy legislation (specifically the Cullom Bill, an antibigamy law designed to dissolve bigamous families), provided an early public platform for Latter-day Saint women to counteract opponents' opinions about their lack of agency.[20] Speakers at those meetings acknowledged that "the world thought we were in the bonds of servitude, which we had no power to break" and asserted that Mormon women must "take a wider sphere of action" and "express our feelings and not remain silent beneath such a flood of falsehood."[21] Eliza R. Snow expounded on the agency, liberty, and authority of Latter-day Saint women at the Great Indignation Meeting held on January 12, 1870:

> Our enemies pretend that in Utah, woman is held in a state of vassalage—that she does not act from choice, but by coercion—that we would even prefer life elsewhere, were it possible for us to make our escape. What nonsense! We all know that if we wished,

> we could leave at any time—either to go singly or we could rise and now en masse, and there is no power here that could or would ever wish to prevent us. I will now ask this intelligent assembly of ladies: Do you know of any place on the face of the earth, where woman has more liberty, and where she enjoys such high and glorious privileges as she does here, as a Latter-day Saint? "No!" . . . Were we the stupid, degraded, heartbroken beings that we have been represented, silence might better become us; but, as women of God,—women filling high and responsible positions—performing sacred duties . . . we not only speak because we have the right, but justice and humanity demand that we should.[22]

Women in her audience probably recognized the limitations of Snow's assertions. They knew it wasn't quite so easy to leave Utah and their family, friends, and social safety nets. How might a woman comfortably rooted in Utah support herself elsewhere in the 1870s? But Snow's audience also likely agreed with her. They believed that the church met their highest priorities in terms of agency because of key doctrines and because their church activities broadened woman's sphere—they were "women of God . . . filling high and responsible positions . . . performing sacred duties." Their stewardships further generated their agency.

As Latter-day Saint women continued speaking out in their own defense and engaging in a wider sphere of activities throughout the 1870s, they provided persuasive testimonies regarding their agency to act, to access spiritual power, and to exert influence within the structure of the church. Within weeks of the January 1870 protest meetings, the Utah territorial legislature passed a bill granting suffrage to Utah women. Thus, women in Utah first obtained the right to vote more than fifty years before the Nineteenth Amendment extended that right to all American women. In response to women's suffrage in Utah, Phebe Woodruff exulted, "God has opened the way for us . . . the yoke on women is removed." Bathsheba Smith also linked suffrage with agency, concluding "there is nothing required of us that we cannot perform."[23]

In addition to acting on divine inspiration, LDS women also exercised gifts of the spirit such as speaking in tongues, prophesying, testifying, teaching, receiving promptings, and healing. Practicing spiritual gifts gave church members direct access to spiritual power. For instance, women and men from the early days in Nauvoo until the early twentieth century exercised the gift of healing. They saw people healed as a direct result of their efforts to anoint an ailing person with oil, place their hands on her head, and call on God to heal and to bless. Women also ministered to one another through a laying-on-of-hands blessing before childbirth. Such ministrations among women were frequent during the 1870s. In 1875, Mary Ann Burnham Freeze wrote in her diary, "I have been with Sister E[llis] Shipp, to wash and anoint Mrs Louie Felt, who is very low with lung fever, but she seemed much relieved when we got through. Could breathe easier."[24] Church practice and belief made it possible for Freeze and Shipp to ease a fellow church member's suffering. Lula Greene Richards similarly recorded in 1878, "Sisters E. R. Snow, Zina D. Young and E. B. Wells have been to see me today, and to wash, anoint and bless me, preparatory to my approaching confinement. We have had an excellent time."[25] The *Woman's Exponent* recorded the following incident relayed at an 1878 Relief Society meeting in Heber, Utah: "A doctor was sent for to set a bone for a little girl, and he said she would be a long time before she would walk; but the sisters of the Relief Society washed and anointed her, and she recovered fast."[26] The widespread use of such spiritual gifts during this period provided women with a significant degree of unmediated access to spiritual power.

Just as receiving the endorsement of male leaders was essential to establishing the Primary organization, orthodoxy required that male leaders authorize the practice of women performing healings. While male church leaders specifically set some women apart to heal the sick, they often encouraged all women in the church to exercise the spiritual gift of healing. Joseph Smith first preached about widespread access to spiritual gifts when he instructed the Female Relief Society of Nauvoo "respecting the propriety of females administering to the sick by the laying on of hands," teaching that "these signs, such as healing the sick, casting out devils &c. should follow all that believe whether male or female."[27] Eliza R. Snow later reiterated that all worthy women in the church had authority to officiate in laying on of hands to restore health:

> Any and all sisters who honor their holy endowments, not only have the right, but should feel it a duty, whenever called upon to administer to our sisters in these ordinances, which God has

> graciously committed to His daughters as well as to His sons; and we testify that when administered and received in faith and humility they are accompanied with almighty power.[28]

Exercise of the gift to heal provided a meaningful avenue for women in the church to assert their agency through spiritual power.

Participation in the Relief Society also expanded agency and promoted cooperation between men and women. Emmeline Wells joined others who believed the founding of Relief Society had paved the way for improvements in women's station more broadly. She asserted her perception of this process in a January 1880 *Woman's Exponent* editorial:

> The organization of the Relief Society in Nauvoo, Ill., in March, 1842, opened perhaps one of the most important eras in the history of woman. It presented the great woman-question to the Latter-day Saints, previous to the woman's rights organizations, which have created such extensive agitation of the subject since . . . The question did not present itself in any aggressive form as woman opposed to man, but as co-worker and helpmeet in all that relates to the well-being and advancement of both, and mutual promoting of the best interests of the community at large. It has given to woman in its rise and progress, influence on almost all aspects that pertain to her welfare and happiness, and opportunities for expressing her own thoughts, views and opinions.[29]

Wells's statement not only situates Relief Society as paving the way for other women's rights organizations but also specifies that solutions to the "woman question" would come through cooperation between men and women who worked for "the well-being and advancement of both."

For LDS women in the 1870s, working within church structure was one way to counteract the typical separation of male and female spheres. Rogers's depiction of her experience illustrated the choice that many LDS women made to work within, rather than against, the hierarchical religious structure to accomplish their purposes. She determined how to work within the existing system to create positive change in an organization to which she was devoted, thinking over her concern until she conceived a solution, then orchestrating a way to make that solution happen. Her description of the event demonstrates this, but it also minimizes moments of independent thought and action to reinforce the story's ethos of cooperation.

To illustrate, Rogers recalled that Eliza R. Snow and Emmeline B. Wells stopped by her house for a visit on their way to the train station. Why did they stop by? As the head of Relief Society and editor in chief of the women's periodical, these were the most powerful women in Utah; they were neither her relatives nor close friends, and they did not need to visit her on account of church business. She must have invited them. Once her visitors arrived, Rogers likely initiated the conversation about "the rough, careless, ways of the young men and boys."[30] And that topic gave her an opportunity to present her idea to the women in the church who were most capable of enacting change and making her solution a reality. When Rogers's bishop later invited her to preside over an organization for children in Farmington, she readily agreed—she would since the organization was her idea.

Eliza R. Snow's part in the story also sheds light on women's agency during the period, and their choice to work in a cooperative spirit with men in the church. Snow would remember that working in a noncooperative spirit severely diminished women's ability to act. She witnessed firsthand in Nauvoo the disintegration of Relief Society in 1844 when Brigham Young closed down the organization, and did not reinstate it churchwide for over twenty years (1844–1867).[31] Snow did not only value cooperation out of a sense of fearful pragmatism, however. She and other Latter-day Saints believed that Zion should be built by men and women working together. When Snow saw merit in Rogers's idea, she took it to the First Presidency. When she was sure of their support, she wrote to Rogers's bishop, suggesting he call her to a position overseeing the new organization's local development. In another instance, Snow recommended a man, a Brother Perkins, to assist in establishing the Primary organization in the Salt Lake Sixteenth Ward.[32] Thus, Snow established the Primary organization by working in cooperation with men through official channels and protocols. By working through these institutional patterns, even as the patterns themselves were in the process of development, Snow's labors had substantial impact on the form of the church.

In Rogers's case, the Relief Society facilitated agency because it provided a pattern through which Rogers's idea could take shape as part of the official church institution. Relief Society also impacted women's agency because of all it asked women to do. Relief Society women sewed clothing and gathered supplies for the poor, collected and stored wheat, raised silkworms to make silk, farmed, opened and ran stores, taught one another, agitated against provoking political legislation, fought for suffrage, and pursued higher education.[33] Each of these activities required members to develop powerful expertise and to take action. Medical care was one striking example. Throughout the 1870s, church leaders, including Eliza R. Snow and Brigham Young, encouraged women to obtain medical training. Relief Societies raised funds to help women pay for this education. Some women who went to medical school in the East returned home both to attend patients and to train Relief Society members to be nurses and midwives.

Becoming doctors made women into prominent citizens and increased their sphere of influence; in addition to being known for their medical practice, they served on general church boards and wrote for local periodicals. Dr. Martha Hughes Cannon served as the first female state senator in the country. Leaders encouraged women to get this training, but women followed through according to their own discretion. Maggie Curtis Shipp enrolled in the Woman's Medical College in Philadelphia in October 1875, but she chose to return home after one month because of extreme homesickness. Her sister-wife, Ellis Reynolds Shipp, took Maggie's place in Philadelphia and attended medical school from 1875–1878. Ellis Shipp spent the summer before her last year of medical school in Utah. When they learned she was pregnant, her husband and sister-wives thought she would stay home, but Ellis chose to finish school and delivered her fifth child the day after her last exam. After Maggie Shipp's own children were older, she returned to medical school and earned her degree in 1883.[34] The expertise these women attained by responding to Relief Society requests allowed them to widen their sphere of influence and activity even further throughout the rest of their lives.

LDS women conceived of their liberty as providing them agency to act in, and to enlarge, what they called "woman's sphere." Words from a Relief Society presidency in small, rural Hyrum, Utah, illustrate their perspective well:

> Although the outside world may number us with the "poor, oppresse[d] women of Utah," we experience great pleasure in

> saying, we have lived in the States and in the old world, but prefer living in, and enjoying the glorious liberties of Utah and her "Mormon" institutions, and in seeking to fill woman's mission as wives, mothers and daughters, aiding suffering humanity wherever found.[35]

Like many other activists of the nineteenth-century women's movement, LDS women's vision of liberty was predominately the "freedom" to more fully accomplish traditional female roles.[36] However, general Relief Society president Eliza R. Snow's instructions suggested an even broader vision of "woman's sphere" when she taught: "We believe in eternal progression. It will not do to say that we have so much to do that we cannot do any more, because the works and duties for women in Zion are constantly increasing."[37]

Snow recognized that her enthusiastic assertions reflected an ideal instead of actual practice. She further explained: "Although we are not at present living up to all our privileges, and fulfilling all the duties that belong to our sex, the field is open before us, and we are urged to move forward as fast as we can develop and apply our own capabilities."[38] However, her teachings corresponded with earlier encouragement from Brigham Young for women to expand their sphere and engage in higher education, trades, and professions. Five years later, Snow's distant cousin, apostle Erastus Snow, also spoke of expansive destinies:

> We have come to the understanding that every soul of man, both male and female, high and low, is the offspring of God, that their spirits are immortal, eternal, intelligent beings, and that their entity depends upon their agency and independent action, which is neither trammelled by God himself nor allowed to be restrained by any of His creatures with His sanction and approval; that the whole theory of God's rule and government in heaven and on earth is founded upon this principle of agency—self, independent action.[39]

His notion that "their entity depends upon their agency" suggests that according to Latter-day Saint thought, men and women would cease to exist without agency.

Agency never exists independent of hierarchical and social negotiations. But despite these shaping influences, agency almost always exists on some level. In other words, the presence of cultural limitations does not negate the presence of agency. Some scholars have reacted to the work of modern feminist LDS historians (specifically during the 1970s and 80s) as overly positive about the ways polygamy itself functioned to increase women's liberty—sharing responsibilities with sister-wives, for instance—and freed women to pursue higher education and participate in civic causes.[40] Perhaps some portrayals of polygamy were overly optimistic. Nevertheless, scholars still too often have blind spots when it comes to the fact that insiders often see liberty in traditions that outsiders may view as oppressive.

Indeed, many LDS women in the 1870s recognized that they enjoyed certain privileges and saw their membership in the church as the key to their emancipation from the limitations imposed on them by a fallen world. The *Woman's Exponent*, a powerful example in itself of Mormon women's capacity to both think and act for themselves, argued that "Mormon women will lead the van in the questions which are being agitated among the sex, whatever the world may think to the contrary."[41] Utah offered many progressive rights enjoyed by few other women at that time, including women's suffrage, property rights for married women, and opportunities for women to engage in higher learning, professional activities, and leadership roles in both civic and religious organizations.[42] LDS women also found more space to act as direct results of the doctrine of personal revelation, the exercise of spiritual gifts, and participation in Relief Society. No wonder Susa Young Gates declared in 1879, "My sphere of usefulness is being enlarged."[43]

Notes

1. Aurelia Spencer Rogers, "History of Primary Work," *Life Sketches of Orson Spencer and Others, and History of Primary Work* (Salt Lake City: George Q. Cannon and Sons, 1898), 205–8, reprinted in Jill Mulvay Derr et al., eds., *The First Fifty Years of Relief Society: Key Documents in Latter-day Saint Women's History* (Salt Lake City: Church Historian's Press, 2016), 431–32.
2. Ibid.
3. Eliza R. Snow to Aurelia Spencer Rogers, August 4, 1878, in Rogers, "History of Primary Work," 209; see also Derr, *The First Fifty Years of Relief Society*, 433.
4. Catherine A. Brekus, "Mormon Women and the Problem of Historical Agency," *Journal of Mormon History* 37, vol. 3 (Summer 2011): 59.

5. *Oxford English Dictionary Online*, s.v. "agency," accessed December 18, 2014, www.oed.com.
6. Moroni 10:4–5; Joseph Smith frequently taught this principal, explaining, "It is the privilige of the children of God to come to God and get Revelation . . . God is not a respecter of persons. We all have the same privilige." Joseph Smith Discourse, ca. July 1839, in Willard Richards, Pocket Companion, 75, 78–79, Church History Library, Salt Lake City, Utah.
7. Rogers, "History of Primary Work," 207; see also Derr, *The First Fifty Years of Relief Society*, 431.
8. For additional discussion regarding the "cult of domesticity" and "separate spheres ideology" prevalent in the nineteenth century, see Robyn Ryle, *Questioning Gender: A Sociological Exploration* (Thousand Oaks, CA: SAGE/Pine Forge Press, 2012), 342–43.
9. Joel Perlmann and Robert A. Margo, *Women's Work?: American Schoolteachers, 1650–1920* (Chicago: University of Chicago Press, 2001), 90 (citing the annual reports of the United States Bureau of Education, founded in 1867, which noted the gender of teachers in each state, beginning in 1870). "[W]omen accounted for four out of five public school teachers in every region of the country except the South by 1910." Ibid., 91. See also William J. Reese, *America's Public Schools: From the Common School to "No Child Left Behind"* (Baltimore: Johns Hopkins University Press, 2005), 61.
10. Mary R. Clark and Patricia Lyn Scott, "From Schoolmarm to State Superintendent: The Changing Role of Women in Education, 1847–2004," in *Women in Utah History: Paradigm or Paradox?*, edited by Patricia Lyn Scott and Linda Thatcher (Logan: Utah State University Press, 2005), 228. In 1870, 45 percent of Utah teachers were female, compared to 60 percent of teachers nationwide. By the turn of the century, women teachers in Utah had increased to almost 64 percent but the state still had a significantly higher proportion of men teachers than the national statistics. See also Perlmann and Margo, *Women's Work?*, 91 (analyzing regional trends of feminization in school teaching and noting that Utah lagged behind even other Western states after the turn of the century due to its unique Mormon subculture). President Brigham Young acknowledged the need to hire more women teachers in Utah in 1869, indicating that these ratios did not reflect official church policy: "We have sisters here, who, if they had the privilege of studying, would make just as good mathematicians or accountants, as any man; and we think they ought to have the privilege to study . . . We have as good teachers as can be found on the face of the earth, if our bishops would only employ and pay them, but they will not." Brigham Young, July 18, 1869, *Journal of Discourses*, 13:60–61, quoted in Clark and Scott, "From Schoolmarm to State Superintendent," 128.
11. Reese, *America's Public Schools*, 44.
12. Ibid., 47.
13. Catharine E. Beecher, *Woman's Profession as Mother and Educator: With Views in Opposition to Woman Suffrage* (New York: Maclean, Gibson, 1872), 175.

14. A study of nineteenth-century female teachers in Wyoming explained that "compared to such alternatives as nursing, seamstressing, and domestic service, teaching conferred greater status and independence than many young women had known before." Charles E. Rankin, "Teaching: Opportunity and Limitation for Wyoming Women," *The Western Historical Quarterly* 21, vol. 2 (1990): 150.
15. Rogers, "History of Primary Work," 207; see also Derr, *The First Fifty Years of Relief Society*, 431. The Young Men's Mutual Improvement Association (now known as "Young Men") was organized in 1875, and continues to serve as the church's official organization for young men ages twelve through eighteen.
16. Rogers, "History of Primary Work," 212.
17. See Samuel Bowles description of Mormon women as downtrodden and enslaved, Samuel Bowles, *Across the Continent: A Summer's Journey to the Rocky Mountains, the Mormons, and the Pacific States, with Speaker Colfax* (Springfield, MA: Samuel Bowles, n.d.; New York: Hurd and Houghton, 1865), 107. See also John Cradlebaugh, "Utah and the Mormons," in *Appendix to the Congressional Globe: Containing Speeches, Important State Papers, and the Laws of the Third Session, Thirty-Seventh Congress*, edited by John C. Rives (Washington D.C.: Congressional Globe, 1863), 119–25; Horace Greeley, "An Overland Journey. Two Hours with Brigham Young," *New York Daily Tribune*, August 20, 1859. See also Catherine Brekus, chapter 1 in this volume.
18. James Taylor, "An Address. By Miss Eliza R. Snow. Delivered in the Tabernacle, Ogden, at a Relief Society Meeting, Thursday Afternoon, August 14th, 1873," *Woman's Exponent* 2, no. 8 (September 15, 1873): 62; see Derr, *The First Fifty Years of Relief Society*, 382–83.
19. Zina D. H. Young, Tenth Ward Relief Society Minutes, January 22, 1874, Church History Library.
20. On the Cullum Bill, see Sarah Barringer Gordon, *The Mormon Question: Polygamy and Constitutional Conflict in Nineteenth-Century America* (Chapel Hill: University of North Carolina Press, 2002), 273.
21. "Minutes of a Ladies Mass Meeting," January 6, 1870, Relief Society Minutes and Records, vol. 1, 1868–1873, Fifteenth Ward, Salt Lake Stake, Church History Library; see also Derr, *The First Fifty Years of Relief Society*, 307.
22. Eliza R. Snow, "Minutes," Salt Lake City, Utah, January 12, 1870; *Deseret Evening News*, January 14 and 15, 1870; "Proceedings in Mass Meeting of the Ladies of Salt Lake City, to Protest against the Passage of Cullom's Bill," pamphlet, January 14, 1870 (Salt Lake City: 1870); see also Derr, *The First Fifty Years of Relief Society*, 323–24.
23. "Minutes of the 2nd Meeting of the Ladies Co-operative Retrenchment Society," February 19, 1870, Relief Society Minutes and Records, vol. 1, 1868–1873, Fifteenth Ward, Salt Lake [Riverside] Stake, Church History Library; see also Derr, *The First Fifty Years of Relief Society*, 346–47.
24. Mary Ann Freeze, Diary, June 14, 1875, Church History Library, quoted in Jonathan A. Stapley and Kristine Wright, "Female Ritual Healing in Mormonism," *Journal of Mormon History* 37, no. 1 (Winter 2011): 14.

25. Louisa Lula Greene Richards, Journal, June 9, 1878, 2–7, Church History Library, quoted in Stapley and Wright, "Female Ritual Healing in Mormonism," 15.
26. Zina D. H. Young, "R. S. Reports," *Woman's Exponent* 7, no. 7 (September 1, 1878): 50.
27. Joseph Smith, Nauvoo Relief Society Minutes, April 28, 1842, 36, 41, Church History Library; see also Derr, *The First Fifty Years of Relief Society*, 55, 59.
28. Eliza R. Snow, "To the Branches of the Relief Society," *Woman's Exponent* 13, no. 8 (September 15, 1884): 61. For similar statements by church leaders just prior to the 1870s regarding women's ability to administer to the sick, see Brigham Young, "Building Up Zion—Temperance in Eating and Drinking, Discourse by Brigham Young, Delivered in the Tabernacle, Salt Lake City, November 14, 1869," reported by John Grimshaw, *Journal of Discourses* (Liverpool: Albert Carrington, 1869), 13:155 ("It is the privilege of a mother to have faith and to administer to her child; this she can do herself, as well as sending for the Elders"); see also Ezra T. Benson, Cache Valley Stake Relief Society Minutes 1868–1881, June 18, 1868, 14, Church History Library (teaching that "the sisters who had been ordained had the power to rebuke diseases and that we could all have the same power if we would exercise faith").
29. "Women's Organizations," *Woman's Exponent* 8, no. 16 (January 15, 1880): 122; see Derr, *The First Fifty Years of Relief Society*, 447–48. See also Sarah M. Kimball, *Woman Suffrage Leaflet* (Salt Lake City: January 1892), 3 ("[T]he sure foundations of the suffrage cause were deeply and permanently laid on the 17th of March, 1842").
30. Rogers, "History of Primary Work," 208; see also Derr, *The First Fifty Years of Relief Society*, 432.
31. Derr, *The First Fifty Years of Relief Society*, 168–71.
32. Snow to Rogers, "History of Primary Work," 210–11; see also Derr, *The First Fifty Years of Relief Society*, 433–34.
33. Jill Mulvay Derr, Janath Russell Cannon, and Maureen Ursenbach Beecher, *Women of Covenant: The Story of Relief Society* (Salt Lake City: Deseret Book, 1992).
34. Claudia L. Bushman, ed., *Mormon Sisters: Women in Early Utah* (Logan, UT: Utah State University Press, 1997), 60–61; Vicky-Burgess-Olson, *Sister Saints* (Provo, UT: Brigham Young University Press, 1978), 369–70.
35. Christina Liljenquist, Martha Ward, and Lucy Wilson, "F. R. Society Reports," *Woman's Exponent* 1, no. 11 (November 1, 1872): 82.
36. For discussion of the "ideology of 'woman's place," see Anne Firor Scott and Andrew MacKay Scott, *One Half the People: The Fight for Woman Suffrage* (University of Illinois Press: Urbana and Chicago, 1982), 17.
37. James Taylor, "An Address. By Miss Eliza R. Snow. Delivered in the Tabernacle, Ogden, at a Relief Society Meeting, Thursday Afternoon, August 14th, 1873," *Woman's Exponent* 2, no. 8 (September 15, 1873): 62–63; see Derr, *The First Fifty Years of Relief Society*, 382.

38. Eliza R. Snow, "Latter-day Saint Ladies of Utah," *Deseret News Weekly*, July 26, 1871; see Derr, *The First Fifty Years of Relief Society*, 369.
39. Erastus Snow, "Discourse by Apostle Erastus Snow. Delivered in the Tabernacle, Salt Lake City, Friday Afternoon, (Annual Conference), April 6, 1883," reported by Gibbs and Irvine, *Journal of Discourses* (Liverpool: Albert Carrington, 1869), 24:69, quoted in Carol Cornwall Madsen, *An Advocate for Women: The Public Life of Emmeline B. Wells, 1870–1920* (Provo, UT: Brigham Young University Press, 2006), 80–81.
40. See Catherine Brekus, chapter 1 in this volume.
41. "Home Affairs," *Woman's Exponent* 6, no. 1 (June 1, 1877): 4. The *Woman's Exponent* provided a forum for Latter-day Saint women to express their views on a wide variety of political, religious, social, and cultural topics, and served as a platform for women of the church to represent themselves to the women's movement and the world. Upon the creation of the *Woman's Exponent*, the *Salt Lake Herald* announcement proclaimed, "The women of Utah are today unquestionably more the subject of comment than those of any other portion of the country, or indeed of the world. As they have long exercised the right to think and act for themselves, so they now claim the right to speak for themselves through the potent medium of the types." "The New Woman's Journal," *Salt Lake Herald*, April 10, 1872, 3.
42. The Utah Territorial Legislature passed a progressive Married Person's Property Act in 1872 that protected a married woman's right to property that she had owned prior to the marriage. See Lisa Madsen Pearson and Carol Cornwall Madsen, "Innovation and Accommodation: The Legal Status of Women in Territorial Utah, 1850–1896," in Scott and Thatcher, *Women in Utah History*, 48–49.
43. Susa Young Gates to Lucy Bigelow Young, April 18, 1879, quoted in Derr, Cannon, and Beecher, *Women of Covenant*, 108.

11

"The Best Social Practice"

Mormon Women and the Professionalization of Reform

MATTHEW BOWMAN

In January 1920, two women stood before the desk of Heber J. Grant, the president of the Church of Jesus Christ of Latter-day Saints. The younger, forty-seven-year-old Amy Brown Lyman, had come to defend her slow reformation of the social service efforts of the church that brought Mormon efforts increasingly in line with the rapidly professionalizing world of American social work. In the last weeks of his presidency, which ended in November 1918, Joseph F. Smith had initiated creation of a new church Social Service Department, and Lyman, appointed to head it by Grant, proved a remarkably vigorous leader. She quickly hired multiple workers and began systematically training Mormons in congregations in Salt Lake City in the methods of modern social work, learned from such august institutions as the University of Chicago and the national Charity Organization Society.

The older woman, sixty-three-year-old Susa Young Gates, feared Lyman's reforms were damaging to what she believed made the church's organizational efforts vital and distinctive: a particular spiritual commitment that fueled a devout amateurism, an ethos that had guided Mormonism since its birth. In the wake of Lyman's reforms, it seemed as though Gates was attempting to staunch a tidal wave—and yet, she was determined to try.[1]

The dispute between the women was certainly in part about Mormonism itself, reflective of the growing pains the church struggled with as it tried to adjust from the theocratic, polygamous communalism of

FIGURE 11.1. Amy Brown Lyman in the early 1920s, soon after meeting with Susa Young Gates and Heber J. Grant. Public Domain.

the nineteenth century to full participation in twentieth-century American democratic capitalism. But, at the same time, their confrontation revealed that Mormon women were already participating in a transition that was sparking growing pains nationwide. David Hall has observed that Lyman's methods reflected the most cutting-edge social work techniques of the age, and Gates understood herself not merely to be protecting the techniques she was familiar with, but an entire worldview.[2]

For much of the nineteenth century, American women had invoked the particular qualities of femininity as they entered the sphere of politics, social reform, and public activism. Americans—even these women—often assumed that women were naturally more nurturing and spiritual, more concerned for children, orphans, and the otherwise abandoned. Hence, they were specially equipped to ease pain and teach the foundational virtues underlying American democracy. Under the aegis of phrases like "social housekeeping," many nineteenth-century women entered the public square to pursue social welfare and political reform, blurring the difference between political advocacy and moral transformation.[3]

Many of these reform efforts were explicitly predicated upon the supposed natural virtues of women, and often defined themselves against the dry bureaucratic professionalism of the presumably male-dominated public sphere. The "deaconess" movement of the late nineteenth and early twentieth century was a case in point. Inspired by fleeting New Testament references to female officers in the church, many Protestant denominations in Europe and the United States founded "deaconess" orders, whose women were roughly comparable to Catholic nuns. In the United States, deaconesses' feminine authority was seen as a solution to the challenge of the rapidly urbanizing, immigrant-filled American city.[4] The great revivalist Dwight Moody reportedly said, "Give me women! . . . The only hope and possibility of elevating and saving this class of the population in our great cities lies in the unselfish and devoted activity of such women."[5] Isabelle Horton, a Methodist deaconess leader, argued that deaconesses' feminine power allowed them to appeal to immigrant Catholic communities. "The Catholic Church does not fear the Methodist Church, nor the Presbyterian Church, nor the Mennonite Church," Horton said. "But it does fear these women in little bonnets with white strings who are followed in the street by the children and who go into the homes and win the hearts of the mothers."[6]

Horton and other evangelicals who supported the deaconess movement believed that the moral authority of their gender and class uniquely equipped them to effect reform in the city. The New York Baptist Leighton Williams, who ordained deaconesses in his Amity Baptist Church, claimed that, "The work of women in the church in our day is recognized far more than it has been in earlier days . . . Much of the weakness of our churches today is doubtless attributable to a failure to discern and utilize their gifts of the spirit."[7] Horton said that the maternal gifts of women meant that the deaconess "becomes herself a sort of peripatetic settlement," serving all the needs of the poor because of the holistic nature of her gifts.[8]

Horton, and other deaconesses, followed Gates in emphasizing that their authority did not derive from formal training, but from moral authority. They stood midway between Catholic nuns and the well-trained progressive reformer; as good middle-class Protestant Americans, they insisted their authority should be derived both from their gender and their faith. Deaconesses took vows and wore uniforms and lived apart like nuns, but they also were supposed to embody the maternal, cultured, and civilized Protestant woman. One advocate for the deaconess movement wrote, "The Sisterhood affords a sphere for refined, educated women who with their superior privileges and wider outlook can accomplish work."[9]

Thus, the deaconess's ability to serve was not drawn from any training they held, though deaconesses did receive some education. The Chicago Training School Horton attended was the most famous of the deaconess schools, but Leighton Williams and several other Protestant leaders opened schools in New York as well.[10] But these schools focused on traditional topics for Protestant missionaries: theology, evangelism, and the Bible, with only a few rudimentary skills like nursing, cooking, and sewing added on.[11] According to Isabelle Horton, the deaconess brought "the skilled touch of the nurse and the loving heart of Christian womanhood to the service of the neediest."[12]

By the early twentieth century, the deaconess movement—like many other female-led reform efforts—was facing a changing world. Older arguments about the spiritual authority of Protestant womanhood began to seem nebulous as the progressive era's fascination with expertise, training, and professionalism began to take hold. In New York City in 1926, Sophia Fahs, recently appointed principal of the Union School of Religion—an experimental Sunday school affiliated with Union Seminary—complained about what she deemed "amateur" workers who had directed most church work to date, and insisted that the teachers at the Union School receive training from the Seminary or Columbia Teachers' College.[13] Fahs's emphasis on professionalism had seeped into other fields as well. Social work, for instance, had long been particularly dominated by female activists. Its earliest advocates, like Mary Richmond, proudly defended a "holistic" vision of social improvement that sought not merely to relieve poverty or correct institutional ills, but also to pursue moral reform, regenerate the ethical capacities of the poor who required aid, and ultimately guide them toward Victorian respectability. Richmond is often credited as a founder of the discipline of social work. For nearly forty years she worked with the Charity Organization Society in New York, helping to develop the "case work" method, in which "friendly visitors"—ideally, trained, respectable women capable of providing an example as much as information—knocked on the door of those in need, and more than merely providing relief, guided them toward greater responsibility, improved behavior, and deepened virtue.[14]

However, Richmond's commitment to the personal cultivation of morality, like the enthusiastic devotion of the deaconesses, drew increasing criticism as the twentieth century proceeded. As early as the 1890s, Jane Addams worried that COS's methods were scolding and exhibited overconfidence that individual moral improvement could heal systemic and institutional problems of poverty and negative moral environments.[15] In 1922, Richmond published *What Is Social Case Work?* The book opened with an argument that the ability to be a good case worker was as much gift as training, and invoked Anne Sullivan's mixture of "true instinct," "sympathy" and ability to improvise with Helen Keller's lived environment as the critical factors in her success.[16] The same year, in a deeply symbolic event, Richmond lost an election for the presidency of the National Conference of Social Work.[17]

Richmond lost, in part, because social work itself was changing in gendered ways. In 1912, activists who bore a resemblance to Fahs persuaded the federal government to create the U.S. Children's Bureau, and direct it to investigate and provide aid for the welfare of American children. It did so in areas ranging from child labor to pensions for poor single mothers. And yet, as the Bureau began to implement its work, it became clear that there was a division among its supporters, the very women who had lobbied for the creation of the Bureau in the first place. Increasingly, well educated women less sympathetic to Richmond's Victorian ideals came to dominate the ranks of female reformers—and, ironically, institutions like the Children's Bureau came to be dominated by educated men trained in the social sciences.[18]

It is important that these distinctions not be taken too far, or too simply: Mary Richmond was as committed to social reform as was the

Children's Bureau or Jane Addams. All would have called themselves "progressives," interested in political and social change. More, Richmond's *What Is Social Case Work?* was indeed a training manual; she believed that training and education were necessary. However, like the deaconesses—or, like Susa Young Gates—Richmond feared that too much professionalism, too much bureaucracy, too much instruction would lead to jargon, exclusion, and sapping the soul of both the cared for and the caregiver. The fundamentally Protestant background of many of these women convinced them that moral cultivation lay at the foundation of all such work, and they feared that too much education would render it ineffective.

In 1902, while traveling across the country with her husband en route to his education at Cornell University, Amy Brown Lyman met Jane Addams in Chicago, and studied the case work method with her. In 1916, while serving as general secretary of the women's Relief Society, Lyman joined the Salt Lake City branch of the Charity Organization Society, which Richmond still dominated, and began to introduce the case work method to various Latter-day Saint organizations.[19] That she moved so easily between Addams and Richmond's influence indicates that the dispute between the two was not as philosophically rigorous in practice as it seems in retrospect; nonetheless, Lyman steadily moved toward professionalization. In 1918, President Joseph F. Smith asked Lyman to organize a Social Service Department in order to coordinate the various efforts of the church; several months later, after Smith's death, his successor, Heber J. Grant, affirmed the request. Several times between 1917 and her 1920 confrontation with Gates, Lyman traveled to Denver to receive training in social work methods: during World War I, the Red Cross hosted a meeting in the city for representatives throughout the West in order to coordinate war relief.

Denver was important not merely for its convenient location. After 1912, when the reformer Gertrude Vaile took a seat on the city's Commission of Charity and Corrections, the city's welfare program was massively overhauled and eventually placed under the control of a Bureau of Charities, which Vaile ran until she joined the Red Cross in 1917. Vaile had studied in Chicago with Jane Addams and had worked with Mary Richmond at the Russell Sage Foundation in New York City. She had embraced the case work method, but fused to it an emphasis on professionalization and strong, efficient bureaucracy. The new recordkeeping and case management procedures Vaile implemented required the sort of training that she insisted upon: Vaile hired only college graduates who intended upon social work as a profession, rejecting political appointees and using volunteers only under supervision.[20]

This is the system Amy Brown Lyman encountered when she traveled to Denver to study social work. Subsequently, as Lyman proved particularly effective at administration, the Relief Society Social Service Department became the clearinghouse for nearly all the work of the church, and more community agencies were turning to Lyman for aid and direction. During World War I, Lyman's department facilitated relief efforts for families struck by the global influenza epidemic in Utah, coordinated delivery of relief to European war zones, monitored pensions for widows, helped to erect milk kitchens for orphans and single mothers in Salt Lake City, and apparently took over administering the welfare needs of at least one LDS stake.[21] As her office took on heavier duties, Lyman herself insisted on ever-increasing levels of professionalism, what she called "the best social practice."[22] The Social Service Department began hiring full-time employees beyond Lyman and her initial single assistant, and Lyman grew convinced that it was necessary for her workers to have the same training she had received. She sent several to Denver, and in the spring of 1919 began organizing training sessions in Salt Lake City.[23]

Joseph F. Smith and Heber J. Grant had vigorously supported Lyman's efforts, believing that the church would benefit from improved administration. Indeed, both men—Grant particularly—were of the progressive era, believers in rationalized discipline, education, and organization. But Mormonism had thrived precisely because Mormons believed their church was distinct from all other human ventures. Though in many ways Mormonism mirrored the evolution of other churches of the era in its gradual embrace of auxiliary institutions and social programs, Mormons still preferred to think of themselves as set apart and distinct. Thus, both Smith and Grant were sensitive to such internal criticism as Grant heard from Relief Society leader Annie Wells Cannon in 1928—that Lyman's reorganization of the Relief Society meant that "the spirit of the gospel and religion seem to have disappeared, and it seems to be a social welfare organization."[24]

Susa Young Gates felt similarly, and her complaints illustrate that the gulf between her and Lyman mirrored the wrenching changes occurring nationwide. It is important not to make too much of the differences between the two women. Like Lyman, Gates believed that the women's organizations of the church had an important role to play in the betterment of society. "No one will deny that the women of the church have been magnificently disciplined by their various organizations," she declared happily. "There is much to encourage the sociologist in the steady improvement and progress of the women of the church." More, she believed that the progressive era offered a unique opportunity, claiming that "the present age is the admitted women's age," that demands "as many progressive, intelligent, and capable women as can be found among the Latter day Saints." Thus, she said, the aim of her organization was the "shaping of strong, self-reliant, and original characters," that were best formed through participation in Mormonism itself.[25] Like Lyman, Gates acknowledged, gratefully, the guidance she received from national women's organizations, citing in particular her experience at the 1893 World's Congress of Representative Women, where she met May Sewell—a feminist and pioneer in women's education—whom Gates consulted with on both the Young Women's organization and female political activism.[26]

And yet, Gates was more like the deaconesses or Mary Richmond than she was a Sophie Fahs, or an Amy Brown Lyman. Like Annie Wells Cannon and innumerable female activists before her, Gates certainly absorbed the ethos and mood of Progressivism, but remained skeptical of its cult of expertise, training, and bureaucracy. Rather, Gates was a child of nineteenth-century Mormonism's kinship-based community, and was consistently suspicious of attempts to modernize, professionalize, or train Mormons to do anything. For Gates, the power of the Mormon community lay in its relational bonds. She believed in the Relief Society as a natural outgrowth of the congregation, and that each Mormon community possessed within itself the resources and knowledge necessary to draw its members closer to their divine inheritance. This had been characteristic of the Relief Society ever since Emma Smith rejected the name "Benevolent Society" at the first meeting of the organization because, as she said, the sisters of the Society "do not wish to have it call'd after other Societies of the world."[27] Nearly a century later Emmeline B. Wells echoed the sentiment to Lyman herself, writing that "Relief

Society work . . . unites us in a fellowship grander and holier than the highest educational organizations."[28]

As with Smith, for Gates the strength of the Relief Society was in its presumed difference: the near-universal participation it attracted from Mormon women, and the spiritual force their religious commitments gave them. She worried that professionalization would weaken Mormonism's unique spiritual power. As she said, "Most of the Protestant sects, as well as all the nonreligious persons who are generous minded—and what American is not?—are glad to join forces and turn over to C.O.S. officials" their money and organizational capacities. However, the Mormons were different. Charity for them was not merely about organizational experience and issues of efficiency. She pled with the Relief Society general board, soon after Lyman began sending Mormons to Denver, "Let us not make fundamental changes nor alter the perfect and wise adjustment of our religious organization to match the world's spectacular methods." Here she invoked a version of Mormon restorationism: their church, Mormons believed, was not a mere human approximation or attempt to match God's will—rather, its structure was divinely inspired; as she phrased it, "the most perfect social and religious machinery known to mortal man."[29]

This meant that Mormon charity work was not simply charity work; its success did not derive from expertise or efficiency. Indeed, Mormon charity work was a religious, not a procedural act. As Gates claimed, it was "neighborly," done in compassion and personal warmth. The Mormons, she sighed with relief, "have not commercialized their charity." She warned that the indexing, training, and institutionalizing of charity that Lyman advocated would destroy the divinely inspired, spiritual nature of Mormon charity work. "If it is harmful for charity to be given by paid institutions and organizations," she warned, "it is quite as harmful to the paid agent." She looked into the future and saw a Mormon Relief Society dominated by paid, trained agents, all of whom lacked what she called the "moral spirit" that volunteer work cultivated, and were afflicted instead by "the commercial spirit [that] soon or late dominates the transaction." The human, personal, spiritual element would soon depart, and that which made Mormonism's charity unique would be lost. "If you pay a woman to do case work," Gates asked, "how can you refuse to pay our poor sisters who do the neighborhood visiting? And on and on." Far better to keep Mormon charity work amateur, and to preserve its distinctiveness.[30]

Perhaps Gates knew that in her protest she echoed Mary Richmond's own pleas. In 1922, at almost exactly the same time Gates voiced her pleas, Richmond wrote "relief in and of itself has no moral qualities, and least of all is it capable of achieving the quality of democracy."[31] She meant by this that relief simply given with no care for the moral health of the giver or the recipient, did nothing to cultivate self-sufficiency in the receiver, nor truly moral compassion in the giver. Amateur, rather than professional, case work would solve this problem by making the two partners in the social uplift of the needy. Gates feared the same. Professionalized social work would undermine those moral qualities that made the Relief Society the agent of divine care that it was. Nonetheless, though some slight alterations in Lyman's plan were made because of Gates's protests (it was ensured, for instance, that no agencies outside the church would administer church welfare), Lyman's vision of bureaucracy and training won out, and Gates soon resigned her position in the Relief Society. It may seem that the church today relies far more on Gates's vision of a lay sisterhood than on Lyman's, but the spirit of organization, procedure, and centralization that Lyman advocated remains that of LDS Church welfare today.

Notes

1. For Lyman's efforts, see David Hall, "Anxiously Engaged: Amy Brown Lyman and Relief Society Charity Work, 1917–1945," *Dialogue* 27, no. 3 (Summer 1994): 80–81. For an overview of the specific practices that distressed Gates, see Hall, "From Home Service to Social Service: Amy Brown Lyman and the Development of Social Work in the LDS Church," *Mormon Historical Studies* 9, no. 2 (Fall 2008): 67–88.
2. See Hall, "From Home Service to Social Service," 84–88.
3. On the politics of social housekeeping see Elizabeth Perry, "Men are from the Gilded Age, Women are from the Progressive Era," *Journal of the Society of the Gilded Age and Progressive Era* 1, no. 1 (January 2002): 25–45; Kathryn Kish Sklar, *Florence Kelley and the Nation's Work* (New Haven: Yale University Press, 1995); Theda Skocpol, *Protecting Soldiers and Mothers: The Politics of Social Provision in the United States, 1870s–1920s* (Cambridge: Harvard University Press, 1992); and Patricia R. Hill, *The World Their Household: The American Women's Foreign Mission Movement and Cultural Transformation, 1870–1920* (Ann Arbor: University of Michigan Press, 1985).

4. Christian Gelder, *History of the Deaconess Movement in the Christian Church* (New York: Jennings and Pye, 1903) is the most comprehensive history of the deaconess movement. See also *The American Deaconess Movement in the Early Twentieth Century,* edited by Carolyn De Swarte Gifford (New York: Garland Publishing, 1988); Susan Hill Lindley, *You Have Stept Out of Your Place: A History of Women and Religion in America* (Louisville: WJK, 1996), 127–34; and Dana Robert, *American Women in Mission: A Social History of Their Thought and Practice* (Macon: Mercer University Press, 1997), 154–59. Mary Agnes Daugherty, "The Social Gospel According to Phoebe: Methodist Deaconesses in the Metropolis, 1885–1918," and Virginia Brereton, "Preparing Women for the Lord's Work," in *Women in New Worlds: Historical Perspectives on the Wesleyan Tradition,* edited by Hilah Thomas and Rosemary Skinner Keller (Nashville: Abington, 1981), 178–219, date the evangelical deaconess movement to the founding of the Chicago Training School founded by Lucy Rider Meyer. This section draws on Matthew Bowman, *The Urban Pulpit: New York City and the Fate of Liberal Evangelicalism* (New York: Oxford University Press, 2014), 134–40.
5. Gelder, *History of the Deaconess Movement,* 488.
6. Isabelle Horton, *Home Mission Study Course: The Burden of the City* (New York: Revell, 1904), 144.
7. Leighton Williams, "The Deaconess: Her Calling, Her Work, Her Support," in Leighton Williams Papers, box 1, Baptist Deaconess Society folder, American Baptist Historical Society, Mercer University, Macon, Georgia.
8. Horton, *Home Mission Study Course,* 144, 129–30.
9. Horton, *Home Mission Study Course,* 130; Gelder, *History of the Deaconess Movement,* 193.
10. "The Ministry of Women in the Episcopal Church," *Outlook* 57, no. 7 (October 16, 1897): 442–43.
11. Leighton Williams, "Baptist Deaconess Home," Leighton Williams Papers. Grace Episcopal's curriculum is discussed in "Ministry of Women," 443. See also Brereton, "Preparing Women for the Lord's Work," 184–90.
12. Horton, *Home Mission Study Course,* 128.
13. Cited in Susan Harlow, "Sophia Lyon Fahs: Religious Modernist and Progressive Educator," in *Faith of our Foremothers: Women Changing Religious Education,* edited by Barbara Keely (Louisville: Westminster/John Knox Press, 1997), 18–19. On Fahs's theology see L. A. Nolon, "Seeing What Is Not There Yet: Sophia Lyon Fahs, Entelechy, and the Religious Education Association," *Religious Education* 99, no. 3 (Summer 2004): 247–72, which argues that by the 1920s, Fahs's language had little overt metaphysical or religious content. On professionalization see Ann Taves, "Feminization Revisited: Protestantism and Gender at the Turn of the Century," in *Women and Twentieth-Century Protestantism,* edited by Margaret Lamberts Bendroth and Virginia Lieson Brereton (Urbana: University of Illinois Press, 2002), 304–24; and Margaret

Lamberts Bendroth, *Growing Up Protestant: Parents, Children and Mainline Churches* (Rutgers: Rutgers University Press, 2002), 71–73.

14. On Richmond see Elizabeth Agnew, *From Charity to Social Work: Mary Richmond and the Creation of an American Profession* (Urbana: University of Illinois, 2004); and Julia Rauch, "Women in Social Work: Friendly Visitors in Philadelphia, 1880," *Social Service Review* 49, no. 2 (June 1975): 241–459.
15. See, for instance, Jane Addams, *Twenty Years at Hull-House* (New York: Macmillan, 1911), 169–75; Jane Addams, "The Subtle Problems of Charity," *Atlantic* 84 (February 1, 1899): 166–73.
16. Mary Richmond, *What Is Social Case Work?: An Introductory Description* (New York: Russell Sage Foundation, 1922), 22–23.
17. Agnew, *From Charity to Social Work*, 168–88.
18. For accounts of the Children's Bureau and the tensions it created, see Robyn Muncy, *Creating a Female Dominion in American Reform, 1890–1935* (New York: Oxford, 1991); Regina Kunzel, *Fallen Women, Problem Girls: Unmarried Mothers and the Professionalization of Social Work* (New York: Oxford University Press, 1995); and Molly Ladd-Taylor *Mother-Work: Women, Child Welfare, and the State* (Cambridge: Harvard, 1994). Muncy and Ladd-Taylor divide up differently the various groups who struggled for control of the Children's Bureau, but describe the tension between committed technocratic professionals and what Ladd-Taylor calls "maternalists," who subscribed to the home-centered Victorianism of Mary Richmond. Kunzel explores the tensions that developed between evangelical reformers and professional social workers over the best way to combat out-of-wedlock births and aid women who became unwed mothers.
19. Thomas G. Alexander, "Between Revivalism and the Social Gospel: the Latter-day Saint Social Advisory Committee, 1916–1922," *BYU Studies* 23, no. 1 (Winter 1983): 26–27; David Hall, "Anxiously Engaged," 78–79.
20. Thomas Krainz, *Delivering Aid: Implementing Progressive Era Welfare Reform in the American West* (Albuquerque: University of New Mexico Press, 2005), 75–82; Gertrude Vaile, "Public Administration of Charity in Denver," *Proceedings of the National Conference of Charities and Corrections* (Chicago: Hildmann Printing Company, 1916), 412–19.
21. Amy Brown Lyman, "Social Service Work in the Relief Society, 1917–1928," Amy Brown Lyman Collection, 6–8, Special Collections, Harold B. Lee Library, Brigham Young University; Janath Russell Cannon and Jill Mulvey Derr, "Resolving Differences/Achieving Unity: Lessons from the History of the Relief Society," in *As Women of Faith*, edited by Mary E. Stovall and Carol Cornwall Madsen (Salt Lake City: Deseret Book, 1989), 122–47.
22. Lyman "Social Service Work," 3.
23. Hall, "Anxiously Engaged," 80–81; Lyman, "Social Service Work," 6.
24. Heber J. Grant diary, February 24 and 27, 1928, cited in Alexander "Between Revivalism and the Social Gospel," 37.

25. Susa Young Gates, *History of the Young Ladies Mutual Improvement Association* (Salt Lake City: Deseret News, 1911), 36, 49, 58.
26. Paul Peterson, "Modern Lysistratas: Mormon Women in the International Peace Movement, 1899–1939," *Journal of Mormon History* 15, no. 1 (1989): 59–89.
27. Relief Society Minute Book, March 17, 1842, 8, Church History Library, Salt Lake City, Utah.
28. Emmeline B. Wells to Amy Brown Lyman, October 6, 1909, Amy Brown Lyman Papers, L. Tom Perry Special Collections, Brigham Young University. Cannon and Derr, "Resolving Differences," 127–32.
29. Susa Young Gates Papers, Relief Society File, Church History Library.
30. Ibid.
31. Richmond, *What Is Social Case Work?*, 172.

III

CONTEMPORARY SOCIAL SCIENCE PERSPECTIVES

12

LDS Women's Attitudes toward the Church

Satisfied with the Status Quo or Restless for Reform?

DAVID E. CAMPBELL

Listen to the talks delivered by LDS leaders and it would appear that Mormon women are happy with their role in the church. Read the posts in the "bloggernacle" (LDS blogs) and there is often a strain of discontent, or at least a desire for women to have greater voice. This chapter examines what rank-and-file LDS women think about their place within the church, and within society more broadly. Are Mormon women satisfied with the status quo or restless for reform?

Viewed from one perspective, one might think that the gendered division of labor within the church leaves many LDS women unhappy, as evidenced by the recent advocacy of some Mormon women—notably, those associated with the organization Ordain Women—that they receive the priesthood.[1] The excommunication of Ordain Women's founder, Kate Kelly, has focused attention—both inside LDS circles and out—on the role of women within Mormonism, and surfaced discontent among some LDS women about their place within the church as an institution and Mormonism as a culture. Because of the all-male priesthood, many church roles are closed to women, from highly visible positions of ecclesiastical leadership to less-visible assignments like serving as a ward (congregational) financial clerk. Furthermore, the LDS style of vertical hierarchy has also brought a high degree of uniformity across congregations. Women unhappy with their place within the church, but who nonetheless wish to participate in Mormonism, have no other choices available. Unlike Judaism, there is no "Reform" wing of the LDS church. Women, and men, unhappy with gender roles in the church can either stay and try to effect change through the exercise of voice—difficult in a hierarchical organization—or they can exit, a painful decision for many who find much to love within Mormonism.[2]

Viewed from another perspective, however, there is reason to think that LDS women find their role within the church, and Mormon culture generally, rewarding. The expansive lay participation within Mormonism allows women to have many opportunities to invest their time and energy into church service including, but not limited to, the all-female Relief Society. Furthermore, the church places great emphasis on the need to gain a personal conviction that the LDS Church is governed by God, through continuing revelation (i.e., "gaining a testimony"). For many LDS women, such a conviction likely includes an affirmation that women's role in the church is as God intends, and so to suggest change would be to defy God's will. This sentiment is clear from the comments left on the LDS-run website, Mormon.org. For instance, consider the following representative response to the question, "What are Mormon women like? Do Mormons believe in equality of men and women?"

> Women have a divine role, as designed by Heavenly Father before we came to earth. We were given the sacred opportunity to be mothers and to work alongside the brethren of the church to serve, uplift, and strengthen others . . . Women and men are different for divine purposes.[3]

Still others may not have given the issue much thought, since the status quo is all they know.

A priori, a plausible case can thus be made either that Mormon women are content with the way things are, or they are looking for change. To find out which better reflects the attitudes of women within contemporary Mormonism, this chapter considers three questions:

1. How *active* are LDS women in the church?
2. What do LDS women think about *authority* in the church?
3. What do LDS women think about *gender roles* within the church?

As these three questions all deal with the present, the chapter concludes with speculation about the future by considering the possible implications of the recent decision by the LDS Church to lower the age at which women can serve as fulltime missionaries. This policy change, I suggest, could have far-reaching implications for gender roles within Mormonism.

How Active Are LDS Women in the Church?

One gauge of women's satisfaction with their role in the church is their level of religious activity. One reason for this is the theory of "social exchange," often employed by social scientists to explain why individuals participate in groups of all sorts. According to this perspective, people give their time and treasure to organizations because they feel their contribution is "worth it"—they receive something in exchange. In a society where religious affiliation and involvement is a matter of choice, we would expect people unhappy with their religion to "vote with their feet" (or time, or dollars) and withdraw from participation.[4] This logic is not merely the province of social scientists, however, as LDS general authorities have employed it when discussing gender roles within LDS homes and the church. In a recent General Conference talk, Elder Quentin Cook invoked the high levels of religious activity among LDS women to underscore his point that, on the whole, they are content with the status quo.[5]

While many religions encourage their members to be active by attending worship services, the term "activity" has particular meaning within Mormonism. Indeed, Mormons regularly differentiate among church members as "active" or "inactive"—emphasizing the strong behavioral expectations within the faith. To be an active, devout Mormon is to do what Mormons are supposed to do. This list is long, as it includes attending three hours of meetings every Sunday, a "calling" (assignment) that typically requires a few hours of service each week; monthly visits in the homes of other church members; a minimum financial contribution of 10 percent of one's income (plus further contributions); participation in a monthly fast; regular participation in the rites of LDS temples (which are separate from Sunday worship services); holding a weekly "family home evening" within one's home; daily personal prayer and scripture study; doing genealogical research—and this hardly exhausts what it takes to be considered a fully active Latter-day Saint. Activity within the church is therefore an excellent, arguably the best, barometer for Latter-day Saints' engagement with their faith.

To examine rates of activity within Mormonism, I rely on a scientific, nationally representative sample of Mormons.[6] It is important to note that a survey like this only includes people who self-identify as LDS, and thus omits those who might appear on church records but do not consider themselves to be members of the faith. Therefore, the data include a slice of the LDS population that is at least nominally connected to the church, and thus is undoubtedly missing those who are most disaffected with the faith.

While other research has established that Mormons have extraordinarily high rates of church activity, however measured, the focus here is on comparing women and men.[7] Are both genders *equally* active? If men are more satisfied with their role within the church than women, we would expect them to be more active—and vice versa.

The answer is that there are only a few gender differences. Specifically, in our survey LDS men are more likely to hold a calling (LDS lingo for a church assignment) and pay tithing. Seventy-one percent of men indicate that they have a church calling, compared to 60 percent of women; 80 percent of men report that they pay tithing (lingo for financial contributions to the church), while 69 percent of women do.

In interpreting these two indicators of LDS activity, note that women are more likely to be married to a nonmember of the LDS Church and, even if married to a fellow Mormon, to report that their spouses are not active in the church. Both holding a calling and paying tithing are more difficult in a household where both spouses are not equally committed to the church, perhaps especially for women who may have household responsibilities that make it difficult to hold a calling or are not the family's wage earner. When, in a statistical model, the church activity of one's spouse is controlled—i.e., accounted for—there are no longer any differences between women and men. In other words, if a male and female Mormon are both married to spouses of equal activity in the church, they are each equally likely to hold a calling and pay tithing.[8]

There is no difference between women and men in other indicators of church activity, including frequency of church attendance, temple attendance, scripture reading, or personal prayer. Nor do women and men differ in their strength of identification as a Mormon. The survey measured respondents' strength of "Mormon identity" with a series of questions modeled on indices used to gauge racial or ethnic identity. Respondents were asked whether they agree or disagree with the following statements:

TABLE 12.1. Survey of Activity within Mormonism, 2012.

Survey Question	Women(%)	Men(%)
Attending church once or twice a month or more	77	81
Attending the temple once or twice a month or more (of temple recommend holders)	33	35
Reading scripture daily	42	36
Praying daily	71	72
Those who agree: When I talk about Mormons, I usually say "we" rather than "they"	90	91
Those who strongly agree: When someone criticizes Mormons, it feels like a personal insult	69	74
Those who strongly agree: I'm like other Mormons in many ways	84	85
Those who strongly agree: Being a Mormon is an essential part of who I am	64	63

- When I talk about Mormons, I usually say "we" rather than "they"
- When someone criticizes Mormons, it feels like a personal insult
- I'm like other Mormons in many ways
- Being a Mormon is an essential part of who I am

Women and men do not differ on any of these statements and thus have an equal degree of attachment to Mormonism.[9] (See Table 12.1 for details).

In short, both Mormon men and women are highly engaged with their faith—and equally so. Given the logic of social exchange theory, LDS women are presumably not sitting on their hands out of dissatisfaction with their role within the church.[10]

What Do LDS Women Think about Authority in the Church?

While indicators of church activity show LDS women and men to be equally engaged in their religion, this does not necessarily mean that they view every aspect of the church the same way. There are nuances within Mormonism, as two equally devout Latter-day Saints can have differing views on various aspects of the faith. These subtleties are often hidden when Mormons are asked general-purpose questions on surveys designed to cover the entire U.S. population, including people of myriad religious backgrounds. Because we designed our study specifically for Latter-day Saints, our results uncover nuances within Mormonism by asking about concepts unique to the faith using Mormonism's distinctive argot.

In our survey of Mormons, men and women differ most on questions pertaining to the role of authority within the church, a central aspect of the faith. Mormonism contains within it two doctrinal emphases that could be described as either complementary or in conflict. Leaders teach that Mormons should simultaneously obey church authorities while also seeking personal inspiration.[11] In his essay, "What the Church Means to People Like Me," Richard Poll famously employs two symbols from LDS scripture to discuss these two dimensions of Mormonism. Those who prioritize adherence to authority are best described by the "Iron Rod" referred to in the *Book of Mormon,* to which one must hold fast in order to stay on the strait and narrow path to God. Mormons who seek personal guidance from God, over obedience to hierarchy, are symbolized by the "Liahona," which the *Book of Mormon* describes as a divine compass, activated by faith in God, that guided a family of travelers through the wilderness. While the Iron Rod implies a top-down style of religion—God's instructions transmitted through church authorities—the Liahona refers to a bottom-up model, whereby individuals seek out God's direction for themselves. Mormon approaches to authority include both the Iron Rod and Liahona models, but church members rely more on one symbol than the other.[12]

To differentiate between Iron Rod and Liahona Mormons, the surveys asks respondents which of the following two statements better reflects their opinion.

> "A good Latter-day Saint should first seek his or her own personal revelation as the motivation to obey." [Liahona]

or

"A good Latter-day Saint should obey the counsel of priesthood leaders without necessarily knowing why." [Iron Rod]

Note that both options include the concept of obedience to authority, a term that many outside of Mormonism may find jarring but is fundamental to the LDS worldview. The question at hand is not whether to obey, but what obedience means: "following orders" or "finding your own way." While the question refers not to the respondent but to a "good Latter-day Saint," the implication is clearly that each statement refers to what is normative within the church—what Latter-day Saints *ought* to do.

In sharp contrast to the measures of religious activity, where women and men show few differences, they differ dramatically on the question of whether inspiration should trump unquestioning obedience. While 48 percent of men say that a good Latter-day Saint should obey without knowing why, only 31 percent of women choose this option, instead favoring personal revelation.

In other words, women are more likely to see church counsel as something to be confirmed through personal communication with the divine—without mediation by priesthood leaders (i.e., men). More women than men are Liahona Mormons.

A similar gender difference appears for a question about observance of the Sabbath Day (Sunday), which we chose because this is a subject on which Mormons often legitimately disagree. Some Mormons point to LDS statements and policies to make the case that the church has drawn bright lines differentiating between activities that are, and are not, appropriate for the Sabbath. Other Mormons see Sabbath observance as a matter of individual inspiration. They will cite statements from church leaders about the need for personal discretion in observing the Sabbath, as well as the oft-told lesson that the biblical Pharisees were unduly focused on the letter of the Sabbath law at the expense of its spirit. (Mormons frequently repeat the story of how the Pharisees dictated the number of steps that could be taken on the Sabbath.) The point is simply that unlike many other standards of Mormonism, faithful Mormons may agree that one should keep the Sabbath Day holy, but choose different means to reach that end.

As before, the two options address the distinction between Iron Rod and Liahona Mormons:

> "Obeying the Sabbath means deciding for yourself what is appropriate." [Liahona]

or

> "The Church has specific standards for obeying the Sabbath." [Iron Rod]

Women are again more likely than men to choose the Liahona option that observing the Sabbath is a matter of personal discretion: 40 percent versus 33 percent of men.

Women and men also differ in their perspective on whether Mormons should prioritize avoiding sin or serving others. In one sense, this is a false choice. Just as Mormonism contains elements of both the Iron Rod and the Liahona, Mormonism writ large emphasizes both individual righteousness and a strong communitarian ethos. But what happens when Mormons must choose between individualism and communitarianism? Who puts a priority on one versus the other? To find out, the survey asked respondents to choose between these two statements:

> "To live the gospel, it is most important to avoid doing sinful things yourself."

or

> "To live the gospel, it is most important to help other people."

Women are more likely to put providing service ahead of avoiding sin. Fifty-five percent of women choose this option, compared to 47 percent of men. This communitarian perspective complements their emphasis on bottom-up personal inspiration over top-down hierarchy. While men more often have a vertical perspective on Mormonism, seeing it in terms of hierarchy and sin, women tend to take a more horizontal view, emphasizing inspiration and service. Given that the LDS Church places such emphasis on obedience to the authority of a priesthood leadership structure, it is striking—if perhaps not surprising—that the gender ineligible to hold those positions of authority places less emphasis on hierarchy and more on individual inspiration.

What Do LDS Women Think about Gender Roles within the Church?

The fact that Mormon women and men have different views on authority within the church suggests that they might also differ in their view regarding gender roles within the church. However, asking church members about a fraught issue such as gender requires care. A question like, "Should women be able to hold the priesthood?" risks being interpreted as a litmus-test statement of belief in the church as a whole, since the nature and organization of the priesthood is integral to the LDS faith. For many church members, to question the organization of the priesthood would be tantamount to heresy. Therefore, our questions on gender were subtler. One consists of the statement: "The fact that women do not hold the priesthood sometimes bothers me." The second was the statement, "Women do not have enough say in the church"—phrasing meant to dovetail with the recent emphasis on ensuring broad participation in ward (congregational) councils (committees). LDS leaders have quietly encouraged greater involvement of women in these council meetings. Because of this push within the church, members who believe that women's voices are muffled or ignored can express that opinion without necessarily worrying that they are expressing disloyalty or disbelief in the church.

Relatively few Mormons say that the all-male priesthood ever troubles them. But to the extent that they do, more women say they are bothered: 20 percent, compared to 7 percent of Mormon men. Likewise, women are more likely than men to agree that women do not have enough say in the church, by a slightly smaller margin. Among women, 20 percent say that they do not have enough voice, compared to 12 percent of men who say the same.

To borrow an analogy from physics, there are two "opposing forces" among LDS women. The stronger force pulls most women into satisfaction with the status quo. Roughly 80 percent of Mormon women are not bothered by the all-male priesthood, nor think that they should have more say in the church. Another force, though, pushes about one in five LDS women toward the opposite view.

While these data clearly show a high level of contentment with the church as it is, recall that these data are from self-identified Mormons, which raises the possibility that the women—and men—who are most dissatisfied with the role of women in the church have "voted with their feet," exercised the exit option, and left the church. If respondents have parted ways with the LDS Church, they are not likely to identify themselves as such in a public opinion survey. And if the people who leave are the most discontented with church policies, these results may overstate the overall level of satisfaction with the status quo.

A massive survey of religion in America done by the Pew Forum on Religion and Public Life, a leading research institute in the study of religion, provides insight into the attitudes of people who have left the LDS Church. The Pew survey was so large that it is possible to look at the attitudes not only of Mormons—a relatively small share of the population—but former Mormons, an even smaller group.[13] I define former Mormons as people who report being raised in the LDS Church, but no longer identify themselves as Latter-day Saints.

The Pew survey did not specifically inquire about the role of gender, either in religion or society, but it did ask about whether one's religion should

- preserve its traditional beliefs and practices
- adjust traditional beliefs and practices in light of new circumstances
- adopt modern beliefs and practices

While these options do not address gender per se, someone who believes women should play a greater role in their religion would presumably agree that it ought to adjust traditional beliefs or adopt modern ones.

Sixty-eight percent of Mormons believe that their religion should preserve its traditions—higher than members of any other religious tradition in America. (Evangelicals come closest to Mormons, at 59 percent.) By way of comparison, only 35 percent of Catholics and 26 percent of Jews favor tradition over change. However, *former* Mormons sharply contrast with *current* Mormons. More (50 percent) former Mormons believe that their religion should either adjust or discard traditional beliefs than stick to tradition (44 percent). Among women, 21 percent of ex-Mormons specifically endorse "adopting modern beliefs and practices," (rather than adjusting traditions) compared to just 6 percent of men who have left the church.

There is no way to know whether former Mormons are thinking of the LDS Church when answering this question, especially since many have found new faiths. But even if ex-Mormons are thinking of their current, not former, religion, the fact that a relatively high percentage favor change over continuity suggests dissatisfaction with the traditionalism of the LDS Church—including gender roles. It is especially striking that one in five female former Mormons believes in adopting modern ways, not just tweaking traditional practices. That is a higher percentage than women in any single religious tradition.

One must be careful in interpreting the attitudes of former Mormons, as it is tempting to conclude that they show cause and effect. Correlation is not causation. With these data it is impossible to tell whether former Mormons left the LDS Church because they wanted change, or whether they came to believe that change was necessary after leaving. Whatever the reason for their departure from the church, there is a sharp disjuncture between the attitudes of current and former Mormons, at least when it comes to the need for change within their religion. And this disjuncture is sharpest among women.

Conclusion

Are Mormon women satisfied or disgruntled with their place in Mormonism? In terms of their church activity, Mormon women are highly involved in the church, which does not suggest widespread alienation. LDS women and men, however, differ on their views toward authority within the church. Women are more likely to see Mormonism as a faith grounded in following personal revelation, instead of adhering to hierarchy. They are also more likely to view the gospel in communitarian terms, and thus place priority on providing service to others over avoiding sin by oneself. Yet notwithstanding these different tendencies of women and men, roughly four out of five Mormon women are untroubled by the role of women in the church, and thus presumably not restless for change. Perhaps this is because their reliance on personal revelation eases any discomfort with male authority.

Change, however, need not only spring from discontent. Even in the context of a church membership largely—albeit not uniformly—satisfied with women's roles, the winds of change have begun to blow because of a momentous policy amendment by the LDS Church. In October 2012, the church lowered the age of eligibility for female missionaries, from twenty-one to nineteen. This single act is likely to result in many mutually reinforcing effects on the position and perceptions of women in the church. More women will have the "credential" of having served a full-time mission, an important marker within Mormon culture. Even more important, a higher proportion of LDS women will have gained leadership experience in the mission field.

In the short term, the immediate effect of the age change has been to dramatically increase the number of women serving full-time missions.[14] While this initial spike is undoubtedly due to the pent-up demand for missionary service among women who were waiting to turn twenty-one—and thus will not be sustained—the long-term effect will nonetheless be a boost in the percentage of female missionaries within the LDS population. The two years between nineteen and twenty-one are often a critical life juncture, as missionaries-to-be are faced with opportunities for advanced education, careers, and marriage.[15] By lowering the age of eligibility for women interested in serving a mission, they can serve a mission *before* facing these life choices—just like their male counterparts.

As more women serve missions, Mormonism's signal rite of passage will no longer be as dominated by men, thus increasingly "normalizing" women's place in this highly visible part of Mormon culture. More and more converts to the church will have been taught by women. More of the wards and branches in the "mission field" that lean heavily on missionaries will now rely on women to shore up their fledgling congregations. Upon returning home after completing their missionary service, this expanded corps of female missionaries will bring considerable church experience to their local congregations. All of these changes suggest that women will inevitably come to play a different role in the church. Perhaps they will even have more say within it.

While no one knows precisely how the rising number of female missionaries will affect Mormonism, the changes are likely to be subtle yet profound. As we have seen, women often have a different perspective on LDS doctrine, especially the nature of authority, than men. While today most Mormon women are satisfied with the status quo, going forward the question is what the new status quo will be.

Notes

1. Kristen Moulton, "Mormon Women Shut Out of All-Male Priesthood Meeting," *Salt Lake Tribune*, October 5, 2013, http://www.sltrib.com/sltrib/news/56963037-78/women-mormon-church-priesthood.html.csp.
2. Albert O. Hirschman, *Exit, Voice, and Loyalty: Responses to Decline in Firms, Organizations, and States* (Cambridge, MA: Harvard University Press, 2004).
3. Accessed March 22, 2015, http://www.mormon.org/faq/gender-equality.
4. Robert D. Putnam and David E. Campbell, *American Grace: How Religion Divides and Unites Us* (New York: Simon and Schuster, 2010).
5. Quentin L. Cook, "LDS Women Are Incredible!," April 2011, accessed March 22, 2015, https://www.lds.org/general-conference/2011/04/lds-women-are-incredible?lang=eng.
6. I conducted the survey in collaboration with my colleagues Quin Monson of Brigham Young University and John Green of the University of Akron. In December 2011 and January 2012, we commissioned YouGov, an internet survey firm, to interview five hundred self-identified Mormons. Five hundred may not sound like a lot, but for a scientific poll of a relatively small group like Mormons, this is a large enough sample size to provide reliable results. Note that this survey relies on a nationally representative, scientifically drawn sample of the LDS population in the United States, and thus differs from surveys that rely on convenience and/or opt-in samples, such as those distributed through Facebook. Convenience samples can be internally valid, but their external validity is questionable.
7. Putnam and Campbell, *American Grace*; David E Campbell, John C. Green, and J. Quin Monson, *Seeking the Promised Land: Mormons and American Politics* (New York: Cambridge University Press, 2014); David E. Campbell and J. Quin Monson, "Dry Kindling: A Political Profile of American Mormons," in *From Pews to Polling Places: Faith and Politics in the American Religious Mosaic*, edited by J. Matthew Wilson (Washington, D.C.: Georgetown University Press, 2007), 105–29; Ram Cnaan, Van Evans, and Daniel W. Curtis, *Called to Serve: The Prosocial Behavior of Active Latter-day Saints* (University of Pennsylvania School of Social Policy and Practice, April 17, 2012), www.sp2.upenn.edu/docs/people/faculty/cnaan_lds_giving.pdf.
8. Specifically, when either the payment of tithing or holding a calling are regressed on a binary variable for "female," the coefficient is negative and statistically significant—meaning that women are less likely to do either. However, when a variable measuring the religious activity level of a respondent's spouse is added to either model, the coefficient for female ceases to be statistically significant—indicating that the apparent gender difference is actually a spurious statistical relationship. What appears to be an effect of gender is

really an effect of a spouse's level of religious activity. The full results of this analysis are available upon request.

9. Throughout this chapter, the statement that women and men do or do not differ is based on whether the "gender gap" reaches statistical significance—in other words, whether it can be distinguished from chance. I employ the conventional threshold of statistical significance, namely that the result would not have occurred by chance 95 percent of the time (i.e., $p < .05$).
10. Furthermore, when compared to the "gender gap" in virtually every other religious tradition, the mostly equal rate of religious engagement among Mormon women and men stands out. As for why men are equally active, I suspect that this is due to Mormonism's combination of expansive lay participation and a male-only priesthood. Not only are there many roles to fill, current church policy requires that many of them must be filled by men. As those men serve in the church, they strengthen a commitment to the faith that is manifested both in their behavior and their beliefs.
11. Terryl L. Givens, *People of Paradox: A History of Mormon Culture* (New York: Oxford University Press, 2007).
12. Richard Douglas Poll, "What the Church Means To People Like Me," *Dialogue: A Journal of Mormon Thought* 34, no. 1–2 (2001): 11–22.
13. For more details on the Pew Religious Landscape Survey, see http://religions.pewforum.org.
14. Peggy Fletcher Stack, "Mormon Missionary Applications Explode 471%; Half Are Women," *Salt Lake Tribune*, October 22, 2012.
15. Marriage is a particularly salient concern, as Latter-day Saints tend to marry at a younger age than the national average. See Xiaohe Xu, Clark D. Hudspeth, and John P. Bartkowski, "The Timing of First Marriage: Are There Religious Variations?," *Journal of Family Issues* 26, no. 5 (July 1, 2005): 584–618.

13

Mormon Women in Europe

A Look at Gender Norms

CARINE DECOO-VANWELKENHUYSEN

Introduction

I thought I had a Mormon identity until I moved to Utah. A convert at age fourteen in Belgium, I spent the next twenty-six years mainly in that mission field, served in a variety of callings, and married in the temple. After our family moved to Provo in 1999, I became conscious of two dissimilarities of identity between myself and other Mormons around me that rasped against my core Mormon identity, which I had thought I shared with all Mormons worldwide.

The first was the open fusion of Mormon identity with right-wing conservatism and Republican Party affiliation. In the mission field, converts normally retain their pre-Mormon loyalties to parties and unions and typically pass these on to their children. It results in a diverse ideological spectrum among Latter-day Saints, certainly in countries with an array of political parties.[1] In church, these loyalties remain hidden; unity there should not be endangered by politics. In Provo, however, I lived among the sweetest of Relief Society sisters who quietly assured me that George W. Bush was a man of God and that the Democrats were present-day Gadianton robbers. It was disorienting to hear devout women, who were intensely dedicated to family and church, professing what my background identified as bigoted nonsense. These women elaborated on ideals of womanhood and family values in an exclusivist mode, convinced that outside their realm families were being destroyed. I learned that voicing even cautious nuances was not appreciated, certainly not by a convert and, moreover, a foreigner from socialist Europe. Smiles and silence salvaged sisterhood.

Could I find kindred spirits among Mormon feminists active in blogs and independent symposia? There I stumbled on the second identity difference. Though I could comprehend some of the frustrations of these women, my own Mormon identity was imbued with the sense of female equality that the Belgian social order had given me. Feminism was a word from the past. Battles for gender equality were now in problematic countries and communities identified in programs of the United Nations or UNESCO. The grievances of Mormon feminists in Utah made me realize that I had grown up in a society where gender equality was fairly well institutionalized on all levels. But that realization also confronted me with questions: Then why had I never, during my twenty-six years of church membership in Belgium, been bothered by the patriarchal priesthood? Why did no woman in our mission field seem to question the male leadership dominance? Was it the same among Mormon women in other European countries?

The outline for the 2012 conference, "Women and the LDS Church: Historical and Contemporary Perspectives," in Salt Lake City, stated that "the experience of being an LDS woman in the United States is deeply marked by American life and culture," and referred to "Victorian gender norms" that molded the language of femininity in the church. The call for papers asked how LDS women elsewhere framed their experiences in comparison. To answer the question I would have needed a large-scale survey of European Mormon women, scattered over some fifty countries, requiring church consent and cooperation on multiple levels. This proved impossible. I therefore used a limited qualitative approach—personal inquiries through an expanding network of contacts, with open answers and follow-up questions and discussions. I was able to work with some sixty Mormon women from seventeen countries, covering all of Northern and Western Europe, Portugal, Spain, and Italy. Their ages ranged from twenty-one to eighty-five. I had only a few responses from Eastern Europe, where the church is still very young. In all I collected some twelve hundred answers. The samples in this chapter represent only a fraction and do not do justice to the breadth and depth of the responses. For each comment, I added the age of the respondent, her country, and whether she was a convert (1st generation) or was born in the church (with the number of generations).

The topics focused on marriage, children, education, employment, gender equality, priesthood, modesty, dating, and sexual education. As far as relevant, I compared answers with data from a number of frameworks. For women in general, I used the Global Gender Gap Report, the World Survey on the Role of Women in Development, OECD Well-Being Indicators, and Geert Hofstede's dimensions on masculinity and power distance.[2] For Mormon women, I used as frameworks the American Religious Identification Survey, the Pew Research study of Mormons in America, and various studies as cited further in this chapter.[3]

Note that there is no European equivalent (yet) to the feeling of "being American." Respondents speak for their country. Some respondents even emphasized they were Scottish, not British, or North Italian, not from the South.

Marriage, Children, and Education

I asked my respondents:

- Do you think a woman should marry young? Should she become a mother as soon as possible?
- How important is higher education and getting a degree for a young woman?

The overall advice of the respondents was to pursue education and not marry young. They also advised that couples wait to have children until a few years after marriage. These attitudes reflect a general Western trend, both in North America and in Europe, where the age of first marriage has constantly been increasing since the 1960s due to a number of factors; including longer schooling, easier dependence on continued parental support, the desire to have a stable relationship and financial security before having children, and apprehensiveness about marriage and parenthood.[4] Moreover, in Europe, partners are about four years older than in the United States when they first marry—thirty-two for men and thirty for women. Within the United States, Utah has the lowest average age of first marriage—about two years under the American average—twenty-six for men and twenty-four for women.[5] Mormon women in Europe reflect the European trend. Sample responses to the questions included:

> I am glad my older daughter has not married yet at twenty-four. She has a degree and has travelled the world. She has much to offer her future husband and children. (age fifty-one, U.K., 1st gen. since 1975)
>
> I married when I was thirty and I am happy I did. When I finally married I knew who I was and could better identify the man who best matched me and vice-versa. (age forty, Netherlands, 2nd gen.)
>
> Thank goodness the trend these days among the young women in the church in Sweden is to continue with school. My daughters, twenty-six and twenty-two, both have, and so have most of their friends. (age fifty-three, Sweden, 1st gen. since 1975)

Quite a few respondents extrapolated from personal and anecdotal experience that marrying young increases the chance of divorce. They also argued that the limited number of Mormon men and the time it takes to meet other young adults at occasional conferences lead to later marriages.

Regarding educational achievement, survey data for France, the United Kingdom, and Ireland, indicate that both Mormon men and women have higher levels of education than the overall population.[6] This might be due to missionary work patterns. Mormons in Europe are concentrated in large urban areas where people tend to have more schooling than in rural areas. Sociologists Tim Heaton and Cardell Jacobson found the same in Mexico, Brazil, and the Philippines.[7] Members pass the impact of their education on to their children, thus promoting a relatively high education level for the next generation. We do not have similar reliable survey data for other countries.

Employment

In the United States, 48 percent of Mormon women work outside the home—25 percent full-time and 23 percent part-time.[8] The figures in

Europe are significantly higher. Sociologist Christian Euvrard's study in France revealed that 74 percent of Mormon women are employed.[9] All my respondents confirmed that most women work outside the home, with ratios between 70 and 80 percent. This means that the employment rate of European Mormon women is even higher than European women in general, which hovers around 60 percent according to the OECD figures. Again, the urban factor seems to play a determinant role here.

The reasons my respondents gave for employment were partly economic, but also social; namely, they expressed a need to feel involved with society, to put professional qualifications to use, and even to do missionary work. They also explained that the state's social provisions—universal health care, paid parental leaves, child support allocations, the right to part-time employment adjustments, and guaranteed return to full employment—help mothers to balance their work and family responsibilities.

In the United States, this topic was highly debated in 2012 when journalist Anne-Marie Slaughter stated that it is not possible for successful women to have time for both work and family.[10] Riane Eisler and Valerie Young responded to Slaughter: "The shocking truth is that the United States lags way behind every other developed nation in helping parents care for their children . . . The United States is the only developed nation on earth that does not guarantee paid sick days or paid parental leave."[11]

My survey also inquired: "In Europe, most countries have protective laws for women and an elaborate social system (family allowances, maternity leave, etc.). This is considered as a form of socialism in the United States. What is your opinion?" Representative answers included:

> I think it is wonderful. These provisions allow mothers to stay at home with their children and give fathers the similar opportunities in case needed. They confirm that the government sees the family as the central unit in the society. I think these laws are needed in today's world. (age twenty-six, Finland, 1st gen. since 2006)

> Yes, it is socialism, but not only blessing women, but the whole family, therefore I adhere to this system of positive discrimination which allows parents to take care of their family in a dignified

way. (age twenty-five, France, 1st gen. since 2006, originally from Ivory Coast)

We do not sufficiently appreciate how blessed we are in Europe thanks to these social laws and this financial aid we receive when we have children. (age forty-two, Luxemburg, 2nd gen.)

A system to promote more births cannot be called socialism. (age forty, France, 1st gen. since 1997)

Honestly, I think Americans should stop being so skeptical to everything that is not American. Wake up and look at people instead of systems and money. If they think this is socialism, they haven't seen socialism yet. (age fifty-two, Denmark, 2nd gen.)

Being a socialist myself I don't see anything wrong with this and again, I fail to understand the meaning of this question. I've never really understood why socialism is considered to be a bad thing in the United States. (age thirty-five, Finland, 2nd gen.)

Some respondents resented that I used the term "socialism."[12] To them, these provisions are basic rights financed by their taxes. They consider it a token of solidarity that singles and parents without children sustain the system through their higher taxes. They insist that these social provisions are not welfare: they are directed to productive, employed citizens so that people can aspire to "have it all."

Gender Equality

According to the latest report of the Global Gender Gap, which measures items such as equal pay, education levels, health, female representation in leadership, and other items related to gender equality, the United States comes in twenty-second, out of one hundred thirty-five countries surveyed.[13] Among the twenty-one countries preceding the United States, thirteen are Western European countries. The first five in the ranking are all in West Europe.

How does increased social equality, as achieved in these European countries, affect the feelings of women in the church? One question in my survey asked: The church is often considered "patriarchal." Does this provoke feminist reactions with some of the sisters? Nearly all the respondents said "no" and gave several reasons.

First, some respondents felt that gender equality has mostly been attained in European society (hence feminist demands for it are waning):

> We rarely have "feminists" because in my country the real militant feminist fights have mainly been fought by the previous generation of women. The battles we tackle now are against things like violence, war, poverty, hunger, etc. (age thirty-nine, Italy, 1st gen. since 1995)

> Living in Europe I have not often had the "feminist" reaction you describe, but when I lived in Utah I saw it often. It didn't have to do with the Patriarchal order, but with the conduct of Priesthood bearers. (age sixty-three, Norway, 1st gen. since 1966)

Second, in the terms of Hofstede, many European countries are low on so-called "masculinity," meaning citizens place less emphasis on competition, ambition, visibility, and winning, and more on cooperation, consensus, and compromise.

> An American sister made the suggestion that we should call the Relief Society president with the title "president," as we do with male presiding officers. I think that is nonsense. It would be better to abolish the president title for men and call them all brother. (age fifty-three, Belgium, 1st gen.)

Many European countries are also low on Hofstede's dimension of "power distance," meaning that people have more candid interactions with leaders. Directly or indirectly, women participate in much of the decision-making process.

> In thirty-six years of church membership I hardly heard any feminist reaction but I have observed, more than once, that women take the lead. In the church, women are determined, take initiatives, direct, teach. (age fifty-eight, France, 1st gen. since 1976)

> I struggle sometimes with the patriarchal set up, but only when they go hand in hand with unrighteous dominion. I myself will stand up and voice my opinion when I witness unrighteous dominion. I esteem it not only my right but also my responsibility to do so. (age fifty, Belgium, 2nd gen.)

> Men and women have equal worth in the church. The women in my ward are used to retort, in all kinds of meetings and discussions. (age fifty-five, Netherlands, 1st gen.)

This does not mean that all respondents are happy with certain situations. One repeated suggestion is to have more women speakers in sacrament meetings and in stake conferences.

One of the reviewers of this chapter wondered why Mormon women in Europe, empowered in their secular lives, do not question their seemingly subservient church role. The reviewer questioned, "Could it be that European women are not that far removed from, and buying into the same notions of separate-but-equal, pedestalizing women, and benevolent patriarchy as American women are?" I subsequently submitted the following to my respondents: Would you agree with this statement, "Mormon girls and women are often being told they are special, precious, and important, but such 'honoring' of women is also a way to maintain them in their assigned role."? Of the respondents, 62 percent rejected the statement. Only 12 percent agreed. Other women gave nuanced comments. They agreed that such pedestalizing may indeed have some effect on gender role formation, but that character, family, and environment function as much stronger determinants for one's personality and degree of self-esteem. Several mentioned that European girls and women will not take pedestalizing seriously unless it is correlated with real responsibilities and impact in decision-making.

Women and Priesthood

When asked the question: Would it be a good idea if the church gave women the Priesthood?—the unanimous response was "no." This response can be seen in light of the reasons just mentioned: societal equality is felt to have been attained, involvement is already high, and feelings of competition and empowerment are low. Quite a few respondents also gave the traditional explanation: giving men the priesthood keeps them in line and active in the church.

More recently I decided to probe if the respondents would remain consistent in their overall disinterest in receiving the priesthood if they were presented with authoritative and attractive hypotheses about holding the priesthood. A first question tried to mollify defensiveness by changing the perspective: If the prophet announced that from now on women can also receive the priesthood, (a) would you agree? (b) would you be happy? The (a) part has been suggested for other surveys, but (b) invited reflection on feelings and consequences. With one exception, all respondents agree with (a). However, many commented that they would find it "very strange" or "never to happen" because it would contradict the divine order of things. The response to (b) was remarkable, as 53 percent of the respondents said they would not be happy to receive the priesthood. Quite a few commented that they were not eager to get even more work and responsibilities, or that having the priesthood would not change anything in their relationship with God, or that it would entail the risk of less church activity among men. Others conceded they would be happy with the priesthood "only because the prophet decided it," not because they wanted the priesthood themselves.

Three other questions asked respondents to assess situations where female priesthood was presented as appealing or beneficial.

The first question asked: Would you like to see your twelve-year-old daughter, or any other faithful girl, pass the sacrament along with other boys and girls? Of the respondents, 69 percent answered no, 31 percent yes. Among those who responded negatively, comments stressed the inalterability of the revealed practice and the importance of "service" to be learned by boys. Those respondents answering affirmatively hailed equality. Some referred to the development in the Catholic Church, where altar girls now serve along boys on equal footing. A few decried the automatism to give the priesthood to twelve-year-old boys: the criterion should be maturity and understanding, and it should be equally applied to boys and girls.

The second question queried: Would it be good if a single mother (or a mother whose husband is often away) could anoint and bless her sick child with priesthood authority, without having to call the home teachers? The divergent responses reveal that each woman reacted from her personal situation and experience, as 41 percent (almost all married respondents) rejected the idea of a single mother holding priesthood authority, while 31 percent (most single mothers or speaking from past experience as a child in a single-mother home) approved of the idea. Respondents answering no, commented that the present system provides home teachers with opportunities to serve, fosters feelings of Mormon community, and brings father figures into single-mother homes. Those who responded yes, commented that a child in a single-mother home should be able to receive the anointing and blessing from her mother as the most trusted person, rather than from an outsider. Holding the priesthood was also mentioned as a source of positive self-esteem for single mothers. Finally, 28 percent did not answer yes or no, but insisted that even without formal priesthood ordination, women always possess the power of faith and of prayer, and could even lay on their hands to bless.

The third question asked: If women received the priesthood, would it help the image of the church and be good for missionary work? Two-thirds of the respondents answered no, with some of them explaining that the church should never give in to the norms of the world. Those who responded yes, stressed that the church is a dynamic entity, constructively adapting to societal developments, just as it has done in the past with polygamy, and with blacks and the priesthood.

These additional, more provocative, questions triggered more explicit traditionalism and defensiveness. Significantly, many comments did not allow for change in the church. In a world of protest and turmoil, it seems the majority of active Mormon women in Europe experience the church and the gospel as an immutable anchor, and see no reason to disrupt an order they have accepted as perfect. Only a minority of respondents (from their comments, clearly those with more background in church history) see the normalcy of evolution within the church.

According to a study by Verlyne Nzojibwami, American Mormon feminists treat the patriarchal system of the Mormon Church as peripheral to their faith, reconstruct Mormon theology to better fit their feelings, and seek personal empowerment.[14] Based on the responses I obtained, Mormon women in Europe seem to minimize or ignore the alleged tensions. None seem aware of feminist reconstructions of Mormon theology. Their secular empowerment, and their belief in both gender equality and women's contributions to the church, provide important context for this attitude of acceptance.

Modesty

All respondents supported the principle of modesty, but many expressed caveats:

> I am in favor of encouraging modesty but I oppose a strict dress code that could become a byproduct of the pressure of cultural acceptance amongst women in the church. (age fifty, Belgium, 1st gen. since 1989)

> I don't like it how girls are taught that the reason to dress modestly is to keep the boys from having immodest thoughts. I think everyone is responsible for their own thoughts . . . I find it disturbing that the pamphlet "For the Strength of Youth" focuses a lot more on modest dressing for the girls than it does for the boys. (age thirty-five, Finland, 2nd gen.)

> The way modesty has been emphasized lately really bothers me! Women should not be told that it is their fault if men lust after them. It is my duty as a parent to teach my sons to always respect women no matter what, and that they are responsible for their own thoughts and actions. Girls these days have enough body issues. The "witch hunt" of being told that they have clothes too tight, showing too much cleavage, leg or shoulder can be devastating for them! They should be taught to stand tall and be proud of their body, not feel that they are "slutty" or "walking porn." And the same principles should be taught to both boys AND girls! (age fifty-three, Sweden, 1st gen. since 1975)

Norms for modesty are culturally bound. Comments about modesty betrayed a fondness for fashionable clothing—hence some disdain for the "standard" conservative dress of women in the general presidencies of the Relief Society, Young Women, and Primary, whom Europeans see at general conference broadcasts and in church magazine pictures. I have observed that Mormon women's Sunday dress often includes wearing dress pants in Belgium, France, and the Netherlands. I assume it is similar in other European countries. Many Mormon wards in Europe also welcome underprivileged individuals, some of whom don't care or cannot afford to observe Sunday dress norms. Overall this mix encourages leaders to pay little attention to the delicate issue of female dress standards. However, among the more normative members, the emphasis on modesty in church instructions, lesson materials, and church magazines can foster fixations in their attitudes and lead to fundamentalism.

Dating

One question pertained to dating traditions, and particularly addressed those women who have also lived in the United States and could compare dating there with that in their own countries. All responses loathed the American system (as European women perceive it) where the man initiates contact, invites, can "date" several women, and finally proposes. A concept of dating, whereby a man invites a woman to go out, and goes out with another a week later, is considered unbecoming. In European countries teenagers and young adults typically go out as a group of friends. Both young men and young women can suggest activities and invite others to participate. If a young man or young woman is interested in a certain person, he or she will use the group to foster better acquaintance. Only after months, and even years, a couple within the group of young adults may develop a one-on-one relationship. That relationship will be relatively long-standing, again lasting many months or even years, before a step is taken toward engagement, marriage, or cohabitation. Some comments:

> When I lived in America, I noticed how big of a deal for a man it was to propose. For us, it always seems ridiculous, because the decision to marry grows out of a long relation and much communication. (age thirty-one, Belgium, 5th gen.)

> In Finland it is not accepted to go on dates with several people at the same time. If someone asks me out or I ask someone out and we go on a date, we are not supposed to go on dates with other people until we've find out if it works between us two. So one can only date one person at a time, and this is same for both men and women. Dating several people is considered cheating. (age twenty-six, Finland, 1st gen. since 2006)

> We don't have such a date system. Most often in the church we go out as a group or with someone alone whom we know very well already. Also if there is a dance and we don't have a boyfriend, we just go together as a group of friends to the dance, prom, etc. (age thirty-one, Germany, 3rd gen.)

> Girls and boys can come to events alone. My husband did not really propose. We both knew we wanted to marry. We just talked about this. To my mind we are equal individuals. There is no need to play too many roles. Mormonism may keep some roles alive. But I tend to say that German girls know who they are and what they want. Divine daughters should not be expected anything else, I think. (age forty, Germany, 3rd gen.)

> I have been to the United States many times, and I saw women in wards and in LDS congregations. They looked kind of "Victorian" to me. I mean, it seems to me that girls are always waiting for the man to step up and start dating, or to propose or say something. Women here [in Italy], married or not, study, participate in all kind of cultural and fun activities, express themselves as unique persons. They don't wait for something external to take their lives in their hands. They just do it. (age forty-three, Italy, 1st gen. since 1998)

Sexual Education

In European countries, sexual education is part of the mandatory school curriculum. Guidelines come from the European Commission Directorate for Health and Consumer Protection, as part of the SAFE project, but each country has its own forms of implementation. In most European countries sexual education is holistic, meaning that next to the physical aspects, attention goes to relational, emotional, and ethical aspects, such as self-esteem, responsibility, respect for others, prevention of risky behavior, the fight against violence, sexual exploitation, and homophobia. The educational principle is that, because young children hear about and see sex in the media, it is better to provide them with knowledge to handle and place that information. Of course, not all teachers handle sexual education equally well.

Though most of my respondents favored sexual education at school, some expressed reservations if the lessons were only technical and did not provide a context of values and responsibility.

> Both school and parents must provide sexual education. But not all parents are able to do this well. The important thing in both realms is that, next to technical explanations, values and norms, and mutual respect for each other are being discussed. (age fifty-nine, Belgium, 1st gen. since 1979)

> It is clearly the parents' responsibility, but they are not very good at it. They should teach their children as much as they can. The youth have a lot of questions but parents are often unable to answer. (age fifty-two, Denmark, 2nd gen.)

> Americans in general think of Holland as the modern Sodom and Gomorrah. Indeed, in Holland we are very open and we are rebels by nature. So yes, liberal thinking and we openly talk about sex and drugs. But that liberty does not lead to more problems. Teen moms are a rare thing in Holland and drug use by young people is lower than anywhere else in Europe. (age forty, Netherlands, 2nd gen.)

This Dutch pride was not misplaced. Numerous studies show that, of all industrialized countries, the United States has the highest rates of teen pregnancy, births, and abortions, while the Netherlands has the lowest.[15] Other European countries, in particular those with early and holistic sexual education, are also very low on teen pregnancies, teen births, STD's, and abortions.[16] Therefore, in most European countries, "sex" is not perceived as such a threatening problem. Mormon women in Europe clearly reflect that global attitude.

Conclusion

The main finding of my qualitative survey was that the Mormon women in Europe whom I interviewed reflected the gender norms of their own education and of evolving societal standards. This is the same conclusion of Dutch anthropologist Walter van Beek who found that Mormons in Europe are more "Mormon Europeans" than "European Mormons" because their national identity often weighs more in terms of values and norms.[17] Euvrard reached a similar conclusion for French members.[18] Moreover, inasmuch as these Mormon women were aware of Mormon feminism in the United States, they could not identify with it. In their view, local feminist fights had been fought and equality had been attained. Low "masculinity," with its emphasis on cooperation and consensus, and low "power distance" between women and men give Mormon women in Europe the conviction of having an impact on local church leadership.

At the same time, these women are diverse in many respects, including education, life experience, and critical attitudes—just like Mormon women in the United States.[19] Because of this, many American Mormon women will probably agree with many of their European counterparts' comments. Surveys could confirm that impression. The main difference between the American and European realms seems one of a palpable divide. In the United States, the division between "Molly Mormons" and "feminists" is pronounced. In the European realm such a divide is not apparent, perhaps because Mormons in Europe do not want to exacerbate tensions. Membership in the church already creates a number of tensions with the non-Mormon environment (mainly the membership in a "bizarre" church, Word of Wisdom observance, and Sabbath prohibition to participate in communal events). Adding to these tensions by adopting more "Victorian" gender norms is not appealing. Stressing differences between Mormon women in Europe and in the United States should not overshadow fundamental similarities. These include: sharing a fundamental female distinctiveness with the same physical issues and comparable challenges of gender relations; belonging to a worldwide church that expects conformity to feel part of it; and sharing a testimony of the gospel. With only one exception, all of my respondents expressed their love for the gospel and their dedication to the church. In that sense the differences I mentioned become marginal.

Reading the answers from my respondents and corresponding with many of them has been a deeply moving experience. I thank them for their willingness and candor.

Notes

1. For France, see Christian Euvrard, *Socio-histoire du mormonisme en France* (Paris: École Pratique des Hautes Études, 2008), 458–62; for Belgium,

Wilfried Decoo, "Mormonism in a European Catholic Country: Contribution to the Social Psychology of LDS Converts," *BYU Studies* 24, no. 1 (1984): 61–77. Even for the United States, Fox claims a greater variety than usually sampled, but "international and multicultural sampling will reveal even more diversity." Jeffrey C. Fox, "A Typology of LDS Sociopolitical Worldviews," *Journal for the Scientific Study of Religion* 42, no. 2 (2003): 286.

2. Ricardo Hausmann, Laura D. Tyson, and Saadia Zahidi, *The Global Gender Gap Report 2012* (Geneva, Switzerland: World Economic Forum, 2012); United Nations, Department of Economic and Social Affairs, *World Survey on the Role of Women in Development* (New York: United Nations, 2009); Organisation for Economic Cooperation and Development, *Compendium of OECD Well-Being Indicators 2011* (Paris: OECD, 2011); Geert Hofstede, Gert Jan Hofstede, and Michael Minkov, *Cultures and Organizations: Software of the Mind*, 3rd ed. (New York: McGraw-Hill, 2010).
3. Barry A. Kosmin and Ariela Keysar, *American Religious Identification Survey (ARIS 2008), Summary Report* (Hartford: Trinity College, 2009); Pew Research Center, *Mormons in America: Certain in Their Beliefs, Uncertain of Their Place in Society* (Washington: Pew Research Center, 2012).
4. Frank F. Furstenberg, "On a New Schedule: Transitions to Adulthood and Family Change," *The Future of Children* 20, no. 1 (2010): 67–87; Karen Henwood, Fiona Shirani, and Joanne Kellett, "On Delayed Fatherhood: The Social and Subjective 'Logics' at Work in Men's Lives," in *The Future of Motherhood in Western Societies*, edited by Gijs Beets, Joop Schippers, and Egbert R. te Velde (Dordrecht: Springer, 2011), 159–75; Matthijs Kalmijn, "The Influence of Men's Income and Employment on Marriage and Cohabitation: Testing Oppenheimer's Theory in Europe," *European Journal of Population* 27, no. 3 (2011): 269–93.
5. See surveys of Pew Research Center, UNICEF, and Eurostat.
6. Euvrard, *Socio-histoire*, 437–40. Personal communication with David M. Morris; the data are based on his "UK and Irish LDS 2012 Survey" (unpublished research).
7. Tim B. Heaton and Cardell K. Jacobson, "The Social Composition of Mormonism," in *The Oxford Handbook of Mormonism*, edited by Terryl L. Givens and Philip Barlow (Oxford: Oxford University Press, 2015), 312–14. See also Tim B. Heaton, Stephen J. Bahr, and K. J. Cardell, *A Statistical Profile of Mormons: Health, Wealth, and Social Life* (Lewiston, NY: Edwin Mellen Press, 2004).
8. Rick Phillips and Ryan T. Cragun, *Mormons in the United States 1990–2008: Socio-Demographic Trends and Regional Differences. A Report Based on the American Religious Identification Survey 2008* (Hartford: Trinity College, 2008).
9. Euvrard, *Socio-histoire*, 442.
10. Anne-Marie Slaughter, "Why Women Still Can't Have It All," *The Atlantic*, June 13, 2012, accessed July 21, 2012, http://www.theatlantic.com/magazine/archive/2012/07/why-women-still-cant-have-it-all/309020/.

11. Riane Eisler and Valerie Young, "From the 'Mommy Wars' to a Caring Economy," *Huffington Post*, June 28, 2012, accessed July 1, 2012, http://www.huffingtonpost.com/riane-eisler/mommy-wars_b_1630872.html.
12. These reactions clearly stemmed from the concern that the word "socialism" has different meanings in different countries, and that in the United States it is often understood as related to communism, implying perilous government domination. Conceptual boundaries between left and right shift according to cultural backgrounds. Cf. André Freire and Kats Kivistik, "Western and Non-Western Meanings of the Left–Right Divide across Four Continents," *Journal of Political Ideologies* 18, no. 2 (2013): 171–99.
13. Hausmann, Tyson, and Zahidi, *The Global Gender Gap*, 8.
14. Verlyne Nzojibwami, *Creating Space: How Mormon Women Reconcile Their Feminist Attitudes within a Patriarchal Religion* (master's thesis, University of Calgary, 2009).
15. Margaret Brugman, Sandra L. Caron, and Jany Rademakers, "Emerging Adolescent Sexuality: A Comparison of American and Dutch College Women's Experiences," *International Journal of Sexual Health* 22, no. 1 (2010): 32–46.
16. Melissa S. Kearney and Phillip B. Levine, "Why Is the Teen Birth Rate in the United States So High and Why Does It Matter?," *Journal of Economic Perspectives* 26, no. 2 (2012): 141–63; John S. Santelli and Andrea J. Melnikas, "Teen Fertility in Transition: Recent and Historic Trends in the United States," *Annual Review of Public Health* 31 (2010): 371–83; Carmen Solomon-Fears, *Teenage Pregnancy Prevention: Statistics and Programs* (Washington: Congressional Research Service, 2012).
17. Walter E. A. van Beek, "Mormon Europeans or European Mormons?: An 'Afro-European' View on Religious Colonization," *Dialogue: A Journal of Mormon Thought* 38, no. 4 (2005): 3–36.
18. Euvrard, *Socio-histoire*, 497.
19. Lori G. Beaman, "Molly Mormons, Mormon Feminists and Moderates: Religious Diversity and the Latter-day Saints Church," *Sociology of Religion* 62, no. 1 (2001): 65–86.

14

Culture and Agency in Mormon Women's Lives

MELISSA WEI-TSING INOUYE

What is the relationship between culture and agency in Mormon women's lived religious experiences? How does a woman's cultural context influence her perception of the truth of Mormonism's religious claims and the efficacy of its practices? Does culture tend to constrain or to create opportunities for Mormon women's spiritual expression?

Culture can be understood both as the language, customs, and learned behavior patterns of people in a given country or ethnic group, and also as the particularized, lived expression of universal religious claims. Documenting and understanding culture in this dual sense was one of the major goals of the Asian American and Asian Canadian Oral History Project run by the LDS Church History Department.[1] I was the principal oral historian for this project, which involved visits and interviews in cities hosting high concentrations of Mormons who were born in Asia but who had immigrated to North America, including Vancouver, Toronto, San Diego, and Washington, D.C., to name a few. From fall 2003 to fall 2004, I conducted over 140 oral history interviews. In this essay, I summarize highlights from these women's narratives in the Asian American and Asian Canadian oral history collection, and discuss how greater awareness of the experiences of Mormon women born outside of North America can change the sort of questions that we ask about women, culture, and agency in general.

In popular understanding, culture in both its national and religious forms is often viewed as a collectively created set of norms that can restrict individual agency by pressuring people to conform. For instance,

Hollywood films often celebrate the feisty young protagonist's struggle to break free of stifling cultural norms. Similarly, popular discussions about Mormon women, such as threads found online in Mormon and ex-Mormon blogs and discussion groups, frequently treat culturally inflected teachings as a less perfect form of Mormonism than teachings specified in the text of scripture. Culturally inflected Mormonism—that is, maxims, norms, and practices that aspire to enact universal gospel truths but that are also shaped by certain assumptions, norms, and practices distinctive to a group of people in a specific place, time, or relational circumstance—is often discussed as a subjective and often flawed interpretation of gospel truth that circumscribes or diminishes the spiritual authority and agency that Mormon doctrine actually allows for women.

To illustrate, in a recent posting on the popular blog Feminist Mormon Housewives, prominent blogger Hannah Wheelwright drew a distinction between church teachings about personal dress for women and a woman's belief in Jesus Christ: "Why should I stay in a church that seems to care more about whether I get a third piercing in my ear than in whether or not I have a testimony of the teachings of Christ?"[2] In weighing cultural and doctrinal perspectives, Wheelwright privileged universal claims ("the teachings of Christ") over culturally inflected teachings (the correct number of ear piercings) and deemed the latter harmful to women's spirituality.

The constraining power of norms within Mormon culture is unmistakable, especially in places like Utah, where Mormons are a demographic majority and Mormon doctrines and beliefs have a more visible role in influencing popular local culture. While the prescribed norms of Mormon culture often carry this negative connotation of constraint, thinking about culture in a larger frame of reference opens up new possibilities for thinking about culture and women's agency. The constraining power of culture (ethnic, religious, or otherwise) on individual behavior is greatest when an individual has only experienced one set of cultural norms, and least when an individual's experience of multiple sets of cultural norms raises awareness of the particularistic and conditioned nature of such norms.

This is why Asian Mormon women in North America have such an interesting perspective. Unlike a Thai Mormon woman in Bangkok or an American Mormon woman in Salt Lake City, who may both take certain culturally contingent aspects of their religious practice for granted, women who have negotiated between sharply contrasting cultural realities often expressed an expanded sense of possibility and authorship in shaping their lives.

In the Asian North American oral history interviewees' accounts of their lives' meaning and value, Mormonism emerges as an important and indispensable source of ideological and cultural authority that is, nevertheless, not hegemonic. It coexists (and competes) with multiple other cherished points of reference from which the interview subjects triangulated their sense of the world and how to do the right thing.

Below I will give an overview of how cross-cultural perspectives can help to reframe discussions of Mormon women's agency by drawing on a few examples from the Asian American and Asian Canadian oral history project. First, I show that conversions based on the practical, as opposed to doctrinal attractions of Mormonism, show that conversion is a two-way exchange in which women choose Mormonism on their own terms and according to the values of their native cultural frame of reference. Second, I cite ways in which "Mormon culture" (usually North American Mormon culture) can also provide a vehicle for furthering women's agency and serving women's larger cultural priorities. Third, I argue that Asian North American Mormon women's acceptance of patriarchal structures does not signal a lack of awareness or abdication of their spiritual agency. I conclude with a discussion of the urgent need for scholarly perspectives that take into account the experiences of women in Mormonism's non-North American majority.

On Their Own Terms: Practical, Not Doctrinal, Motives for Conversion

The majority of the women in the Asian American and Asian Canadian oral history project were converts to Mormonism. Of these women, many said that they had joined the LDS Church not for doctrinal reasons but because the moral values taught within local church communities resonated with those of their native culture.[3] Aspects of Mormonism that seem distinctive or countercultural in a North American context may already be deeply embedded in an Asian cultural context influenced by Confucianism and Buddhism, including socially conservative attitudes toward sexuality and gender roles, emphasis on the extended family unit, the value of self-cultivation and self-discipline, and prohibitions on alcohol and substance abuse. While the official church narrative for why people should convert to Mormonism centers on God's restorationist message to Joseph Smith Jr., and the restoration of lost theological truths and priesthood authority, such doctrinal distinctions seem to have factored little in the women's decision of whether or not to join the church. Instead of a totalizing ideological overhaul, conversion for these women was a process of engaging with Mormonism according to their understanding and within the context of their preexisting priorities.[4]

The language barrier may have played a role in making Mormonism's moral culture more attractive than its doctrines to immigrant Asian women. Sai Wai Lau, who immigrated to Utah as a young bride in 1949, said that her level of English ability made it hard for her to understand the missionaries' various theological discourses. Because language took the theological perspective on conversion off the table, her decision to be baptized came down solely to more practical considerations based on her preexisting values:

> First we just thought, Maybe it'll be good for the children. And so thinking about the future and about our children, that's why we decided to join the Church . . . There are a lot of things that I don't understand. I don't read a lot. But Jerry understand, and he'd just tell me.

Now a member of nearly half a century, with four grown children who are all active Mormons, Sai Wai Lau still thinks of her decision to be baptized in terms of the practical effect that she feels the church had on her family.

> I think we made the right decision to join the church. None of our friends joined the church. None in Salt Lake. But I think it's a little bit different. The children have learned more. I think our friends had a lot of kids that didn't get married. Our best friends, the daughter's Jessie's age. They didn't get married. They didn't have the church activities. I think it's really good for the children to learn. Compare the family, and you can tell that our life is more happier than their lives. The kids are more happier than their kids, and more . . . Well, we are a little different, you know. I don't know

> why. But compare with the families . . . So I'm proud of myself for making the right decision to join the Church.[5]

Callie Sukhee, a Mongolian woman living in Arlington, Virginia, recalled that when she joined the church she had only a spotty understanding of what the missionaries were teaching in English, but that her husband had been favorably impressed:

> [My husband said,] "This is a good church. I heard that they are very good people and this is a good church. Let's join it." Just like that . . . Mostly they taught us in English. It was very complicated. Sometimes you would understand what they said, and sometimes it's just foggy—you didn't understand what they say. Then we set the baptism date, and just four weeks later we got baptized.

Sukhee continued to go to church after her baptism, even after her husband's activity tapered off. Six years later, when she had the opportunity to return to Mongolia, she attended church at a little rural branch. She recalled that attending church services in her native land and in her native tongue was a powerful spiritual experience, unlike the confused discussions that had led her into Mormonism in the first place: "The Spirit was very strong, and I felt it and listened to the gospel in my own language. It struck my heart strong, like pointed things. Every single word would melt in my heart. It was very strong."

For Sukhee, the intense spiritual experience that is often presumed to be a requirement for conversion occurred several years after her decision to be baptized as a Mormon. It also occurred in a different cultural context. That her conversion experience was the reverse of the church missionary program's ideal of the so-called "golden investigator" shows not that she was a "silver" or second-class convert, but that she joined the church on her own terms. Over time, and as she developed a heightened awareness about the role of culture in inflecting spiritual experience, her language as a Mongolian Mormon woman and the language of Mormon charismatic narratives gradually converged.

Many Asian interviewees reported being attracted by conservative Mormon social norms because they overlapped with their Asian cultural values. This support for pushback against mainstream, more liberal North American culture may have been very attractive for members of a minority culture striving to maintain their distinctiveness and sense of tradition.[6] The relative significance of orthopraxy instead of orthodoxy within Mormonism helps to explain why it was so easy for the women to convert and participate in the church without articulating strong theological opinions.[7] The Asian women in the study wielded agency in choosing a religious tradition whose theological claims interested them far less than the refuge it provided for their existing morals and values.

Mormon Language Units: Communities of Culture

The influence of North American culture—and in particular, the culture of the U.S. Intermountain West—in shaping the worldwide ecclesiastical culture of the LDS Church is undeniable. In 1999 I sat in on a training meeting for church translators and interpreters in Taipei and watched a training video. In this video, a white male church employee in a suit sitting at a desk with an American flag behind him, advised the Taiwanese interpreters to purchase a book on American pop culture so they would be better prepared to interpret anecdotes about American sports, high school experiences, music, literature, and the like. Grace Kwok's recent study of Hong Kong women has shown that they struggle with their internalization of idealized versions of Mormon womanhood that have been shaped by North American norms. Kwok's informants list aspects of this ideal Mormon womanhood as "good at scrapbooking," "willing to bear a lot of children," and "responsible for staying home and taking care of the children." All three of these ostensible marks of womanly perfection are alien to Hong Kong's competitive, fast-paced society, in which most families have one or at the very most two children, and all but very wealthy women work as a matter of financial survival.[8]

However, despite the drawbacks of an organizational culture that can be strongly shaped by North American cultural norms, this close and sometimes nearly indistinguishable link between culture and doctrine within Mormonism can also be used to sustain minority cultural traditions. Mormon women of Asian descent, discussing the values and teachings that were most important to them, revealed that values often claimed by Mormons, such as family-mindedness and hard work, are in actuality Asian values.[9] Indeed, in many cases it seemed that "mainstream" Mormon approaches to family-mindedness and hard work may not have gone far enough for these members of Asian descent.

In units with a high proportion of members from Asian nations, these traditions tend to shape definitions of Mormon belief and practice. For instance, one of the characteristics of Mormonism that tends to be most attractive to people from a Confucian background is the high value placed on the family unit.[10] This family emphasis (not Joseph Smith's First Vision, or living prophets and apostles, or various other doctrinal distinctions that speak audaciously to longstanding Western theological debates but that are nothing special from a Buddhist or Shamanic perspective) can come to dominate members' interpretation of Mormon belief. This shared understanding of "first things" diverges from official interpretations in church materials published in North America and reflects the priorities of Asian units' native culture over North American Mormon norms.

Reversing the usual equation in which culture functions to achieve a religious ideal, Mormon women in Asian language units used Mormon religious structures (the branch or ward community organization) as the vehicle for achieving an ethnic cultural ideal. Anne Jensen, a Hmong born in Laos who immigrated to France and later to the United States as a young girl, married Kyle Jensen, the Hmong-speaking missionary who had baptized her family in central California. She and her family had been members of typical Mormon wards (geographically defined congregations with all meetings conducted in English), but at the time of the interview they were members of a special Hmong language ward, called the Nong Shala Ward, where her husband was bishop. Speaking of her preference for the Nong Shala Ward, she said:

> From the Hmong culture I like the fact that Hmong are very supportive one of another—not to say that Americans are not, that's not what I'm saying. For example we've been attending mainstream wards, and we've been in the Nong Shala Ward for almost three years now. I really love it, and I want my children to stay in this ward because a lot of the parents are still raising their children in the traditional way.
>
> For example, when my husband and I want to go out for a date and we need a babysitter, then we'll ask the young women

> [teenage girls] to come and babysit for us. We've offered money, and they'll say, "Oh no. Please don't pay. We just want to offer help." I think that in the mainstream ward—not that it's bad—they could expect you to exchange that for maybe, you know, like babysitting fees. Would you agree? . . . In our ward a lot of the young women just won't accept being paid, they want to do that. Or, I've done it where the mothers will say, "Oh now, please don't pay my daughters. I want them to be hard workers." Or sometimes I've asked the mother if the girls could come and watch the kids, and her typical response is, "Never hesitate to ask my girls to come and help. I don't want them to be idle. I'd rather them be spending time doing service projects than staying home."

The Nong Shala Ward teenage girls' refusal to be paid for babysitting suggests a distinctive community culture in which social capital is more important than actual money, and in which members closely and self-consciously link this social capital to the idea of a common Hmong cultural heritage. While Jensen said that it was not "bad" that babysitters in a "mainstream" English-speaking ward would want money for their work, she preferred the Nong Shala Ward because of its ethic of hard work and self-sacrifice that exceeds typical North American Mormon standards.

This anecdote also points to the dual role of LDS "language" units such as Hmong-language wards in Sacramento, Cambodian branches in Seattle, and Chinese wards in Toronto. Officially they exist merely to facilitate the administration of a non-English-speaking congregation. At the same time, like the ethnic enclaves in these cities, language units also provide a community of culture in which converts' religious education takes place in a culturally familiar setting. Within these communities of culture, members' human capital such as leadership ability, education, and so on can be fully utilized.[11] In Asian-language congregations within North America, church meetings in native languages take on a special importance in providing an immersion environment for the second generation.

The Lesser of Two Patriarchies: Mediating between Mormon and Asian Gender Hierarchies

Many conversations in the academic field of women and religion center on the problem of women's disproportionate participation in patriarchal religions, including Mormonism.[12] These studies, conducted among a majority white, North American demographic, generally show that patriarchal authority within Mormonism is often viewed either as a negative that is mitigated by other positives, or as an apparent negative ("people might think that Mormonism doesn't value women, but actually . . .") that must be situated in explanations of complementarism between divinely appointed male and female roles. Among the older generation of women raised in Confucian cultural traditions, however, patriarchy is often accepted unapologetically as simply a fact of life. This hierarchical view of gender roles long preceded their contact with Mormon patriarchal values, and in this context Mormonism is actually "patriarchy lite." In many cultures where strong norms of male dominance prevail, Mormonism and other conservative Christian traditions may be relatively progressive in their emphasis on male spiritual headship as a divine directive for men to behave responsibly. In her work on evangelicals in Latin America, Elizabeth Brusco argues, "The Pentecostal message provided the best way [women] could see to effect a genuine change in their family relations, to get their men to forgo some of the macho posturing the popular culture encourages, and to reorder priorities on how limited family income was spent."[13]

Catherine Brekus recently called for approaches to Mormon women's history that show their agency not just in challenges to existing community structures, but also in the reproduction of these structures.[14] In the cases of the Asian American and Asian Canadian Mormon women, who are reproducing not only Mormon religious structures but also Japanese or Cambodian or other Asian cultural structures, we gain insight into the complex relationship between patriarchal hierarchy and spiritual power. While feminist scholars might be inclined to view religious patriarchy as something that always limits or dampens women's spirituality, these patriarchal assumptions often provide the warp on which some of the Asian interviewees' most far-reaching and vivid spiritual experiences are woven.

In some of the Asian Mormon women's stories, it seems that God colluded with patriarchal Confucian tendencies; in others, it seems that God gently corrected them. Angela Wu was in Hong Kong when she prayed for the birth of a son (a major prerogative in Chinese Confucian-influenced family culture) and felt that God answered her prayer:

> I really want a son. I really want a son because my husband is Chinese. I want a son for him to carry the name. I also want a son to let me have the experience to know what it would be like to be the mother of a son. So I prayed to Heavenly Father, I promise you that if you give me a son, I promise you that I will try my best to bring him under your light, to teach him all the things you want to teach a boy, but please give me one. Then as I kneeled down and prayed, right at that moment, Heavenly Father answered. And in my heart I got this warm feeling all over my body, and I knew that he answered my prayer. I will conceive. So it was at that very night I conceived.

While Angela Wu's petition for a male offspring was met with a feeling of spiritual affirmation, and also a feeling that she would indeed conceive a son, the plea of Ellen Tsui was met with a similarly affirming spiritual experience, but accompanied with a different premonition.

Ellen Tsui was born in Hong Kong but later immigrated to Canada. She recalled that when her first child was born, a girl, her in-laws were very happy because it was their first grandchild. As she was expecting her second child, however, she felt a great deal of pressure to produce a son to carry the family name and fulfill her in-laws' expectations. She prayed that this second child would be a boy, even up to the night that she was in labor in the hospital.

> I remember one night I stay in the hospital, waiting. She is coming. I kneeled down in the window. I prayed to Heavenly Father, "Please, I know, I know," I told Heavenly Father, "I know if she is a girl for you. You can make she be a boy." So I asked Heavenly Father, "Please promise me: give me a boy." When I finished my prayer, in my mind I saw a picture. A picture is a really, really happy picture. I saw two little girl. They hold their father together, one hand and another hand from two daughters. They are very, very happy, and in the street they say good-bye to their daddy; they kiss. One daughter kiss this face, and another kissed another face. Come to my mind is said, "Two daughters they grow together. This is very good to them. They know each other; they can help each other." So this really, really happy picture in my mind. That

> moment, I am very happy, too. But after that when I went back to my bed, I lie down. Suddenly I realize that's Heavenly Father. He tell me this is a daughter. So when, that night my daughter was born, so I know she's a daughter. So I knew, but still have a little disappointment. Now is 21 years later, and I knew that's good. That's really good to them, and the picture in the hospital I saw this, the picture. Some years later, one day when I, my husband and two daughter we go to school, we went to take them together. Because he missed to go right way and go to the intersection, he need to say good-bye with them. The two daughters kissed his cheeks, then that picture: I remember I saw this before.

In this instance, Tsui drew on her Mormon faith in a God who answers prayers to express her Confucian desire for a son. In her narrative, God responded to the prayer of faith in a miraculous way that also refuted the Confucian emphasis on male offspring. In this way, Mormonism softened—not strengthened—Confucian patriarchal priorities.

Even as many of the Asian Mormon women affirmed patriarchal authority, they simultaneously circumvented it through seeking direct personal revelation from God. Kee Park Chang from South Korea, saw her courtship and marriage to her husband in almost purely religious terms. When she decided that the time had come to get married, she was daunted by the thought of dating and concluded that the best way to find the man that she was to marry was to simply ask God. She fasted for one day and during that fast saw a vision in which she saw the side of a man's face (but not enough to be recognizable). She subsequently decided that a forty-day fast would be most efficacious, since Jesus had fasted for forty days. She fasted on the first day and on the last, and during the days in between she tried to be absolutely perfect. At the end of this fast she saw another vision in which she saw a man whom she recognized. It was a male acquaintance of hers from church, a man in whom she'd never had any romantic interest:

> I pray, "Why him?" I don't want it, but I know I have to listen to the Spirit. I call him, I met him, I told him, "I'm going to marry you." He was so surprised because I never date. I never talk about anything. He said he was really surprised, but he said yes because

> he was my home teacher at that time.[15] He know me, I know him, but I never wanted to him dating . . . But anyways, he did the yes, and then I called my branch president, all my friend, "I'm going to marry him!" Everybody's "You're kidding me." . . . I never met him, but I know I'm doing right way because of the Spirit. I listen Spirit, it is right. Until now I really appreciate I marry him. He is so opposite from me, that's why I can learn more from him. Because of everything doesn't go same way to think, but I always try to because he is my heaven. He is kind of my lord because we are supposed to listen my husband. So I learn from the Church. So I try to listen him—not [just] 100 percent, [but] 200 percent, [he is] my school.

According to this narrative, Chang married a man entirely as a result of a religious vision and not as the object of romantic attraction, in the process overturning established South Korean cultural norms. Yet, for all the assertiveness that she demonstrated in finding a man to marry, she is surprisingly submissive within her marital relationship. In the same account, she volunteers that her husband is her "heaven," her "Lord," her "school." To a certain degree this unseats our expectations: she starts out looking like an aggressive, overbearing woman who pushes her husband around, and ends up looking like a meek object of patriarchal domination. Of course, she is neither. She is simply a woman who inhabits a multidimensional world shaped by complex cultural and spiritual realities.

Conclusion

In this essay I have sought to discuss culture in a broad comparative context, acknowledging the powerful cultural gravity that exerts a force on how people think and behave in a given regional and religious context. In culture's larger realms, Mormon women whose life experiences have led them across the borders of Asian and North American culture are perhaps more aware than others of the magnitude of cultural (ethnic) authority as a counterpoint and complement to Mormon belief and practice. With this broadened perspective on ethnic and religious cultural structures as powerful resources for shaping one's life experiences, Mormon women's agency expands.

Despite the fact that a majority of Mormon believers come from outside of North America, it is somewhat bemusing that the topic of. "Mormon Asian women" may have an eclectic or exotic air. In such a paradigm, Salt Lake City is the sole center of Mormondom, where mostly white, North American men oversee the production of the gospel message in spoken and printed word. From here, it is carried to the periphery, translated and received (but not produced) in numerous diverse and colorful settings. In such a paradigm, the North American version of the church is the main course, and outposts outside of North America are like the side dishes and garnish that complete and transform the meal.

Perhaps this is the case in terms of the ongoing North American editorship of nearly all the church's official cultural productions, including General Conference talks and correlated lesson manuals. But, when it comes to actual numbers and people, the broad distribution of Joseph-Smith's-First-Vision-believing, Spirit-of-God-singing, Book-of-Mormon-reading, Sabbath-sermon-speaking, churchgoing Mormons outside of North America are not merely the garnish but part (54 percent) of the main course.[16] Far from being mere consumers, as is often assumed in the "religious market" model, religious individuals within Mormonism are producers of religion through their worldviews, practices, and social presence in the lives of others. If more than half of all Mormon experience and community is produced outside of North America, then it behooves us to scramble to catch up so that the production of Mormon studies scholarship reflects the globalized and gendered aspects of this production.[17]

One great challenge to the emergence of global studies of Mormon women is that the church outside of North America is extremely fragmented, a collection of small pockets of believers who do not speak each other's language (after English, Spanish, and Portuguese, the fourth through seventh most common languages spoken in the church are three Filipino dialects and Japanese).[18] Another challenge lies in the fact that men produce nearly all officially authoritative, ecclesiastical discourse within Mormonism (such as General Conference sermons). Without a turn at the microphone in the form of strong individual leaders, the collective voices of Mormon women churchwide blend into an indistinguishable murmur. If it seems daunting enough to lump Asian Mormon women together into one research category, how much more difficult would it be to collectively study women in the larger "European, African, Asian, and Australian" contingent that makes up 16 percent of church membership worldwide?

One solution to this challenge is to engage in focused studies of Mormon women that avoid utilizing the center-and-periphery orientation, whereby the experiences of non-North American Mormon women supply "diversity" that plays a complementary role in relation to a more uniform "norm" of North American Mormon women. It is true that the administrative center of The Church of Jesus Christ of Latter-day Saints is Salt Lake City, Utah. But in many other ways, the relationship between this administrative center in Salt Lake City and a local unit in Taiwan is fundamentally the same as that between a local unit in Salt Lake City and a local unit in Massachusetts. The women in these Mormon units all participate in a complex church community shaped by local norms and subject to constant negotiation. Diversity in Mormonism is to be found not only by crossing geographic borders, but also by each circle further removed from the central administrative chain of command.

This essay has shown that geographic border crossing expands Mormon women's agency in authoring their religious and cultural lives. The experiences of Asian Mormon women in North America show culture's potential as a source of liberation, and not just constraint. If certain ethnic or religious cultural norms or values are strong enough, instead of being pulled into the gravity of a stronger competitor, they simply hold their place in the firmament, forming a fixed but multidimensional constellation by which an individual can confidently navigate. These women, whose multicultural perspectives increasingly define twenty-first-century Mormon womanhood, use the compelling authority of both ethnic and religious culture to actively shape their lives. Through conversion on their own terms, the creation of local communities that reflect their distinctive values and priorities, and affirmation of the reality of a plane of revelatory experience that cuts through all cultural circumstances, these Mormon women draw creatively on resources of authority to define and pursue life's meaning.

Notes

1. "Asian" as a panethnic category can be nearly meaningless beyond general physical similarities upon which outsiders rely to lump people together from

diverse ethnic backgrounds, but on the other hand, "Asian" ethnic groups themselves have embraced panethnic categorization for their own purposes. See Yen Le Espiritu, *Asian American Panethnicity* (Philadelphia: Temple University Press, 1993), 2–6.

2. Hannah Wheelwright, "Understanding Our Differences: Younger Mormons and Leaving the LDS Church," *Feminist Mormon Housewives,* August 17, 2013, accessed September 15, 2013, http://www.feministmormonhousewives.org/2013/08/understanding-our-differences-younger-mormons-and-leaving-the-lds-church.
3. Other studies have addressed this question of overlap between Mormon and other cultures. In one study comparing attitudes toward the Mormon health code, or Word of Wisdom, among Mormons in North America and Guatemala, Thomas Murphy found a "coexistence of patterns." He observed that "proscriptions in the Mormon health code generally fit into a preexisting cultural pattern in Guatemala," specifically Latin American folk beliefs about the qualities and effects of various foods. See Thomas W. Murphy, "Guatemalan Hot/Cold Medicine and Mormon Words of Wisdom: Intercultural Negotiation of Meaning," *Journal for the Scientific Study of Religion* 36, no. 2 (June 1997): 302.
4. In contrast to this totalizing point of view, scholars of Christianity such as Robert Hefner and Fenella Cannell have proposed that religious conversion is not so much a systematic reorganization of personal meanings, but a new locus of self-identification, a multifaceted shift in orientation. See Robert Hefner, *Conversion to Christianity: Historical and Anthropological Perspectives of a Great Transformation* (Berkeley: University of California Press, 1993); Fenella Cannell, introduction to *The Anthropology of Christianity* (Durham: Duke University Press, 2006).
5. Sai Wai Lau, interview, Asian American and Asian Canadian Oral History Project, Church History Library, Salt Lake City, Utah. All interviews with Asian American and Asian Canadian Mormon women in this essay are part of this oral history project.
6. See Armand Mauss, "Can There Be a 'Second Harvest'?: Controlling the Costs of Latter-day Saint Membership in Europe," *International Journal of Mormon Studies* 1, no. 1 (2008): 1–59.
7. For more on the Mormon focus on orthopraxy over orthodoxy, see James Faulconer, "Why a Mormon Won't Drink Coffee but Might Have a Coke: The Atheological Character of the Church of Jesus Christ of Latter-day Saints," *Element* 2, no. 2 (Fall 2006): 21–37.
8. Grace Ka Ki Kwok, "Mormon Women's Identity: The Experiences of Hong Kong Chinese Mormon Women" (master's thesis, University of Hong Kong, 2012), 20–22.
9. Mormon public identification with an emphasis on the strength of the family unit in recent years is evident in the near-canonical status of "The Family:

A Proclamation to the World," first introduced in 1995. The Mormon emphasis on the importance of the traditional, nuclear family also came to the fore in its public support of Proposition 8 in California (2008) and other same-sex marriage ballot initiatives. Family themes account for over a third (five out of fourteen) of the church's "Pass-Along Cards" (public relations tools used to share certain key Mormon teachings with interested parties). In 2007, then Relief Society general president Julie Beck gave a talk in the semiannual General Conference that was later widely cited, titled "Mothers Who Know." This talk emphasized the importance of family life and stressed, among other things, hard work: "Working beside children in homemaking tasks creates opportunities to teach and model qualities children should emulate." Julie B. Beck, "Mothers Who Know," General Conference of The Church of Jesus Christ of Latter-day Saints, October 2007.

10. For example, the bumper sticker "No Success Can Compensate for Failure in the Home" is a best seller among church members in Taiwan and often appears on the doors or vehicles of people who are not members of the church.
11. Rebecca Kim, "'Made in the U.S.A.': Second-Generation Korean American Campus Evangelicals," in *Asian American Youth: Culture, Identity, and Ethnicity*, edited by Jennifer Lee and Min Zhou (New York: Routledge, 2004), 243.
12. See Lori Beaman, "Molly Mormons, Mormon Feminists and Moderates: Religious Diversity and the Latter-day Saints Church," *Sociology of Religion* 62, no. 1 (2001): 77; John Heeren, Donald B. Lindsey, Marylee Mason, "The Mormon Concept of Mother in Heaven: A Sociological Account of Its Origins and Development," *Journal for the Scientific Study of Religion*, 23 no. 4 (1984): 396–411; Jeanne Kay Gulke, "Mrs. Gardner's World: Scale in Mormon Women's Autobiographical Writing," *Area* 39, no. 3 (2007): 274–75.
13. Elizabeth Brusco, *The Reformation of Machismo: Evangelical Conversion and Gender in Colombia* (Austin: University of Texas Press, 2010).
14. Catherine Brekus, "Mormon Women and Agency," *Journal of Mormon History* 37, no.2 (2011): 59–87.
15. A male priesthood holder, who in partnership with another priesthood holder, is assigned to regularly visit specific members of a congregation and to watch over their spiritual and temporal wellbeing.
16. "A Global Christ-Centered Faith," http://www.mormonnewsroom.org/article/infographics.
17. Gender matters in understanding locally produced Mormonism around the globe because gender is such a critical factor in defining a functional, local Mormon community (i.e. the need for a certain number of male priesthood holders in key leadership positions). Particularly useful would be the gathering of some good, hard data showing the relationship between gender and church conversion and retention rates around the world. I suspect that gender ratios within Mormon communities in Asia, for instance, are even more skewed toward women than those in North America. How do Mormon

women exercise authority and influence within congregations where they generally predominate in number, but not in official leadership?

18. "A Global Christ-Centered Faith," http://www.mormonnewsroom.org/article/infographics.

15

Mormon Women's Sexual Agency in Patriarchal Culture

Women Who Suffer and Women Who Thrive

JENNIFER FINLAYSON-FIFE

While researching my dissertation subject of sexual agency among Mormon women, and currently as a private practice therapist working with Latter-day Saint (LDS) couples on sexual and relational issues, I have been exposed to the psychological challenges and strengths of many LDS women.[1] My dissertation explored the question of Mormon women's sexual agency within the patriarchal and sexually conservative institution of our faith. Utilizing a feminist framework for its critique of patriarchy, and the postulated deleterious effect on women's agency, my research sought to understand the relevance of the critique to LDS women. While the narratives of most Mormon women in my research and clinical practice reflect the predicaments and threats to agency that the feminist critique postulates, a subset of women demonstrate that the law of chastity in its purest theological form can actually support Mormon women's sexual agency. While a combination of cultural influences, including church leaders' statements about gender and sexuality, often thwart this potential positive outcome, these women's interpretations of LDS theology offer a way for Mormon women to use their faith to promote and sustain their psychological and sexual well-being.

I will first outline the utilized feminist critique, as well as demonstrate its relevance to Mormon women—including how LDS women have suffered because of the cultural narratives surrounding gender and sexuality. I will then discuss the nonapplicability of the critique to a portion of LDS women, and discuss how these individuals demonstrate sexual and personal agency within and because of LDS teachings and principles.

I employed a perspective postulated by radical feminism. While the word "radical" is sometimes used in the vernacular to express feminist extremism, I am referencing a specific theory within feminist thought that arose in the 1960s and 70s. Radical (meaning "root") feminism asserts that male-led institutions (or patriarchies) are at the root of women's oppression.[2] According to radical feminism, women's agency, and in particular women's sexual agency (meaning the ability to act on one's behalf in the sexual realm), is undermined in patriarchy.[3] Patriarchal (or male-biased) ideologies, in the radical feminist view, undermine women's sexual agency by delegitimizing female desire. In this theoretical perspective, invalidating a woman's relationship to her sexuality is a particularly potent form of female oppression; it not only undercuts her relationship to her body, her self-knowledge, and her capacity for pleasure, but it diminishes the clarity and autonomy that comes from that self-awareness.[4]

The primary oppressive mechanism of patriarchy, in radical feminist thought, is the ideology of gender roles.[5] Patriarchal gender scripts assert that women are nurturing, selfless, gentle and kind, and naturally less sexual than men. They also construct erotic desire as unfeminine—upholding female sexuality as inherently chaste, and morally superior to the supposed depravity of male sexuality. While superficially approving of women's nature, this cultural prescription leaves women little room to legitimately experience, express, or integrate erotic desire. To be feminine is to suppress or disconnect from sexual desire, or feel ashamed of its presence. The prescribed rejection of embodied experience necessarily undermines clarity and self-confidence, in the radical feminist perspective, as women must reject a part of themselves in order to be seen as legitimate.[6]

While gender role ideology teaches women to disown sexual desire, it encourages them to pursue sexual *desirability*.[7] Enhancing desirability includes striving to meet expectations of proper female comportment (such as kindness, self-effacement, and attention to the needs and desires of others), as well as standards of female beauty. However, these often unattainable standards undermine agency further as they foster women's nonidentification with their own bodies and desires, and encourage women's overidentification with men's wishes and men's approval.[8] Thus, patriarchies instruct men to desire, an agentic position, and women to be desirable, a nonagentic position; or similarly stated, men learn to be the subjects of desire in patriarchy, and women the *objects* of it.

Furthermore, patriarchal ideology, in the radical feminist view, not only undermines agency by teaching women to be the objects of male desire rather than the subjects of their own, it inhibits sexual subjectivity by holding women disproportionately responsible for shared sexual activity. As "good" women supposedly lack erotic feeling, patriarchies give women the cultural mandate to manage the sexual behavior of men.[9] As unfair as this may be, it is made worse by the fact that women must live up to this mandate within the restrictive dictates of proper feminine behavior that prescribe women's deference to men and attention to men's needs as inherent female virtues. These ideals make it exceptionally difficult for women to succeed in safeguarding the cultural limits of sexual behavior, as they must fend off men's sexual assertiveness or aggression while being at the same time kind and attentive.[10] Given that women are seldom able to navigate these contradictory cultural dictates, they are vulnerable to feelings of shame for participation in sexual behavior that devalues or blemishes them, as well as feelings of guilt for not having stopped the behavior. These cultural burdens further undermine women's confidence, clarity and psychological autonomy.[11]

Radical feminist theory as outlined above is compelling when considering Mormon women's experiences since there is reason to believe that LDS women's sexual agency may be constrained in ways that the critique theorizes. The Church of Jesus Christ of Latter-day Saints is a patriarchal religion both organizationally and ideologically. In addition to belief in a male deity, religious leadership comes through men as they comprise the primary authoritative structure of the church. Women occupy some leadership roles over women and children, but that leadership is always overseen by men. Furthermore, there is asymmetry in attributed authority between husband and wife, as men are taught to lead in the home, and women are taught to defer to that (righteous) leadership. As a result of this patriarchal structure, women have limited institutional agency in Mormonism as men in the church (as priesthood holders and leaders) have greater authority to interpret theology and implement policy than women do, as well as the ability to define many spiritual and temporal realities for women.

Central to these male-defined spiritual and temporal realities is the prescription of gender assignments and temperaments. Current

Latter-day Saint teachings construct women as less agentic than men, as women learn that their divine role is to support the righteous desires and efforts of men. In a current manual written for new members of the church, President Brigham Young is quoted in a section entitled "The Role of Women." He states, "One thing is very true and we believe it, and that is that the woman is the crowning jewel of the man." President Young goes on to say: "When I reflect upon the duties and responsibilities devolving upon our mothers and sisters and the influence they wield, I look upon them as the mainspring and the soul of our being here. It is true that man is first . . . But when Mother Eve came she had a splendid influence over [Father Adam]."[12] While this statement outwardly honors women as necessary and even the "crowning jewel" of man, it reinforces men as the reference point for women's value, behavior, and sense of self. Similarly, as stated in a General Conference talk entitled, "The Divine Nature and Destiny of Women,"[13] women play a "sacred role . . . in the sanctification and purification of men." Men are the actors, women are the support staff for men's actions and agency. Consistently, the cultural assumption of nonagency for women is evident in the manuals used for the Young Men's and Young Women's organizations from 1984 until late 2012. The curriculum titles demonstrate the difference in perceived power between the genders: In the Young Men's manual a lesson on marriage is entitled "Choosing an eternal companion" (demonstrating an agentic position), and the reciprocal lesson for the young women is entitled, "Preparing to become an eternal companion" (demonstrating a nonagentic position).[14] Evident is the supposition of male agency, as men actively seek a wife of their choosing, and the presumption of female nonagency as women in relative passivity prepare to be chosen.

Consistent with the radical feminist perspective, LDS women learn not only to be passive relative to men's subjectivity, but also their nonagency is further reinforced by the doctrinal emphasis on desirability or esteem earned through fulfillment of these prescribed roles. For instance, Apostle James E. Faust taught young women to listen to their "natural desires" in making life decisions, implicitly defining for them the narrow scope of their legitimate choices:

> There are ever-increasing demands on women that challenge their traditional role as caregivers. But as women, the roles of

> wife and mother are in the center of your souls and cry out to be satisfied. Most women naturally want to love and be loved by a good man and to respond to the God-given, deepest feelings of womanhood—those of mother and nurturer.[15]

Authoritative statements not only reinforce that wifehood and motherhood are the most (if not only) esteemed roles for women, but that women will be valued for their willingness to fulfill those roles. "I have been very careful, and am very careful, to treat my wife with the respect and reverence that is due her in performing that thing that is of most worth for a woman in this life: to live the gospel, to be the wife and the mother of the children of a worthy holder of the priesthood."[16] Previous president of the church, Gordon B. Hinckley, said to women, "Please know how much we appreciate you. You bring a measure of wholeness to us."[17] While openly affirming, his statement underscores the fact that woman's value in the church lies in her service to men and men's needs.

Additionally, church curriculum emphasizes the importance of female desirability through sexual purity. In the theology of the church, both men and women should be chaste until marriage, and both sexes take this seriously. As such, there is no double standard—meaning no greater expectation of sexual innocence in women than men. That said, women's virtue is heralded in scripture and church instruction as a defining characteristic of true womanhood. In his talk, "Near to the Angels," Apostle Faust taught young women that the "virtue of young women should be equal to the angels."[18] Apostle Richard G. Scott instructed LDS men that "of all the creations of the Almighty, there is none more beautiful, none more inspiring, than a lovely daughter of God who walks in virtue."[19]

While control of sexuality is clearly expected of men in the church—and there are social and spiritual costs if they do not comply—the notion of a "virtuous man" is not explicitly linked to sexuality.[20] By comparison, the notion of a virtuous woman is common, and is used primarily in reference to her sexual behavior and her value, as in the oft repeated scripture: "Who can find a virtuous woman? For her price is far above rubies."[21] The threat of lowered desirability through female sexual behavior is evident in Apostle Faust's claim that, "young women should realize that young men they date will not honor and respect them if they have been involved in moral transgression."[22]

In line with this disproportionate focus on women's sexual purity, it is often implied that young women in the church should manage the sexual desires of the young men they are with through their own modest dress and behavior. Apostle Dallin H. Oaks remarked, "Young women, please understand that if you dress immodestly, you are magnifying this problem, by becoming pornography to some of the men who see you."[23] Or, as Elder Tad R. Callister of the Quorum of the Seventy stated in the *Ensign*:

> The dress of a woman has a powerful impact upon the minds and passions of men. If it is too low or too high or too tight, it may prompt improper thoughts, even in the mind of a young man who is striving to be pure . . . Women particularly can dress modestly and in the process contribute to their own self-respect and to the moral purity of men. In the end, most women get the type of man they dress for.[24]

Perhaps, not surprisingly, most women that I interviewed had internalized a sexual double standard (in spite of a doctrinal single standard around sexuality). Many women believed that a sexual transgression was not as serious for men as it was for women; they offered more forgiveness for their husbands' past transgressions than they felt they themselves deserved. And, in spite of having repented and feeling confident that God had forgiven them for past sexual conduct, many women did not disclose premarital sexual activity to their husbands, given the uncertainty that they would be forgiven or esteemed as worthy if their nonsanctioned sexual behavior were known.

Consistently, a majority of the women in my study expressed feelings of responsibility for men's sexual behavior, or for not successfully stopping an unwanted advance. When one woman's boyfriend pushed beyond a limit that she desired, she felt responsible "because [she] didn't stop him immediately." In line with the radical feminist critique, this social expectation is particularly complicated given the cultural expectation that women defer to and care for men. Many women expressed in interview the conflict between wanting to please their boyfriend and feeling pressured to defer to his judgment, while knowing that they would be judged for their sexual behavior if they continued. They also found it difficult to stop an unwanted advance, as they did not know how to do it without offending or hurting the feelings of their suitor. Very few women in my dissertation research navigated this complex of expectations and emotions well. Usually they submitted to the pressures of the male, and went further sexually than they actually wanted, then felt guilty and blemished for having consented. Many women reported feeling disproportionate guilt and shame for having engaged in sexual behavior, even when the advance was fully unwanted on their part.

The narratives associated with sexual nonagency dominated my dissertation interviews, and are present in most of my clinical discussions with LDS women as well. Consistent with the radical feminist critique, many LDS women internalize a sexual double standard, believing in their hearts that femininity and eroticism are incompatible. The cultural expectations of gender and sexuality inhibit many women's ability to act on their own behalf in the sexual realm, even when their desire is to obey the law of chastity premaritally and to be sexual maritally. Expressed as excessive responsibility for men's feelings and desires, disownership of their own eroticism, and engaging in sexual behavior out of obligation, many LDS women do not fare well in the sexual realm. This suggests a strong need to reexamine the ways that gender and sexuality are communicated to LDS women in the church.

However, it is also worth understanding the subgroup of women who demonstrated high levels of sexual agency and thrived within the teachings of the church.[25] In contrast to the group with lower levels of sexual agency, women in this group modeled greater explicit ownership of the law of chastity, seeing the principle as something that worked in their favor. While all interviewed believed that living by the law of chastity was important, this subset of women believed it would enhance the quality of their lives. They saw the law of chastity as a communal expectation that worked to their advantage. In a cultural system where men of the church prove their masculinity, in part, through sexual self-control and family commitment, the law of chastity promises a context of sexual expression that these women most desired: namely a context of commitment and fidelity.[26] This possibility stood in sharp contrast to the larger cultural expectations of men. Many LDS women saw sexual liberalism as a negative for women overall. They perceived that men could, and would, more readily take advantage of them sexually when sex was culturally divorced from commitment. They believed the law of chastity allowed

LDS women to expect more of men, offering a potential protection from male exploitation.

Latter-day Saint women with high levels of sexual agency further claimed that this cultural reality fostered trust in their sexual relationships and allowed them to more fully express and explore sexual desire. As one participant said, "I really feel strongly about married sex . . . because when there is that trust, it just gets better." And as another woman shared:

> I have complete confidence in the person I married. I trust him one hundred percent . . . I really have a sense that he cares about me in a way that is just amazing. I was really worried before I got married . . . like a lot of women, I had a body image phobia going. I hoped he would still think I am okay, when I don't have any clothes on. But with Bill, I felt it was a very easy transition, because overwhelmingly, I felt we had this very deep connection and the physical connection was just a natural part of that. So it was much more natural than I had even ever supposed.

Furthermore, women with greater sexual agency saw the law of chastity as a gender-neutral expectation, as it is in its purest theological form.[27] While most women in my research and clinical practice bought into the sexual double standard, those with greater agency did not. Women with high levels of sexual agency did not hesitate to defend sexual limits that they claimed for themselves. As one interviewee expressed, "I really felt like I should be able to be in control of that and that I didn't have to accept any unwanted stuff and so I had a lot of guys try to kiss me and I would physically block them." Similarly, women expressing greater agency did not believe that they owed men caretaking, particularly when it was at their own expense. They saw it as men's responsibility to manage their own sexuality relative to the law of chastity, and to manage their own feelings if they were disappointed by romantic or sexual refusal. Apostle Jeffrey R. Holland articulated:

> I have heard all of my life that it is the young woman who had to assume the responsibility for controlling the limits of intimacy in courtship because a young man cannot. Seldom have I heard any point made about a subject that makes me want to throw up more than that . . . To say that a young woman in such a relationship has

> to bear her responsibility and that of the young man's too is the most discriminatory doctrine I have ever heard.[28]

Consistent with Elder Holland's perspective, one participant said to her dating partner, "Listen, my relationship with you is not there, and if you want any kind of relationship, you need to stop." Even though it "really hurt his feelings," she said this "was more his problem than mine."

Additionally, Latter-day Saint women with high levels of sexual agency did not remain chaste to earn some future man's respect. They remained chaste because it fit with their own values; they were obeying the law of chastity because it represented the way they wanted to orient to their premarital sexuality, and it represented their relationship to God, not a future man. When these women did not live up to the law of chastity, their concerns were for their own commitments and their relationship with God, not for the men that might judge such behaviors as unfeminine or as a threat to their masculinity.

Finally, women with greater sexual agency moved relatively comfortably into marital sex. They saw sex within marriage, including desire and pleasure as fully legitimate for them. Rather than seeing sex as something one does out of duty to one's husband, they related to sex as an important and meaningful part of their lives, and as a God-given capacity that they enjoyed and looked forward to.

Why did some LDS women thrive within patriarchal, cultural, and religious realities while others did not? There are no demographic differences such as age, education level, or even claimed ideology that account adequately for the disparity in sexual agency among the participants. That said, women with greater sexual agency demonstrated agency in other parts of their lives as well. They were unapologetic for their beliefs, desires, and passions in life. Even if they overtly held to gender scripts (such as "my husband is the leader of our home"), they functioned in egalitarian marriages where power and decision making were genuinely shared.[29] Their behaviors reflected teachings such as Apostle L. Tom Perry described: "There is not a president and vice president in a family. We have co-presidents working together eternally for the good of their family . . . They are on equal footing. They plan and organize the affairs of the family jointly and unanimously as they move forward."[30] Importantly, these women also embraced their relationship with God to reinforce their strength, using belief in their divine nature, as well as prayer and personal revelation for validation of their legitimacy and their (sometimes nontraditional) choices. These women found in their relationship to God the ability to desire and live unapologetically, even when their choices went against church and cultural norms. As Apostle Quentin L. Cook taught, "Our doctrine is clear: Women are daughters of our Heavenly Father, who loves them. Wives are equal to their husbands."[31]

Finally, another expression of agency that I see among LDS women—while less optimal or mature than what I just described—further challenges the radical feminist perspective that women in patriarchy are powerless or vulnerable to mindless subjugation. This expression is agency as resistance to oppression within marriage. Some LDS women navigate male sexual entitlement by using the gender role script in their favor. In claiming their prescribed lack of desire or vulnerability (expressed sometimes as depression or self-doubt), women can invoke the reciprocal script of a benevolent patriarch in their husband and fend off unwanted sexual pressure. Women's culturally dictated vulnerability pressures men in Mormonism to be selfless and deny their own sexual longings. In "putting off the natural man," LDS men are pressured to prove their Christlike nature.[32] Albeit, a form of rebellion within a traditional marriage, it is an act of agency and nonsubmission, nonetheless.

In my clinical work with LDS women with limited sexual agency, I draw upon theological narratives and teachings that encourage us to embrace equality between the sexes, as well as embrace the body and its capacity for pleasure. To illustrate, I speak to women about the fact that we believe in embodied Parents in Heaven, and that LDS theology teaches that gaining a body, with all of its parts and passions, is critical to our spiritual development. Unlike some theologies, where the body (carnality) is seen as a threat to one's spirituality, Mormonism recognizes the essentialness of the body to becoming more like God, inclusive of our sexuality. While sexuality is a powerful currency and worthy of our respect, it is theologically inherent to our development as marriage partners and as children of God. I also discuss the sexual double standard and the nontheological nature of that accepted duplicity, as well as the legitimacy and importance of women's desires and perspectives in creating honest, intimate marriages and strong families. Additionally, I talk to women about being responsible for their own sexuality and attending to their own desires, rather than approaching sexuality from a framework of duty or passivity, lest they never find pleasure in sexuality for themselves.

In conclusion, a minority of the Mormon women I interviewed found ways to use LDS theology to their advantage by embracing the restrictive, sexual ethic precisely because it has the potential to secure them sexual fidelity and greater relational security through the cultural expectations of Mormon men. Latter-day Saint women with high levels of sexual agency also interpreted LDS theology as egalitarian and gender neutral, and took confidence in their own legitimacy as sexual beings and as daughters of God. Some Mormon women resisted simple submission to the sexual desires of their partners and found ways to use the gender role script to justify that resistance.

My clinical experience and dissertation research demonstrate that the radical feminist critique of patriarchal effect on sexual agency is relevant and worth considering for the damaging messages communicated to LDS women. These gendered messages affect many LDS women negatively, undermining their relationship to themselves and their sexuality. How to dispel these cultural false traditions and teach notions of sexuality that promote agency and the ability to embrace our God-given sexuality is worthy of our thoughtful consideration.

At the same time, the radical feminist critique is also too simplistic in that it doesn't account adequately for the ways that LDS women express their agency within patriarchy, and the ways that women embrace (a patriarchal) theology to their advantage. Expecting Mormon men to observe the law of chastity, LDS women can anticipate sexual loyalty and find greater sexual freedom in the safety of that reality. Mormon women also can access the LDS teaching of gender equality, God-given value, and personal revelation to find divine legitimacy for nonconventional choices and desires, thereby securing greater psychological and sexual agency amidst patriarchal expectations.

Notes

1. Jennifer Finlayson-Fife, "Female Sexual Agency in Patriarchal Culture: The Case of Mormon Women" (PhD dissertation, Boston College, 2002).
2. Catharine A. MacKinnon, "Feminism, Marxism, Method and the State: Toward Feminist Jurisprudence," *Signs: Journal of Women and Culture in Society* 8, no. 4 (Summer 1983): 635–58.

3. Rosemarie Tong, *Feminist Thought: A More Comprehensive Introduction* (Boulder: Westview Press, 1998).
4. Audre Lorde, *Sister Outsider: Essays and Speeches* (Trumansburg: Crossing Press, 1984); Catharine A. MacKinnon, "Feminism, Marxism, Method and the State: An Agenda for Theory," *Signs: Journal of Women in Culture and Society* 7, no. 3 (Spring 1982): 515–44.
5. Laura Hengehold, "Between Rape and 'Desired Sex': Making a More Complex Difference," *Journal of the Psychoanalysis of Culture & Society* 3, no. 2 (1998): 27–39; Gerda Lerner, *The Creation of Patriarchy* (New York City: Oxford University Press, 1996).
6. Judith Daniluk, "The Meaning and Experience of Female Sexuality: A Phenomenological Analysis," *Psychology of Women Quarterly* 17, no. 1 (March 1993): 53–69; Judith Daniluk, *Women's Sexuality: Across the Lifespan* (New York City: Guilford Press, 1998).
7. Sandra Lee Bartky, *Femininity and Domination: Studies in the Phenomenology of Oppression* (New York City: Routledge, 1990).
8. Ibid.; Daniluk, "The Meaning and Experience of Female Sexuality."
9. Deborah Tolman and Tracy Higgins, *How Being a Good Girl Can Be Bad for Girls* (New Brunswick: Rutgers University Press, 1996).
10. Susan Brownmiller, *Against Our Will: Men, Women, and Rape* (New York City: Simon and Schuster, 1975); Tolman and Higgins, *How Being a Good Girl Can Be Bad for Girls*.
11. Deborah L. Tolman, "Adolescent Girls, Women and Sexuality: Discerning Dilemmas of Desire," *Women & Therapy* 11, no. 3 (1991): 55–69; Deborah L. Tolman, "Doing Desire: Adolescent Girls' Struggles for/with Sexuality," *Gender & Society* 8, no. 3 (September 1994): 324–42; Sharon Thompson, "Putting a Big Thing in a Little Hole: Teenage Girls' Accounts of Sexual Initiation," *Journal of Sex Research* 27, no. 3 (August 1990): 341–61.
12. *Latter-day Saint Woman: Basic Manual for Women, Part A* (Salt Lake City: The Church of Jesus Christ of Latter-day Saints, 2000), 91.
13. Glen L. Pace, "The Divine Nature and Destiny of Women," *Church News*, March 9, 2010.
14. "Choosing an Eternal Companion," *Aaronic Priesthood Manual* 3 (Salt Lake City: Church of Jesus Christ of Latter-day Saints, 1994), 127. "Preparing to Become an Eternal Companion," *Young Women's Manual* 3 (Salt Lake City: Church of Jesus Christ of Latter-day Saints, 1994), 14.
15. James E. Faust, "How Near to the Angels," *Ensign*, May 1998, 96.
16. Boyd K. Packer, "Priesthood Power in the Home," *LDS.org*, February 2012, accessed October 31, 2013, https://www.lds.org/media-library/video/2012-02-1030-priesthood-power-in-the-home?lang=eng&category=worldwide-leadership-t.
17. Gordon B. Hinckley, "Women of the Church," *Ensign*, November 1996, 70.
18. Faust, "How Near to the Angels," 95.
19. Richard G. Scott, "The Sanctity of Womanhood," *Ensign*, May 2000, 36.

20. David Clark Knowlton, "On Mormon Masculinity," *Sunstone* 16, no. 2 (August 1992): 19–31.
21. Proverbs 31:10, King James Version.
22. Faust, "How Near to the Angels," 95. "Moral transgression" is a Mormon euphemism to imply nonsanctioned sexual behavior.
23. Dallin H. Oaks, "Pornography," *Ensign*, May 2005, 90.
24. Tad R. Callister, "The Lords Standard of Morality," *Ensign*, March 2014, 47–48.
25. Sexual agency was measured through qualitative analysis of LDS women's narratives, looking for congruence and incongruence with the radical feminist perspective. I conducted three- to four-hour interviews with sixteen active, married LDS women. The purpose of a qualitative study is to look in depth at the themes that emerge within a representative group. While most of the women that I interviewed demonstrated themes of sexual nonagency, we cannot legitimately extrapolate that most LDS women lack sexual agency. From this research it can only be concluded that some Mormon women interpret the theology in destructive ways, and that other Mormon women interpret the same theology in more constructive ways. This study gives us the opportunity to learn from both interpretations.
26. Knowlton, "Mormon Masculinity."
27. David A. Bednar, "We Believe in Being Chaste," *Ensign*, April 2013, 43.
28. Jeffrey R. Holland, "Of Souls, Symbols, and Sacraments," (speech presented at a devotional address at Brigham Young University, Provo, Utah, January 12, 1988). Copy in author's possession.
29. While church teachings around marriage in recent decades were unabashedly patriarchal, more recently, messages from church leadership emphasize equality between husband and wife. Notions of gender equality, however, continue to be contradicted by ongoing teachings that men should "preside" in the home and women should commit to obey their husbands. This theological contradiction has meant that many Mormon couples negotiate this discrepancy on their own terms, with many couples claiming notions of male leadership while functionally sharing marital decision making.
30. L. Tom Perry, "Fatherhood: An Eternal Calling," *Ensign*, April 2004, 70.
31. Quentin L. Cook, "LDS Women Are Incredible!," *Ensign*, May 2011, 26.
32. Knowlton, "Mormon Masculinity."

IV

CONTEMPORARY PERSONAL PERSPECTIVES

16

Agency in the Lives of Contemporary LDS Women

CLAUDIA BUSHMAN

Agency is one of three great Mormon feminist principles; the other two being revelation, and the belief in a Heavenly Mother. These principles give us power and scope as women. We have a female model in heaven, however we may choose to define her. With personal revelation women have a direct route to, and a connection with, deity that bypasses all marital, ward, stake, priesthood, and general authority. With agency, we have the right and ability to choose between different options. Agency is the strongest of these three feminist principles and goes beyond thinking into action—granting human choice. I will discuss here agency in belief and agency in practice.

When I was young, I thought that agency was a managed, not a free, choice. While the principle of choosing was clear, I thought that I could only choose between good and bad. My choice was to follow along, do what I was taught was right, and to obey orders as they were given, or to make a stupid, rash, thoughtless choice and be zapped for eternity. Church teaching in my young days centered on trying to guarantee that young people would make the right choices and guard them against making the wrong choices—for choosing wrong was not only disastrous, but irreversible, leading us down the slippery slope to immortal disaster. Repentance was discussed theoretically, but not really seen as likely or possible. There were only two choices: the right way, and the wrong way.

But my later life experience and observations suggest that we all have endlessly rich and malleable choices. We not only make choices, we have the right—or at least we have appropriated the right—to define the alternatives we choose. That is, we not only choose *between* the alternatives, we *choose* the alternatives, writing the complex scripts of individual choice. Our possibilities are not laid out for us and are limited only by our imaginations. That's tremendous freedom. That's tremendous power. We are free agents in the great scheme of things.

Mormonism has a daunting long list of beliefs and practices that assume more or less importance as times change. All these beliefs, rules, and commandments paradoxically coexist with the assertion that we do not have any complete definitive creeds or set of rules. We accept the Ten Commandments and the Articles of Faith, but neither contains the fullness of the gospel. Some like to consider "The Family: A Proclamation to the World," as definitive, but no one has claimed that it is revelation and it has not been canonized. The questions asked for temple recommends are changed and modified from time to time. The requirements that can be found in the church's teachings are so many and varied that we must individually decide which are most important and which we wish to follow. We have the agency to choose between simple or complicated lists of things we might or should do. We also choose how to interpret our choices, whether they are punishments, limitations, opportunities, creations, or pleasures. Some people consider Mormonism oppressive, but if it is oppressive that, too, is a choice we have made.

Although we have great freedom to choose, in the practice of Mormonism we believe that there is still an orthodoxy, with some variations, that we hold in common. We believe that the Bible, the Book of Mormon, the gospel as taught, and the church are "true" and that the stories of righteous men and women can be distilled for rules we can follow to our edification and improvement. One convenient measuring device for our own virtue is the nonscriptural temple worthiness questionnaire, administered by members of the bishopric and stake presidency, which we must take to determine whether we feel we are worthy to hold a recommend to enter the temple. This is a specific list of questions, but it is not found in the scriptures, and the queries have evolved and changed in our lifetimes. However, here, agency comes down to specific forms of behavior.

These questions are full of code phrases that can be interpreted in varied and complex ways. Some Mormons have decided that simple answers to these questions are the best answers, that these interviews are rituals preceding ritualistic temple ceremonies in which the "correct" answers are expected and presented. Others of us shade our positive answers with nuance. "No, I am not involved in any radical groups—except the University of California where I am a student." "Yes, I obey the Word of Wisdom, the same way that Joseph Smith and Brigham Young did." In temple interviews we choose between the complex answer and the simple, positive reply. When we are finally asked to say whether we think we are worthy to attend the temple, the question is posed with the expectation and hope that we will say that we are worthy, however we have answered the questions or feel about them.

Using our agency we choose the type of Mormon we wish to be: We can choose to be oppressed or liberated by the demands that are offered to us. We are free to determine our relative virtue or vice. We can choose to try to do everything, or to pick and choose from among all the injunctions we receive. As a practical matter, we already choose our level of obedience to the commandments and teachings. We can't obey them all with equal intensity. We all have our favorites.

The writer Walter Kirn, in his "Confessions of an Ex-Mormon: A Personal History of America's Most Misunderstood Religion," offhandedly described this stance: "My stated excuse for sneaking away from Mormonism was skepticism about its doctrines, but I'd learned that most Mormons don't grasp all the teachings of Joseph Smith—nor do they credit all the ones they do grasp."[1]

Mormons pick and choose; they select the doctrines they feel fervent about, and then choose their level of commitment. And there are plenty of commandments, rules, teachings, and suggestions from which to pick and choose.

This has all become increasingly clear to me as I study the interviews in the oral histories of Latter-day Saint women that we have collected at Claremont Graduate University. As we try to record what contemporary LDS women of all stripes have to say, we see them interpreting teachings and creating personal doctrine for themselves, making and justifying their choices based on their own preferences and circumstances.

We have many statements that show this choice, this combination of agency and personal revelation. Below is a simple statement from a sister who maintains that each member creates her own church. She sees each person's LDS religion as unique to herself. Each person follows an individual path, in this case, for her own comfort and salvation.

> I feel like there are twelve million LDS [Churches], that we all filter the teachings of the Church through our own personality traits and our life experiences. I think that's OK . . . We all have our own direct relationship with the Church, where we find those things that are important and that bring us closer to God and bring us peace and wisdom.[2]

Another statement from a mother addresses her daughter's agency. Church participation for her children is very important to this mother, but she values her daughter's freedom beyond her own preferences.

> I so much believe that God meant us to have our free agency that while it would break my heart, [to have my children leave the church,] because I believe [in] it, I fully believe that my children are here to have their own experience. I cannot have it for them. They are going to make their own choices. I relish the fact that they get to make their own choices. Hopefully I will have given them enough information to be able to say that [the church] is something worth holding on to because it makes me happy. But if it doesn't make [my daughter] happy, I can't and I wouldn't choose it for her. I want her to make her own choices.[3]

She "relishes" her daughter's freedom to choose, enjoying it more than her power to compel her daughter's obedience to her own views.

Our oral histories are full of this kind of expansive talk. We not only hear the statement in general, but in particular as women frequently interpret and speculate about religious topics. Speculation about a Heavenly Mother is especially common because so little official information is available about this nebulous figure. Mormon women try to make sense of the role that a Heavenly Mother plays in their individual lives and in their religion. As they long to know their Mother, and feel frustration at the silence that surrounds her, they develop personal beliefs in their quest to tap into hidden truths that, for them, provide convincing precedent or consensus. Familiar to church members is the idea put forth from the highest levels as restated by one of our narrators: "I personally feel that the reason we don't read about [our Heavenly Mother] is that our Father in Heaven loves her so dearly that he will go to any lengths to protect her. She is so treasured by him."[4] This familiar idea is not scriptural, but it has achieved a place in folk belief from its frequent repetition.

In our oral history collection, about half the women regarded the silence about Heavenly Mother as a protection for her. They think and pray about these matters and feel that they have received testimonies of the positions that they adopt. The others argued against this silencing of the Heavenly Mother. Many women dismiss the idea of the protected Heavenly mother because it echoes the paternalistic, Victorian, patronizing, Mother's Day chivalry that men use to praise women while keeping them under control.

Nevertheless, this kind of nonscriptural argument is of great interest to church members, and its existence leads to further personal doctrinal creation. All of us can engage in this speculation. The creative activity of others encourages us to try out new ideas to see if they work for us. One woman said, "I don't believe that we don't know about her because Heavenly Father is trying to protect her. She's a God; surely she can take care of herself and whip some butt if she needs to."[5]

Once a person begins this sort of doctrinal freethinking she can go in many directions. A little free thinking of my own led to speculations like the following ones. I wonder if, perhaps, Heavenly Mother is unlike some other Gods in that she, in a motherly way, cares for her children without the need to be worshipped by them. Perhaps, in another of my imaginative, mythical forays, Heavenly Mother has so evolved, that like the Queen Bee, she has no other purpose than reproduction. Perhaps, she is only a million uteruses, having lost her head, hands, and heart in heavenly evolution. Perhaps, and I prefer this explanation, the Heavenly Father and Mother, being perfected, have fused into a single perfect being and that they reproduce by asexual parthenogenesis, far more efficient than the messy, long-term, and painful reproduction practiced on Earth. In that case, the voice of the Father would be their voice and that would explain the silence of the Heavenly Mother and the otherwise inexplicable phrase that God created man in [their] own image, both male and female created he them. A biblical clue to support this hypothesis comes from Matthew who quotes Jesus as asking husband and wife to become "one flesh."[6] Perhaps he meant that literally and the conjoined heavenly parents is the favored state. My musings are attempts to make sense of the scriptural material that we have been given.

Clearly, choice is not only available, it is unavoidable. The absence of specific information about Heavenly Mother leads us to interpretation and can be seen as an advantage, encouraging us to create the female deity that we need and want. Women imagine the wise and loving mother figure who provides comfort and support in times of need, and many have testified that they feel her presence.

Power to see and imagine infinite alternatives includes the power to choose among those alternatives. Our belief in free agency and the multiple possibilities presented to us invite us to think broadly and openly.

In the church we sometimes categorize teachings as doctrine, that is God-given theology; or as policy, something that met a need at a certain time and has become traditional. The growth of the global church has highlighted cultural differences and caused the church to reconsider and discontinue practices that had once been considered dogma. So we have dogma, policy, and culture that have varying calls for obedience, and it is not always clear which is which. We have examples in our history where what was clearly described as dogma (God's word) gradually changed its official designation, passing through years of justification, followed by years of silence, with occasional softening along the way. What was once abhorred is later embraced. The people who had doubts early on and were sometimes punished for their unorthodox stances were justified. There is no question that evolution can be traced in LDS beliefs and teachings. The lesson from this is that we would do well to keep a dual faithfulness, trusting in God's messengers and spokesmen, while continuing to listen to and lean into our own understanding. Agency offers a full banquet of possibilities from which to choose our positions. Our own views are likely to evolve along the way even as church teachings and interpretations have evolved.

Examples from our oral history collection illustrate people in the process of defining their relationships to church teachings. Our own interpretations of teachings and circumstances allow us to make peace with the church teachings that may be too demanding, or that seem to lack harmony with present circumstances. In the following example, we find a very busy professional woman accentuating the spirit of the law, rather than the letter. If she cannot do all the busy work suggested, she can still manage the higher acceptance of the spirit of her work that brings her peace, having assured herself that she is doing the best she can, and that all her efforts are in harmony with God's will for her.

This woman has carried on a demanding professional life since she graduated from college. She married, supported her family while her husband was in graduate school, and has borne and raised five children. She defines herself, and the people she helps in her calling as less than perfect, but worthy of God's love in their imperfection.

> Right now [she tells us] I'm compassionate service leader in our ward, [a busy and demanding responsibility] and I wouldn't say I do everything, definitely not, but I'm more aware of what goes on behind the scenes with visiting teachers and what they do for certain people, just the acts of service and the love that extends out from that, and just that God really does love all of his children no matter what they're doing, no matter how crazy they are, and if you can tap into that and try and see people how God sees them then life is a lot less stressful.

She uses the remarkable image of commandments as "a leash around [her] neck" even as she denies that she is so led. She justifies her choices as in harmony with God's plans for her, knowledge that has come from prayer and revelation.

> I've never felt that I have a leash around my neck, like by way of commandments or anything like that, I've always felt, maybe because my choices always reflect what I think Heavenly Father wants me to do, but I always know there's a choice.

She feels great freedom as she looks forward to her future life, a less demanding time of child raising. She will define her choices by her personal preferences rather than as good and bad.

> Our youngest is five, she'll be in kindergarten next year and for me I'll have more time to learn and to grow, it's kind of exciting because I'm getting into this phase of just learning. It's exciting,

> I want to learn more about gardening and mulching, there's all these things that I'm starting to get books and to learn about, about nutrition and all these things, so it's an exciting point in time of learning.
>
> I wouldn't think of that as free agency necessarily, but I've thought of the gospel and all of this as learning and trying to find truth wherever it's found, and not necessarily about good and bad choices. I don't know why, just this excitement of being on earth to learn and to grow and to understand, and to try and see the bigger picture as God sees it. The more I try and do that, the less stressful I am because there's so many things in life that you can stress about that don't matter in the big picture, I mean my house is a mess right now, but I would let Christ in my front door. Why? Because of the feeling we have in our house.
>
> I would make space on the couch for him to sit down. I know that's a common thing, "Oh you want your house to be perfect when someone comes by" but to me that's not what it's about. I remember when I was in the ward, going to visit someone because I was in the Relief Society presidency at the time and I went to visit one of the Relief Society teachers. I knew that this person wouldn't let the Relief Society president in her house because she somehow felt inferior, but she let me in her house and it was a little messy and such, but I just commented to her about what a great feeling there was in her house, and she was surprised. She was like "but it's so messy" I said, "but it's so beautiful," I mean just the feeling in her house. She was taken aback by that, and I thought, "Why won't she let the Relief Society president in her house?" To me it's not about the clutter, it's about something inside—a feeling.[7]

This woman is at peace in her life because she feels that the choices she makes are approved. This woman is comfortable with the church teachings—which she firmly believes—and thinks that she is exempted from some of the responsibilities. She is in harmony with the church and God's will.

But not all women have the assurance that they are doing right in working through the demands of agency and choice. In this account the narrator describes an intense interfamily drama, a feud with her sister. The narrator shows several aspects about agency: her sister's anti-agency stance, her own attempt to reconcile herself to her sister's values, and finally the reversal of her need to honor her sister's demands. The issues on which the sisters differ are not specified, but both sisters seem to be somewhat orthodox believers in their religion. Agency is the issue. The sister not only disapproves of the narrator's decisions, she questions the Lord's decision in allowing free agency.

> It's taken me several years to come to peace with what has happened between me and my sister N. She has disowned me three times; she has called my husband a tool of the devil. It's been hard, because growing up, she was like a second mother to me; so discovering that her love wasn't unconditional—that it was in fact conditional upon me making the same decisions she has made—was a blow to my soul. But through that I have learned a couple of very important lessons. N told me once that the biggest mistake Heavenly Father ever made was giving us our free agency. And I think that is really why she behaves as she does—she wants to force us to make what are, in her eyes, the correct decisions, the decisions that will bring us back to Heavenly Father. Because of my struggles with N I have learned the value of free agency—I have come to understand that by trying to force myself into her life, I am calling into question her own free agency. Walking that thin line between trying to keep open any chance of communication, and respecting her wishes to have nothing to do with me, is difficult. For the most part I try to limit my contact with her to small tokens for her children—if I make something for the other nieces and nephews I include her children, knowing that she may well throw it away but not wanting them to think that I have forgotten about them, even though I've never met them.
>
> N has also taught me more than I ever wanted to know about forgiveness. Ultimately, forgiveness is not about healing the other person—it is about healing ourselves.
>
> Ten years ago, I went through this thing where I continually prayed to Heavenly Father to show me what was wrong with me. I knew that N had to see something I couldn't see, I knew that she

> was right and I was wrong and I prayed for Heavenly Father to show me this flaw, this horrible thing about myself, so that I could fix it and make N love me again. The prayers were always left unanswered and so I pleaded harder and harder, convinced that I was so flawed, so horribly wrong that Heavenly Father couldn't even begin to show me what was wrong. I pleaded and begged and promised that if he would show me what I needed to fix, I'd fix it. Finally one day when I was out in the shed working refinishing a piece of furniture I collapsed in tears and prayed again: Please Heavenly Father, show me what is wrong, let me fix it. And then this small thought entered my mind: What if there is nothing wrong?
>
> For me that was the beginning of forgiving N. Opening myself up to the idea that there was nothing wrong with me—How do I say this? Acknowledging that perhaps N was wrong, allowed me to acknowledge that N wasn't perfect, that she was facing her own set of challenges and that this was the way she was trying to address those challenges. It gave me the space to try to forgive her. It was still not an easy process and sometimes I find I have to go back and readdress it; there was definitely a challenging time when she made her peace with my parents and other sisters but has continued to want nothing to do with me. But this lesson I have learned, about forgiveness, is one that I cherish.[8]

Even as her sister writes her off, forgiving everyone but her, the narrator comes to an acceptance of herself. She prays for help and gets an answer in words, apparently from some source outside herself. The narrator justifies herself in her independence from N. who had felt that she had earned the narrator's obedience by her devotion. When the narrator exercised other views, N. could not accept her. N. thereby delineated the limits of free agency. Our agency is free to the point when it confronts the agency of another. We have the power to choose, but not to coerce. Each person is responsible for herself.

In a dramatic climax, the narrator switches her assessment of what is wrong. She had assumed that she was guilty of something, but in a moment of comprehension—realizes she is not.

In attempting to achieve reconciliation, the narrator comes to two important conclusions: that she cannot take on herself the trials of another person who is free to choose, and that forgiveness means forgiving herself as well as someone else. She carries her respect for individual choices into the area of trials. Each person has her own collection of challenges and trials and must make her own way. As she says,

> I think I have learned the importance of trials . . . Each trial has its lessons. So many times I have prayed to Heavenly Father to be able to remove a trial from a loved one. Each time the answer has come back, "Don't be selfish. This is their journey; these are their lessons."

The wonderful collection of oral histories that we have been gathering shows some of the ways women think and make their decisions, how they wrestle and make peace with the tense issues of their lives. LDS Church teachings make clear that all members have their agency. The question is how members deal with that agency.

Agency is a redemptive doctrine. As this last instance shows, a person can find peace and reconciliation with God and herself by recognizing agency. It can free us from destructive judgments and is a way of recognizing our own personhood and the personhood of others. Agency allows us to create our own perspective on doctrine and conduct and thereby make the gospel more individual.

Notes

1. Walter Kirn, "Confessions of an Ex-Mormon: A Personal History of America's Most Misunderstood Religion," *The New Republic*, July 13, 2012, 7–10.
2. Claremont Mormon Women's Oral History Collection, no. 29 (2009), 16, Library of the Claremont Colleges, Claremont, CA, hereafter cited as COHC.
3. Ellen Comp, (presentation in a Columbia University class, "Contemporary Mormonism," taught by Richard and Claudia Bushman, March 17, 2012, and transcribed by Claudia Bushman).
4. COHC, no. 046 (2010), 14–15.
5. COHC, no. 107 (2011), 15.
6. Matthew 19:5.
7. COHC, no. 158 (2011), 12–13.
8. COHC, no. 107, 18–19.

17

My Book of Mormon Story

P. JANE HAFEN

Hopi children grow up being socialized by ritual through Kachina dancers. The Kachinas are sacred beings who participate in the holy stories of the Hopi and other Pueblo tribes. When the children are about eight years old, the Kachina dancers are unmasked and revealed as fellow members of the tribe, rather than holy spirits. This process is disenchantment. After learning a new truth, the children then have a choice—exercising their agency and participating in the tribal community by continuing the Kachina tradition and becoming the dancers, or rejecting that knowledge and separating from the tribe.[1]

I was invited to participate in this book project with the instructions to examine personal agency in contemporary Latter-day Saint women's lives. I hope that my discussion about agency, disenchantment, and values will elucidate the power of story and faith, and survival from colonialism. Even though we are raised in the church to bear testimony and bare our souls, I have been reluctant to "bleed in public." I have hesitated to tell my own story partly because it involves others and I wish to respect their privacy, as well as my own. Terry Tempest Williams says "We all have our secrets . . . To withhold words is power. But to share our words with others, openly and honestly, is also power."[2] From my perspective as a Taos Pueblo Mormon woman, I will examine how I was raised in the LDS Church, had challenges, and tried to remain faithful.

My life began in contradiction to the ideal of a "happy family." I was born to a Taos Pueblo Indian man, who would later receive the Spencer W. Kimball Service Award, and to his twenty-year-old secretary—who was not his wife. I was raised in a reservation border town by a woman who was Mormon and her non-Mormon alcoholic husband. I was acutely aware of the racism that occurs in border towns, and was familiar with seeing intoxicated Indians and hearing disparaging remarks about "lazy Indians" or "drunk Indians." The city park was unusable because of the number of inebriates who were there all hours of the day. As a mixed race person and from a different tribal nationality than the local tribe, I did not identify with most of the Indians at school. Neither did I identify with the non-Indians. I was called names and harassed. When I was in high school, young men would talk about "rolling Indians" for their weekend entertainment.

My senior high school English teacher was LDS. He let us read pretty much whatever we wanted. I remember reading *Jane Eyre, Wuthering Heights*, and the Book of Mormon. I was aware of Book of Mormon mixed messages that in some places spoke of a chosen generation of Lamanites, but elsewhere described dark skin as a curse and partook in behavior stereotypes. I was not sure I was either.

Growing up, the church offered me a fairly uncomplicated social stability by contrast. I do not remember any Indians who attended our ward. There were periods of civil unrest, however, when members of the ward were advised to take routes avoiding the reservations to attend meetings at the stake center.[3] I grew up as an earnest believer in the literal church, believing simple stories and binary opposites of good and evil without shadings or complexities of human existence. Even at a young age I understood the value of love through the example of Jesus Christ. At age seventeen, I headed to Brigham Young University. There was a large population of Indian students in the early 1970s and a thriving Indian Education program. My junior year I accompanied the Lamanite Choir, a group of Indian students who performed in concert and church settings rather than the entertainment dances of the Lamanite Generation (another campus performing group). We performed some ambitious choral pieces including "The Gloria" by Frances Poulenc and Randall Thompson's "Alleluia." We also sang Indian style hymns arranged by our director, John Rainer Jr., and traditional Native songs. A highlight for the choir was singing for President Spencer W. Kimball at a special devotional. He was presented an elk skin inscribed with the words to the song, "Go My Son," by Arlene Nofchissey Williams and Carnes

Burnson.[4] I received scholarly recognition from the American Indian Education program and did feel respected and honored.

At the same time, though, I was a curious student. I spent hours in the library researching anthropological documents that described my tribe and my family like scientific specimens. I ran across a report in *Akwasasne Notes* (a tribal newspaper) that criticized the assimilative practices of the Indian Placement Program where young Indian children were baptized, removed from reservations, and then placed in homes of non-Indian LDS members.[5] Through my study and independent reading, I became aware of the violent history between the United States and Indian Nations. Although I did not have the critical vocabulary at the time, I was learning about colonialism, the ways in which agency for indigenous peoples is consumed by the dominant culture. As Dakota scholar Waziyawatin (Angela Cavender Wilson) explains: "Colonization refers to both the formal and informal methods (behaviors, ideologies, institutions, policies, and economies) that maintain the subjugation or exploitation of Indigenous Peoples, lands, and resources."[6] I knew about colonialism firsthand from my border town upbringing, and from my increasing education.

My BYU experience included learning about both the chosen and the oppressed, noble inheritance and being treated as savages. Nevertheless, I followed the happy Mormon family script: I married an outstanding returned missionary, Jeff Hafen, and we started our own family. As an undergraduate, Jeff was working with a group on the Spanish language text for the Missionary Training Center. When the group was fairly well into their project, the word came down from the Missionary Committee that what they were doing needed to be scrapped and they were to start over. There was no explanation or reasoning, just the instructions to follow the directive. This was my first experience with seemingly arbitrary church authority, a "because I said so" moment.

This incident was not life changing, nor did it affect my faith, but I saw the unveiling of institutional power. That humanizing of absolute authority was a disenchantment, a recognition of the human beings in the Lord's church. Using agency to continue in an institution that created cognitive dissonance, a collision between heart and mind, placed value on the community over individualism. For me, disenchantment with the Missionary Committee illustrated human fallibility in the authority structure. I understood the disparities, but they were not sufficiently significant to lead me away from activity in the church. I used my agency and remained committed to the community.

Mormon children who were socialized about Indians rarely experienced a disenchantment. Colonialism emerged in commercial products targeted for children where the Lamanites were dark skinned and savage in illustrations and action figurines. There was no social mechanism for correction of these stereotypes as they became entrenched in the culture. All of this is still true today. Among the worst perpetrators of colonialism was the primary song, "Book of Mormon Stories."[7]

As a musician, I have regularly served in church callings that have not required a lot of contemplation but have called for skill. I have only been Primary chorister once, though, and it was when I was young and attending a family ward at BYU. A great time filler in Primary was letting the children choose what songs to sing, and one of their favorites was "Book of Mormon Stories." As we sang, the back rows of preadolescent young men added their own rhythms: "Book of Mormon stories that my teacher tells to me (me, me), Are about the Lamanites in ancient history (ry, ry)," and so on, imitating tom-toms. I cannot remember now what I did in the situation. I did know that the boys were mocking and playing out stereotypes of Indian music. Unfortunately, the song lent itself to the parody through both the accompaniment rhythms and the pentatonic-like melody.

The lyrics of the song's second verse were especially problematic. "Lamanites met others who were seeking liberty, And the land soon welcomed all who wanted to be free." In reality colonizers soon impaired the agency of the land's original inhabitants by appropriating land, confining Indians to reservations, and restricting original religious practices. The song's main idea followed naturally from Book of Mormon prophecies:

> . . . in the latter days, when our seed shall have dwindled in unbelief, yea, for the space of many years, and many generations after the Messiah shall be manifested in body unto the children of men, then shall the fulness of the gospel of the Messiah come unto the Gentiles, and from the Gentiles unto the remnant of our seed—
>
> And at that day shall the remnant of our seed know that they are of the house of Israel, and that they are the covenant people of the Lord; and then shall they know and come to the knowledge

> of their forefathers, and also to the knowledge of the gospel of their Redeemer, which was ministered unto their fathers by him; wherefore, they shall come to the knowledge of their Redeemer.[8]

Again the contradiction of "dwindling in unbelief" contrasted with redemption of the "covenant people;" how could a community be both cursed and saved? However, in the song, simple and plain as it is, the master American narrative of conquest was played out as a palliative (welcoming) with the imperative of settler colonialism seizing "the land." Thus the salvation of the remnants of Book of Mormon peoples (more on who they were later) depended on mediation by the very people who took the land and liberty (agency) from them.

In the ensuing years, I have been a Primary accompanist on many occasions. I use my own agency and refuse to play "Book of Mormon Stories." I am nice about it and just say "Sister Hafen cannot play that song, please choose another." I do not want to think about myself as a Lamanite in this song's context. I certainly do not want my children, and now my grandchildren, to think about themselves in such a stereotypical fashion.

The underlying racism of "Book of Mormon Stories" worked its way into my master's thesis in humanities at BYU. I had three small children and was expecting a fourth. In order to save their lives and my own, my husband encouraged and supported my work in graduate school. My thesis was about Mormon institutional discrimination toward Indians. I was a good girl. I listed positive examples of art by American Indian Mormons and did not directly criticize the church, but I did identify artistic colonialism in Mormon arts. I looked at older hymns that have since been removed or revised; I discussed literary representations of American Indians; and finally, I looked at visual representations. What was largely unknown then, and I believe is still unknown now, is that major American Indian artists, like Fanny Nampeyo, a world renowned Hopi potter, are Mormon.

This project raised a number of issues. Clearly, most of the non-Indian artists were well-intended and playing out their own understandings of both the historicity of the Book of Mormon and American historical images of Indians. They followed the patterns Robert Berkhofer described as *The White Man's Indian*.[9] Indians were romanticized nobility who still possessed savagery. In doing the research and work for my thesis, I had to confront the gap between artists' depictions of Indians and the unfiltered self-representations of Native artists themselves. Non-Indian Mormon artists had a tendency to romanticize and objectify Native topics and removed Indian agency by speaking for Natives. On the other hand, indigenous artists reflected their own tribal values, stories and images, thus exercising agency as subjects rather than objects. I chose to tell myself that Mormon artists were reflecting their historical bias and their culture, which was separate from what I believed was the Gospel of Jesus Christ. The title of my thesis: "A Pale Reflection: American Indian Images in Mormon Arts."[10]

During this period of my life, I read and studied many statements by leaders of the church, many of which connected Lamanites from the Book of Mormon to indigenous peoples of the Western Hemisphere. Much of the so-called archeological evidence seemed like text-proofing or selective pieces that did not tell the whole story. To illustrate, I had heard that Quetzalcoatl, the feathered serpent, was proof of Christ in America. However, the story of Quetzalcoatl also included human sacrifice and incest, certainly un-Christlike actions. I was exposed to legalistic arguments about linguistics, geography, and Middle Eastern similarities with the Book of Mormon that seemed to leave behind the gospel principles of hope, faith, and charity as the scriptural and spiritual core.

Additionally, an official 1981 editing of the Book of Mormon changed the descriptive wording of the redeemed remnant of Book of Mormon peoples from "white and delightsome" to "pure and delightsome," thus seemingly negating the racial imperatives of the text.[11] However, the "skin of blackness" that came upon the disobedient did not disappear.[12] A reading of the long narrative arc of the Book of Mormon shows that eventually the (good) Nephites and the (bad) Lamanites were not fixed categories. Conversions and crossovers led to the (bad) Nephites eventually being destroyed.

I cannot pinpoint my own metamorphosis, but at some point I no longer considered myself racially aligned with a group from the Book of Mormon. American Indian cultures were too varied, both culturally and linguistically. The number of indigenous peoples in the Western hemisphere did not match the narrative. I was relieved to learn that Elder Spencer W. Kimball had observed that some of the ancestors of Native peoples may have come to the continent outside the Book of Mormon narrative: "Through the centuries of movements, discovery, exploration, settlement, and colonization of the people of this land, it is not impossible that there could have seeped across the Bering Strait a little Oriental blood, as claimed by some people, and possibly a little Norse blood may have crossed the North Atlantic."[13]

However, Kimball still adhered to the idea of Indians as descendants of Lehi and saw a paternalistic responsibility in helping them with their burden. A Symposium on Archaeology of the Scriptures discussed multiple origins and populations as early as 1978.[14] Additionally, Elder Dallin H. Oaks noted, "The Book of Mormon is not a history of all of the people who have lived on the continents of North and South America in all ages of the earth."[15] Despite these hints about Indians' varying origins, the general cultural narrative has been that American Indigenous peoples play a role in Mormon cosmology.

My transition from believing in all-encompassing definitions of Lamanite may have been a disenchantment, like the unmasking of the Hopi Kachinas, but it was gradual. I did not broadcast my thoughts; I continued being faithful and participating in the church because I had and still have a basic belief. I felt hope in this Book of Mormon scripture: ". . . and [the Lord] inviteth them all to come unto him and partake of his goodness; and he denieth none that come unto him, black and white, bond and free, male and female; and he remembereth the heathen; and all are alike unto God, both Jew and Gentile."[16] However, I no longer felt part of a "chosen" people, nor did I bear the burden of theological racial inequality. This is not to say that I abandoned my sense of resistance to bigotry and institutional racism.

A major disenchantment came several years later when Navajo general authority George P. Lee was excommunicated. At the time, the general consensus was that Lee had openly challenged racism in the church, especially in and around reservations. Likewise, I had challenged the racist ways Mormon culture represented Indians in my master's thesis. Although my thesis was (and still is) obscure, I had to question whether or not I had misstepped. I knew that my Mormon values led me to represent what I considered true, and I believed my critiques were honest. I had hoped they would be used as educational tools against racism.

A few days after Lee's excommunication, my husband (then a full-time employee at the Missionary Training Center) and I attended dinner, as we often did, with some General Authorities and their wives. This particular evening we sat at a table where there was a flippant, verbal one-upmanship about how and where these couples had received their calls. The illusions of infallible church leaders were long gone to me. In my heart, an elephant in the room was the unspoken and unacknowledged tragedy of Lee's excommunication. Only one person seemed to have a sense of gravitas on that occasion and that person was newly called general authority Jeffrey R. Holland.

The disenchantment I felt over George P. Lee's excommunication did not distance me from the church. I recognized there was truth in some of his criticisms, but after years of association with BYU and church administration, I also knew to use propriety in addressing those issues.[17] I was further aware that my agency and my voice are my own, regardless of the power of the church. I did not and do not fear speaking the truth, but I also know the power of silence.

We moved to Nevada; we lived on the Arrowhead Trail and attended the Arrowhead Ward. I completed my doctorate with a dissertation about American Indian Literatures. I was Relief Society President and then taught Sunday School Gospel Doctrine classes—my husband was bishop. A ward member told me I was the fulfillment of prophecy for the Lamanites. While I was living my life in the small community of my ward, subtle shifts were moving the discourse and attitudes about Indians.

A year after Lee's excommunication, an article in the January 1990 *Ensign* highlighted five Indian couples with strong, positive statements about Indians in the church. One partner in each marriage had been a success story of the Indian Placement Program. The word "Lamanite" was not mentioned.

By the time the church was confronting challenges about DNA and the Book of Mormon in the late 1990s, I had already distanced myself from believing in a literal lineage.[18] The redefinition from hemispheric historicity to a limited geography model did not surprise me. The most official change came in 2007 when the introductory page of the Book of Mormon changed from "the Lamanites, and they are the principal ancestors of the American Indians" to "the Lamanites, and they are among the ancestors of the American Indians." This is a significant change, especially considering living prophets' earlier pronouncements about Lamanites.

One of the appeals of Mormonism is the idea of continuing revelation. One of the frustrations is that change comes without historical contextualization, explanations, or apologies. For instance, the 1978 Official Declaration "extending priesthood and temple blessings to all worthy male members of the Church," offered no explanations. The context, beyond the immediacy of the process as explained in the Proclamation, was left to scholars and others to interpret until the recent publication of clarifying "Gospel Topic Essays" at lds.org. However, little is yet discussed for the changing definition of the Lamanites. This change was not a disenchantment for me. Nor did it affect my agency.

Twenty-three years after the excommunication of George P. Lee, Larry Echohawk (Pawnee) was called as a general authority in 2012. He had a distinguished career as a lawyer, public servant, BYU law professor, and Commissioner of Indian Affairs. His initial talk in October 2012 general conference was an earnest story of his conversion predicated largely on his testimony of the Book of Mormon. He referenced the new language of the Book of Mormon introduction and declared its historicity:

> On the title page I read that it is "written to the Lamanites, who are a remnant of the house of Israel; and also to Jew and Gentile." In the introduction to the Book of Mormon: Another Testament of Jesus Christ, it says that the Lamanites "are among the ancestors of the American Indians." As I read the Book of Mormon, it seemed to me that it was about my American Indian ancestors. It tells the story of a people, a part of which were later described as "Lamanites," who migrated from Jerusalem to a "land of promise" (1 Nephi 2:20) about 600 B.C.[19]

I understand being raised with that belief. What is also interesting, though, is the personal tribal history that he related:

> My great-grandfather Echo Hawk, a Pawnee Indian, was born in the mid-1800s in what is now called Nebraska. When he was 19 years of age, the Pawnee people were forced to give up their

> 23-million-acre (9.3 million ha) homeland to make room for settlers. In 1874 the Pawnee people were marched several hundred miles south to a small reservation located in the Oklahoma Indian Territory. The population of Pawnee people had declined from over 12,000 to less than 700 upon their arrival in Oklahoma. The Pawnee, like other tribes, had been scattered, smitten, and nearly destroyed.[20]

In terms of literary criticism, Echohawk is demonstrating a tribalography;

> Native stories, no matter what form they take (novel, poem, drama, memoir, film, history), seem to pull all the elements together of the storyteller's tribe, meaning the people, the land, and multiple characters and all their manifestations and revelations, and connect these in past, present, and future milieus (present and future milieus mean non-Indians).[21]

Echohawk does this by bringing in the history of his tribe, the Pawnee. He notes the land loss and tribal displacement and removal. He also connects this tribalography to the Book of Mormon, but not like the "Book of Mormon Stories" song that embraces settler colonialism. His retelling of Pawnee history asserts, through tribal sovereignty, a sense of survival of the Pawnee people. He believes that his conversion to the gospel through the Book of Mormon is central to the past, present, and future.

The structure and tone of Echohawk's talk is not colonial, and given the history and context of Indians with the church, he opens the door to a number of issues. Is he claiming a literal or a metaphorical history for the Lamanites?[22] The implications could be that just like not all Indians met Columbus, but all were impacted by him; not all indigenous peoples are Lamanites, but they are impacted by Book of Mormon prophecies and promises. Is there a way of rethinking the responsibilities of Europeans (Gentiles) to the "Lamanites" that is ethical rather than colonial? Louise Erdrich, Ojibwe writer, observed that "conversion . . . [is] a most ticklish concept and a most loving form of destruction."[23] Echohawk's church service and his public career seem to suggest that he survived that conversion, just as his tribe survived colonialism. How can the blessings of the gospel be offered while still respecting the "other"?

My experience is that change, agency, and overcoming racism is not structural or institutional, but most often occurs on a personal level. I know that many Primary choristers will continue to sing "Book of Mormon Stories," but in the wards where I have participated, they generally do not. When I explain my discomfort to choristers, they experience disenchantment and that is individual, not institutional. The persuasion is not because of my opinions but because they appreciate the impact of the stereotypes on my children and grandchildren. Change comes gradually, personally, and sometimes in small steps.

I have reconciled my ethnicity with my Mormonism. Young academics I know who are Native and Mormon have told me that being a "Lamanite" is "not such a big deal" and is a construct. As Armand L. Mauss observed: "For some, this [Lamanite] identity is never really internalized and therefore has no real 'use' in their lives."[24] On the other hand, scholars like Elise Boxer (Dakota) have closely examined the historical racialization of the idea of "Lamanite" and have used their agency to unmask the institutional ways that racism continues.[25]

The story of my own disenchantment with the Book of Mormon leads me back to faith and hope in the community. However, after our returned missionary son told his father and me that he is gay, I encountered a major disenchantment over homosexuality and the church. My experience is that in my ward there is a general homophobia. I painfully absorb when a Relief Society sister talks about her gay neighbors as deviants. I stay silent. I stay silent. A number of people, including a bishop, have dismissively said to me that the atonement would take care of my gay son and then have disengaged from conversation and association. Longtime friends have fallen off the radar or no longer ask about our children. I stay silent. A family member who was a general authority, officially said that gays would be resurrected straight. I stay silent. The community I once depended on is no longer there in terms of the church. In my local congregation I choose silence rather than defensiveness. I acknowledge the paradox that traditionally, indigenous peoples have a unique vocabulary for two-spirits and hold them in sacred regard.

As a gospel doctrine teacher, I have used my agency to focus on what I consider to be the basic values of the gospel I love: faith, hope, charity, kindness, and love for one another. I do not address issues of historicity or talk about topics that reinforce Mormon exceptionalism. I continue to work against racism toward American Indians in many aspects of my life. In a fall college course I taught, I used the film *Twilight* as an example of racial appropriation and institutional discrimination.

As I look to the future, I have hope. I have hope that the racist misunderstandings from the Book of Mormon will be overcome. I have hope in this verse from the Book of Mormon: "Yea, come unto Christ, and be perfected in him, and deny yourselves of all ungodliness; and if ye shall deny yourselves of all ungodliness, and love God with all your might, mind and strength, then is his grace sufficient for you."[26] I survive by invoking the paradoxical vision of Oglala holy man, Black Elk, who stood at the center of the universe and who saw unity in diversity: "And I saw that the sacred hoop of my people was one of many hoops that made one circle, wide as daylight and as starlight, and in the center grew one mighty flowering tree to shelter all the children of one mother and one father. And I saw that it was holy."[27] I have no fantasy that my voice is significant in the larger discourse of the church. I utilize my agency to try and navigate a place where I can overcome my disenchantment and still have hope despite my own human errors and the humanity of members of the church. I am honored to be invited to speak on some of these issues, where mine is not the only voice but one of many.[28]

Notes

1. See Sam Gill, "Disenchantment," *Parabola* 1, no. 3 (1976): 6–13, reprinted in *I Became Part of It: Sacred Dimensions in Native American Life*, edited by D. M. Dooling and Paul Jordan-Smith (New York: Parabola Books, 1989), 106–19.
2. Terry Tempest Williams, *When Women Were Birds: Fifty-Four Variations on Voice* (New York: Sarah Crichton Books, 2012), 18.
3. In 1974, in Farmington, New Mexico, young white men targeted, murdered, and mutilated three Navajo men. There was a subsequent civil rights investigation. See Rodney Barker, *The Broken Circle: A True Story of Murder and Magic in Indian Country* (New York: Simon and Shuster, 1992).
4. Armand L. Mauss notes that "Go My Son" refers to Natives as an "'Indian Nation' rather than as Lamanites." See Armand L. Mauss, *All Abraham's Children* (Urbana and Chicago: University of Illinois Press, 2003), 131.
5. Beth Wood, "The Mormon Southwest: LDS Indian Placement Program," *Akwesasne Notes* 10 (Winter 1978): 16.
6. Waziyawatin (Angela Wilson) and Michael Yellowbird, *For Indigenous Eyes Only: A Decolonization Handbook* (Santa Fe, NM: School of American Research Press, 2005), 2.

7. Elizabeth Fetzer Bates and Nancy K. Daines, "Book of Mormon Stories," *Children's Songbook* (Salt Lake City: The Church of Jesus Christ of Latter-day Saints, 1989), 118.
8. 1 Nephi 15:13–14.
9. Robert F. Berkhofer Jr., *The White Man's Indian: Images of the American Indian from Columbus to the Present* (New York: Alfred A. Knopf, 1978).
10. P. Jane Hafen, "A Pale Reflection: American Indian Images in Mormon Arts" (master's thesis, Brigham Young University, 1984).
11. 2 Nephi 30:6.
12. 2 Nephi 5:21, Alma 3:5–7.
13. Spencer W. Kimball, "The Lamanite: Their Burden, Our Burden," February 9, 1967. For audio of this talk see https://speeches.byu.edu/talks/spencer-w-kimball_lamanite-burden-burden/.
14. "Ancient News: Symposium on Archeology of the Scriptures," *Ensign*, March 1978, http://www.lds.org/ensign/1978/03/news-of-the-church/ancient-news-symposium-on-archaeology-of-the-scriptures?lang=eng&query=bering+strait.
15. Dallin H. Oaks, "The Historicity of the Book of Mormon," Foundation for Ancient Research and Mormon Studies Annual Dinner, Provo, Utah, October 29, 1993, http://maxwellinstitute.byu.edu/publications/transcripts/?id=30
16. 2 Nephi 26:33.
17. "The Lee Letters," *Sunstone* 13, no. 4 (August 1989): 50–55. Lee was later convicted of child abuse in 1993 and that, along with changing attitudes toward the literalism of the Book of Mormon, has diffused the impact of his criticisms.
18. See P. Jane Hafen, "The Being and Place of a Native American Mormon," in *New Genesis: A Mormon Reader on Land and Community*, edited by Terry Tempest Williams, William B. Smart, and Gibbs M. Smith (Salt Lake City: Gibbs Smith, 1998), 35–41.
19. Larry Echo Hawk, "Come unto Me, O Ye House of Israel," https://www.lds.org/ensign/2012/11/come-unto-me-o-ye-house-of-israel?lang=eng.
20. Ibid.
21. LeAnne Howe (Choctaw), "The Story of America: A Tribalography" in *Clearing a Path: Theorizing the Past in Native American Studies*, edited by Nancy Shoemaker (New York: Routledge 2002), 29–48.
22. For a discussion of ethnic metaphors, including skin colors, see Steven L. Olsen, "The Covenant of the Chosen People: The Spiritual Foundations of Ethnic Identity in the Book of Mormon," *Journal of the Book of Mormon and Other Restoration Scripture* 21, no. 1 (2012): 14–29.
23. Louise Erdrich, *The Last Report on the Miracles at Little No Horse* (New York: HarperCollins, 2001), 55.
24. Mauss, *All Abraham's Children*, 134.
25. Elise Boxer, "'To Become White and Delightsome': American Indians and Mormon Identity," (PhD dissertation, Arizona State University, 2009).

26. Moroni 10:32.
27. John G. Neihardt, *Black Elk Speaks* (Lincoln: University of Nebraska Press, 1979), 43.
28. Thanks to Jeff Hafen, Tom Plummer, Jim Faulconer, and Amber Featherstone who read and conversed about parts of this essay. Thanks also to Matt Bowman and Kate Holbrook for their suggestions. I am especially grateful to Kate for her encouragement and for tracking down the original Kimball speech.

18

Filling the Page

Women's Choices in the Context of Gospel Boundaries

NEYLAN MCBAINE

I believe in telling stories. I've been actively engaged in telling the stories of Mormon women for over seven years. As the founder and editor-in-chief of the Mormon Women Project, I have published interviews with more than three hundred Mormon women from twenty-two countries at www.mormonwomen.com.[1] I've developed a testimony of telling stories the same way one develops a testimony of a gospel principle: by observing the positive effect of stories upon myself and those around me when I examine them, share them, and lean on them. The reasons stories matter are almost as varied as stories themselves, but in almost all cases the bottom line is that stories transform. They affect the way we make choices in our lives, influencing us to take one path when we otherwise might have taken another.

Some time ago, I was talking to the wife of a general authority, a woman whom I deeply admire as a spiritual and intellectual force, and an influence for good. I asked her about her initial personal reaction to her husband's calling. What instructions had she been given when her husband had been set apart to set aside his livelihood and devote himself full time to the church? How was she directed to use her own time? Her answer stuck with me. She told me,

> Neylan, at first I was frustrated. My husband was given detailed instructions on how to spend every minute of his day, but I was left largely on my own. Couldn't I be useful too? But as we got into the field, I recognized that I'd been given a great gift: I'd been given the Lord's trust to use my time as I wanted. I'd been given

a blank sheet of paper to fill with good things as I pleased; a page with borders, with limitations, yes, but with the freedom to fill in the way I wanted, according to my own promptings and desires.

The image of a blank piece of paper returns to me again and again as I read and edit new interviews for the Mormon Women Project. At some level, each interview answers the question, "How does this Mormon woman fill the blank page of her life?" Each life, like a blank page, has its borders: commandments that must be followed, values to be upheld and promoted, circumstances that shape choices. But each woman has filled that metaphorical page with something, and more often than not, I am humbled by the vibrancy and honed beauty that practically leaps up in three dimensions from her stories and reflections.

Despite having fewer constructs in place—when compared to men—by which to define their responsibilities and influence within the institutional church, many of the women profiled in the Mormon Women Project have a confidence in their spiritual lives and in their identities as Mormon women that allows them to see that blank paper as a gift (as my friend above did), rather than as an indication of underuse or neglect. The very nondeliniation perceived by some as underuse or neglect looks very much like opportunity to others. Through exercising agency on how to spend their time, women settle into a sense of themselves—their strengths and weaknesses—and magnify their relationships with diety.

Ironically, it is this very nondelination that can also be the wedge that drives a woman and God apart. I am familiar with how frustrating it can be to figuratively stare at that blank piece of paper that is our lives and wonder what should go on it. I know the puzzlement we can feel as women when we read Doctrine and Covenants 107 in which the Lord outlined responsibilities for the church in the latter days, and yet, there is no mention of a woman or her responsibility. Where are the women? I don't know. I don't have the silver bullet to ease the ache caused by that question, but I choose a faith-based perspective when staring at that blank page myself. I choose to see it as a vote of confidence in my ability to exercise my agency. I choose to see a doctrinal commitment to agency borne out in this nondelineated space. I choose to rely on the confidence I feel as a daughter of God to move ahead, crafting a life that I believe fulfills my potential and pleases him.

Because I have chosen to move forward in this confidence, my efforts to represent, support, and encourage other women in the church reflect this same perspective. The Mormon Women Project features interviews with LDS women who are positive examples of filling up the blank page of their lives with spiritual power, earthly pursuits, meaningful relationships, and family contributions. These women work outside the formal framework of duties and responsibilities that our men work under, but have created a spiritual scaffolding in their own lives through deliberate choices and an active relationship with God.

Without the framework of priesthood governance, without the ability to readily identify ourselves in scriptural narratives—or in many of the personal experiences of our male leaders—women's stories about themselves, such as stories on the Mormon Women Project, become the sacred tools we use to settle into our own identities. Persuasive storytelling is the way to model how we can take full advantage of the nondelineated trust we've been given to share in God's power as we are personally, not institutionally, directed.

I received an email from a reader that I felt beautifully stated the longing each woman has to see how other women have filled their pages:

> Marie Wilson, Founder and President Emeritus of the White House Project, has said, "You can't be what you can't see." There is a huge void in society today when it comes to showing us strong accomplished women. We are bombarded with misleading media about women where they are portrayed as objects, petty and foolish. We are largely left out of history books and when we go to church, a place where we should see strong female role models, we largely only see women of one type. Stories of women in the scriptures and in our lesson manuals are also scarce. They often fall into two categories: the saintly mother or the devilish temptress. Where are the real women? Complex women who strive to do their best in all they do? Who are spiritual, powerful and accomplished and also have weaknesses? With no clear image of Heavenly Mother and very little in regards to women everywhere else in our lives, I am hungry, no ravenous, for the stories of my fellow sisters. When I read these stories, I am buoyed up and gain a clearer image of what I can accomplish. I find strength in others. I can be more like what I see.[2]

The stories of contemporary Mormon women do indeed fill a craving among LDS women today to grasp onto realistic role models that demonstrate a range of ways to craft meaningful lives.

The women featured in the Mormon Women Project self-identify as currently active in their church participation. By establishing this criteria for an interview subject, I recognize that I am choosing to publish and promote the stories of LDS women who most often feel positively towards their Heavenly Father and the institutional church. Of particular interest to me as I study these faith-promoting stories is why these women—who have faced some of life's greatest trials and derailing challenges—continue to rely on God and on the church, while many others do not. Is remaining faithful really simply a choice made in a moment of self-awareness and self-crafting? Or is the decision to trust God and continue association with his church the result of cumulative experiences, convictions, and personality characteristics? In other words, why have the women interviewed for the Mormon Women Project embraced the blank page of their lives as a symbol of trust and love from their Heavenly Father, rather than as a sign of worthlessness? What makes these women different from the ones who walk away?

These questions have no easy answer, but I find that identifying themes among the interviews puts me on a path to understanding the decision-making process that leads to faith rather than disillusionment. Finding thematic similarities helps isolate those factors that might prompt a woman to embrace the metaphorical blank page as a vote of divine confidence in her agency, and thus a commitment to God, rather than as a sign of her uselessness in his eyes.

I start with the theme of affliction. For many women, the opportunity to craft a deliberate life arises from the ashes of a trial or tragedy; they are initially acted upon either by another's poor choices or simply by a blameless tragic occurrence. Being acted upon unwittingly inevitably gives the woman ample opportunity to actively assess responses that either build or destroy reliance on deity. Kimberly White found herself in this very active state of choosing when she learned at a doctor's appointment that her full-term fetus had no heartbeat:

> I was in my house alone, sitting on the ground with my phone, waiting for my husband to come, waiting for the situation to

> resolve itself somehow. I remember having this distinct sense that since I hadn't broken down and cried or responded emotionally yet, I was completely capable of going one of two directions. I could say, "This is not fair. The Lord has betrayed me. I didn't deserve this." And I would be fully justified. No one would blame me. That way was fully open to me.
>
> But next to this there was an option that I could say, "I know the Lord and I trust him and I'm just going to bow my head and do this thing that He apparently has called me to do." I decided that, while I might be justified in being angry and upset, there was nothing to be gained in that. It wasn't clear to me how there could possibly be any purpose in losing a child, and in losing a child in this way. But I decided I was just going to give the Lord a chance to show me that it was okay.
>
> When something like that happens, you spend years having up days and down days. As much as I think the Spirit confirmed to me that this fully-gestated seven and one half pound human female was a real person with a real spirit who would be resurrected and saved like everyone else, other than having that assurance, I never, ever from the Spirit or from any other source got any inkling or indication or even foggy idea of what sort of purpose this might serve. It doesn't make any sense. And frankly, if you gave me the reason, I probably wouldn't like it. But, as it became clear that there just wasn't going to be a reason given for this one, my husband and I decided that if the Lord was giving us a trial that wasn't going to have an explanation, that it was up to us to find a way to get a benefit.

Being forced into a corner by others' hurtful actions is a variation on this theme: misfortunes caused by other people place women in positions to choose paths that lead them away from victimhood or the dissolution of their personal agency. The pattern of these stories includes an initial limitation or challenge from the poor choice of a spouse, child, parent, or friend. For instance, Catherine Humphrey discovered after twenty-eight years of marriage that her husband had embezzled money from clients and was being disbarred. He was a changed man from the mission president he had been years earlier. In her interview, she says,

"[I] showed my kids the importance of education and the importance of a woman being self-reliant. I'd just started my Ph.D. when the divorce was finalized. I showed the children, 'This is how you manage. You get the most education you can and you take care of business yourself.' Women cannot be helpless."

Making conscious spiritual choices in the face of others' hurtful actions is also a theme that resonates through the deliberate lives of women on the Mormon Women Project. For instance, Sahar Qumsiyeh of the West Bank, Palestine, must cross Israeli checkpoints to attend church each week at the Jerusalem Center. She claimed her power to exercise spiritual agency in the following episode. She said in her interview:

> One day when I was trying to go through the checkpoint to attend church, one of the Israeli soldiers told me to go back; he said I wasn't allowed in. I looked into his eyes and remembered a scripture I read in Matthew that morning in which the Savior said, "Love your enemies." It occurred to me that I didn't love the Israelis, and it really bothered me that I could not obey one of the Savior's commandments. I struggled with that and didn't know how to overcome those feelings. I came across a scripture in Moroni—chapter 7, verse 48—which talks about charity as the pure love of Christ. It reads, "Pray unto the Father with all the energy of heart, that ye may be filled with this love." I decided that this was the only way to gain love for my enemies; I couldn't love them through my efforts alone. I needed help from my Savior who had perfect charity for everyone. He was able to love and forgive the very soldiers who crucified Him. If anyone knew how to love, He did, and I knew He could teach me. I decided to ask Heavenly Father to help me because living with anger and hatred damages the soul. I prayed for this for a long time, and I thought He didn't answer, because I didn't notice a particular change. But about a year after I started praying, I was passing through one of the checkpoints and I looked into the eyes of a soldier (who told me to turn back) and felt an amazing love for him. I knew that we were all children of God, and we don't have to hate the people who do bad things to us; we can just hate their actions, but we don't have to hate the people themselves. It was a tremendous

comfort to me to learn that when Heavenly Father tells us to do something, He provides a way for us to obey His commandments.

In many of the examples of tragedy or victimization, women imply or state openly that anger and dissolution of spiritual worth could easily have been their innate response—the "natural man" response. There seems to be a moment, or series of moments, in these women's lives in which they see themselves defaulting to a state of bitterness. They make an active choice to pull themselves out of a destructive default and onto a path of rehabilitation.

What actually prompts some women to pull themselves out—like Sahar, Kimberly, and Catherine—while other women find themselves unable to make similar choices? Sahar indicated the answer was her familiarity with the scriptures and her desire to follow the Lord's commandments literally. Kimberly implied she trusted the Lord—she wanted to give him a chance. For Catherine, being an example for her children was motivation enough. Common links suggest each woman is aware of her ability to form a deliberate response and each is confident enough in the Lord to include him in it.

Some women profiled on the Mormon Women Project feel that their pages start off even blanker than others': even the few constructs that we rely on to define what it means to be a daughter of God seem challenged or missing in their lives. Those who struggle to become mothers, for instance, cannot embrace what is probably the clearest delineation of responsibility for Mormon women. What do they put on their page when even the delineation of motherhood is absent? An internal driving force, such as struggling with an eating disorder or defining oneself as homosexual, can feel like drawing on the blank page with the nub of a pencil. Women of color can feel at a disadvantage in a predominantly white community. For these women, there is something in their lives beyond their control that impacts their experience of agency, and yet the women we've profiled who follow this theme have still chosen to respond to their "otherness" from a position of faith rather than alienation.

As an example, Sui Lang Panoke is of Hawaiian descent and identifies with Mormon women of color, of which she sees few even in her ward in Washington, D.C. In her interview, she explains that her race could drive a wedge between her and the church, but, instead, she tries to use her difference as an opportunity to understand the gospel from a fresh point of view:

> One of the things I've struggled with in the Church is the history of its treatment of African Americans. My daughter's father is African American. Most of the men I've dated have been African American . . . But I have learned a lot about the gospel and what it really means through these relationships. Me, being politically progressive but religiously conservative, finding myself drawn to African American conservatives actually makes perfect sense to me. I believe that when each of us is able to get to the point where we can sit down with people of opposing views and genuinely seek to understand where their beliefs are coming from, this is how our country—and, ultimately the world—will be healed. It is very difficult to get to that point, and it always ultimately begins with us. I feel that the gospel is what's going to get us there. Or at least it is what's gotten me to where I'm at right now spiritually. I haven't always been as open and accepting as I am now . . .
>
> When our stake got reorganized, Elder Holland came out to assist in the transition and it was the first time that an apostle had come to the Greater Washington Area in twenty years, so it was kind of a big deal . . . It ended up being the most spiritual meeting I've ever been in. I think this is why: oftentimes I find myself looking up at the pulpit in sacrament meeting, stake conference, or General Conference and observing that the leadership of our church residing on the stand are overwhelmingly, if not all, "old white men."
>
> This meeting was different, because in this meeting, though I found myself looking up on the stand and once again seeing all white men, this time I was inspired to look beyond what meets the eye. And I didn't see them as "old white men"; I saw them as men of God who just happened to be white. One after another they each testified of their love for their wives, their love for our Savior, and their love for each and every one of us there. Although they were sitting above all of us on the stand, I knew that in the

> hearts of these men, they did not set themselves above any one of us in the room; their leadership roles were more lateral than hierarchical. Each one of them came from a place of humility, meekness, and gratitude. It dawned on me that all of these years, I was hoping and waiting for the demographic of the leadership in the Church to change, when in fact, the Lord was waiting for me to humble myself to the point where I could switch my focus from viewing those around me through the eyes of the world to genuinely seeing those around me through the eyes of the Lord. It doesn't matter what any of us looks like on the outside; what matters is what's in our hearts. In fact, this is the only thing that matters to the Lord. It was the most powerful meeting that I've ever been in.

Despite falling outside the customary expectation of what a Mormon woman *looks* like, Sui Lang came to a place where she embraced what being a Mormon *feels* like, even to the point of being able to see beyond the skin color, or the feeling of otherness that could have thwarted her choice to be a part of the Mormon community. Tina Richerson came to a similar peace when she chose to renew her involvement with the Mormon community, even though as a gay woman she falls outside the usual paradigm for self-identification within the church:

> I was living with a Buddhist here in New York and he had this incredible library of Buddhist books. He practiced zazen or meditation every day; he taught me how to practice zazen too. We talked a lot about Zen and Buddhist precepts. I began to read these books and the Zen Buddhist approach really helped me embrace the suffering. My mom was also really sick with cancer at that time too. So, I started to redevelop my spiritual side through Zen Buddhism and through music. So, I just sunk deeper into music and my spirituality which was really powerful and wonderful. Buddhism is actually what brought me back to the church.
>
> I was reading a book by Thích Nhất Hạnh, who is one of my favorite Zen Buddhist authors, called *Living Buddha, Living Christ.* In the book, he talks about the jewels of our traditions and how important it is to accept our own tradition. He says:

> When we respect our blood ancestors and spiritual ancestors, we feel rooted. If we can find ways to cherish and develop our spiritual heritage we will avoid the kind of alienation that is destroying society and we will become whole again. We must encourage others, especially young people, to go back to their traditions and rediscover the jewels that are there. Learning to touch deeply the jewels of our own tradition will allow us to understand and appreciate the values of other traditions and this will benefit everyone.

And when I read this I was so struck knowing that I had to go back to my tradition, to my Mormon tradition. I was like, oh, crap! Really? This information sat inside of me for about six months before I had the courage to go back to church, to be whole again, but I knew I had to do it.

I knew at that point it was time to go back to church. I was going to honor my tradition. I went back to church. The very first Sunday back was fast and testimony, the very first Sunday of the new year (2011). I got up and bore my testimony to my congregation. I said I hadn't attended the church for nine years but I've always known it was true. I just bore testimony that I know that Jesus is the Christ and that this is the restored gospel. I didn't announce that I was homosexual. I think it was pretty obvious though. You know, I showed up with a tie and a button down shirt and nice slacks on. I bore my testimony and everyone was so kind and loving and I was like, okay this is cool. And I just began to work with my Bishop. I continued to practice zazen and I continued to read Buddhist books. I continued to practice mediation and mindful living but I slowly incorporated reading the scriptures, starting with the New Testament because I felt like I needed to get to know my Savior more. I began to pray more to Heavenly Father as opposed to just mediating or chanting. It only took about five or six months before the Lord showed me that I could totally incorporate my zazen and scripture reading. I still chant. I think it's something really important that our culture doesn't teach but it is a very strong tool and I chant what people would praise in church like: "Praise God," "Thank you, Jesus,"

> "Thank you, Father in Heaven." Just chant like that because it is very powerful. So, I still keep that in my personal practice . . .
>
> The Great Creator can make us into whatever he wants of us. If we move ourselves in [the] slightest right direction he will take it and he'll magnify it for our good. I feel like I've been blessed to be at such peace about this. I have this incredible relationship with the Lord and with the Spirit. I'm just so peaceful. Peaceful! Joyful! I will take the gifts of the Spirit over the gifts of the flesh any day of the week. I'm all about it . . .
>
> My desire to feel the Spirit got me to this point. My desire to know the truth. My desire to align myself with the Lord's will. My desire to not be afraid and say—hey, I'm a homosexual. I'm the big bad word. I was created this way. It's not an affliction. I was created this way. And I was given the ability not to be afraid of that any more.

Identifying why these two women see a place for themselves in their church membership when others in similar situations do not may be as individual as the women themselves. Both Sui Lang and Tina seem to recognize—perhaps through the Spirit, perhaps through conditioning from past experiences—that the Lord does not withhold his love from them because they do not conform to an established norm. Both of these women did spend time away from the church, which may have led to a deeper appreciation of the gospel's warm embrace once they returned, but both seemed to appreciate the metaphorical blank page as an invitation to be true to themselves within the borders the Lord had established. Within those borders, they both fashioned identities as daughters of God that were uniquely their own.

Lastly, these interviews contain a prominent theme of women who are called to a ministry: a specific purpose outside of their homes or families to serve or be involved in their communities. In the Mormon Women Project, we have featured remarkable women who have started ambitious global service organizations, from Rising Star Outreach in India, which serves those affected with leprosy; to the Women's World Health Initiative, which provides life-saving medical resources to birthing mothers in Senegal; to Elevita, an organization run out of the founder's home to sell handmade goods from developing countries. I also place in this thematic category those women who feel a drive to a particular profession, area of study, or engagement in their communities. One of our most-read interviews on the Mormon Women Project is with Elaine Bradley, the drummer for the popular rock band—the Neon Trees. In her interview, Elaine talked about how she learned to trust her drive towards music, and trust that music—specifically drumming in a rock band—was actually the Lord's specific will for her. Elaine said:

> I really try to include God in my decisions about music and the band. I ask Him to open doors or close doors as necessary. I kind of keep an open heart about it. Before, I was too afraid to talk to God because I didn't want to get a "no" answer. I think I've learned through my life's experiences to be more honest with Heavenly Father. I used to think of praying as something that I had to be in the mood for or that I had to say just the right thing. I felt like I couldn't tell Him that I was scared. Now, I tell Him that I'm scared but I want to do the right thing . . . It's hard to have that personal relationship with God if you can't be honest with Him . . . It's a process. It's getting to know somebody. Learning how to trust somebody with your deepest, darkest most special thoughts and feelings.

For these women, the blank page doesn't just represent opportunity within their roles as mothers or church workers; it represents their opportunities in the larger world. These are women who seem to crave a big life, a highly engaged life, and many of them see their academic, professional, or volunteer pursuits as working hand in hand with their spiritual development, not in conflict with it. They learn, as Elaine did, that the page's borders are not fences keeping them from engaging with the broader world.

While examining these stories may not offer one clear answer as to why some women stay engaged in church activity and others do not, their narratives of commitment, engagement, and action allow us as readers to see potential paths played out in others' lives before enacting them in our own. Through contemplating these stories, we can create life choices spiritually before creating them temporally, following the divine pattern of creation described in Moses 3. A story's ability to influence our personal decision making is as fundamental as the scriptures themselves. Scriptures are sacred stories of families and individuals, and sometimes those stories themselves point the way to specific decisions and ways of being that are in keeping with the Lord's will. But just as often—and probably more often for women who are less likely to relate to the male heroes of our canon—those sacred stories simply open up a portal to personal revelation. Something about the act of reading those particular stories, even if they're as distant from our own personal experiences as a military captain in ancient Mesoamerica, opens up paths of thinking in us that allow us to see possibilities for ourselves. While not sacred in a canonical sense, the deeply personal stories of our women in the Mormon Women Project can similarly open up paths of possibilities for readers, even paths for the Spirit to help determine what should be written on the page of each woman's life. I hope that these stories are a clear answer for a woman who finds herself wondering whether the blank page is a divine dismissal of our contributions or, on the other hand, a gift.

Notes

1. All interviews cited in this essay can be found at this website.
2. Personal communication with the author.

19

Narrating Agency

AIMEE EVANS HICKMAN

In her talk at the 2012 Women and the LDS Church conference, Neylan McBaine recounted a conversation with a general authority's wife, who contrasted her own schedule with that of her husband's. This sister expressed the sense of freedom she felt at not having the hours and minutes of her days tied to an ecclesiastical leadership agenda the way her husband's were. As a woman unbound by priesthood and leadership duties, she expressed a sense of relief at having a "blank page" on which to define her daily routine. McBaine referred to this as agency that is "personally, not institutionally directed," a distinction she implied holds true for all Mormon women. Free from the strictures and schedules of ecclesiastical duty, McBaine asserted that the only parameters for Mormon women's agency are the page borders themselves.[1]

As the editor-in-chief of *Exponent II*, a publication that has devoted its forty-year history to the publishing of Mormon women's writing, I am naturally drawn to McBaine's metaphor of a blank page. But, as McBaine acknowledges, a blank page does not signify infinite choices. The cultural norms that a Mormon woman encounters often define the margins of this metaphorical page. To be a faithful Mormon woman has often meant that women need to be not only good Mormons but good *women*. Or, to put it more strongly, to be a good Mormon—for someone who is gendered female—is by some lights precisely to be a good *woman*, where the category of "woman" has been filled with what Mary Bednarowski aptly calls "cultural platitudes and pieties" about femininity.[2] Within a Mormon cultural context, the question of women's agency is often a question of how women accept or subvert cultural norms that emphasize marriage and motherhood, often to the exclusion of careers outside the home, as the ultimate expression of what it means to be a *good* Mormon woman.

Against the backdrop of these cultural pressures, Mormon women are also seeking divine revelation for their own lives. Yet these cultural values are often articulated so vigorously that they substantially mediate incoming revelation, making it hard to distinguish God's will from the felt imperatives of being a good Mormon woman. As so many of the narratives submitted to *Exponent II* attest, personal revelation becomes the fulcrum for a Mormon woman's life: Will her revelation align her with or against the Mormon cultural framework?

For some women, personal experience and belief confirm cultural demands. These women experience a harmonious marriage between institutional and cultural expectations with their own personal revelation and lived experience. But for others who face choices or circumstances that may not complement those institutional and cultural expectations, a tension is exposed—is it more faithful to adhere to the cultural script, or to privilege personal promptings and divine revelation? Mormon women's narratives are shot through with this tension and offer us an invaluable resource as we consider how "personal and institutionally directed" notions of agency play out in the lives of many Mormon women.

This tension is apparent in a question that underlies almost every submission to *Exponent II* that I encounter: How does the concept of personal agency interact with a deeply embedded notion that God has a plan for each of us? The way women answer that question often indicates how they exercise agency in other facets of their lives. In her remarks at the Women and the LDS Church conference, Claudia Bushman recalled how in her own youth she was "taught that agency was a managed choice, not a free choice." Choose obedience and be blessed, or disobey and suffer the consequences. She went on to discuss how a more mature view of agency realizes that we "not only make choices, but we have the right to define the alternatives among which we choose. That is, we not only choose between the alternatives, we choose the alternatives from which we choose."[3] If one interprets the Plan of Salvation to mean that each significant life experience has been providentially plotted out and one's spiritual work is primarily divining that predetermined path (a la *Saturday's Warrior*), then the alternatives available to choose from are limited. Whereas, interpreting the Plan of Salvation as a broad exercise in free agency in which there are numerous alternatives, even on matters as important as when/whom/if one marries, multiplies options that may all contribute to individual eternal progression.

As an editor, I am interested in how Mormon women understand the scope of their agency, as well as how they acknowledge the spiritual and cultural forces that inform the choices they ultimately make. Do they narrate their actions as deliberate decisions that attempt to balance desires and beliefs against a backdrop of multiple options, or do they portray them as exercises in obedience to a single, clear-cut command? The rhetorical choices Mormon women make when narrating episodes from their lives have the capacity to broaden the scope of possibilities for future choices they and their readers will encounter or turn those stories into fixed devotional objects with a moral imperative all their own. The effect our narrative choices produce may matter as much as the forces that informed those choices in the first place.

The Will of God and Personal Agency

A Mormon woman's understanding of the extent of her own agency is intimately bound to the kind of God she worships, and the kind of answers she feels God gives when inquiring about her own decisions. Does she worship the God who dictates her desires (however lovingly) or the God who consecrates them? Mormon scripture and teachings are rife with examples depicting God in these two roles. Classic Book of Mormon examples of the dictating God, like God commanding Nephi to kill Laban in order to recover the brass plates, contrast with examples of a God who asks his people to creatively determine their own course with the promise that he'll consecrate, or bless, their righteous efforts—like the Brother of Jared's innovation to illuminate barges by asking God to touch a set of stones. Modern Latter-day Saint efforts to address this dichotomy are found in teachings like the Bible Dictionary's definition of prayer: "Prayer is the act by which the will of the Father and the will of the child are brought into correspondence with each other.[4] The object of prayer is not to change the will of God, but to secure for ourselves and for others blessings that God is already willing to grant, but that are made conditional on our asking for them."[5] This definition is symptomatic of the dichotomy, exemplified in the often inevitable slippage from a genuinely dialogic relationship between God and humans—"the will of the Father and the will of the child are brought into correspondence *with each other*"—to a one-way dictation—the will of the child is brought into correspondence with the will of Father. This unresolved tension between what it means to exercise free will, while simultaneously aligning one's individual desires with the will of God, is often at the crux of one's personal relationship to God within the LDS Church.

What I want to suggest in this essay is that in the case of Mormon women this tension may be likelier to resolve toward one end of the spectrum than the other. As evidenced by official proclamations and the church structure itself, a Mormon woman's world is presided over by men, whether in the ward house or in her home.[6] Such conditions may predispose Mormon women toward a divine dictation model in their own narratives. While the spiritual practice of bringing divine and human wills into correspondence, however understood, is common to both men and women in the LDS Church, the fact that the church is quite openly and self-professedly a patriarchal structure makes for a fundamentally different experience for women. Because the primary decision-making bodies of the church are currently comprised of men, many Mormon women are acculturated to locating authority—the power to decide—outside rather than within themselves. This is not to suggest that men aren't equally as bound by the parameters of church hierarchy and views about what constitutes the ideal Mormon man, but men (who are also a product of this patriarchal culture) set those parameters, and are seen as the dispensers of revelation for people both within and outside their own homes. These structural limits on Mormon women's authority within Mormonism itself can skew them toward a certain kind of providentialist narrative in which their spiritual virtue is always conditional upon the flexibility of their personal agency vis-à-vis a male authority figure. This creates a vicious circle that can prevent women from asserting their own agency against those institutional constraints. In effect, Mormon women can be conditioned to construct their lives as controlled by anyone but themselves.

Dictation

A submission I received early in my tenure as editor of *Exponent II* exemplifies the effects that a narrow definition of the will of God can have as one makes choices and reflects on those decisions. The writer (who for the purpose of this essay I'll call Jane) was an early thirty-something mother of six writing about the circumstances leading to the pregnancy of her seventh child.[7] Jane, who was living on the East Coast of the United States, recounted a feeling of judgment she encountered every time she went to the supermarket with her six children and pregnant belly on display. She craved to return to the West, to Zion, where, she hoped, more people would better understand why she had chosen to have a large family at a young age. She wanted people to know that her choices were "based on [her] belief and desire to have a large family, not on an inability to understand contraception." I cheered her as I read these words. If feminism has taught me anything it's that we must respect the woman who has deliberately chosen to devote herself to motherhood full-time—as we do the woman trying to balance work and family, or the woman who is in the midst of pursuing professional aims. Deliberate choices deserve our deliberate support.

Jane then recounted how after the birth of her sixth child she experienced nearly immobilizing depression for months. She felt overwhelmed, exhausted, and depleted. Her husband's long work hours, combined with the isolation she felt while homeschooling her children and attending to the many other domestic tasks of parenthood, were taking a toll she hadn't anticipated resulting from righteous choices. Yet, here she was, feeling "the prompting that another child was supposed to come into [their] home." Jane didn't understand how God could ask this of her when she felt she was at her psychological and physiological limit. In desperation she turned to her bishop for counsel. The bishop assured her that if she followed the prompting, she would be blessed. With a husband in full agreement, their seventh child was soon on the way. "Thy will, not mine be done," were the final words of her essay. In essence, the choice she faced was one of obedience to a divinely dictated order—a managed choice to fulfill God's plan and "the measure of [her] creation"—or not, which was not *really* an option for Jane.

I share this story not to contest whether the feelings Jane experienced were divinely inspired, but to examine critically how personal agency interacts with God's will in her narrative. Jane, and every person she counseled with (who happened to be male authority figures), supported her following this spiritual prompting even though she expressed feeling overtaxed and unprepared. Because her prompting corresponded with traditional Mormon ideals that esteem motherhood and large families, the chances that demonstrating righteous agency by not bearing another child at this time were diminished within Jane's cultural context. To have taken another course would have required its own special dispensation—a personal witness that going off script has divine sanction.

Jane's understanding of God's will, as well as the spiritual culture to which she turned to reveal God's will, dictated the limits of her agency. In Jane's narrative, exercising agency is an Abrahamic test—a managed choice in which she sees an opportunity to prove her commitment to the will of God over her preferences and mortal limitations. Her narrative is not one of feeling free to act as an independent agent open to a variety of possibilities, but of proving her faith by limiting her own desires.

Of crucial significance is the fact that turning her agency over to this dictated plan relieves Jane of responsibility for this choice. God's will can fend off judgment from those in the grocery store, her congregation, or even herself.

In almost direct contrast, an article from the summer 2014 issue of *Exponent II* shares the following story:

> Several years ago, in a stake conference in Pittsburgh, a woman in the congregation asked the visiting general authority what she should do about a specific problem in her life. His answer was, I don't know you, and I can't presume to tell you what to do. I'm a general authority, and I give general advice.
>
> Another friend of mine was very happy to hear this. She was pregnant with her first child, after being told she couldn't conceive; she was in law school and her husband was working on his Ph.D. She had prayed about what to do: should she still continue with law school? The answer she got was, "You are going to be a lawyer. This is what I have for you to do." Of course, this flew in the face of some general advice that she had heard over the pulpit, and even some advice she had heard in Young Women and Relief Society lessons. But she was comforted to hear that general advice is merely that: general.[8]

Both actors relied on personal revelation and the counsel of ecclesiastical leaders to make their decisions, yet one used those authorities to suppress her own will, while the other used them to enact hers. The differences in their stories are manifold—Jane had a prompting that contradicted her desires, while the law student was seeking confirmation for hers; Jane's ecclesiastical leader did not offer general advice but specific advice that she would have disobeyed if she had followed her desire, while the law student received an ecclesiastical endorsement of her own revelatory capacity. In both cases, however, extraordinary personal revelation was their ultimate trump card.

But what happens when that divine dictation model is so totalizing that it preempts personal revelation altogether? In the winter 2010 issue of *Exponent II,* author Crystal Bever narrates a childhood growing up in "an unusually strict Mormon household," which included a mandate that all the girls wear dresses and heavily restricted the whole family's access to media.[9] Bever recounts that at the age of nine she was "told at home and at church what to think, what to believe, what to wear, what to say, and who to emulate." Sheltered from the world by her parents' design, Bever's "alternatives among which we choose" were narrowly defined, charting a course for a feminine Mormon identity that demanded obedience to gendered ideals of twentieth-century domestic life.

Bever describes beginning to grasp the limitedness of the possibilities available to her after a family move to a poor, urban neighborhood on the San Diego/Mexico border. Experiencing the culture shock that came from being "one of three white girls in [her] elementary school," Bever stood "enthralled" on the playground as she watched her male peers break-dancing on the school asphalt. She recalls

> watching those boys and envying the fact that they owned their bodies and they knew themselves well enough to create their own style, their own way of talking, their own way of moving, in blatant defiance of authority. After a lifetime of being taught to copy others, I understood for the first time in my life that it was possible to be an individual, to discover who I was, what I liked, what I thought, what I wanted, independent of anyone else . . . Watching the boys break-dance, strut and brag, I felt suffocated, an imitation, a hardly substantial copy of my mother, my sisters, my church congregation. I didn't know until that time that I could choose to be different.

Bever describes a particularly harsh Mormon upbringing that stifled individuality and privileged authority even when the authority was abusive. Fearing she would "never be strong enough to be [her]self or find [her] own identity," Bever's "existence was spent in denial, in voicelessness, in a determined erasure of thought, will or feeling."

Due to the stifling nature of Bever's parents' religious practice, Bever identified them and the teachings of their church as the source of her oppression. She chose rebellion from a culture, home, and institution too entangled to delineate. God's will, so often wielded as a weapon against her in childhood, is understandably absent from her narrative of liberation; she pairs rejecting institutional and cultural oppression with God's absence. Does it always have to be that way?

Consecration

The previous narratives set up a dichotomy between agency and authority, implying that they're often incompatible, and that agency always pushes against authority. In contrast, Suzette Smith's fall 2010 essay, "My Faith's Journey," offers us a way of thinking about agency that works in harmony *with* rather than *against* authority, when that authority is imagined differently.[10]

Smith, thirty-three years old and a devout member of her adult singles congregation, found herself unexpectedly discouraged in her graduate studies and unsettled about future plans. She recalled feeling "distant from God and was confused by this, considering my faithful obedience. I read my scriptures and prayed daily as I always had. I paid tithing, went to church and served in the temple. Despite my efforts, I felt little comfort and found few answers for my growing doctrinal questions."

Smith's account demonstrates how obedience to church practices and commandments functioned like a contract in which her faithfulness was rewarded with comfort and blessings. In effect, this contract operated like a measuring stick, gauging her spiritual welfare by recognizing the blessings she received.

To move through this spiritual low point, Smith turned to a trusted church leader and was advised to "dig deep into the scriptures to look for answers." Smith took this advice, "spending a full quiet hour each morning in study, thought, and prayer. The process was challenging and took sacrifice and patience, but my spirit began to fill and I felt the budding of a greater faith . . . I began to navigate life, my exams, and my gospel questions with more confidence, and felt I was standing on a more solid foundation." Confirmation that God was indeed directing her life toward a happy outcome as a result of her obedience, came in the form of a budding romantic relationship. Smith describes how

> at thirty-three I felt that my trust in the Lord was being rewarded with this new relationship. I believed that God had intended this man for me and as I had followed His prompting, He had led me to him. After the years of waiting and wondering, this new life with Tom was just the right fit. Love was sweet and my prayers were full of gratitude to God for showing the way . . . I believed this answer to my "marriage prayer" was proof that I could trust God completely.

In a culture in which being a faithful Mormon woman has often meant early marriage and a child or two by age thirty, Smith was beginning to see herself fitting into her institutionally and culturally appointed place.

But then the relationship ended, and Smith found herself mending not only a broken heart, but reeling from a sense of divine betrayal writing, "I wanted an explanation for my suffering. Why was I denied an understanding when I had followed the Lord? How had I misread the inspiration from heaven?" Smith's underlying belief that God's will for her life was detailed down to her spouse, and that her own agency was best exercised by divining and acting on promptings that fulfilled that predetermined plan (a divine dictation model), defined the parameters of her agency. The failed relationship rocked these foundational beliefs. Smith's "rebuilding" came as she began to adopt "a faith centered simply *in* Christ and not on life's happy results." Smith began to believe in a divine correspondence with God that was not conditional on either her unquestioning obedience, or his carefully calculated blessings of compensation. She wrote:

> Perhaps my trust in God is its own reward. Perhaps that trust alone could give me security and peace . . . I have come to focus my faith more securely on God alone and that genuine goodness and love, rather than believing heaven's blessings are proof of

> that love or a reward for my faithfulness. If my faithfulness brings me anything, it is a greater sense of who God is and who I am, a deeper relationship, which is its own reward.

For Smith, the possibilities for self-understanding and genuine dialogue with God were expanded when she released herself from strict institutional, cultural, or even personal definitions of God's will for her life. Seeing God as a partner whose love would consecrate her efforts and desires without manipulating outcomes, rather than as a dictator to the faithful, or dispensary of disaster to the disobedient, was key to her healing and taking greater responsibility for the choices ahead of her.

Conclusion

As the narratives here attest, the expectations of what it means to be a "good Mormon woman" give shape not just to the hours and minutes of a day, but of a lifetime. While I am hopeful of the scope a blank page may offer Mormon women, I question the assertion that because a Mormon woman's choices are not bound by an ecclesiastical leadership schedule, institutional and cultural expectations are not still capable of dictating her choices in rather fine detail. The conclusion that Mormon women are blessed with freedom particular to their sex precisely because they are distanced from priesthood authority and ecclesiastical leadership, fails to take into account how the page borders themselves are delineated by those very powers from which they are distanced.

The nature and extent of women's agency in the LDS Church is in need of our collective inquiry. I do not mean to suggest that should women become fully integrated into the institutional leadership structure of the church those women would suddenly redefine currently established Mormon gender norms. Indeed, if the current discourse among Mormon women about increasing the visibility and authority of women in the church is any indicator, we may find that female contributions further cement longstanding ideals! But the very presence of women in the church's governing bodies could mean a significant shift in the way a Mormon woman might see her relationship to God: to understand on a personal level as well as an institutional one that her agency is not eternally mediated by men and maleness. There would be hope, at least for some, that as women participated in delineating the page margins, the "alternatives among which we choose" might better reflect the breadth of feminine experience, and therefore present a more expansive vision of righteous choices. The current absence of such a vision may cause many to write on pages even smaller than our gospel deems necessary.

Notes

1. Neylan McBaine, "Filling the Page: Women's Choices in the Context of Gospel Boundaries" (paper presented at the Women and the LDS Church: Historical and Contemporary Perspectives Conference, Salt Lake City, August 25, 2012).
2. Mary Farrell Bednarowski, "Soul Sisters: Intersecting Paths in the Journeys of Mormon and Roman Catholic Feminists" (paper presented at the Women and the LDS Church: Historical and Contemporary Perspectives Conference, Salt Lake City, August 25, 2012).
3. Claudia Bushman, "Agency in the Lives of Contemporary LDS Women" (paper presented at the Women and the LDS Church: Historical and Contemporary Perspectives Conference, Salt Lake City, August 25, 2012).
4. The LDS Bible Dictionary is an adaptation of an Anglican Bible dictionary from Cambridge University Press, edited for an LDS audience. See Philip L. Barlow, *Mormons and the Bible: The Place of the Latter-day Saints in American Religion*, (New York: Oxford University Press, 1991), 208–12; Robert J. Matthews, "The New Publications of the Standard Works—1979, 1981," *BYU Studies* 22, no. 4 (1982): 387–424.
5. Bible Dictionary, The Holy Bible (Salt Lake City: The Church of Jesus Christ of Latter-day Saints, 1979), s.v. "prayer."
6. "The Family: A Proclamation to the World," delivered by President Gordon B. Hinckley, September 23, 1995, https://www.lds.org/topics/family-proclamation?lang=eng.
7. Jane withdrew her essay before it underwent editorial review and it was never published in *Exponent II*. Because of this, I have changed the author's name and a few details of the story to preserve her anonymity.
8. Libby Potter Boss, "Understanding God: A Riddle," *Exponent II* 34, no. 1 (Summer 2014): 14–17.
9. Crystal Bever, "Telling the Truth: Culture Shock, Hip Hop, and the Power of Authentic Self-Expression," *Exponent II* 30, no. 3 (Winter 2010): 9–11.
10. Suzette Smith, "My Faith's Journey," *Exponent II* 30, no. 2 (Fall 2010): 10–12.

20

Soul Sisters

Intersecting Paths in the Journeys of Mormon and Roman Catholic Feminists

MARY FARRELL BEDNAROWSKI

I began reading *Dialogue* and *Sunstone* in the 1980s when I discovered how helpful they were for conveying the ways Mormon intellectuals were responding to the challenges of modernity and postmodernity: issues of authority, scripture, history and historiography, organization, gender, sexuality, and distinctiveness of identity in tension with the pulls—positive and negative—of broader American religious and cultural values. I was surprised by how familiar and intriguing the discussions and analyses felt to me as a Roman Catholic woman. Although the particulars of our traditions differed, there was much recognizable overlap with respect to emphasis on family, community, tradition, story and ritual, and "saints."

The multiple affinities I discovered then, and that I continue to encounter, have focused most powerfully on the work of Mormon feminists. If at one time in our histories Mormon and Roman Catholic women might have seemed unlikely conversation partners, over the years it has become increasingly compelling to me how much we have to learn from each other: about gender dynamics and institutional structure, our common struggles, and how we exercise distinctive forms of creative moral and theological agency in our communities.

I now take this phenomenon of connection for granted, and I seek it out. Mormon and Roman Catholic feminists are alike in that participation in our communities has had profound influences—not just on our spiritual lives, but on our intellectual, psychological, and aesthetic formations. Our religious heritages have been essential to how we understand ourselves at the deepest levels of identity, wherever we may now stand in relation to our church institutions. Our upbringings, steeped in church life, have offered us religious educations, theological vocabularies and worldviews, and ongoing lessons in church history, whether or not we have studied theology or history in formal, academic ways. We are alike in having learned and lived out our histories and our theologies in daily ways. Because of the intensity of our upbringings, our traditions have offered us a great deal of raw material with which to respond creatively and imaginatively, not only to our spiritual lives but to life in general. Creativity, imagination, and resilience are needed in religion and theology just as they are in any other human discipline.

We also experience ourselves similarly as women in male-dominated, hierarchical traditions that continue to deny us access to priesthood and to most arenas of publicly acknowledged power. As in previous centuries, since the early years of Second Wave feminism, LDS and Catholic women have sought more egalitarian ways of understanding and engaging authority. We have had to fight to find our voices and to have them heard at all levels of our traditions. We have learned only too well that it is "body," and not lack of ability or calling that circumscribes our places in our traditions. But through that painful learning we have also discovered the satisfactions of our own gifts for theological creativity. We are good at it. Being female is not a bar to learning, teaching, and writing about theology and religion. We also hold in common the bewilderment of offering these same gifts to our communities only to find ourselves received as dissenters, apostates even, rather than as welcomed participants.

We have been ignored, admonished, warned, uninvited, silenced, investigated, "brought in," censured, disfellowshipped, handed ultimatums, and excommunicated. We have argued against dead-end theologies of complementarity—male and female in Catholicism and motherhood and priesthood in Mormonism—that combine essentialist overadulation of women's gifts and virtues with institutional obstructions to the expansion of women's leadership roles. We continue to feel the disorientation but also the theologically and intellectually stimulating realities that come of being simultaneous insiders and outsiders in our communities. Years after reading it for the first time, I continue to feel the power of Lutheran theologian Gail Ramshaw's statement that women have been "paradoxically richly nurtured by a church that constrained us."[1] Laurel Thatcher Ulrich said something similar of Sonia Johnson: that she rose to prominence because she was a "feisty Mormon," but that she was dismissed by the community that had shaped her. If religion, theology, and various forms of ministry are for some of us the arenas of creativity that draw us most powerfully, then LDS and Catholic women have a lot to work with and just as much to contend with.

If the above sounds gloomy, I intend to proceed in this essay in a more hopeful mode. I write as a feminist who is convinced that Mormon and Catholic women have much to tell each other about our religious communities. Our conversations can promote solidarity in our similarities, and reciprocal illumination in the exploration of differences. At the most fundamental level, Mormon and Catholic women share in the number of times we've heard the question, "Why do you stay?" Sometimes the questioner asks this with such incredulity that I am not motivated to engage in further conversation. More often, our interlocutors are genuinely interested. Forty years of pondering that question as a Catholic woman has required me to be persistently thoughtful about my identity. In fact, I consider "Why do you stay?" a life-giving question, one that members of any religious community should ask themselves persistently as a form of spiritual practice. I am drawn to the variations on this question that I encounter in the complicated, imaginative, and moving stories told by Mormon women and men in books like Robert Rees's, *Why I Stay: The Challenge of Discipleship for Contemporary Mormons.* Often, the answers are profound in their very simplicity. To illustrate, three of the six reasons Lavina Fielding Anderson gives for staying (in her own way) are these: that she loves Mormonism, she loves Mormon theology, and she loves the Mormon community.[2]

The most obviously significant similarity we share is the fact that LDS and Catholic women do not yet participate in priesthood, however differently priesthood is understood in our respective traditions. At the same time, our theological concerns go well beyond priesthood, and sometimes I wonder whether too much emphasis on achieving priesthood masks the extent to which we care about many other issues—authority, scripture, vitality of doctrine, authenticity, and responsiveness to changing times—all of which are directly related to the future well-being of our communities.

Historically, exclusion from priesthood, from theological studies, and therefore from authoritative teaching, has been a powerful catalyst to the theological creativity of early Second Wave religious feminists.

And it continues to be. But so much emphasis on the struggles against exclusion—ironies abound here—has functioned to conceal, distort, and subvert the extent to which Mormon and Roman Catholic women are contributing to the revitalizing of our traditions by claiming our own authority and moral agency.

As an example, the 2012 headline of the *New York Times* obituary for Ada Maria Isasi-Diaz, the founding mother of *mujerista* (Latina) theology declares: "Ada Maria Isasi-Diaz, Dissident Catholic Theologian, Dies at 69." The writer suggests that Ada Maria, who was once a nun and often said that she would have become a priest were it not for the ban on women's ordination, became, instead, "a dissident theologian for those she considered the neglected spiritual core of the church's membership: Hispanic women like herself."[3] That is one way to look at it. Isasi-Diaz certainly disagreed with the church's stance on women's ordination. However, I believe she is better understood as a woman whose work emerged from within the deepest depths of Catholic social teaching; and from her conviction that the experiences of women, mostly poor women in this case, have as much wisdom to contribute to the church as do those of academic theologians and clerics.

I see Mormon feminists like Lavina Fielding Anderson, Margaret Toscano, Janice Allred, Laurel Thatcher Ulrich, and Maxine Hanks in a similar light. These are women, now considered among the first generation of modern Mormon feminists, whose work has been very influential for my own. Their theological and historical reflections emerge from the lived experience of the heart and mind and burning center of Mormonism. As individuals, they presently inhabit different locations relative to the boundaries of institutional Mormonism. At the same time, I see all of them drawing on the transforming possibilities of Mormon history and theology. These feminists are demonstrating their love for their community and their faith in its depth and capacity to respond to new moments in history, including insights into the complexities of gender. In concert with Catholic women, that means calling their community to account and offering their own testimonies that it can be "more."

I am persuaded that it is precisely because Mormon and Roman Catholic women do not yet participate in priesthood, for reasons we reject as both unpersuasive and false to the history and integrity of our traditions, that we are becoming more sophisticated about how deeply embedded gender biases remain in our traditions. Because the struggle for the full inclusion of women is taking so long, we have begun to realize what I did not know forty years ago (and in my idealism would not have wanted to know): that gender in religion is not a problem somehow to be solved in the near future and put right once and for all. It is an essential category of inquiry, immensely complex and endlessly mysterious, for the exploration of religious experience. But the study of gender cannot be an isolated and isolating experience, that is, by women and for women. Men are gendered, too. Protestant theologian Catherine Keller makes this point cogently and movingly:

> We [feminist theologians] have passions beyond gender, we always did, and the political pieties that seemed to require their disciplined sublimation are fading into the past century. And yet I may speak for the critical mass of women and a goodly number of men when I say that it was only by way of the particular impossibilities of feminism that we have found "our way of approaching" all that matters to us.[4]

If, for the moment, access to priesthood in Mormonism and Catholicism is one of those particular impossibilities, it has, ironically, opened up a great deal of theological creativity about many other matters.

A larger study of the theological and historical work of Mormon and Roman Catholic feminists would need to take into account the very distinctive differences in structure between the male hierarchies of our respective traditions and what those differences require strategically for the full inclusion of women. We could investigate together the differences between a priesthood that is nonclerical and virtually "everywhere" versus an ordained (a term we use in common to mean different things), sacramental priesthood whose members are set apart from the laity and few in number—and getting fewer. We could look into the significance of women's participation in a system where women live in marriage with men who hold priesthood powers and who are in frequent contact with bishops (we have very different kinds of bishops!), in contrast with a church in which bishops are few in number and far away, literally and metaphorically. There are millions of Catholic women who never have been, and never will be, in the same room with a bishop except on the day of their Confirmation (one of the seven sacraments in Catholicism and traditionally conferred by a bishop) or that of their children. There is also the variable of "vowed women religious," that is, nuns and sisters (in popular usage these terms are used as synonyms) in Catholicism, whose various orders have produced many famous, and often embattled, feminist theologians. While that is mostly work for another day, there is evidence that it is already beginning. Panel presentations with Mormon and Catholic participants about women's ordination and more equitable distribution of authority in both traditions have already taken place: one in September 2012, sponsored by the Women's Studies in Religion Program at Claremont Graduate University, and another in Berkeley in March 2013, sponsored by the Sunstone Education Foundation.

To return to similarities and "passions beyond gender" and how they manifest themselves in the works of Mormon and Catholic women, there are two interrelated areas of inquiry I'd like to explore; both are related to ongoing issues in Mormonism and Catholicism concerning who can speak with authority for their communities. And here I don't mean official authority, but rather the authority that comes from articulating with integrity the lived experience of one's participation, and what that experience offers to our communities in order for them to prosper.

One powerful way Mormon and Catholic women are claiming the power of their authority is by setting the terms of their own membership, their ways of belonging to their communities. They are demonstrating by their choices that the effort of religious institutions to establish non-permeable boundaries of membership is not realistic or even possible. At the very least, the days of "love it or leave it" and "be a reformer and stay in or be a radical and get out" are long over. These polarized options are blatantly inadequate for discerning what is really going on in terms of other possibilities.

The creative instabilities of what it means to belong are evident in *Frontiers in Catholic Feminist Theology: Shoulder to Shoulder*, a book of essays by young Catholic feminist theologians, many at the beginning of their careers. They articulate the fluidity of their connections to institutional Catholicism:

> The Catholic feminist may choose one day to claim the space of writing, working, and arguing for the transformation of an unjust

> church, while another day (or that same day) find herself walking away from a community that excludes us, only to return to reclaim a space in a community saturated with grace. It is a vacillation born of ambiguity and hope—hope in the possibility that justice might indeed reign among those who follow Jesus, ambiguity in that we have seen this possibility shattered as often as we have seen it realized.[5]

Wherever they find themselves on a given day, or even at a particular moment, it is clear that these women understand themselves as engaging in theological work for the good of the whole community and, that the community—as they experience it—extends well beyond the boundaries of the official institution. There is, as I see it, a loyal dynamism to their belonging.

Catholic feminists do their work in nonacademic settings as well. The Hispanic women, the *mujeristas*, with whom Ada Maria Isasi-Diaz ministered for so long before her death in 2012, offer a telling example of women who feel deeply that they are part of "church," part of "the people of God," as Vatican II defined the church. They continued to spend their Sunday mornings holding services outside the parish church they consider their own, even after it was closed by the Archdiocese of New York. It would be hard to find a more revealing example, literal and metaphoric, of what it means to be simultaneous insiders and outsiders in a tradition to which they feel deeply that they belong.[6]

I see this same dynamic at work among Mormon women who likewise claim multiple places to stand in relation to the institutional church, and from which to do feminist work. Their stories are very familiar to Mormons, but not as familiar to Roman Catholic feminists who would, I'm certain, find them edifying, instructive, and inspiring. After her excommunication in 1993, Lavina Fielding Anderson, deprived of her temple recommend and the privilege of receiving the sacrament, made the commitment "to being in church every Sunday and being as active as I'm permitted to be—this year, next year, forever."[7] Her assessment of her identity was that she would always be Mormon, but not in the same way LDS. Maxine Hanks, editor of *Women and Authority: Re-Emerging Mormon Feminism*, was also excommunicated in 1993, left the church for many years, and was received back in 2012. Hanks spent years on a spiritual journey that included the study of traditional Christianity and sacramental priesthood. She was drawn back for many reasons, among them Mormonism's lay priesthood and the role of testimony and its creative possibilities for Mormonism and feminism.

Historian Laurel Thatcher Ulrich's interpretation of her life as a fully practicing Mormon and feminist includes her identification with feminists across centuries who have claimed their own gifts. As a Mormon she "embrace[s] ideals of equality and a critique of power that also shaped early feminism."[8] It was, in fact, many years after reading her truly groundbreaking 1976 article on colonial American women that I learned Ulrich is Mormon. I have been instructed as a Roman Catholic ever since by her negotiation and integration of her feminist and Mormon identities. Margaret Toscano was excommunicated in 2000, seven years after her husband Paul. She does not attend church but continues to write about what is at stake theologically and politically for Mormonism in relation to Heavenly Mother and "Heavenly Motherhood." Janice Allred, Toscano's sister, was excommunicated in 1995 and likewise continues to present and publish work on the theological development of God the Mother in Mormonism.

Having the courage to claim religious identity and belonging from locations inside and outside institutional boundaries inevitably inspires women to formulate and internalize—not such an easy task—new understandings of their own authority in relation to their traditions. Often the first step in doing so is to face the reality that our religious communities are not perfect. This acknowledgement would seem to fall into the category of the egregiously obvious, but it can be a long part of one's spiritual journey. Roman Catholic ethicist Lisa Sowle Cahill, has taught for many years at Boston College and is well known for her work in sexuality and gender ethics. She describes her pre-Vatican II upbringing thus: "My childhood in the 1950s and early 60s is suffused with memories of Catholic piety and practice that were at once parochial, romantic, prayerful, stifling, uplifting, fear-inducing, identity-forming, spiritual, hopeful, and sexist."[9] The candor and the implicit humor of this description, taken together, give evidence that the capacity to be realistic, to offer both loving tribute and rigorous critique, is a necessary foundation for spiritual maturity, theological creativity, and reform.

Mormon and Catholic feminists are aware as outsiders and insiders that there are vehicles in both traditions that, creatively employed, should lead to the full participation of women. These are, in fact, meant to function to offset internal excesses of hierarchical authority that run counter to a tradition's best wisdom. Among Roman Catholics, there is the *sensus fidelium,* the sense of the faithful that has been invoked historically at times when the laity deeply disagrees with a teaching of the church. The ban on artificial contraception comes to mind even though official change has not yet occurred. There is also the principle of the primacy of conscience, whereby the individual or a part of the community is both empowered and obligated to go against a teaching of the church experienced as immoral. And there is the phenomenon of the development of doctrine by which we assume that the "fullness" of truth of central doctrines unfolds over time in new historical circumstances. In Mormonism, as I understand it, there are parallel opportunities: for personal and communal testimony and for ongoing revelation. A belief that certainly sounds appealing to many Catholics is that "the heavens are open" and further revelation is both possible and expected.

It would be disingenuous to deny that these strategies are not carefully regulated, qualified, and argued over by each institution out of concern that they will be used to justify what is considered dissent. I acknowledge, also, that it requires brave hearts to claim the right to exercise them. There is no ignoring the power of official hierarchies to affect negatively the lives of women. The stakes are high personally and professionally. And yet we can tell a thousand stories about women in both traditions whose consciences have called them to speak out. Sister Joan Chittester, a prolific author, is a Benedictine sister now in her 70s who has had multiple tangles with ecclesiastical authorities, including defying a Vatican order that she not attend and speak at a women's ordination conference in Dublin several years ago. She recounts in a spiritual memoir, *Called to Question,* a particularly maddening moment when she was given what she considered a ludicrous answer (alas, probably sincere) to a question she asked of a priest. At this point she decided that "answers are cheap. I decided to risk a few ideas of my own." She concluded that "Feminist spirituality demands that women become adults. It's that simple."[10]

And, of course, it's that difficult. The process of women's claiming their own adult authority is tightly tied to matters of doctrine in Mormonism and Catholicism, and doctrine is officially the province of male hierarchy. The theological work Mormon and Catholic women feel called to engage in, in order to bring about their full participation, has required them to question the very nature and authority of doctrine. If popular understanding takes "doctrine" for granted as a tenet that is true and absolute and that must be believed as a requirement for belonging, many women are asking, instead, "What is doctrine *for*, anyway?" Is it a static or a dynamic category? Is it the function of doctrine to hold the line, to insist on the unchanging nature of faith and belief irrespective of historical context and new information about how the universe operates? Or are doctrines resilient repositories of tradition and innovation? We see in recent encounters of Roman Catholic and Mormon feminists with official authorities that the dynamism perspective prevails, even if it doesn't always win.

Consider two recent examples from Roman Catholicism, both of which occasioned national headlines. In late 2008, the Vatican Congregation for Institutes of Consecrated Life and Societies of Apostolic Life announced and implemented an Apostolic Visitation to look into the quality of life of multiple orders of Catholic sisters in the United States. The majority of sisters involved experienced this as an anxiety-producing investigation lacking in reciprocal dialogue, rather than as a pastoral visit.[11] In 2012, in the midst of the visitation, the Vatican Congregation for the Doctrine of the Faith issued what was called a "doctrinal" assessment of the Leadership Conference of Women Religious that called for the renewal of the LCWR under the supervision of several American bishops. The LCWR is the organization of what formerly would have been called "mother superiors" (most orders now have multiperson leadership teams) that represents 80 percent of American sisters.

While the document praised the many contributions of American sisters to both church and society, the authors found evidence of dissent on doctrinal issues, silence on matters of morality such as homosexuality and gay marriage, and infiltration of what they called New Age philosophies and radical feminism. The report "stunned" the sisters. The statement left no doubt about what the writers meant by authority of doctrine: "allegiance of mind and heart to the authority of the bishops." The statement made clear that bishops did not understand sisters' theological contributions to ministries of social justice as offering insights on new and authentic ways to be "church" in the spirit of Vatican II.

Four months later, Pat Farrell, a Franciscan sister, gave the presidential address at the annual LCWR Assembly. It was a response to the document and urged the sisters not to be distracted from their mission of social justice. Citing widespread support from the general public (think of the Nuns on the Bus phenomenon), Catholic lay people, and fellow religious, women and men, Farrell said, "Clearly they share our concern at the intolerance of dissent even from those with informed consciences, the continued curtailing of the role of women." She continued, "We can only go forward in a way that contributes to the good of religious life everywhere and to the healing of the fractured Church we so love."[12]

Although the circumstances and subject matter are very different, I see the same configuration of theological creativity and exercise of moral agency at work in Mormon women's explorations of the need for "more" in relation to the doctrine of Heavenly Mother, and her place within official Mormonism: more theological depth, more ritual, more images, more prayer, more inclusion in the plan of salvation and, in general, less silence about her. Roman Catholic women have much to appreciate in the struggle to expand knowledge of Heavenly Mother and devotion to her. We admire the theological knowledge and depth of life experience required to imagine a Mother who is powerful and compassionate, in ways that both include and transcend "mothering," and at the same time subvert cultural clichés of what it means to be a good mother. How intriguing to contemplate the contrast between the Mormon theological task of filling a symbol that has for so long been nearly empty in Mormonism, and the Catholic effort to empty centuries' worth of accumulation devoted to pieties of passivity, obedience, and indirect influence. We find this theological task elaborated in academic works like those of Margaret Toscano, Linda King Newell, and Janice Allred. They are to be found as well in the efforts of younger feminist Mormons on popular blogs like Patheos, Religion and Feminism, and Feminist Mormon Housewives. Heavenly Mother is very much coming into her own, given life by the creative authority of Mormon feminists.

Just as evocative to earlier generation feminists like myself, is the extent to which younger Mormon feminists are broadening the discussion about women's ordination and fuller participation through social media, like the 2013 letter-writing project directed at LDS headquarters to ask that women pray at general conference. The campaign resulted in the first woman, Jean Stevens, to offer a prayer at the April 2013 general conference: "We spoke up, we acted collectively, and we helped to bring about change."[13] Or the efforts, fostered by the blog, Ordain Women, to allow women to attend the Mormon priesthood session at the 183rd Semiannual General Conference in October 2013. Women were not, finally, permitted to attend, but the session was available online for the first time. Joanna Brooks, author of *The Book of Mormon Girl*, posted an entry on Religious Dispatches (September 30, 2013): "Why the Women's Ordination Question Will Shape the Future of Mormonism." From what I can tell these blogs and letter-writing campaigns are making a significant difference in the feminist work of extending conversation about the full inclusion of women in Mormonism. They are serious, sophisticated, and, often, productively funny as well. I'm thinking here about the "Wear Pants to Church" effort of 2012 that stirred up so much intense conversation about women in Mormonism. And the post by Jessawhy on the Exponent II blog: "So a Mormon Feminist Sits by a Priest on an Airplane." That was, indeed, funny, but serious at the same time as it examined what we learn from people of other traditions, in this case a young Catholic priest. "He knew a little [How could he know only a *little*? I wondered] about Catholic women's push for ordination to the priesthood and was respectful of my views. He even seemed somewhat open to the idea of female ordination, acknowledging that Jesus treated women with radical equality in the Bible." And, she said, "I loved his view of Mary."[14]

The sometimes rueful, but very effective, combination of humor and seriousness in these online sources makes me remember my first encounter with Mormon feminist humor in 1978. Somewhere in a box of research notes from long ago there is a cartoon that appeared in 1978 in what must have been either the *Minneapolis Star Tribune* or the *New York Times*. This was after the revelation that black men could be ordained to the priesthood. In the cartoon, a woman stretches her hand to reach up to then LDS church president Spencer W. Kimball, who stands in a very tall pulpit. She asks, "Did He say anything about us?" "Ah," I thought in instant recognition, "ask God about us, too." In retrospect, I see that experience as a moment of incipient sisterhood that has deepened over the years.

Interestingly, this expanding movement in Mormonism comes at a time when some Roman Catholic women, while still convinced of the necessity of working towards women's ordination, are coming to see it as an effort that may have to be delayed for the sake of accomplishing other goods. In *Conscience and Calling: Ethical Reflections on Catholic Women's Church Vocations*, Anne E. Patrick speculates that "today's Catholic women—especially those of us who are well-fed, educated, and white—can allow our dreams of full equality in canon law to be deferred for a time and focus more attention on the injustices experienced by marginalized and materially poor persons in this country and throughout the world."[15]

I have chosen not to belabor the themes of ambivalence and irony in this essay. They are certainly there between the lines. Ambivalence, often creative, sometimes painful, has to be the middle name of those of us who choose religion and theology as major arenas for our own particular gifts. And irony—well, how could there not be untold ironies in all the ways women's theological creativity is enhancing the traditions that are excluding them from full participation? Rita Gross, one of the first woman scholars of feminist Buddhism in America, speaks eloquently of the ironies, frustrations, and satisfactions of her work. After forty years, she reveals that she agrees "paradoxically" with those who think that gender is a superficial matter on which too much energy has been expended, and, at the same time, with those who claim that it is "of momentous importance." "The one position," she says, "fuels my ambivalence about having needed to expend so much of my intellectual capital writing about sex, gender, and feminism. The other position led to all that writing and reflecting."[16] Mormon and Roman Catholic feminists, I'm convinced, know exactly what Gross is getting at. We wouldn't have missed all that growing awareness, reflection, writing, and activism for the world.

And yet, does the exercise of theological creativity on behalf of the full inclusion of women, by its very nature, necessarily require so much struggle and suffering? In traditions where gender, doctrine, and exercise of official authority are so tightly intertwined that seems to be the case—at least at this moment in history. Signs for the future are mixed. The report of the Apostolic Visitation, more positive than anticipated, was issued in December 2014. While it praised the work of sisters, it did not include an apology, as Mary E. Hunt, a respected feminist lay theologian, suggested it should. Nor did it acknowledge the anxiety, energy, time, and money required of the sisters who were engaged in the process. When the other shoe [the report] dropped, Hunt said, "It was not a red Prada slipper, and the devil is still in the details."[17] The difficulties between the Vatican and the LCWR remain unresolved, but the LCWR did not hesitate to bestow an outstanding leadership award on Elizabeth Johnson, CSJ, at their 2014 assembly in August, in spite of the 2011 indictment of her book *Quest for the Living God* for "doctrinal errors."[18] On the other hand, the change in tone and emphasis that have marked the papacy of Francis I, and his vision of a church more compatible with the social justice values of Catholic feminists, leads many to speculate that, whether or not there are doctrinal changes, there may well be positive movement related to greater inclusion of women. Kate Kelly, founder of Ordain Women, was excommunicated in June 2014, for leading a movement supporting women's ordination in the Church of Jesus Christ of Latter-day Saints. She was accused of apostasy for what she experienced as stating the obvious: that women and men are not equal in Mormonism. The official letter of excommunication stated that the problem lay in Kelly's having "persisted in an aggressive effort to persuade other Church members to your point of view and that your course of action has threatened to erode the faith of others."[19] Her appeal was turned down later that year. But *Exponent II,* a second-wave, Mormon feminist reincarnation of *Exponent I,* a late nineteenth-century/early twentieth-century women's publication, celebrated its 40th anniversary in 2014. Its two editors, Aimee Evans Hickman and Emily Clyde Curtis, are younger than the journal.

In October 2014, in an interview with the *Harvard Gazette,* Laurel Thatcher Ulrich made the statement, "I had the advantage of disadvantage."[20] She was speaking not of her Mormon faith, but of the vagaries of her academic career, an immensely prestigious career, but one that for multiple reasons did not unfold in predictable, linear ways. Much of the history of Roman Catholic and Mormon feminists might be characterized in that same way, marked by the creativity fostered by particular kinds of institutional disadvantage that, at the same time, has fostered a theological creativity that would not have been possible otherwise. In like spirit, the sisters who experienced the recent Apostolic Visitation as a time of trial, nonetheless, claim a renewed love for their vocations, congregations, and way of life: "We have gained strength from our increased solidarity that will fortify our ability to stand together as we take the next steps in the evolution of religious life. We will continue to preach the truth as we are called by the gospel to do, and to do that respectfully, without hesitance, without fear of censure."[21] What more could Mormon and Roman Catholic women ask for each other and for our churches? I am convinced that history will demonstrate that at the same time Mormon and Catholic women are pointing to the limitations of their traditions, they are also living into their depth and resilience. That is the work of the insider who is also an outsider.

Notes

1. Gail Ramshaw, *God beyond Gender: Feminist Christian God-Language* (Minneapolis, MN: Fortress Press, 1995), viii.
2. Lavina Fielding Anderson, "A Coin Balanced on Its Rim," in *Why I Stay: The Challenges of Discipleship for Contemporary Mormons,* edited by Robert Rees (Salt Lake City: Signature Books, 2011), loc. 1229–1245 (Kindle version).
3. Paul Vitello, "Ada Maria Isasi-Diaz, Dissident Catholic Theologian, Dies at 69," *New York Times,* June 5, 2012.
4. Catherine Keller, "The Apophasis of Gender: A Fourfold Unsaying of Feminist Theology," *JAAR* 76, no. 4 (December 2008): 906.
5. Susan Abraham and Elena Procario-Foley, eds., *Frontiers in Catholic Feminist Theology: Shoulder to Shoulder* (Minneapolis, MN: Fortress Press, 2009), 220.
6. Ada Maria Isasi-Diaz, "Hispanic Women: Being Church in the U.S.A." in *Twentieth-Century Global Christianity: A People's History of Christianity,* edited by Mary Farrell Bednarowski, vol. 7 (Minneapolis, MN: Fortress Press, 2008), 107–28.
7. Levi S. Peterson, "Lavina Fielding Anderson and the Power of a Church in Exile," *Dialogue: A Journal of Mormon Thought* 26, no. 1 (Winter 1996): 176.
8. Laurel Thatcher Ulrich, "Border Crossings," *Dialogue: A Journal of Mormon Thought* 27, no. 2 (Summer 1994): 4.
9. Lisa Sowle Cahill, "The Council as Seen from a Catholic Girls' School," in *Vatican II: Forty Personal Stories,* edited by William Madges and Michael J. Daley (Mystic, CT: Twenty-Third Publications, 2003), 22.
10. Joan Chittister, *Called to Question: A Spiritual Memoir* (Lanham, MD: Sheed and Ward, 2004), 4, 165.
11. In the fall of 2014, not long before the report on the Apostolic Visitation was made public, some members of the Leadership Conference of Women Religious (calling themselves the Grassroots Group), published their account of the visitation in *Power of Sisterhood: Women Religious Tell the Story of the Apostolic Visitation,* edited by Margaret Cain McCarthy and Mary Ann Zollman (Lanham, MD: University Press of America, 2014). The book does not include responses from the Council of Major Superiors of Women Religious (CMSWR), a smaller organization of more traditionalist women's orders

whose leaders chose not to participate on the grounds that the visitation had not yet concluded.

12. Pat Farrell, OSF, "Navigating the Shifts," https://lcwr.org/media/news/navigating-shifts-presidential-address-pat-farrell-osf. Two other well-known feminist theologians who have publicly tangled with the Vatican and the American bishops, and whose struggles are illuminating, are Elizabeth A. Johnson, CSJ, criticized in 2011 for *Quest for the Living God: Mapping Frontiers in the Theology of God* (New York: Continuum, 2007,) and Margaret A. Farley, RSM, chastised for *Just Love: A Framework for Christian Sexual Ethics* (New York: Continuum, 2006). Both authors have eloquently and authoritatively defended their views and methodologies. On April 16, 2015, the Vatican Press Office issued a release indicating that the work of the April 2012 Mandate, regarding the doctrinal assessment of the Leadership Conference of Women Religious, had been completed. That same day, several members of the LCWR had a very cordial fifty minute conversation with Pope Francis. Details can be found at lcwr.org.
13. Carolyn Kline, "Making Mormon Feminist Progress: Writing for Change," May 28, 2013, www.feminismandreligion.com.
14. Jessawhy, "So a Mormon Feminist Sits by a Priest on an Airplane," October 14, 2013, www.the-exponent.com/author/jessawhy/.
15. Anne E. Patrick, *Conscience and Calling: Ethical Reflections on Catholic Women's Church Vocations* (London and New York: Bloomsbury, 2013), 171.
16. Rita M. Gross, *A Garland of Feminist Reflections: Forty Years of Feminist Exploration* (Berkeley: University of California Press, 2009), 8.
17. Mary E. Hunt, "American Nuns and the Vatican: More Pain than Promise," *Religion Dispatches*, December 18, 2014.
18. A link to Johnson's acceptance speech, "Let a Woman Speculate," in which she said it would be "disingenuous" not to mention the controversy over *Quest*, can be found at ncronline.org. See also Dan Stockman, "Johnson to LCWR: Sisters Ahead of Hierarchy in Living Vatican II Renewal," August 15, 2014, http://ncronline.org/news/sisters-stories/johnson-lcwr-sisters-ahead-hierarchy-living-vatican-ii-renewal.
19. "Notice of Decision," *Deseret News*, June 23, 2014, accessed March 22, 2015, http://www.deseretnews.com/media/pdf/1365030.pdf.
20. Corydon Ireland, interview with Laurel Thatcher Ulrich, "I Had the Advantage of Disadvantage," *Harvard Gazette*, October 22, 2014.
21. Zollmer and McCarthy, *Power of Sisterhood*, 207.

21

A Mormon Woman's Journey in Sierra Leone

MARIAMA KALLON WITH RILEY M. LORIMER

My parents lived in a small village in Sierra Leone, West Africa, and because I had a desire to go to school, I grew up mostly in the homes of aunts and uncles and others in the capital, Freetown. I slept on the floor of their homes. I couldn't stay in the village because in the village, it's hard to get an education. Children in the village may go to school through elementary school, but then they drop out, because there is no money and no materials. But I was really ambitious. I really wanted to learn. At the same time, I never enjoyed being a child because for much of the time, I didn't grow up with my parents. Sometimes I didn't even know what village they were living in. To get an education was not a smooth path for a girl in Sierra Leone.

At age seven, I began living with a teacher I barely knew in the city. My family had arranged for me to work for this woman to do a little cooking and cleaning, and in return, I lived with her and went to a school nearby. I was not happy because she was cruel to me and beat me. Later, while I was living in my uncle's home, I was molested by my uncle's wife's brother, but the traditions of our society forced me to endure these traumas in silence. If I had voiced anything out, I would have been driven out of those homes. And if I was driven out, that would have been the end of the education that I was trying to seek. That learning was precious, but for me, it came at a cost.

Just as I was finishing my high school education, my country was consumed by a civil war that would last for eleven years. Between 1991 and 2002, more than fifty thousand Sierra Leoneans were killed, and more than two million were driven from their homes. And during that time, I saw many things that disturbed me.

As Revolutionary United Front (RUF) rebels got closer to Freetown, everyone started to hear about the rapes and the violence. Everyone started getting scared and leaving Freetown to try to make their way somewhere else. That was the time I started heading to my parents' home in the village. I had never gone on foot to my parents' home before, but I traveled inland with about thirty other women who were trying to find a safe place to stay. We walked through abandoned villages and past dead bodies and bloody ground and things I had never seen before. But we kept walking.

We arrived in my parents' village late in the evening. The RUF attacked just two days later.

My family fled into the bush, but none of us escaped. My parents were shot and killed as we ran away. My brother was captured and had his arms cut off by rebels, and he eventually died from tetanus. I ran from the rebels and was raped and terrorized by them until finally my sister and I found ourselves in a line of ten other women, waiting to have our limbs chopped off by rebel soldiers. I tried not to watch as my sister, who was third in line, had her legs chopped off.[1] All around me, women were crying and praying. Silently, I told God that I knew I was no better than my sister or the other women, but I pled with him to save me. And just before my turn came, people started shouting in the distance that ECOMOG soldiers were coming.[2] The rebels fled. God saved me. He saved my life.

I was fortunate after that to meet up with an old friend who invited me to live with her family. At this point in the war, there was little anyone could do for one another but listen. After listening to what I had endured, my friend's neighbor shared her story with me. She said her daughter had been taken by the rebels and had not been seen since. We shared our pain. Then she said, "We have a church that we go to. We go because even though all these things are happening, we still believe there is a God." I think maybe I was gifted with the kind of heart that I have because in those times, it was so easy to believe that there was no God. Because if God was there, why was he letting so many bad things happen? But when that woman told me that she believed in God and that her church gave her hope, I remembered my prayer when I was standing in line. And I felt sure the woman was right and God was there.

On my first day in church in the Kissy First Branch of The Church of Jesus Christ of Latter-day Saints, I was struck first by how quiet it was. My parents were Muslim, but I had attended Methodist and Catholic schools and had been to many different churches with my friends. And in my experience, church was noisy. Five blocks down, you know it's a church. I remember listening for the drums and hurrying toward the Limba Christian Church across from where I lived on Fourth Street in Freetown as a small, small girl. We danced and sang to the drums at every service.

But the LDS Church was quiet. At first, I wondered if I had made a mistake—maybe this wasn't a church at all. The meetings were held in a house—the living room was the chapel, and the bedrooms were auxiliary rooms. I sat down in a folding chair and noticed a lady reading from a blue book I had never seen before. The meeting began, and into that quiet, I remember the voice of the lady reading from that book:

> The spirit and the body shall be reunited again in its perfect form; both limb and joint shall be restored to its proper frame, even as we now are at this time; and we shall be brought to stand before God, knowing even as we know now . . . Now this restoration shall come to all, both old and young, both bond and free, both male and female, both the wicked and the righteous; and even there shall not so much as a hair of their heads be lost. (Alma 11:43–44)

Those were the most beautiful and liberating words I had ever heard. It seemed almost too good to be possible. Suddenly I didn't miss the dancing and the drums. My heart was overflowing. The thought that my parents, brother, and sister could be made whole again overwhelmed me. I felt hope, and that hope was connected to the blue book with "Jesus Christ" on the cover. And when the teacher then taught that we could, by our actions and obedience, choose to be with our families forever, I knew I had to be a part of this church. I was baptized soon after.

In many of the churches I had attended before, I was made uncomfortable by the preachers because it seemed to me that they were trying to force the congregation to feel certain emotions. The preacher would gesticulate or shout, and his sermon was designed to convince you—to bring you over to his point of view. Week after week, the same preacher spoke, and his was the only voice heard. But when I joined the LDS

Church, I was impressed that the members in my small branch took turns teaching from scripture. No one ever pressured me into belief. They simply presented the doctrine. They taught me about agency and personal revelation and encouraged me to make decisions for myself. I was grateful for the freedom to participate in church. For the first time, I felt I had a voice. Rather than sitting down, listening to somebody till the end of the day, and taking whatever they taught me, I would raise my hand; I would participate. I felt like I belonged.

The LDS Church gave me confidence in my own relationship with God. In many of the churches I used to go to, I had to go to the pastors or whoever was leading the congregation to pray for me. It used to make me wonder, *Who am I to God, then? If he says he loves me, why does somebody else have to pray for me?* But the LDS Church taught me that I can go to God—no matter what sin I have committed, no matter who I am, no matter where I come from. To be able to go to God—to kneel down and offer my prayer to him—was both humbling and empowering.

As I came to know the members in my branch better, I recognized that conversion to the gospel had changed the way the men and women related to each other. In Sierra Leone, a man will often say, "How did God create Adam? First. And then Eve. And how did he do it? He took a rib out of Adam's side, so that means the woman is always here" pointing to his side, underneath his arm, "not here," indicating heads at equal height. "If he wanted you to stand side by side, he would have taken a bone from the shoulder." But the church taught that men and women are equal—that we are all children of God.

The church's teachings on the equality of men and women improved the lives of all the members greatly. In the church in Sierra Leone, men took on family responsibilities, helped with cooking and cleaning, and took a greater role in caring for children. Women took on leadership roles in wards and branches, and they were treated as equal partners in families. Where I grew up, it was difficult for women to receive an education because many people think that the more educated women are, the more prideful they become. Traditional Sierra Leonean society believes that education teaches women to want to be above the men. But when I came to the LDS Church, I found a church that values education for men and women equally. I was encouraged to get as much education as I wanted. Having sacrificed so much for education in my childhood, I felt at home.

Part of the process of educating the members was to help us see things in our own society that were contrary to the way of the gospel. There is a common Krio saying in Sierra Leone: *Bad man bɛtɛ pas emhti hos*—"A bad man is better than an empty house." I grew up believing that, as most people did. I knew and loved women who endured so much pain and heartache because they were taught that they were less than men, and should put up with whatever the men did. They believed it was better to have a man who would beat you or maltreat you as long as he was there, because then you have a man. I have an aunt who was married but was unable to bear children. Her husband went outside of the marriage and had four children. There was a big fight in the house when my aunt found out, but she still felt she had to stay because she believed the notion of *bad man bɛtɛ pas emhti hos.* But when I found the church, I learned that proverb is a lie. And I realized she didn't have to choose that. She can choose to be a woman. I am a daughter of God. And I know that God loves me, no matter who I am, and I don't have to suffer silently under maltreatment.

I came to the United States originally as a missionary for the Salt Lake City Temple Square Mission. At the close of my mission, the war was still raging in Sierra Leone, and I had no home to go back to. I applied for and was granted political asylum, and I became a permanent resident of the United States. At some point after I moved to America, my friends started to ask me, "Why are you staying single? Why can't you just have a man and make American babies?" But because I have this church in my life, I know that I do not have to make that choice. I don't need that kind of man. More and more of my Sierra Leonean sisters are realizing this same thing. The gospel gives them the knowledge and confidence they need to say no to the people who would tell them to endure beatings and infidelity instead of loneliness. We are choosing to wait and pray and live our lives. Because we know that things need to be equal, and we will not settle for less.

Notes

1. My sister was sent to a clinic where I could not visit her, and where she died a few years later.
2. Economic Community of West African States Monitoring Group. These forces—made up of troops from Nigeria, Ghana, Guinea, Liberia, Mali, Burkina Faso, Niger, and Sierra Leone (and others)—were major combatants in the Sierra Leone Civil War, fighting against the RUF beginning in 1997.

Acknowledgments

The editors of this volume would like to express our gratitude to the many funding agencies who lent their support to the conference that initiated this book. In particular, we thank Bob Goldberg, director of the Tanner Humanities Center at the University of Utah, and Beth Tracy, administrative manager at the center. The center not only provided generous funding for the conference, but Bob and Tracy shared their wisdom and considerable administrative support, including securing an ideal venue at Ft. Douglas for the conference.

We also thank those whose donations made it possible for exceptional presenters to come from around the country to attend. These included:

- LDS Church History Department
- Utah Valley University
- Charles Redd Center for Western Studies, Brigham Young University
- Neal A. Maxwell Institute for Religious Scholarship, Brigham Young University
- Women's Studies Program, Brigham Young University
- American West Center, University of Utah
- Program in Religious Studies, Utah State University
- Center for Women and Gender, Utah State University
- Leonard J. Arrington Chair of Mormon History and Culture, Utah State University

John Alley, thanks for your faith in and enthusiastic pursuit of this project. Your work as an editor has brought to the fore many key works on Mormon women's history. Hilary Barker helped with meticulous formatting work for an early submission.

We also extend our thanks to our contributors, whose hard work has resulted in what we believe to be a substantial contribution to scholarship on Mormon women in particular, and the larger study of women and religion in general. These pages of your insights will, we believe, help readers to understand the complexity and nuance of women's experiences with religion. Finally, we thank our families and our friends for their love and support.

Selected Bibliography

Allred, Mabel Finlayson. *Plural Wife: The Life Story of Mabel Finlayson Allred*. Edited by Martha Bradley-Evans. Logan: Utah State University Press, 2012.

Archer, Patience Loader. *Recollections of Past Days: The Autobiography of Patience Loader Rozsa Archer*. Edited by Sandra Ailey Petree. Logan: Utah State University Press, 2006.

Bartholomew, Rebecca. *Audacious Women: Early British Mormon Immigrants*. Salt Lake City: Signature Books, 1995.

Beecher, Maureen Ursenbach and Lavina Fielding Anderson, eds. *Sisters in Spirit: Mormon Women in Historical and Cultural Perspective*. Urbana: University of Illinois Press, 1987.

Bradley, Martha Sonntag. *Pedestals and Podiums: Utah Women, Religious Authority, and Equal Rights*. Salt Lake City: Signature Books, 2005.

Bradley, Martha Sonntag and Mary Brown Firmage Woodward. *Four Zinas: A Story of Mothers and Daughters on the Mormon Frontier*. Salt Lake City: Signature Books, 2000.

Brady, Margaret. *Mormon Healer and Folk Poet: Mary Susannah Fowler's Life of "Unselfish Usefulness."* Logan: Utah State University Press, 2000.

Brooks, Joanna. *The Book of Mormon Girl: A Memoir of an American Faith*. New York: Free Press, 2012.

Brooks, Juanita. *Emma Lee*. Logan: Utah State University Press, 1984.

Bushman, Claudia L., ed. *Mormon Sisters: Women in Early Utah*. Logan: Utah State University Press, 1997.

Bushman, Claudia L. and Caroline Kline, eds. *Mormon Women Have Their Say: Essays from the Claremont Oral History Collection*. Salt Lake City: Greg Kofford Books, 2013.

Butler, Judith. *Gender Trouble: Feminism and the Subversion of Identity*. New York: Routledge, 1990.

Campbell, David E., John C. Green, and J. Quin Monson. *Seeking the Promised Land: Mormons and American Politics*. New York: Cambridge University Press, 2014.

Carmack, Effie Marquess. *Out of the Black Patch: The Autobiography of Effie Marquess Carmack, Folk Musician, Artist, and Writer.* Edited by Noel A. Carmack and Karen Lynn Davidson. Logan: Utah State University Press, 1999.

Compton, Todd. *In Sacred Loneliness: The Plural Wives of Joseph Smith*. Salt Lake City: Signature Books, 1997.

Covington, Kae. *Gathered in Time: Utah Quilts and Their Makers, Settlement to 1950.* Salt Lake City: University of Utah Press, 1997.

Crosby, Caroline Barnes. *No Place to Call Home: The 1807–1857 Life Writings of Caroline Barnes Crosby, Chronicler of Outlying Mormon Communities.* Edited by Edward Leo Lyman, Susan Ward Payne, and S. George Ellsworth. Logan: Utah State University Press, 2005.

Cross, Mary Bywater. *Quilts and Women of the Mormon Migrations.* Nashville: Rutledge Hill Press, 1997.

Daynes, Kathryn M. *More Wives than One: Transformation of the Mormon Marriage System, 1840–1910.* Urbana: University of Illinois Press, 2008.

Derr, Jill Mulvay. *Sarah M. Kimball.* Salt Lake City: Utah State Historical Society, 1976. Reprint. Salt Lake City: Signature Books, 1981.

Derr, Jill Mulvay, Janath Russell Cannon, and Maureen Ursenbach Beecher. *Women of Covenant: The Story of Relief Society.* Salt Lake City: Deseret Book, 1992.

Ellsworth, Maria S. *Mormon Odyssey: The Story of Ida Hunt Udall, Plural Wife.* Urbana: University of Illinois Press, 1992.

Ellsworth, S. George. *Dear Ellen: Two Mormon Women and Their Letters.* Salt Lake City: Signature Books, 1974.

Gates, Susa Young. *Lydia Knight's History.* Salt Lake City: Juvenile Instructor Office, 1883.

Godfrey, Kenneth W., Audrey M. Godfrey, and Jill Mulvay Derr. *Women's Voices: An Untold History of the Latter-day Saints, 1830–1900.* Salt Lake City: Deseret Book, 1982.

Gordon, Margaret E. P. *Pansy's History: The Autobiography of Margaret E. P. Gordon, 1866–1966.* Edited by Claudia L. Bushman. Logan: Utah State University Press, 2011.

Hale, Veda. *Swell Suffering: A Biography of Maurine Whipple.* Salt Lake City: Greg Kofford Books, 2009.

Hall, Dave. *A Faded Legacy: Amy Brown Lyman and Mormon Women's Activism, 1872–1959.* Salt Lake City: University of Utah Press, 2015.

Hanks, Maxine, ed. *Women and Authority: Re-Emerging Mormon Feminism.* Salt Lake City: Signature Books, 1992.

Heywood, Martha Spence. *Not by Bread Alone: The Journal of Martha Spence Heywood.* Edited by Juanita Brooks. Salt Lake City: Utah State Historical Society, 1978.

Holzapfel, Richard Neitzel and Jeni Broberg Holzapfel. *Women of Nauvoo.* Salt Lake City: Bookcraft, 1992.

———. *A Woman's View: Helen Mar Whitney's Reminiscences of Early Church History.* Provo, UT: Religious Studies Center, Brigham Young University, 1997.

Kimball, James N. and Kent Miles. *Mormon Women: Portraits and Conversations.* Salt Lake City: Handcart Books, 2009.

Kinkead, Joyce, ed. *A Schoolmarm All My Life: Personal Narratives from Frontier Utah.* Salt Lake City: Signature Books, 1996.

Leavitt, Sarah Studevant, Mary Brown Pulsipher, Adeline Beman Noble, Martha Pane Jones Thomas, and Eliza Dana Gibbs. *Autobiographies of Mormon Pioneer*

Women. Volume 1. Compiled by Ogden Kraut. Santaquin, UT: Pioneer Press, 1994.

Mack, Phyllis. "Religion, Feminism, and the Problem of Agency: Reflections on Eighteenth-Century Quakerism." *Signs* 29, no. 1 (September 1, 2003): 149–77.

Madsen, Carol Cornwall. *Sisters and Little Saints: One Hundred Years of Primary*. Salt Lake City: Deseret Book, 1979.

———. *In Their Own Words: Women and the Story of Nauvoo*. Salt Lake City: Deseret Book, 1994.

———. *Battle for the Ballot: Essays on Woman Suffrage in Utah*. Logan: Utah State University Press, 1997.

———. *An Advocate for Women: The Public Life of Emmeline B. Wells, 1870–1920*. Provo: Brigham Young University Press, 2005.

Madsen, Carol Cornwall and Cherry B. Silver, eds. *New Scholarship on Latter-day Saint Women in the Twentieth Century: Selections from the Women's History Initiative Seminars, 2003–2004*. Provo, UT: Joseph Fielding Smith Institute for LDS History, 2005.

Mahmood, Saba. *Politics of Piety: The Islamic Revival and the Feminist Subject*. Princeton, NJ: Princeton University Press, 2005.

McBaine, Neylan, ed. *Sisters Abroad: Interviews from The Mormon Women Project*. Englewood, CO: Patheos Press, 2013.

Miner, Caroline Eyring and Edward L. Kimball. *Camilla: A Biography of Camilla Eyring Kimball*. Salt Lake City: Deseret Book, 1980.

Morrill, Susanna. *White Roses on the Floor of Heaven: Mormon Women's Popular Theology, 1880–1920*. New York: Routledge, 2006.

Morris, Mary Lois Walker. *Before the Manifesto: The Life Writings of Mary Lois Walker Morris*. Edited by Melissa Lambert Milewski. Logan: Utah State University Press, 2007.

Newell, Linda King and Valeen Tippetts Avery. *Mormon Enigma: Emma Hale Smith*. 2nd ed. Urbana: University of Illinois Press, 1994.

Newell, Quincy D., ed. "The Autobiography and Interview of Jane Elizabeth Manning James." *Journal of Africana Religions* 1, no. 2 (2013): 251–91.

Nielson, Carol Holindrake. *The Salt Lake City 14th Ward Album Quilt, 1857: Stories of the Relief Society Women and Their Quilt*. Salt Lake City: University of Utah Press, 2004.

Olson, Vicky Burgess. *Sister Saints*. Provo: Brigham Young University Press, 1978.

Peterson, Levi S. *Juanita Brooks: Mormon Woman Historian*. Salt Lake City: University of Utah Press, 1988.

Pratt, Louisa Barnes. *The History of Louisa Barnes Pratt: The Autobiography of a Mormon Missionary Widow and Pioneer*. Edited by S. George Ellsworth. Logan: Utah State University Press, 1998.

Putnam, Robert D. and David E. Campbell. *American Grace: How Religion Divides and Unites Us*. New York: Simon and Schuster, 2010.

Richards, Mary Haskin Parker. *Winter Quarters: The 1846–1848 Life Writings of Mary Haskin Parker Richards*. Edited by Maurine Carr Ward. Logan: Utah State University Press, 1996.

Rogers, Aurelia Spencer. *Life Sketches of Orson Spencer and Others, and History of Primary Work*. Salt Lake City: George Q. Cannon & Sons, 1898.

Romney, Catharine Cottam. *Letters of Catharine Cottam Romney, Plural Wife*. Edited by Jennifer Moulton Hansen. Urbana: University of Illinois Press, 1992.

Scott, Patricia Lynn and Linda Thatcher. *Women in Utah History: Paradigm or Paradox?* Logan: Utah State University Press, 2005.

Sessions, Patty Bartlett. *Mormon Midwife: The 1846–1888 Diaries of Patty Bartlett Sessions*. Edited by Donna T. Smart. Logan: Utah State University Press, 1997.

Smith, Lucy Mack. *Lucy's Book: A Critical Edition of Lucy Mack Smith's Family Memoir*. Edited by Lavina Fielding Anderson. Salt Lake City: Signature Books, 2001.

Snow, Eliza R. *The Personal Writings of Eliza Roxcy Snow*. Edited by Maureen Ursenbach Beecher. Logan: Utah State University Press, 2000.

———. *The Complete Poetry*. Edited by Jill Mulvey Derr and Karen Lynn Davidson. Provo: Brigham Young University Press, 2009.

Snyder, LuAnn Faylor and Phillip A. Snyder, eds. *Post-Manifesto Polygamy: The 1899–1904 Correspondence of Helen, Owen, and Avery Woodruff*. Logan: Utah State University Press, 2009.

Stenhouse, Fanny. *Exposé of Polygamy: A Lady's Life among the Mormons*. Edited by Linda Wilcox DeSimone. Logan: Utah State University Press, 2008.

Tanner, Annie Clark. A *Mormon Mother: An Autobiography*. 3rd ed. Salt Lake City: Tanner Trust Fund, University of Utah Library, 1991.

Tong, Rosemarie. *Feminist Thought: A More Comprehensive Introduction*. Boulder, CO: Westview Press, 1998.

Tracy, Nancy Alexander, Eliza Partridge Smith Lyman, Emily Partridge Smith and Young, Mary A. Phelps Rich. *Autobiographies of Mormon Pioneer Women*. Volume 2. Compiled by Ogden Kraut. Santaquin, UT: Pioneer Press, 1994.

Tullidge, Edward W. *The Women of Mormondom*. New York: Tullidge and Crandall, 1877.

Turley, Richard E. and Brittany A. Chapman, eds. *Women of Faith in the Latter Days, 1775–1820*. Volume 1. Salt Lake City: Deseret Book, 2011.

———. *Women of Faith in the Latter Days, 1821–1845*. Volume 2. Salt Lake City: Deseret Book, 2013.

Van Wagenen, Lola. *Sister-Wives and Suffragists: Polygamy and the Politics of American Suffrage, 1870–1896*. PhD diss., New York University, 1994. Reprinted. Provo: Joseph Fielding Smith Institute and *BYU Studies*, 2003.

Warenski, Marilyn. *Patriarchs and Politics: The Plight of the Mormon Woman*. New York: McGraw-Hill, 1978.

Whitley, Colleen, ed. *Worth Their Salt*. Logan: Utah State University Press, 1996.

———. *Worth Their Salt Too: More Notable but Often Unnoted Women of Utah*. Logan: Utah State University Press, 2000.

Whitney, Helen Mar. *A Widow's Tale: The 1884–1896 Diary of Helen Mar Kimball Whitney*. Edited by Charles M. Hatch and Todd Compton. Logan: Utah State University Press, 2003.

Contributors

MARY FARRELL BEDNAROWSKI is professor emerita of religious studies at United Theological Seminary of the Twin Cities. Her teaching, research, and writing have emphasized theological creativity, particularly in relation to gender, as in *The Religious Imagination of American Women*.

MATTHEW BOWMAN is the author of *The Mormon People: The Making of an American Faith* and *The Urban Pulpit: New York City and the Fate of Liberal Evangelicalism*. He holds a PhD in American history from Georgetown University and is associate professor of history at Henderson State University.

CATHERINE A. BREKUS is Charles Warren Professor of the History of Religion in America at Harvard Divinity School. She is the author, most recently, of *Sarah Osborn's World: The Rise of Evangelical Christianity in Early America*.

CLAUDIA L. BUSHMAN is currently Distinguished Senior Scholar in Residence at the American Antiquarian Society in Worcester, Massachusetts, where she is working on a study of Boston in 1870.

DAVID CAMPBELL is professor of political science at the University of Notre Dame and founding director of the Rooney Center for the Study of American Democracy. His most recent book is *Seeking the Promised Land: Mormons and American Politics* (with John C. Green and J. Quin Monson).

REBEKAH RYAN CLARK holds a juris doctorate from the J. Reuben Clark Law School at Brigham Young University. She graduated from Harvard University with a bachelor's degree in American history and literature, where she focused her research on Mormon women in the suffrage movement. In addition to working as an attorney, she has taught history for Brigham Young University-Idaho, researched for the LDS Church History Department, and published various articles and chapters on Latter-day Saint women.

RACHEL COPE is an assistant professor of church history and doctrine at Brigham Young University. Her research interests focus on American women's spirituality and conversion in the late eighteenth and early nineteenth centuries. She is an assistant editor of *Wesley and Methodist Studies*, and the lead series editor of the Mormon Studies Series through Farleigh Dickinson University Press.

CARINE DECOO has been a member of the church since the 1970s. She studied at the University of Antwerp and holds a BA from Brigham Young University. Married to Wilfried Decoo, she spent many years both in Belgium and in Utah.

JENNIFER FINLAYSON-FIFE is a private practice psychotherapist in Chicago who works with LDS couples and individuals on relationship and sexuality issues. She received her PhD in counseling psychology at Boston College and wrote her dissertation on LDS women's sexual agency. She is a frequent contributor to LDS-themed magazines, blogs, and podcasts on the subjects of sexuality, faith, and mental health.

P. JANE HAFEN (Taos Pueblo) is a professor of English at the University of Nevada, Las Vegas. She edited *Dreams and Thunder: Stories, Poems, and The Sun Dance Opera by Zitkala-Ša*, and is author of *Reading Louise Erdrich's Love Medicine* and articles and book chapters about American Indian literatures. She recently edited a collection of essays, *Critical Insights: Louise Erdrich.*

AMANDA HENDRIX-KOMOTO is a PhD candidate at the University of Michigan where she studies the intersections of American religious history, sexuality, and nineteenth-century colonialism. She received her BA from the College of Idaho and has a master's degree in curriculum and instruction from the University of Nevada, Las Vegas.

AIMEE EVANS HICKMAN served as the editor-in-chief of the *Exponent II* magazine from 2009–2015, a publication that has been exploring the diverse experiences of Mormon women since 1974. She is a graduate of the University of Utah and presently lives in Baltimore, Maryland.

KATE HOLBROOK is coeditor of *The First Fifty Years of Relief Society: Key Documents in Latter-day Saint Women's History* and *Global Values 101*. Her dissertation, "Radical Food: Nation of Islam and Latter-day Saint Culinary Ideals: 1930–1980," explores the everyday theological priorities carried in food. She specializes in women's history as a historian at the LDS Church History Department.

MELISSA INOUYE holds a PhD in Chinese history from Harvard University and is a lecturer in Chinese history at Auckland University.

MARIAMA KALLON is a Latter-day Saint born and raised in Sierra Leone. She now lives in Utah, where she frequently works as a public speaker.

NEYLAN MCBAINE is the founder and editor-in-chief of the Mormon Women Project, a continuously expanding library of interviews with LDS women found at www.mormonwomen.com. Her writings have been published in *Newsweek, Dialogue: A Journal of Mormon Thought, Meridian Magazine,* and the *Washington Post*. She is the author of *Women at Church: Magnifying LDS Women's Local Impact.*

SUSANNA MORRILL is associate professor in the Religious Studies Department at Lewis and Clark College where she teaches courses on American religious history. She wrote *White Roses on the Floor of Heaven: Mormon Women's Popular Theology, 1880–1920.*

QUINCY D. NEWELL researches and writes about American religions, focusing on the religious history of the American West. She is the author of *Constructing Lives at Mission San Francisco: Native Californians and Hispanic Colonists, 1776–1821*; the coeditor of *New Perspectives in Mormon Studies: Creating and Crossing Boundaries*; and the author of numerous book chapters and journal articles. After more than a decade on the religious studies faculty at the University of Wyoming, Newell now teaches American religious history at Hamilton College.

JENNIFER REEDER earned her PhD in American history from George Mason University, where she focused on nineteenth-century women, religion, material culture, and memory. She is the nineteenth-century women's history specialist at the LDS Church History Department.

JONATHAN STAPLEY is an amateur historian with a doctorate in carbohydrate chemistry. He is currently serving on the board of the Mormon History Association.

LAUREL THATCHER ULRICH is currently 300th Anniversary University Professor at Harvard University. Her book *A Midwife's Tale: The Life of Martha Ballard, Based on Her Diary, 1785–1812* won the Pulitzer Prize in history, the Bancroft Prize, and several other awards. She is also the author of *The Age of Homespun: Objects and Stories in the Creation of an American Myth* and *A House Full of Females: Mormon Diaries, 1835–1870*. She is past president of the Mormon History Association and the American Historical Association.

KRISTINE WRIGHT has an MA in history from the University of Western Ontario. She has published articles in *Dialogue: A Journal of Mormon Thought* and the *Journal of Mormon History*.

Index

Page numbers in *italics* indicate illustrations. Pages number followed by t indicates a table.